ROBERT ROSSEN

Robert Rossen

*The Films and Politics
of a Blacklisted Idealist*

Alan Casty

McFarland & Company, Inc., Publishers
Jefferson, North Carolina, and London

LIBRARY OF CONGRESS CATALOGUING-IN-PUBLICATION DATA

Casty, Alan.
Robert Rossen : the films and politics of a blacklisted idealist / Alan Casty.
p.   cm.
Includes bibliographical references and index.

ISBN 978-0-7864-6981-9
softcover : acid free paper ∞

1. Rossen, Robert, 1908–1966 — Criticism and interpretation.
I. Title.
PN1998.3.R673C38 2013   791.4302'33092 — dc23   [B]   2013001844

BRITISH LIBRARY CATALOGUING DATA ARE AVAILABLE

© 2013 Alan Casty. All rights reserved

No part of this book may be reproduced or transmitted in any form or by any means, electronic or mechanical, including photocopying or recording, or by any information storage and retrieval system, without permission in writing from the publisher.

Front cover images: Robert Rossen, 1961 (Photofest);
Film and coffee stains © 2012 Shutterstock

Manufactured in the United States of America

McFarland & Company, Inc., Publishers
Box 611, Jefferson, North Carolina 28640
www.mcfarlandpub.com

For Jill

Table of Contents

Preface 1
Introduction: The Films of Robert Rossen—A Legacy Lost 5

Part One: The Writer—Craft, Idealism and Ideology

1. A Matter of Experience—From the Lower East Side to Hollywood
   and the Party 19
2. Stretching the Boundaries of Genre—The First Two Screenplays 29
3. Warner Bros. and the Party—Five Films, Three Years 42
4. Ode to an Era—*The Roaring Twenties* 52
5. The Party Line and the Writer—Two Warner Films in a Shifting
   Political World 60
6. The War and Post-War Worlds on Film—Three with
   Lewis Milestone 72

Part Two: The Director—Success, Doubt and Disillusion

7. The Writer Becomes Director—*Johnny O'Clock* 93
8. The Battle and the Myth, Personal and Political—*Body and Soul* 102
9. Conflicts and Consequences—The First Hearings, 1947 118
10. Power and Betrayal, Personal and Public—*All the King's Men* 126
11. A Time of Tests, Trials and Fear—*The Brave Bulls* 143
12. The Political and Moral Turmoil of the Blacklist Era—
    The Hearings, 1951 153

Part Three: The Director—Blacklisting, Rebellion and Isolation

13. What Is Behaving Decently?—Testifying and Silence 165
14. Starting Anew in Europe—*Mambo* 175
15. Seeking the Power and the Glory—*Alexander the Great* 182

16. The Road Back—*Island in the Sun* and *They Came to Cordura* 194
17. At the Top of His Game—*The Hustler* 211
18. The Forgotten Masterwork and Enigma—*Lilith* 228
19. An Unfortunate Epilogue—The Legacy Denied 244

Chapter Notes 255
Bibliography 263
Index 267

Preface

This is a book about the films of Robert Rossen, but it is a "films-of" book that goes beyond the boundaries of the standard genre—as the films of Robert Rossen went beyond the boundaries of the Hollywood film genres he often worked in. It works within the genre to thoroughly describe and analyze each of his films, and places them in the cumulative arc of his uniquely unified work—his *oevre*. But it proposes, further, that his is an achievement of a significant and valuable body of work that has not been recognized—indeed, has been ignored—in the writing and teaching of American film history. The book is a challenge to this conventional wisdom as it has filtered down through academia, film criticism and history, and the popular media. It seeks to be a "right whale"—in the metaphor of Herman Melville in *Moby Dick*—to offset a tilting of moral judgment, distorting and unjust, and to restore a just sense of balance to moral judgments and to film history and criticism.

In thorough detail, and with extensive quotations of Rossen and others, it presents a full depiction and analysis of the films of his long career, from 1936 until his untimely death in 1964 at the age of 57. It examines his ten early screenplays and the ten films he wrote and directed—their narratives and characterization, dramatic and cinematic techniques, style, their deepening insights and themes, their place in the development of film genres, and the context of the production of each in the studio system. But it particularly places them in the panorama of their times and interprets them as a meaningful reflection of the American scene. It places them in the context of his personal experiences in a manner distinctive among American directors. And, most significantly, it places them in the context of his relationship to communism and the Communist Party.

Robert Rossen was the most accomplished and significant filmmaker who was a long-time active member of the Communist Party. I combine the meaningful interaction between his life in Communist politics and his films, and develop the profound influence of this interaction, in all of its stages, on his films—from his early idealism, the influence on his work of the left-wing theater and Marxist theories, and the ideological ways of analyzing society and its warping pressures to the emotional and painful political and moral dilemmas of the postwar period, and to his break with and disillusionment in the Party, his testifying, and the subsequent impact on his work, his life, his reputation.

As it describes and analyzes the sequence of his films, it intersperses the appropriate and related narrative details of Rossen's actions within, and in relationship to, the Party and its major issues and conflicts — from the mid-thirties through the political and moral conflicts and dilemmas of the period of investigations and the blacklist. In the Congressional hearings of 1951, he discussed his criticism of the Communist Party and Communism, but refused to discuss any of his or other people's memberships or activities. He was blacklisted. After much inner conflict and moral questioning, in 1953 he decided to testify fully. The book is a factual narrative that in its details supports my definition of the complex morality of the issues of the period and its aftermath. I challenge the assumptions of the conventional wisdom about the morality of the period that has influenced the reductive view of Rossen's work and its place in American film history by questioning the unexamined assumption of an absolute dualism that maintains that those who testified were irredeemable betrayers, while those Communists who did not were unblemished moral heroes.

In tracing the stages of his career, I emphasize how his political ideals, and then his disillusionment and final dilemma and decision to testify at the hearings in 1953, were not only an influence on his work, but then produced profound changes in the films after his testimony and "exile." In this, it traces the development and evolution of his continuing and meaningful concerns and themes, the personal thematic unity over the arc of his career. It traces the development and evolution of his distinctive film style — his particular combination of the elements of the patterns and images of *mise en scène* and emphatic editing — in each film, with changes to match the changes in his human concerns and his goals for filmmaking.

His insights and themes, as he gave shape to them in his movies, are still meaningful today in this world and time of fractured values, of extreme and unexamined beliefs or no beliefs at all. I see the defining characteristic of his films — beyond any social, political, ideological issues — as works of probing the person, one's sense of identity, seeking, and motives. In his whole span of films there is a central dramatization of energy and potential misplaced, of a person "reaching," as Rossen said, "for the symbols of his identity, rather than the reality, destroying yet finding himself in the tragic process." Seeking and choosing these illusory symbols of the self, Rossen's searchers reach for power in all its forms — whether through the desire for success, for status and wealth, violence and domination, conquest of continents, or love twisted into violation.

I develop how, for Rossen, this damaging way of life, this misuse of one's power within the pressures of a society that is oppressive or falsely alluring, could be embodied in the concept and self of the hustler. Years before his return to the world of the pool hall in *The Hustler*, and its transfiguration into a parable of human betrayal, this sense of a person of energy being a hustler, *driven* to be a hustler, was present (but as yet undefined) in so many of his earlier films and central characters. And so the inevitable consequence of hustlers on all levels — of the corruption of this way of seeking one's self — is betrayal. Betrayal, in its many masks and guises, is the painful, unrelenting human flaw at the core of the ideas, instincts, and intense emotions of Rossen's films. In their demanding need to win, the all-too-human hustlers betray what they do well, their gift and élan; they betray family, friends, the women that could save them, love itself; they betray even their ideals and the bedrock principles of social justice; they betray the People, the downtrodden masses.

There is in this, of course, his sadly and angrily disillusioned vision of the betrayals within the world of communism, of the destructive alliance of unbridled power and the corruption of ideals into fervent, blind and often terribly destructive idealism. But there is in this pattern a deep personal view of life and what it is to be human. It is striking to note that some form of betrayal is present in his earliest scripts — before his recognition of the destructive deceits and human depredations of communism, before the trauma of the blacklist period and the dilemma of testifying or remaining silent. It was, however, not until the final films of his life, after this tangled and troubled period, that the theme, with all its human ambiguities and tragic results, was fully explored.

In Rossen's films, and in his hopes, the counterpoint to the drive for power and its betrayals is a sudden opening to a sense of redemption, an opening for the *possibility* of redemption. His searchers may be hustlers all, in one way or another, but some of them can learn — can at last see and admit the lost causes and the human beings they've betrayed — and find a kind and degree of redemption, if, too frequently, too late.

I hope, then, that this book captures the drama of the life, the power and energy, the conflicts and dilemmas, and the wounds under the tough exterior of this complex man — an aggressive Hollywood "player" and hustler, and a committed idealist who was eventually torn by his disillusionment and the painful dilemma of choice, was deeply affected by his decisions, and was able to transform his experience into the lasting form of film art.

Introduction: The Films of Robert Rossen — A Legacy Lost

In the dark chill of the New York winter of 1966, Robert Rossen, seriously ill, was, with wishful hope, arranging for the writing of his autobiography with editor and publisher Nan A. Talese. He died the week that she had prepared the contract to bring to him in the hospital. In a letter to Rossen's wife Sue, the noted editor wrote:

> There are few men I have known who really *cared* the way he did — and that kind of caring is so tragic to lose in this world as there is so little of it. It still exists in his work, which is a greater legacy than anyone can normally hope to leave.[1]

It was not to be. It was a legacy lost.

In the sun-drenched summer of 1936, Robert Rossen arrived in Hollywood, having had one play produced, *The Body Beautiful*— and even that for only a short run on Broadway in 1935. The play that brought Rossen to Hollywood — to his success and the complex conflicts and ambiguities of his career, to the eventual painful stations of his political and moral cross — was a comedy. It is one of the many paradoxes of his career, his works, and his life — although undoubtedly the least significant and certainly the least painful — that in all the rest of his hard-driving, pulsing work, whether screenplays written or films written, produced and directed, there is much wise-cracking, street-smart talk, and tough, hard irony and wit. There is, however, hardly a moment of softer comic relief. The world, and filmmaking, of Robert Rossen is a world of intense desires and complex motivations, of struggles for power and control and their inevitable destructive consequences, their betrayals. There are moments of redemption — often earned with pain and tragedy — but in this world the soothing relief of comedy would seem an evasion, an hypocrisy.

Producer-director Mervin Le Roy had seen Rossen's play in New York and sensed his instinctive touch for dramatic structure and narrative drive, and brought him to Hollywood, to Warner Bros. Within his first year at the studio, Rossen had written two of the most significant and memorable screenplays of the mid-thirties; and he had joined the Communist Party. Years later he recalled how it had seemed that "it [the Party] offered every possible kind of thing to you at that time which could fulfill your sense of idealism ... anything that tends toward the realization of the inner man." Years later, however, he realized that "the same reasons why you go into the party are the same reasons which make

On the set of *The Hustler* (1961), Twentieth Century–Fox (left to right): Paul Newman, Myron McCormick, Robert Rossen, Jackie Gleason.

you go out, which is ultimately the discovery that the idealism that you were looking for, the fighting for the ideas that you want, are just not in the party."² In that intricate web of conflict and contradiction are enmeshed many, if not most, of the painful dilemmas of his life and the decades of their destructive consequences — but also many of the deepening insights and explorations of his films.

Rossen's career in Hollywood and his life in the Party provide a quintessential narrative of the nature of a journey through the developments, changes, and conflicts in the motion picture industry, and in the Hollywood studio system, over three tumultuous decades — in which, in unique fashion, the Communist Party played a significant role. It was a career that spanned thirty years and included work as a screenwriter, director, and producer. By the end of his contractual stay at Warners he had written ten screenplays that were filmed; in the early forties he went on to write three more with the unique director Lewis Milestone before writing and directing ten films himself. By 1948, when he was forty, he became one of the first to wear three hats, to act as an independent writer-producer-director of his films.

At Warner Bros. in the thirties and early forties, Rossen was the most influential and prolific screenwriter under contract. He was instrumental in developing what became known as the Warners' style. It was a style of pace — fast-paced actions and scenes, big city rhythms, fast and sharp street-wise dialogue, big-city moods and tones in harsh black and white contrasts. Hit hard and move on, often with the ambiance of gangsters and crime, slums and political corruption. It was a contemporary look at tough guys in a tough world and, surprisingly for the time, tough, independent gals. In this tradition, Rossen's approach was to focus intensely on confrontations of characters with a straight-on power and directness. His sincerity and passion, his often raw, open empathy with his characters, risk the naked display of intense feeling that can sometimes veer into melodramatic excess.

But within this style and within the Warners specialty of popular movie formulas (the genres, as discussed by critics), Rossen was developing an approach that dramatized meaningful and progressive social themes, making some of his scripts the most important films of the period. In his very first film, in *Marked Woman,* for example, he brought the theme of the demeaning role and oppressive treatment of women into the structure of a gangster film. His script at the turn of the decade for *The Roaring Twenties* revisited and re-visioned in moral and human terms the whole iconography of the genre of gangster films of the thirties. In his scripts throughout this period he helped extend the boundaries of this socially-oriented realism, and began to explore the psychological dimensions within both genres and social themes.

Later, from the mid-forties on, refining this approach to character became a basic accomplishment of his mature films as a director. He moved beyond the basic liberal-left pattern, the thirties proletarian and agit-prop conflicts between decent victims and the indecent pressures of society and/or capitalism itself. In Rossen's later films—from *Body and Soul* and *All the King's Men* to *The Brave Bulls, Alexander the Great, The Hustler* and *Lilith*—the pressures are not merely out there, the corrupting forces of society, but are felt within the psychology of the characters, shaping and often disfiguring their potential decency, their attempts to forge a valid identity, and their consequent acts of betrayal. (There is a basis for dramatizing this kind of false and distorted consciousness in traditional Marxist dramatic theory, but other Marxist-loyal screenwriters rarely applied it.) These later films also began to explore a human dimension, that while still central to the social themes, is more and more a moral questioning—uneasy emotional paradoxes of choice and betrayal beyond the social and political.

While his films were discovering a greater sense of the complexities of being human, his filmmaking was maturing in style as well. He developed more artistic and sophisticated visual means for capturing, reflecting, and enforcing the dramatic structure, the narrative development of themes and insights, and of individual psychological states. It was a cinematic syntax that adapted but did not discard the earliest elements of his style, as learned in the practical workshop of the Warners studio system. In the final stage of his career, to a critical crescendo of misunderstanding, he began to venture in style to a more lyrical, evocative, and even ambiguous use of image and narrative structure. His development, and its shifts and changes, exemplified Emile Zola's lucid definition of style in art—in which "a corner of the world is seen through a temperament."

In a particularly significant aspect, this sense of style can be seen in the personal unity of his screenplays, even within the procedures—rituals even—of the traditional studio system. A close look at the screenplays, beyond that usually accorded the written work for the screen, provides a valuable insight into the importance and particularity, the major contribution to the final studio product, of *screenplays* in that period. It is a contribution not usually given the attention it warrants. For within the studio system, the notable examples of these screenplays contained much more of the personal vision of the writer, human and visual, and much more of the aspects of the final film, including imagery and editing patterns, than were provided by scripts written in the later period of independent and personally expressive directors. Despite being assigned subjects and genre requirements, and being pressed by short, rushed schedules, and despite the factory-like patterns of levels of command, the best of these scripts of the thirties and forties, like Rossen's, could provide a personal point of view, even an ideological one, and a thoroughness of detail for the actual translation onto the screen. For also within this system, directors were frequently under even greater pressure regarding time, with schedules, often short, regularly set for films to be directed. Many, like those Rossen often worked with (and unlike Lewis Milestone, whom he later worked with and learned from), were efficient craftsman churning out a number of films a year, sometimes even a month, with a sharp sense of pace, momentum, build-up and climax, but without the time, impulse, or, most importantly, visual creativity to determine and control the visual format for the words and actions in screenplays. When that aspect was provided by the script, they relied on it, and the results are evident. When it was not provided, the resulting film was more flat, mundane, and workmanlike. It is an aspect of the relationship between screenplay and film, screenwriter and director, that Rossen's work in the thirties and forties illuminates in a meaningful and significant way.

In Rossen's scripts that were directed by others there are a striking set of parallels — themes, views of character, visual patterns — that provide the basis for seeing the temperament of the writer working through a consistent, deepening, and maturing point of view. These screenplays became the early stages of a personal body of work, an *oeuvre*. It is a body of work that increasingly reflected an emotional and meaningful inter-relationship with the experiences of his own life, his early political ideals and ideology, and eventually the major stages of his turmoil and dilemmas, and the pain of his disillusionment and rebellion against that ideology. This intense degree of creative inter-action between his life — and particularly his political beliefs and conflicts — and his films was (and remains) unique among American directors.

As his career progressed, he fought, often without clear victories, for the opportunity to produce this significant body of work by mastering the slippery business side of the film industry. "Fighting" is more than a metaphor. Tough and aggressive, he could do battle with the best of them. Working within the mental warfare of the Hollywood system, he was a hustler himself, one who understood the hustlers' game and saw through the guises of those who would hustle him, figuratively breaking his thumbs if they had to (or even just wanted to), as they did those of Fast Eddie in *The Hustler*. He was a power player with a critical insight into power. He used their system, worked his way up, made friends and enemies, hurt a few along the way, gained the three hats and at least some degree of control, lost it, and gained it back through struggle and strategy, endurance and talent, via his own personal manipulation of power. Like so many of his protagonists, he liked to, even needed to, win. Sometimes at whatever the cost. There were those — not even those who became his political enemies — who, looking back, could recall that he sometimes could be a son-of-a-bitch, but an awesome one.

He shared the inner paradoxes of so many of his characters, living a life of intense drama, conflicts, and contradictions. He was an idealist who was active in the Communist

Party to do good in the world, and was active within the Party during World War II — following its current line — to help save the world for democracy. But he was also a driving career realist, an aggressive personal force, skillful at maneuvering and manipulating, and a natural deal-maker — a hustler. Yet again, he remained a growing and maturing and increasingly sensitive artist, a thoughtful, compassionate student of human need and desire, and of human frailty.

Through his Warners period and on into the forties, Rossen was a regular participant in Communist Party activities and crusades. By the end of World War II, in erratic, fitful stages, he had begun to break with the Party. In 1947, however, he was one of the nineteen summoned to Washington for the hearings of the House Un-American Activities Committee — when only the first ten (ever since extolled as the Hollywood Ten), plus the German playwright Bertold Brecht, were actually called to testify. When HUAC began a new, broader round of hearings in 1951, he was one of those who attempted to forge a middle way, answering some questions but not others. The strategy didn't work, and he was blacklisted. In 1953, within the moral morass of the blacklist period, after much soul-searching and attempting to sort out the demands and dilemmas of his own motives, he did testify. He did name names — a few dozen presented on lists. He began to work again and slowly rebuilt his career toward his final two masterful films, *The Hustler* and *Lilith*.

Rossen was the most active member of the Party among those who then turned against the Party and testified. Among the major figures who testified, he was a member longer than any others, including Elia Kazan, who was a member for only a brief period in the mid-thirties. He personifies the whole set of dilemmas, conflicts, paradoxes — and personal anguish — over the choice of testifying or not. His decision to testify had an unrelenting impact on his life. His eventual testimony was thoughtful and principled, yet it left him ostracized by former friends and colleagues, vilified in print while alive and even after his death. It caused the value of his films, of his films as a meaningful and artistic oevre, to be ignored or denied, and left him embittered at this treatment. While continuing to work, he never set foot in Hollywood again. But the crisis and its lingering scars led as well to a growth in his work as a filmmaker, to a deepening complexity of human insight into and compassion for human frailty. His films are particularly an American saga. They illuminate their time in America in a way unmatched, save possibly by those of Kazan.

In 1951, when facing the personal and moral dilemmas posed by the congressional investigations of communism in Hollywood and the developing blacklist, he wrote a personal statement about the intertwining of his politics and his career, which he felt might be coming to an end. The statement was never published. At one point in this text he wrote:

> I tried to be as honest in my portrayal of the American scene as I possibly could, and I believe, now, that whatever success I had was due to the fact that I was so deeply imbedded in that scene, that my roots received the same nourishment as millions of other Americans, that my hopes were theirs, and so were my fears, and that they recognized this quality in my work.... My ability to articulate the silent cry that lay in the throats of so many people for so many years gave me my success.[3]

This full and meaningful body of work dramatized not only the conflicts and paradoxes of American society, but also of capitalism itself. It is a critique that is influenced by the ideology and ideals of the political Left, and the political drama and literature of the thirties. Although he never made a film about Hollywood or the blacklist directly, his movies, more than the films of any others, reflect (even more than he had ever consciously intended) the conflicts and dilemmas, the moral and emotional ambiguities, and the psychological wounds of the world of Hollywood in the time of the blacklist.

In Rossen's Hollywood, betrayal had become as much a part of the climate as the indifferent sun — not only in the political betrayals of ideals or of people (despite the extolling of the People) during the period of the Communist Party in Hollywood, not only in the conflicts and torments during the time of the blacklist, or in the lingering, extreme claims in its aftermath, but also in the everyday, often ruthless times of the business and even the art of making movies, and too often in the personal interactions in the lives of those struggling and even succeeding in the movie business.

For Rossen, this damaging way of life, this misuse of one's power within the pressures of a society that is oppressive or falsely alluring, could be embodied in the concept and self of the hustler. The hustler is more than a professional pool player; he is any player in the destructive game of power, this misuse of one's energy, one's gift, one's élan.

And so the inevitable, perennial consequence of hustlers on all levels — this hustlers' way of living, of existentially being in the world, this corruption of seeking one's self — is betrayal. Betrayal, in its many masks and guises, is the painful, unrelenting human flaw at the core of the ideas, instincts, and intense emotions of Rossen's films. It is embedded, like a deep, stabbing, always embedded burr, in the drive for power and success — their sweet smell (in Clifford Odets' phrase) and the sweet perfume of the women that come with them. It is in winning in some way or other, and at whatever the cost. In this demanding need, the all-too-human hustlers betray what they do well, their gift and élan. They betray family, friends, and the women that could save them — love itself. They betray even their ideals and the bedrock principles of social justice. They betray those whom, at least at the start, they are acting for — the people, the needy and downtrodden masses, Willie Stark's hicks, Stalin and Lenin's proletariat.

And yet there is still more involved in Rossen's vision of this ubiquitous pattern of betrayal than ideological and political conflicts, whether in terms of ideals lost or of the monstrous violations of Jews and millions of others. There is a deep personal view of life and what it is to be human. It is striking to note that some form of betrayal is present in his earliest scripts — before his recognition of the destructive deceits and human depredations of Communism, and before the trauma of the blacklist period and the dilemma of testifying or remaining silent. It was, however, not until the final films of his life, after the impact of the ideological upheavals and moral dilemmas, that the theme was probed with all its human ambiguities and tragic results.

In Rossen's films, and in his hopes in life, the counterpoint to the drive for power and its inevitable betrayals is a sudden opening to a sense of the need for redemption, an opening for the *possibility* of redemption. His searchers may be hustlers all, in one way or another, but some of them can learn — can at last see and admit the lost causes they've betrayed — and find a kind and degree of redemption. Over the course of the sequence of films, and in Rossen's deepening, maturing vision of life, the movement was toward a more earned, more truly felt redemption — in the drama and in the human life depicted. As in the classic tragedy that Rossen admired, the redemption often comes at the cost of the death or destruction of others. It can be said to be earned by the recognition and acceptance of one's guilt in the tragic cost, the price that others have paid. And, as comes with this territory, it is always too late.

It is love that often provides the path and possibility for change and redemption, but it is also love that, in its complexity, can be violated as one aspect of betrayal. It is women who can open the driven men to the possibility of love and its gifts; but it is women who can be the lure to the pathway of false symbols of power and success.

In this climate he began more and more to view his betrayers and hustlers — view us all? — not with righteous judgment but with compassionate understanding. "As for people," he said, "I don't believe that they are ever of one piece. Nothing is all black or all rose-colored. Things are more complicated, and the best we can do is still try to render them in their complexity to attempt to understand them better."[4]

Robert Rossen's career, then, is the epitome of the most successful moviemakers of the era — that mixture of professional skill and talent with business "moxie" (as his characters would say), drive, and energy. It was a battling career, but it is made more distinctive and significant by his central role in the life of the Communist Party in Hollywood, by his personifying the period's unusual interaction of ideology and the business and art of making movies (and later by his painful role as a central target). It was a career that produced a personal and meaningful set of films within the studio system and yet with a core personal unity within their diversity. It is a body of work that provides a valuable counterpoint to much of the over-publicized, over-praised work of those of the old Left in Hollywood who have become romanticized heroes in the writing and teaching of film history.

And yet his valuable body of work has not been seen for what it was and is — if it can be said to have been truly "seen" at all. There has now been more than a half century of the denial of this legacy, of the distorting and ignoring of the value of the unified artistic achievement of his work and career, and its significant place in the history of the American motion picture. Even when a film like *All the Kings Men* or *The Hustler* has been respected and remembered, it has been seen only dimly, even superficially, rather than being seen and understood as a film by Robert Rossen, as part of a significant and meaningful body of work, and as a stage of an expression of a temperament in style and theme.

Behind this neglect there are, it is true, reasons of film theoretics, aesthetics, and fashions. But in his case these are adjuncts to a deeper, stronger, and insistent impact of ideology that has set the assumptions for looking (or, in a sense, not looking) at Rossen and his films.

It is clear that the mocking, nose-thumbing fashions and ironies of postmodern art, of art theory and its even more extensive development in arcane film theory, and of art and film teaching are not exactly hospitable to the traditional straight-on sincerity (beyond the pale!), intense drama, and classic sense of irony of almost all of his work, or his trademark stylistic mixture of classic *mise en scène* and climactic editing. His sincerity and passion did not fit the academic and artistic paradigms of the postmodern cliques, as summarized in another context by the art critic Jed Perl: "But there is a new quality to the skepticism that we are seeing today, for it is not so much a skepticism about the modern orthodoxy — or about classical or romantic values — as it is an unwillingness to believe that anybody ever actually believed in anything." Or as cultural critic Camille Paglia has called it, a "smug, debunking cynicism."

Another factor, with more immediate impact, was a change in film (and other) fashion on the level of popular culture, rather than esoteric theoretics. In the decade of Rossen's death, particularly in the years up into the seventies after his death, American film history took an important sharp, veering turn. The important and noteworthy development of a new style of a independent American filmmaking brought with it a strong exhilarating rush, a fresh and vivid new fashion in American moviemaking and an eagerly accepted new set of values in criticism. It was a creative, if self-satisfied, often even smug, feeling of liberation from the old, whatever that was considered to be.

This American version of the French New Wave was impelled by the rebellions of the sixties and the opposition to the Vietnam War, and vaguely, loosely influenced by the European Theater of the Absurd and the alienation theories and practice of Bertold Brecht. It created a volatile, quirky new style for American films. Impulsive, rebellious, and proudly and creatively contradictory, this style mixed humor and tragedy, unrest and often zany character ambiguities, and social and political protest, whether melodramatic or satirical (or both). Filmmakers discovered and relished the impact and value of ambiguity and discontinuity — of shifts and blurring of tone and mood, of an openness of narrative patterns and sequences, of enigmatic boundaries of scenes, of patterns of editing. There came a discovery as well of "heroes" who were not that "heroic," not maturely focused, nor clearly defined in the narrative. It all resulted in the adoption of a mocking critical stance toward society and traditional filmmaking that had the effect (certainly unintended and un-noticed in the excitement of the new renegade flurry) of creating a new cutting edge of values for the appraisal of, even the perception of, films. Along the way came the accepted assumptions that more traditional filmmakers like Rossen were unworthy of attention. Lost was the ability to notice in his films the valued emphasis on irony and ambiguities of motive and actions, and the complicated mixed nature of his central characters (and without the propagandic simplifications of the anti-authority, anti-capitalist protest of many of the new films).

The excitement, praise, and critical establishment of the new style of film accelerated the distracted bypassing of his work, And it certainly contributed to an initial impetus toward an unconsidered definition of his work as out of touch with the rebellious present.

But all this theory and fashion was only the surface flow and swirl of the vectors of cultural force that produced an assumption, a premise, an image, an accepted definition of a filmmaker and the place of his work in what is deemed important fashion and theory. The new fashion and theoretics would not have had this continuing effect on responses to, or even recognition of, Rossen's work without the deeper emotional and ideological core of personal and artistic criticism that permeated and shaped the responses to him and his work. It was the beginning and unfortunate continuing context for his fall from view and grace.

For he is also, unfairly and tragically, the key representative figure of a significant group of men and women, with mixed and complex motives, who testified. And thus he has borne the distorting and often vicious vilifying impact of ideological bias on the treatment of his morals and character, his reputation, and his work — not only by his former colleagues and comrades, but by the spread of this bias into the unexamined conventional wisdom of the standard historical and critical record.

The prevalent, conventional assumptions established by the Left and nurtured through the generations in academia and film theoretics and history posits an absolute moral dichotomy in the era of Congressional investigations and the Hollywood blacklist (the era from 1947 to, roughly, 1960). It is a dualism of biblical dimensions and righteousness — pure heroes and martyrs who refused to testify, or irredeemable betrayers and scoundrels who testified. In the phrase popularized by Victor Navasky (a leading perpetuator of this mythology of an absolute moral dualism), Rossen committed the unpardonable sin of "naming names" while appearing at hearings held by the House Un-American Activities Committee. In so doing, in another iconic Navasky phrase, he did not "behave decently." And so, beyond redemption or absolution, he is confined and defined within the absolutes of this historical mythology. Rossen, like others who testified, has become nothing beyond the namer of names, the informer, the betrayer.

The relentless, scornful flavor, the fervent religiosity, of this crusade is captured in the biblical allusions used by Navasky in the introduction to his *Naming Names* (1980), a book with a major influence on generations of responses to the issues and conflicts of the period — and to the people and their works:

> The Aramaic word for informer as found in the Book of Daniel is *Akhal Kurtza*, whose literal translation is "to eat the flesh of someone else." The so-called Minean curse, which was introduced as the twelfth benediction to the daily Amidah prayer, says "And for the informer may there be no hope." ... Penalties for the informer range from flogging and imprisonment to branding the forehead, cutting out the tongue, cutting off the hand, banishment, and, most frequently, death.[5]

A minute sampling among far too many vulgar and disturbing examples of vituperative personal attacks on Rossen through the decades might include screenwriter Walter Bernstein's rant in *Tender Comrades* (1999), an anthology of interviews of major blacklisted figures. After complaining about Rossen's alleged mistreatment of him when Rossen, he claimed, supposedly reneged on a deal to hire him, Bernstein said, "I felt there was something essentially corrupt about him on a personal level.... You could tell that there was something slippery about him."[6]

Similarly, writer and director Abraham Polonsky, a central figure among the Hollywood Reds whom Rossen battled with during the filming of *Body and Soul*, said:

> You wouldn't want to be on a desert island with Rossen, because if the two of you didn't have any food, he might want to have you for lunch tomorrow.... He was talented like Elia Kazan was talented, but like Kazan he also had a rotten character. In the end they both became stool pigeons. I figured all along that Rossen couldn't be trusted.[7]

(See further discussion of attacks on Rossen in Chapter 19.)

Others have received the same abuse, particularly director Edward Dmytryk. In the view of the committed Left, his betrayal was felt to be a personal violation, for he had been "one of us." He was one of the original Hollywood Ten, had defied the Committee in the first hearings in 1947, and had gone to jail. That he had done that honorably, even while in great inner conflict over the Party and his connection to it — that he then changed his position on the basis of principles that he had finally determined for himself — this has not been a part of the discussion of Edward Dmytryk, either by the Left or (in the important transmission of these views) the poplar press that has accepted the Left's premises. Typical attacks on him again illustrate the continuing intensity of the vendetta.

For Communist screenwriter Lester Cole, Dmytryk was "so morally degenerate it is almost impossible to comprehend."[8] Screenwriter and major Communist ideologue Albert Maltz wrote again and again about the blow Dmytryk had dealt him:

> [I]t is nauseatingly ugly when someone you have known, someone who fought by your side, went with you into prison—became such an eager wretch, such a fawning informer....
> He has lied and befouled others with his lies; he has traduced the good principles for which he once stood.[9]

As the conventional wisdom of this moralistic dualism has been passed down through generations of cultural "gatekeepers," a crucial important and damaging layer of unexamined assumptions has accrued — that these political betrayals, these moral failures, are, in turn, linked to failures in the films of those who testified. In this accepted and unnoticed climate of opinion, one can remain ignorant of a filmmaker's work with no apologies due or even considered.

With the mixture of moral righteousness and artistic criticism that is typical of him and of this "genre" of criticism, Polonsky commented, "He [Rossen] was talented, but like Kazan he also had a rotten character." After they testified, the films of both, he averred, were "marred by bad conscience."[10] And Bernstein: "It is important, too, what testimony did to his [Rossen's] work."[11]

Comments by noted liberal director Martin Ritt capture the essence of this consistent approach — and are indicative as well of how ideology and long-held resentment can blind an accomplished director to the real accomplishments of another. For Ritt, an effective director of films with good liberal heart but less complexity, such as *Norma Rae*, the moral universe holds only two extreme poles:

> I must say I don't know a single person who behaved, in my view, properly, and who has been any less of a human being for the rest of his life. And I know a lot of guys who behaved badly, and who have not fully realized themselves as artists or human beings since that time.... They [particularly Kazan and Rossen] made a wrong move. They violated themselves.[12]

Those who testified, however, whatever their own complex mixture of needs and motives, were not without the principles and cogent arguments that their detractors denied them. Among the reasons cited for his deciding to testify (in his actual testimony, which, like that of others, is never dealt with in these diatribes against him), Rossen, in one example, referred to his previous action (in not testifying fully) as "what I considered to be a position of individual conscience.... I did a lot of thinking. I don't think, after two years of thinking, that any one individual can ever indulge himself in the luxury of individual morality or pit it against what I feel today very strongly is the security and safety of this nation." Among the things he realized was that in the Communist Party "none of the things that you believe in were being fought for in terms of the ideal itself. They were merely being instruments for some other end in itself."[13] (See Chapter 15 for further discussion of Rossen's testimony and his reasons for testifying.)

Among *his* reasons for testifying, Kazan stated that he wanted "to help break open the secrecy"[14] that the Communist Party thrived on. For him, "the Communists who decry the lack of freedom in this country haven't given thought to the amount of freedom allowed the people of the Soviet Union":[15]

> We must never let the Communists get away with the pretense that they stand for the very things which they kill in their own countries.... The people who owe you an explanation (no apology expected) are those who, year after year, held the Soviet blameless for all their crimes.[16]

When Dmytryk, after serving his sentence for contempt as a member of the Hollywood Ten, finally testified, he stated that he had decided that "defending the Communist

Party was something worse than naming names. I did not want to remain a martyr to something that I absolutely believed was immoral and wrong."[17]

When he had refused to testify in 1947, he had already rebelled against the Party over its insistence on following the Party line and on Party discipline that infringed on his freedom of thought and speech—despite the claims made in those hearings to the contrary. In 1951 he explained:

> The Party has a good explanation for everything that troubles a man. If he says he doesn't have freedom, the great explainer, whoever he is in that locality, will point out that he has the freedom to tell the truth; that the Communist Party has discovered the ultimate truth; and within that limit he can speak. Anything outside of the Party line is a lie. Of course anything capitalistic is basically a lie because it comes from a system they consider dishonest to begin with.[18]

For the righteous and committed, however, there could be no sincere beliefs, no valid principles for testifying. Motives could only be scurrilous, and morally and artistically destructive. Bernstein's comment on Rossen is representative of this kind of denial (and little concern for accuracy): "Rossen had no real belief larger than his ego. He saw informing as pure survival, without any of the justifications other informers found necessary to give.... I felt the same as I did while rereading Kazan's testimony: the two of them didn't believe anything that they were saying."[19]

Early on, prolific screenwriter and pamphleteer Dalton Trumbo, in a letter to Guy Endore in 1956, told him, with his usual epistolary flourish, that if you look at someone who has informed "on friends who have harmed no one, and who thereafter earns money he could not have earned before ... I will show you not a decent citizen, not a patriot, but a miserable scoundrel who will ... if the price is right, betray not just his friends but his country itself."[20] Similarly, screenwriter Ring Lardner, Jr., said this of Rossen: "He had just started a new career as a director when he was subpoenaed for the second time and decided to preserve that career at the expense of his former values."[21]

The Hollywood Reds who attacked those who testified, and who for half a century have been enshrined as pure noble martyrs (and their work in films consistently over-praised), were the same true believers who through the decades remained silent before more than the House Un-American Activities Committee. Even when some accepted some blemishes on the purity of communism, they continued to remain silent about the monumentally destructive realities of the Soviet Union and international communism.

Here follows a typical cross-section:

- Lardner: "[T]he best hope for mankind lay in the Soviets. Only in Russia were massive construction and planning for the future going on."
- John Howard Lawson: "The only truly conscious anti-fascist force during the war years was the Communist Party."
- Polonsky: "[T]he best vehicle for bringing the socialist transformation of society."
- Maltz: "[T]he Party was the best hope for humanity ... the one force which moved the world toward brotherhood."
- Cole: "[T]o reach those goals [brotherhood and equality] required organization, and the Party, whatever its strengths or weaknesses at any given time—and I was aware of both—remained the only viable organization through which to make the struggle."[22]

- Lillian Hellman and Dashiell Hammett made a published "Call" for "the cooperation of this country with other nations and people opposed to Fascism, including the Soviet Union, which has been the most conscious defender of the people."[23]

But all this is the self-righteous ideological and emotional stereotyping of the people, issues, and morality that has held sway for more than half a century. It is a dogma, a dualism that has become accepted and assumed as truth spread beyond its original ideological bias. The consequences of this prevailing paradigm of morality affect the climate of opinion that has, in turn, shaped the writing and teaching of film criticism and history. These assumptions and opinions have, in a further turn, been filtered down and dispersed through academia, film studies and journals, criticism, and history into the image-shapers of popular culture—publishing, the press, television, and movies. Unexamined at the popular level and even unnoticed as accepted truth, this entrenched moral equation has led to the distortion of the history and judgment of films and filmmakers in Hollywood—and of the lingering image of those who testified that is presented as "conventional wisdom" in the popular press.

The biographer Joan Mellen is no ideologue of the Left. Yet in a passing anecdote in her popular and widely-praised book *Hellman and Hammett* (1996) she absorbs and passes on this unnoticed spread into accepted moral parlance and paradigm: "One day as [a group of people] were chatting about the Korean War on the Rosen porch, filmmaker Robert Rossen, a *government informer*, appeared"[24] [emphasis added].

There are, then, many forms of, and many paths to, betrayal—in ways not faced and understood in the decades of moral judgments of the painful drama of the period and its protagonists. If one grants that those who testified did act on principle, they, however, still paid the price—as in all difficult dilemmas—of a kind of betrayal of both principle and people. They named the names of others as members or former members of the Party, and so they became complicit in the actions of the Committee and enforcers of the blacklist. Because of this they were complicit to some degree in the consequences for those who were named. The nature of this betrayal, however, is further complicated, since in almost all cases the names were already known. Their act of naming them did not determine whatever consequences ensued for other people

Those Communists and close followers in Hollywood who did not testify were blacklisted, and suffered the unjust loss of their freedom to work. Their suffering, however, is shaded and mottled into the moral paradoxes of the period by their loud and evasive silence about the monstrous consequences of the communism that was their cause and crusade, and about the destructive deceits of the American Communist Party as a party to those consequences.

Who then were the scoundrels and betrayers of human freedom and human lives? Who betrayed what in the tangled web of "utterly human" contradictions? In that troubled and tormented time, who among them was not a "hustler" of some sort, for some form of beliefs and principles, some crusading version of the truth? Or of ineluctable personal needs and desires? The answers are not all that simple.

The films of Robert Rossen did not give those answers, but through the stages and changes in his career and his life they captured, in deepening complexity, some of the dilemmas suggested by those questions—and not only for the Hollywood world of communism. The films captured his corner of that broader human world, as seen through his temperament but shaping for us in a singular way the temperament of their times.

PART ONE

The Writer—
Craft, Idealism and Ideology

And I don't agree with the *Cahiers* lad, a fine fellow — Marcorelles, I think — who said to me as we were having lunch, that there were no more "hustlers" in Europe. Then I looked at him: at a nearby table were a group of people who were there for the launching of *Jules and Jim*, starlets, businessmen, photographers, and so on. I pointed them out, saying to him: "And they? They are not 'hustlers'? You don't believe that they try to rob one another, to exploit one another, all day long?" — ROBERT ROSSEN

1

A Matter of Experience — From the Lower East Side to Hollywood and the Party

In the nice phrase of the Irish poet Seamus Heaney, in writing about the nourishing springs of poetry, "the art radiated [from] the density of experience that has been lived through." This echoes roundly with Robert Rossen's sense of the influence of experience in a far different art, one often characterized as the product of multiple efforts and forces, even, in the current theoretical jargon, without any determining *intentionality*. But for Rossen, "In our profession everything is only a matter of experience. Good or bad, experiences always leave traces; it is they that inspire us." In this last interview, he told Daniel Stein, "the best kind of pictures you can get are films that are not all intellectually constructed, but drawn out of your experiences and senses."[1]

From the start of his career in the studio system — even while fulfilling assignments demarcated by others, and constrained by the structures and icons of popular genres and the demands of the commercial industry — Rossen's work was something that was developing from within. His work — both screenplays and films he also directed — was filtered through his own nature, the contradictions of his own personality and character, and his own inner conflicts, whether recognized or not. To a degree unique in the Hollywood of his time, his films and themes and deep concerns, his personal sense of his craft, rise from the "traces" of the experiences of his life. These experiences, and his absorbing of them, range from the past through the dramatic impact of his shifting present life — his early life in New York City, his exposure to and participation in the left wing social drama of the thirties, his decades of battles in the Hollywood studio system, his life in and belief in the Communist Party and its ideals, his disillusionment with and break with the Party, and finally the dilemmas and anguish of his decision to testify — and the painful but ironically revelatory, and artistically significant, consequences of doing so.

In 1951, in a statement he wrote prior to his appearance before the House Un-American Activities Committee, he summed up his approach to making movies:

> I have always been very serious about films. I considered them an art form on a level with any other art form and I think I contributed somewhat to the recognition of that idea.... I

tried to be as honest in my portrayal of the American scene as I possibly could and I believe, now, that whatever success I had was due to the fact that I was so deeply embedded in that scene, that my roots received the same nourishment as millions of other Americans, that my hopes were theirs, and so were my fears, and that they recognized this quality in my work....

My ability to articulate the silent cry that lay in the throats of so many people for so many years gave me success.[2]

The films that he felt achieved this kind of humane, emotional success were in a tradition that he admired:

I believe that in one way or another, the great *cineastes*, too, share in this humanist tradition [which he also thought had guided the young Marx]. Take Bergman, for example, the man in search of God; take Fellini; it is always a point of view, a way of relating one's experience, of preserving what one has received, with which one has lived, and a way of transmitting it in terms of relations among human beings. That's Renoir, who attains that more than anyone else. It is an end we all pursue, no matter where we start from.[3]

He expanded on this relationship between film style and life — to capture "the moment of truth" — when talking to Jean-Louis Noames of *Cahiers du Cinema* in 1963:

[T]he task of one whom you call in *Cahiers auteur de films* is to speak of films in a much deeper way, to create a style in the making of films, a style in the service of a content....

It must capture the moment of truth, the moment when things reveal themselves as they are. They open out in virtue of a situation that creates a moment of emotion.[4]

His memories of his early life, the feelings and attitudes it engendered in him, the culture of the Lower East Side that he lived in and with, that he observed and heard about, learned about, imbibed, absorbed, the lore and even the myths — all this became the clay he would shape in his creative work from its beginnings to his last film. It was a world that he used for convincing palpable details, of characters and characterization, relationships and situations, quotidian signs of daily life, iconographic images of the essence of that life, images that conveyed both fact and feeling. But it was more than a milieu of events, people, and physical environment that he could use. It was also a world that shaped the sense of what life basically is that the films project, whatever the subject matter, however commercial or genre-based or personal the project. It is a sense of life as a struggle, of intense confrontation, battle, power and survival — often on mistaken, self-defeating, and even tragic terms. Whatever the later influences and additions — left-wing dramas, commercial genres, ideological concepts, source materials — these experiences were called up or merely rose up instinctively in his work.

Like so many of his own heroes, Rossen himself (born Robert Rosen on March 16, 1908) was from an impoverished area — in his case the Rivington Street section of New York's East Side. His neighborhood was just beyond the limits of the main Jewish ghettoes of the Lower East Side, his family just beyond the painful edge of poverty. But his particular corner of that world shared many of the characteristics of those neighborhoods. Many families, like the Rossens, lived in what were known as "railroad flats" — long, narrow apartments with a string of small windowless inner rooms. These were typically in brick buildings of five or six stories, with a lacing of fire escapes, regularly draped with laundry across their street facades or across alleyways or even streets. Even in this kind of newer building, famed mob boss Meyer Lansky described years later how the rooms were smaller and more suffocating than in their old flat in the Brownsville section of Brooklyn. "Hot in summer, cold in winter," he recalled. "I joined a library as soon as I could."[5] And he hung out there, as did Robert Rossen.

Rossen's parents had emigrated from Russia. His father rebelled not only against the physical hardships and monotony of working in the garment trades, but also against its sapping of one's spirit, one's dignity. He eventually found a greater sense of freedom in being a house painter, but it came with no steady income and even less security. At that time his trade also meant, however, that he had to move his family on occasion to where he was doing a painting job, even to streets and areas where there were few other Jewish families.

During Rossen's adolescence he lost the sense of community of living in a Jewish ghetto, whatever its deprivations. He told Daniel Stein many years later, "I was always living in a hostile environment with Irish kids, Poles, Italians, Germans — I lived in Yorkville for a while — so that I probably had a clearer look at the impact of environment on character and vice versa than I would have had otherwise.... I had a few professional bouts as a fighter, but fighting was a defense just to live in that neighborhood."[6]

Within the tensions and conflicts of the ghettos or the polyglot neighborhoods, the candy store was a kind of haven for boys and young men, a place to hang out, but also a place to have a sense of identity and community. In *Body and Soul* (1947), the parents of Charley Davis own such a candy store. It was a perfect hang-out for the boys — and for the budding gangs. The iconic comedian and actor Eddie Cantor later described his initiation into this world of gangs in the "outfit" of "Pork-Faced Sam." The boys would invade a store and distract the storekeeper while several would then steal items, and then all would flee. "And the next day the leader came down to see him and sold him back his stock of bicycles."[7]

It was in the cigar stores, however, that the real money was made in taking illegal bets, participating in the "numbers" lottery, or being a front for the sale and even the production of illegal liquor during Prohibition. Here was often the testing ground for young men finding their identity — and the siren promise of money, power, and women — in the gangland world of bootlegging, gambling, racketeering. Cafes then became their meeting places, often along Second Avenue, a wide commercial street that was lively day or night, with blocks and blocks of restaurants, theaters, dance halls and some of the newer apartment buildings. A well-known example was Segal's Café. Its "habitués" were a cross-section of established and neophyte gangsters, from Irish Patsye Keegan, a "mack" (pimp), and Dopey Benny, a for-hire gunman/strong-man/arsonst (arson was popularly known as Jewish Lightning), to Charley Pearlstein, strike-breaker and sometime doorman, and Little Mikie Newman, a full-fledged mobster.[8]

By the twenties these racketeers had moved in to almost completely control the prostitution business. Along with the control of bootlegging and gambling, control of whores was one of the bases of the rise of gangland powers in the neighborhoods and the trigger for gangland battles. One of the most successful of these gangster-pimps was Motche Goldberg. Known as the "King of the Vice Trust," he spread and developed his "business" until he controlled a dozen or so whorehouses and more than a hundred women on a number of streets of the neighborhood, including Rivington. He — like others in the prostitution, gambling, bootlegging, and protection rackets (and Vanning in *Marked Woman* and Eddie in *The Roaring Twenties*, 1939, and many other filmland gangsters) — sought to use their accumulating wealth to move out into legitimate businesses and become true capitalists, true American successes.[9]

Goldberg's rackets, and those of every other racketeer and mobster, depended on the bribery of police and public officials, a corruption of law and order, and a betrayal of the justice system that was an open and constant facet of life in the neighborhoods.

In the twenties of Rossen's youth, the violence, the very terms and incidents, of this gang rivalry had been a constant neighbor on the Lower East Side. Just as Eddie and George do in *The Roaring Twenties*, Meyer Lansky and Benny "Bugsy" Siegel had started in the neighborhood riding shotgun to protect liquor convoys, as did the powerful gang leader Longy Zwillman. One commentator noted that they were a "group of killers so tough even the Dutchman [Dutch Schultz] shied away."[10] They moved on to taking over a few convoys themselves (again like Eddie and George), and as they gained more power, they acquired a string of speakeasies and ran a number of gambling joints. Selling the "suckers" their whisky, they thus made money two ways.

One of the most notorious open battles of the real "Roaring Twenties" occurred on Norfolk Street, in the block between Delancey and Rivington. Little Augie had achieved notable success (so much so he was talking about retiring soon) by hijacking liquor convoys and warehouses and setting up speakeasies, night clubs, and gambling joints. But those he had stolen from had marked him for death. While he was out on the sidewalk with his bodyguards, including Legs Diamond, a black sedan swept up, and slowed down. In a hail of bullets, Augie was killed; he was buried in the rain. The silver plate on his massive cherry-red coffin read: "Jacob Orgen, Age 25 years." He was thirty-three. Eight years earlier, when he had taken control of the gang, his father had announced that, for him and his family, Jacob Orgen was dead.[11]

Surviving with one's dignity intact in this volatile, often hostile and dangerous world contributed to the development of Rossen's own aggressive, driving, forceful nature. But it also influenced his constant concern for and probing of what it meant to have a true sense of oneself and one's powers — of the need for one's own power in a threatening world, and yet the dangers and violations that power could bring.

During these hectic twenties, Rossen attended New York University for several years; but he left to fulfill a literary bent that he had developed early in life, in great part by his own escapes into the world of libraries and local reading rooms. This direction for what was clearly a natural talent was instilled and encouraged by his mother and her side of the family. His grandfather was a rabbi, an uncle wrote poetry in Hebrew, another was a sometime writer and journalist, and another was a professional translator. In Russia they had been drawn to socialist organizations as a bulwark against anti–Semitism. In their apartments in New York their talk often turned to the appeal of the socialist movement and the better way of life they envisioned it could bring. For them socialism meant no anti–Semitism. These discussions resonated deeply within Rossen when he was drawn to the ideals of the Left and eventually joined the Communist Party.

The strongest artistic and political influence on Rossen and his work was the communist-oriented social protest drama of the late twenties and early thirties. It was a dynamic, hopeful, and "fruitful" time — new plays and playwrights, theater groups, theater magazines, ardent talk and theorizing, forums and lectures, all energized by the synergy between political and artistic idealism, Marxism and Modernism. Even the central Communist Party political magazine *New Masses* regularly carried not only extensive (and doctrinaire) theater reviews, but also theoretical pieces by such central American figures as Mike Gold and John Howard Lawson, and translations from Russian and European theorists.

When Rossen began to work in theater, his first job was as an assistant stage manager for *Precedent*, a social protest play about the Mooney-Billings trial. Nonetheless, while he was drawn to this kind of protest play and affiliation with left-wing ideas, he was also already intent on getting somewhere in his career, on being a success. This was the integral two sides of him: thinking and feeling, committed but also hustling, battling to get ahead and do more than merely get ahead. Through intent and circumstance his next connections were with theater groups not affiliated with the Left, including work with the Washington Square Players and a season with the Maverick-Woodstock Players in Woodstock, New York. At Woodstock he directed several revivals, such as Kenny Nicholson's *The Barkers*. He began, however, to move further into the burgeoning theater of the Left. By 1931 he was directing serious plays of the Left in New York City, including Richard Maibum's *The Tree* in 1931 and then Maibaum's anti–Nazi play (an early example of this theme) *Birthright*.

About the time of his work on Maibaum's *The Tree*, Rossen was introduced to the script of a protest play by Paul Peters called *Wharf Nigger*. He was immediately attracted to, and firmly believed in, its political idealism and proletarian dramatic structure. He invested some time and even money (his and others) in trying to get it produced, but with no result. In fact, he was forced to let the project go after he was attacked in the *New Masses* for being a bourgeois director because of the plays he had directed at Woodstock. It was the first of many of his encounters with the ideological fervor of the Communists. The play, re-named *Stevedore* and re-written by Peters and George Sklar, was later produced by Theatre Union and was one of the seminal left-wing dramas of the thirties.[12]

In 1932 *The Daily Worker* carried brief articles on February 6 and February 16 that on February 17 Robert Rossen would direct the protest play *Steel*, written by John Wexley, under the auspices of *The Daily Worker* and the Workers School, a Communist Party organization.[13] By 1932 Wexley was already active in New York radical circles, including the Workers Theater. Two of Wexley's topical protest plays were among the most discussed, and attended, of that era. In 1934 his play about the Scottsboro boys (and the CP's touted defense of them against the racist injustice of their trial in the South), *They Shall Not Die*, was produced in New York. His play *The Last Mile*, an attack on capital punishment as an extension and tool of capitalism, was produced to strong acclaim and led to his own move to Hollywood. He was later one of the most prominent and outspoken of the CP members in Hollywood. While blacklisted, he wrote *The Judgment of Julius and Ethel Rosenberg*, which proclaimed their innocence, as Wexley then continued to do through the years, despite all the evidence to the contrary.

Wexley's plays of topical protests are not actually within the central structure and motifs of the Marxist proletarian drama and its theories that so attracted and influenced Rossen and many of his co-workers in the Writers' Building at Warner Bros. in the thirties. In line with the theories and practice of plays in Russia and Europe, the basic form was based on the central Marxist concept of consciousness, alienated and warped or authentic and fulfilled—first written about in terms of art and theater by Leon (Lev) Trotsky in one of the rich and often contradictory veins of his thinking.

The dramas that were developed were of two basic types. One was the more central and accepted; the other was generally more sophisticated and artistically mature, but (probably inevitably and expected) often subject to Party-line criticism.

In the central iconic form, individuals within groups are isolated, their consciousness stunted and false, their energies dissipated. They are alienated from a true sense of self but most importantly from a true, life-enhancing sense of their relationship to the group. And so the group itself is emptied of energy, belief, solidarity, and the ability to act. In these plays the group is dominated and oppressed, and individuals are reduced and shaped to indecision and inaction. An occurrence — an act of brutality and murder by the oppressors, often producing a martyr — and the growth of consciousness in an individual or two lead those figures to ignite the rest to a belief in the importance and power of the group, and to meaningful action on the basis of their newfound solidarity. With alienation now dissipated, the *people* can act against the aggressor and oppressor — usually some form or aspect of capitalism and capitalists. In solidarity, all are now committed to the common cause of the proletariat and Communist ideals.

Rossen's 1938 screenplay *Racket Busters* (unfortunately much edited before its release) follows this pattern more than any of his other works. The narrative arc of the film traces the raising of the consciousness of the central character (played by George Brent) to act in social ("revolutionary") protest and inspire others to do the same. As he leads the men to stand up to the gangsters who control their union, he tells them, "We've got to stick together." It is the kind of statement and the kind of narrative structure of raising the consciousness of men to join together and fight injustice that was becoming the political as well as moral emblem of so much literature, drama, and film of the Left. During Ernest Hemingway's brief honeymoon with the "Cause" at this time, Harry Morgan's dying words in *To Have and Have Not* show his (and Hemingway's) recognition of the mantra, "No man alone ... no man ... no man alone ain't got no ... ain't got no chance."

This narrative structure rising to a visual crescendo of increasing numbers of people, often coming in from all directions, was a staple at the climax of major Soviet films of the twenties and early thirties. Through patterns, movements, and editing, Sergei Eisenstein mounts several rousing variations in *Battleship Potemkin*. When the body of the martyred sailor is placed in state on a jetty, first one and then more and more people pass by, flowing in from all directions in long graceful lines. When the sailors on board the ship successfully rebel, crowds of people build on the shore and steps, and small boats of all kinds sail rhythmically to bring supplies, joining the sailors in the solidarity of righteous action. In his *The General Line*, the exultation of the *politicalization* of farm workers, who had previously been only aware of their own individual, even selfish, problems, is captured in similar montages, as well as a brilliantly edited sequence of tractors swarming together in carrying out the new collectivization of the farms. In V.I. Pudovkin's film *Mother*, when her son is shot and falls to the street with others also slain, his *mother* picks up the fallen red flag. Brandishing it like a sword, she leads the burgeoning throng of the marching masses against the soldiers of the Tsar.

Rossen was to transform these patterns into visual correlatives for rebellion against the Nazis in his World War II script for *Edge of Darkness* (1943), and then he used variations with scathing irony in *All the Kings Men* (1949).

Peters and Sklar's *Stevedore* (1934) is a classic instance of the central iconic structure and its chief attributes. In it, the topical issue of oppression of workers is interwoven with the racial prejudice of the thirties South. But the broader, deeper issue and structure is raising the consciousness of alienated individuals to take collective action against (clearly capitalist) oppression. A black union worker and union leader, Lonnie, is accused of raping a white woman. As racial and strike tensions mount, he hides at a lunchroom where black and white stevedores eat and congregate. When strike-breaking goons enter the lunchroom, a black stevedore is killed. The men are panicked, frozen. But Binnie, the woman who owns the lunchroom, grabs a gun and shoots one of the gangsters; the others flee. Always a flamboyant talker, Binnie now exhorts them all to action, and joins them — and more and more workers — at a barricade for the climactic battle with the gangster goons of the bosses.

As critic Mike Gold gushed in *New Masses*, "When big, lovable, motherly Binnie, who runs a lunchroom and bosses the husky stevedores with her spicy tongue, picks up an old gun and pops off one of the gangsters, the audience cheers. It cheers not only because a brute is dead, but because something has happened in the soul of a working-class mother."[14]

In the most popular of these American agit-props, Clifford Odets' *Waiting for Lefty* (first staged late in 1934), a cabbie, Joe, is weak and indecisive (as are others) about going out on strike. His wife threatens to leave him unless he acts for solidarity and his rights: "Get those hack boys together! Stand up like men and fight for the crying kids and wives. Goddamit! I'm tired of slavery and sleepless nights." The play has been a series of vignettes about the oppression and indecision of the cabbies. At the climax, when they are told that Lefty has been killed, all the characters unite and line up at the front of the stage. Arms raised, in unison they shout, "Strike! Strike! Strike!" And, solidarity spreading, the audience rises and, arms raised in unison, shouts, "Strike! Strike! Strike!" In *New Masses* (January 1935), Nathaniel Buchwald found that "propelled by his burning revolutionary fervor, and by an essentially clear guiding idea, this young playwright swept the audience off its feet."[15]

Even Lillian Hellman, whose plays were generally of a quite different nature, in 1932 wrote her (though still more character-oriented) version of the agit-prop labor union play. In *Days to Come*, strike breakers oppress the working class, and in a melee shoot the child of a worker. At this, even the wavering middle class protagonist is impelled to join the proletariat — the Workers, the People — in rebellion.

In the thirties this fervor and idealism of the theater of the Left had their echoes in the zeitgeist of popular culture and its response to the problems and events of the Depression. The iconic example is the decade-ending film of John Steinbeck's, *The Grapes of Wrath*. The Darryl F. Zanuck–John Ford version transforms the left wing structures and preachments into the popular vernacular of liberal social uplift (replete with images of spic-and-span FDR-implemented camps for uprooted farmers). At the end, the Joads drive off in their ramshackle truck — one of a long line on the highway of beaten-down trucks of the people — to at least the hope of a better future. And Ma announces for us all, "We're the People, Pa, we're the People." During World War II, in the theatrical review *Meet the People*, the Communist Left in Hollywood turned this iconic phrase, the tradition of Clifford Odets' *Waiting for Lefty*, and all the bag and baggage of the movement, into a satirical yet sentimental view of the rather comic foibles of the powerful and the undeterred energy of We, the People. At several points — and in celebration and friendliness rather than the fervent demand in *Lefty*— the cast comes to the front of the stage and sings, "Step up, meet the People, meet the Common Man. You'll find him wonderful."

The second type of the social dramas of the thirties focuses more on an individual — alienated, uncommitted, wavering with indecision or making faulty choices, and following a society-shaped inauthentic sense of self. This individual then betrays others (or ideals) and himself, and may end tragically (either dead or isolated, frozen, deadened), or he may be allowed an individual growth of consciousness (or at least a possibility of one). When these plays (and films in this structure) emphasized the tragic trap of these figures, they were often criticized by the Party press and theorists as defeatist, un–Marxist, and not emphasizing the positive potential of the individuals or groups, particularly the working class.

Albert Maltz's union play of the thirties, *Black Pit*, illustrates this second basic type of Marxist-inspired play. However, it was one of those that generated controversy and criticism for being un–Marxist and not positive enough — even though the play still had the requisite insistent counter-display of the usual exploitive evils of the bosses, and a final movement toward true consciousness and group action. After he had toured mining towns in the South and done several articles for the *New Masses*, Maltz wanted to promote true class consciousness by indirection: showing the pain and terror of its opposite, depicting the tragedy of a man who is forced to sell his soul to the bosses by betraying his union comrades. Later Maltz was to fiercely insist that Rossen and others had betrayed their Hollywood comrades.

Within the tragic aspect of the Maltz play, the role of women contrasts in two characters. Joe's wife is pregnant, and also weak, and she is one of the reasons he turns informer. On the other hand, his sister Mary, along with her husband, is one of the leaders in uniting the workers in their resolve to fight the bosses. Their actions and their speeches help Joe see the error of his sacrifice, accept his guilt, and realize that it is the union and the strike that bring hope for his baby. In the play's attempt at folk dialogue, Joe recognizes, "What good get t'ings by be false to odern miner? ... Bett'r to starve, bett'r be live in hole lak animal." For as stalwart brother-in-law Tony tells him (foreshadowing the final soliloquy of Hemingway's Harry Morgan), "Miner no can get by self ... when cohmpany got every-t'ings you got go wit' odern miner, tak cohmpany by t'roat, fight."

There are strong echoes of both of these forms in Rossen's films, but he was certainly more personally drawn to the depiction of the difficulties and dilemmas of choosing one's authentic self, of choosing actions within the complexity of motivations, of facing the almost inevitable forms of betrayal. As he summed it up in an interview, he traces "the impact of social environment on character."[16] Still, in his films there is still almost always the possibility, or at least the hope, of redemption.

In the mid-thirties Odets himself, the young "golden boy" of agit-prop, turned to more complex and deeply human plays. With the production of *Awake and Sing, Paradise Lost, Rocket to the Moon*, he turned to capturing the damaging impact of social and economic pressures on the energy and spirit, the true sense of a harmonious self in middle class families. And he was consistently rebuked in the Party press. A typical example of this application of strict Marxist ideology was Stanley Burnshaw's take on *Paradise Lost* in *New Masses* in 1936 (though clearly echoing a recent series of articles by Lawson): "It is the lack of Marxism which has deprived the play of its fundamental social truth.... It is regrettable to see a left writer proceeding on an utterly false premise, portray as doomed objects of decay that very middle class which will be enlisted as a vigorous ally in the growing people's front against Fascism and war."[17]

Odets, nonetheless, persisted, and went on to write *Golden Boy*, which was produced by the Group Theater. (The Group Theater was the most important theater group of the period artistically and the most prominent of these groups in the commercial theater world, though never financially secure. It was not a Party affiliated group, though it had an active and directly Party-controlled Communist clique among its members.) *Golden Boy* was the most successful left-wing play of the thirties — and Odets' ticket to Hollywood. In an emotionally winning fashion, it combines elements of Odets' family plays and both the tragic-betrayal and up-beat forms of the proletarian drama. It also includes motifs of thirties gangster films. This is one aspect of the significant and interesting interaction of motifs from films influencing the theater, and of motifs, themes, and political commitment of the theater influencing the films. It comes in a flux that makes it difficult to determine which came first, the chicken or the egg. In Maxwell Anderson's poetic plays *Winterset* and *Key Largo*, the gangster is the evil impetus for the new resolve of alienated, wavering protagonists. In Robert E. Sherwood's *The Petrified Forest* (T.S. Eliot's *Wasteland*?) the gangster Duke Mantee is the catalyst for the new commitment and action of the alienated intellectual.

In both venues, as in *Golden Boy*, the gambler/gangster often not only becomes the tangible face and force of evil, but of the evil of capitalism. The play's golden boy does not betray his fellow workers; he betrays his gift, his artistry as a violinist, and his family. He sells out to the gambler/gangster and the allure of a woman, and becomes a winning boxer. He does see the light, but it is too late. With the woman in the car that represents what he has sold himself to, and for, he is killed in a high speed highway accident.

The play foreshadowed motifs used in a number of later Hollywood films, and has particularly interesting ties to *Body and Soul* (1947), an original script by Abraham Polonsky directed by Rossen.

Lawson, who both mentored and attacked the young Odets, later was the dogmatic leader of the Party in Hollywood for many years. He was the most dynamic and inventive of the playwrights and theorists among the left-wing dramatists. From the twenties into the early thirties he experimented with the new forms of drama burgeoning in Europe while attempting to balance the Marxist dramatic structure of oppression, raised consciousness, and solidarity with his own personal, internal conflicts over the difficulty of commitment.

Lawson wrote plays that epitomize both of these forms of left-wing drama. For example, in the very Soviet *The Internationale* (1928) the *people* of a generalized oil-rich Asian country are oppressed by stereotypical imperialist capitalist force and brutality. Typically in a Lawson play, a woman leads both the tormented intellectual and the wavering, indecisive "masses" toward commitment and ideological action. Nonetheless, at play's end the intellectual, David, is still torn, still wavering — as was typical of Lawson's central characters. "How do I get home?" he asks. "Christ, for the love o' pity, where do I go home?"

Lawson's final play, *Marching Song*, was not completed and produced until 1937, after he had been writing screenplays for several years. In its Soviet-style epic form (truly a Marxist extravaganza), it encompasses all the ideological precepts for authentic proletarian art that Lawson had absorbed and transmuted as his own. It includes practically every element, device, symbol, caricature, narrative pattern, and cliché of the genre. Sadistic gangsters are brought in to break the strike of the electrical workers. The workers are raised to allegorical levels of the proletariat's movement toward solidarity and action — raised to revolutionary consciousness by events: a strong wife energizes her wavering husband, a baby is killed, groups are attacked with gun and gas bombs. After a union organizer is tortured to death by sadistic company strike-breakers, the workers, carrying his body proudly, are inspired (*à la* Eisenstein's film *Battleship Potemkin*, which Lawson analyzed extensively in one of his books of theory) to march against their oppressors. A black worker, who himself has been changed from scab to revolutionist, exhorts the people as they mass and the power is turned off: "Power is people!"

Oddly, as he had moved toward his own conversion to a devout belief in communism, Lawson wrote what may be his best play, a realistic dramatization of the "anguish of choice" highlighting the personal, inner corruptions and the painful betrayals of ideals that capitalism produces. In *Success Story* (1932) the central character, Sol, sells out his ideals and his soul, and violates his family for money and success. And there is no conversion.

For the rest of Lawson's career, in the movies and in the Party, he was to deny the value of this most valuable aspect of his own plays — whether in art or in political life.

In later years in Hollywood, Rossen was to work with Lawson in the Party — in organizational fights, in the important Hollywood Writers Mobilization, and in several more special, even secret, tasks. And then in 1949 at a meeting called by Lawson, he, and *All the King's Men*, were to bear the brunt of attacks based on the very kind of dogma and doctrine espoused by Lawson in the thirties.

In 1934, however, Rossen, working on his first plays, was writing *The Body Beautiful*. While he was absorbing all of these controversies, ideological issues and fervor, and while he was moving toward his own commitment to the ideals expressed in the plays and theories, at the same time he was nonetheless following his own instincts, his nature. Seeking ideals but holding on to his tough, skeptical, world-wise roots, he, too, like a divided Lawson character, was drawn toward success and turned toward the commercial theater to start to build a career. Among his works at this time was an unproduced play with a pool-hall setting based on his own experience entitled *Corner Pocket*. Some forty years later it became the raw material he mined and refined with great success and significance in *The Hustler*. The one play of his that was produced, *The Body Beautiful*, was strictly, and hopefully, commercial. He also directed the play, which was produced by Sidney Harmon. It lasted for seven or so performances (depending on which recollection) in the fall of 1935, the year that he was married. Despite the brevity of its run, it received positive notices as a "workmanlike farce."[18] The reviews garnered some interest by people in the movie industry, attracting the attention of director Mervyn LeRoy. Rossen's articulate and aggressive salesmanship did the rest. Once he was established in the writers' building at Warners, his innate talent burst forth, full grown, without, it seemed, any need for an apprenticeship at all.

His Hollywood career had begun, just as he hoped and, in his way, determinedly planned. The career itself continued to add to the experience that affected and "inspired" his works — as did, with devastating personal anguish, his life in and then against the Communist Party (and all the later consequences of that tangled and troubled period of betrayals that were real, merely perceived or denied).

2

Stretching the Boundaries of Genre — The First Two Screenplays

Robert Rossen's screenplays for Warner Bros.—from the two screenplays in his first year at the studio—work within the helix-like intertwining of the conventions of social problem films and the conventions of the standard popular genres. These social-problem pictures, both in the thirties and later, were often dramatized within the patterns, formulas, and iconography of the standard genres that the industry was developing, such as the gangster film or western. In a turn of the circle, these hybrid films have been influential in shaping the basic conventions and structures of social realism within which many later American films of social criticism have been created.

The genres within which these social problem pictures are embedded can be approached from several directions of typical discourse. Early in its history the film industry recognized the commercial value of developing repeated types, formats, and subject areas of movies—formulas, later to be denoted *genres*. By the thirties the elements of specific types of films, the genres, had become standardized based on workable formulas of efficient production and successful salesmanship. There was money to be made—and production efficiency and economy to be achieved—in capitalizing (as Warner Bros. particularly did) on headlines and history, on the audience's interest in and understanding of contemporary events and situations (from prohibition to war), or of the traditional icons or myths of the past. There was marketing value in building and fulfilling expectations, developing repetitions of subjects, situations, structures, conflicts, and characters that audiences can recognize—but still with variations within the formulas that maintained and heightened interest. Formulas, or genres, are not self-contained and exclusive; they are not exactly definable and limited, like a law of physics. And so in practice they may be mixed; or elements of one type—for example, a gangster film—can be found in tough guy films, slum boy films, labor films, newspaper films, or even westerns.

As theories of genres have developed in published criticism and academia, however, these standard formats were defined and interpreted beyond mere marketing formulas. It was recognized that the structures created for these formulas, and their popularity, were based on conventions and structures of society. Genres, as one theorist aptly phrased, were an assimilated "field of reference" for a cultural milieu, as well as a physical and narrative setting that condensed the conflicts, hopes, fears, mores, and standards within the real world on which they were, with great imaginative license, based. And so, in reverse, the real world — its social conventions and structures, its values — could be interpreted in the conventions and structures of the films. In this circular process the genres could be seen as a particular interpretation of that society at a particular time. For some critics and historians, those cinema interpretations were inevitably seen as defenses of the society's (capitalist) structures; for others they could be critiques — often indirect and ironic — of those structures.

As society (its issues and values, its culture) changed, as the nature of its conflicts and issues changed, so did the nature of the interpretations of that society that the genres presented — that is, the forms of acceptance or criticism given shape by the films. In the sixties and early seventies, for example, detective stories mutated; they, took on structures in which the detective, private or public, did not solve or settle anything, or even if he or she did, it seemed to make little difference. In gangster films mobsters actually became a part of the standard business world and did not merely imply the allusions to business found in traditional gangster films. In westerns all was not put right by the actions of the lone hero or group, even if villains were killed. Previous moral and social standards were questioned, and new issues raised, whether racial prejudices or urban growth, civic corruption or business encroachment.

Back in the days of the standard genres, 1936, Rossen's first two films nonetheless used genre structures and motifs in a similar, though less extreme, revisionist way. They brought into question the conventional values and attitudes that genre can sometimes, or indeed often, serve to inculcate. They challenged its expected codes of meaning. But, furthermore, as he contributed to the establishment of the standard conventions of the forms in the thirties, he also showed an instinctive adeptness at subverting the conventions of genre itself as a form — that is, adapting, going beyond and re-ordering its expected narrative structures, emphases, and characterizations by introducing other themes and tones into ordinary genre formulas.

In his first two screenplays he worked within the expected conventions of the courtroom and crusading district attorney genres. Normally within these conventions, things, at least on the surface, are usually set right and justice prevails. In these two screenplays — with differing degrees and types of subversion — the assumptions of the prevailing "hegemony" are challenged. In *They Won't Forget*, justice itself is betrayed (as well, of course, as the victim) in the conviction and killing of an innocent man. The other, *Marked Woman*, combines the D.A.-justice structure with the gangster genre. In it, the system does succeed in convicting the right man, the evil gangster; but the film's uniqueness is that the system, and its authorities, its power figures, fail to find a broader social justice for the women who help in the case. It betrays them indirectly when there is no recognition of the need to change the assumptions of male-dominated standards. The irony is bitter in both films — broader in the former, more nuanced in the latter.

In these two films the balance between the exposure of social injustice and the examination of an individual's motives and the illusory or authentic symbols of one's self tilts toward the pole of social criticism, as would be expected within the Warner tradition and Rossen's place in it at that time. Nonetheless, in both films the corruption of alleged social ideals, such as justice, is a product of both social attitudes and individual motivations and drives — the seeking of power, control, success. These personal motivations contribute to the particular kinds and degrees of betrayal dramatized in the screenplays. They remain a striking foreshadowing of Rossen's themes through the years.

On the level of method and technique, in the production of these two films, Rossen was working with two directors, Mervyn LeRoy and Lloyd Bacon, who are not known for their attention to visual imagery, but rather for their efficiency and savvy in moving scenes and the plot along deftly, with the pace and verve of a Warners film. Working with them, Rossen had his first experience of expertise in the practical process of making movies. But while working with them he was also able to apply his own sense of the use and power of visual imagery as a means of expressing emotion, character and meaning.

Rossen's debut was unique. Both of his first two screenplays were produced and released in one year, 1937. *They Won't Forget*, his first assignment, was for a film directed by LeRoy. It was released in July. *Marked Woman*, however, was released first, in April.

LeRoy was one of the key figures at Warners. Versatile and efficient — and a strong personality — he had a sharp eye for what was current, what would sell. More than that, he could spot what would fit, and then influence, the *zeitgeist*, the public mood of the time. By 1937 he had directed 37 silent and sound movies — six, as sound had become dominant, in 1932 alone, including *I Am a Fugitive from the Chain Gang*. In 1930 he helped institute the major gangster film movement of the thirties with *Little Caesar*. As musicals grew in prominence and popularity, he directed *Gold Diggers of 1933* (in coordination with the father of ultimate musical extravaganzas, Busby Berkeley) while directing four other movies in the same year. He set a style with a successful Joe E. Brown comedy, *Elmer the Great*, and contributed historical epics (with their popularity at the end of the decade) like *Oil for the Lamps of China* and *Anthony Adverse*. He promoted and directed three British-style quality films with Greer Garson just before and during World War II, including *Mrs. Miniver*. His war films included *Thirty Seconds Over Tokyo* and (later) *Mister Roberts* (finishing the film when John Ford had to bow out due to a gall bladder attack). He crowned the postwar trend of costume epics with the 171-minute *Quo Vadis*, made the bleak *The Bad Seed*, and helmed the jovial film that set the screen and television image for Andy Griffith, *No Time for Sergeants*.

Despite his great eye for what was *au current* (or should be), LeRoy, like most directors that Rossen worked with, was not known for having an eye or creative touch for visual imagery. For that he relied on his screenwriters and, of course, cinematographers.

They Won't Forget—which, at least on one occasion, Rossen said was his favorite among his Warner screenplays — was one of the most outspoken attacks on entrenched injustice of the period. *Time* saw it as "the most devastating study of mob violence and sectional hatred the screen has yet dared to present." The valuable critic Otis Ferguson in *The New Republic* praised it as one of the best of the "pictures with social teeth in them." In the *New York Times*, Frank Nugent praised the "quiet intensity of its narrative ... [its] courage, objectivity, and simple eloquence."

Within the studio system of organized and controlled production, a kind of mass production process applied to filmmaking. Writers were under contract for time periods, not specific films. It was a standard practice to have at least one additional writer on a film, sometimes with credit, sometimes not. On *They Won't Forget*, Rossen worked with Aben Kandel, who had been brought to Hollywood after the critical praise of his urban novel *City for Conquest* (filmed later, with a screenplay by John Wexley that Rossen worked on). Kandel had only a minor career subsequently, with no distinctive approach, themes, or style (and actually no opportunity for the development of these). He eventually went to England in the sixties to write a number of the popular British horror movies of the time. While the film does not use the big city background of either man, Rossen does bring to it a cynical sense of the corruption of the justice system that he had experienced both in life and in the social drama of the thirties. The screenplay is adapted from a novel by Ward Greene, which was in turn loosely based on an earlier real-life episode, the 1915 case of Leo Frank, a transplanted New York Jew. In its depiction of the violation of law and human life by political greed and mob hysteria, the film is a strong and unrelenting attack on the dynamics and momentum of injustice — climaxed by a lynching. It is a model of the Warner Bros. tradition of taut, fast-moving narrative structure; focused, compacted scenes; and direct and intense confrontation.

But it is a mark of the film's, and the time's, strange mixture of careful evasion and radical cynicism that the man lynched in this Southern town is white, not black. The studio was not ready to depict the lynching of a black man (or a Jew, as in the actual event). In the screenplay, however, Rossen still manages to capitalize on that basic kind of reality in a trenchant exposure of the indecent drive for personal success of a local Southern politician. On (fittingly) Confederate Memorial Day, a girl (Lana Turner, in her first role and in a sweater) is murdered (and, through vague indirect implication, possibly raped) in a near empty secretarial school. The police take the obvious first step and arrest the black janitor. But for the politically greedy district attorney, Andrew J. Griffin (Claude Rains), that is not good enough. It would be easy to get him convicted, but to convict and hang a "Negro janitor" was too easy, too commonplace. He needs something more striking and unusual to gain him the publicity and fame to energize his campaign for governor against the liberal incumbent. He turns instead to the prosecution of a new young teacher at the school, an outspoken "do-gooder" from up North (pure-white, no Jew) — a modern-day "carpet-bagger" who the town's good citizens are quite happy, indeed thrilled, to condemn.

Rains' D.A. does not serve justice; he serves his own drive for power. He is smooth, smugly "logical," cynically self-contained and controlled. He is the first example of Rossen's development of men with power — whether within the law or outside of it — who will do what they must to dominate, to win. In this case he is not obsessed beyond control of himself; on the contrary, he is cool, calculating, and manipulating, seeming to enjoy his own chicanery. While the law is not a matter of zealous belief for him, he does betray at least his professional task and duty to uphold justice; in so doing, he violates the life of another human being.

But he is not alone in the film's pattern of corruption and betrayal of justice, and, finally, murderous violation of a person's life. Strong emphasis is placed on the hounding of the "murderer" by the news media, both out of zealous crusading and the commercial benefits of rabble-rousing, audience-pleasing tabloid sensationalism. The press is used by the D.A. for his benefit, but it needs no encouragement from him to carry out its own agenda. (LeRoy also directed a less meaningful, satirical look at muckraking journalism in *Five Star Final*, with Edward G. Robinson.) In typical Rossen montages, newspaper headlines inflame the masses and reporters callously violate the dignity of individuals. In one instance, a press photographer is bending over the collapsed body of the suspect's wife after she has fainted upon hearing the news of her husband's arrest. A gleeful vulture in for the kill, he hovers over her, flash bulb popping.

2. Stretching the Boundaries of Genre—The First Two Screenplays

They Won't Forget (1937), Warner Bros. The people of the town, as they become a mob, gather outside the courtroom at the trial of the accused (and innocent) murderer.

It is the townspeople, the Marxist and left-liberal's beloved People (see, for example, John Ford's *The Grapes of Wrath* and the indomitable Ma Joad at its stirring ending: "We're the People, Pa; we're the People") who are, in the most bitter irony, the ultimate betrayers. When a private detective is sent by a Northern newspaper to investigate, he is beaten by the mob. At the trial, a lawyer brought in from New York eloquently exposes the injustice and prejudice. His emphasis on "prejudice" is a kind of short-hand allusion to the lynching of blacks that is like the unnoticed elephant in the room. He reasonably demolishes the lies, the false and doctored evidence of the prosecution's case; but the press sneers, and the crowd jeers. His polished Northern effrontery is seen as confirming the most biased impulses of the members of the jury. They nod their approval when the judge, smoking a pipe, interrupts the defense attorney and when the audience in the courtroom applauds the statements of the D.A., who is sweating through his shirt, wearing the iconic suspenders of the Southern prosecutor.

After the inevitable conviction and death sentence, the liberal governor (the D.A.'s future opponent) commutes the death sentence. Throughout the state he is attacked by the press and the indignant populace. The move pleases Griffin. For the D.A. and everybody else know the Governor's career is now over. It is bitter double message: There are men of integrity in government; their integrity loses them their career.

It is the People, now a mob, who commit the final betrayal, the ultimate violation of human life. They take "justice," as they see it, into their own hands. When the teacher is put on a train to be taken to prison, the mob drags him from the train and carries him off to be lynched. In a fine parallel visual metaphor for the brutality of the act, a speeding train comes roaring down the track, extinguishing the screams of the crowd. As it sweeps by the station, with a heavy, jarring clunk, it snatches a sack of mail hanging from its yardarm, its gallows, like a lynched body.

There is a final double message in the final words of a reporter and Griffin. On the one hand, they too are shown to have an honest doubt. But on the other, this conventional softening allows a further last bitter irony, an implication of even more distasteful corruption. In Griffin's office the reporter says, "Now that it's over, Andy, I wonder if Hale really did it." Rains turns and looks out the window; his face, his final expression and revelation of self—if any were to be allowed or felt—are hidden from us. He replies, "I wonder." As structured in the film, the declaration adds a cynical dimension of awareness to his exploitation of justice for his own success. There is not a glimmer of redemption in that musing and almost amused "wonder."

Novelist Graham Greene, at the time regularly writing film criticism, called it "a film of truth and tragic value ... better, less compromising than [Fritz Lang's] *Fury*."[1] The Lang film depicted the attempted lynching of an innocent man (Spencer Tracy), who escapes during a fire set in the jail. It has its own brand of Langian irony when Tracy becomes obsessed himself with wreaking his own personal justice on those who had violated him. But the ironic view of human frailty and complexity is severely undercut by the film's conventional ending. Tracy's fiancée, who he was traveling to see when caught in the vicious web of the town, prevails upon him (with all the sweetness of Sylvia Sidney) to release his anger and cease his vendetta.

Of Rossen's two 1937 films, *They Won't Forget* received more attention at the time, but *Marked Woman* has proven the more significant. Although it too is based on historical fact and is more directly patterned within the Warners' tradition of the gangster genre and courtroom dramas, its screenplay is more complex and intricate in shaping the clash of various elements of society and the impact of this clash on human beings, particularly women.

Marked Woman's director, Lloyd Bacon, was, as usual, staunchly faithful to the shooting script. Bacon had to be. From 1926 to 1954 he directed nearly 100 movies, and with startling chameleon-like competence, movies in many genres and at all levels of "seriousness." In 1940 alone he directed the serious family (and injustice) drama *A Child Is Born* (also written by Rossen), the conventional crime-slums (with two brothers) drama *Invisible Stripes*, the lightweight *Three Cheers for the Irish*, the worthy gangster comedy *Brother Orchid* (with Edward G. Robinson), and the legendary *Knute Rockne, All-American* (with Pat O'Brien and Ronald Reagan as the Gipper). In the same year as *Marked Woman* he directed *Gold Diggers of 1937*, and earlier *Footlight Parade* and *42nd Street*—iconic thirties musicals with flamboyant production numbers choreographed, staged, and given their visual form by Busby Berkeley.

Rossen worked with Abem [sic] Finkel, another ex–New Yorker familiar with life in the big city. Finkel, who had worked on three B-movies previously, became known as a good technician, a workmanlike adjunct on writing teams that featured more significant writers who stamped their own personalities and concerns on the script. He worked, for example, with John Huston and two others on *Jezebel*, and with Huston, Howard Koch, and Harry Chandlee on *Sergeant York*. Again, even as Rossen shares credit with a co-writer whose career developed no personal imprint or continuity, the film not only prefigures many of Rossen's central themes and concerns, it displays early versions of some of his basic methods: emotional confrontations; strong meaningful juxtapositions for dramatic impact and thematic meaning; dialogue that works dramatically yet indicates thematic concerns; and a relating of environment and specific places to the lives and conflicts of characters, with physical settings given their sharpest focus as visual metaphors that are allusive yet part of the dramatic action.

While *Marked Woman* is one of a line of films capitalizing on the public's interest in both the justice and gangster genres, it was originated as a result of another basic Warner practice — responding to what was in the newspaper headlines. The specialist in generating movie ideas from what was in the news was producer and script supervisor Lou Edelman. One colleague commented, "Lou's specialty is the headlines, which also give him ready-made plots." Another colleague put it more bluntly, stating Edelman "really specializes in free plots." To a reporter, Edelman himself explained his rationale: "Anything worth newspaper space is worth a picture."[2]

The legal case on which this project is based was famous at the time. It was the trial of Charles "Lucky" Luciano, who not only had cornered the continuing liquor (even after the demise of Prohibition) and gambling market in New York, but the exploitative world of brothels as well. A state task force, headed by the crusading and admired Attorney General Thomas E. Dewey (later governor and two-time Republican candidate for president), went after Luciano (as well as others). Dewey focused on the prostitution racket as the most direct way to bring Luciano to trial. Brothels were raided, and close to a hundred women were arrested as potential material witnesses. Luciano was convicted. While in prison he continued to organize the rackets of the mob, including the control of the New York–New Jersey longshoremen unions. During World War II he was allowed to emigrate to Italy, ostensibly to arrange for Mafia assistance in the invasion of Sicily. While he was there, this government "mission" allowed him to initiate the organization of the modern international drug trade.

While the original case did, in part, involve the gangsters' control of prostitutes and the testimony of prostitutes at the trial, the screenplay went far beyond merely translating the topical material into movie form. In the conventional aspect of *Marked Woman*, this headline event is used within one of the usual structures of the gangster genre. Here, the crusading assistant district attorney is pitted against the powerful racketeer who controls night clubs, gambling, and prostitution. But the script's striking innovation shifts the expected narrative pattern to a dramatic emphasis on the women and their lives, not merely as adjuncts to the case and the lives of the men. It focuses on developing the cross-section of personalities, conflicts, and needs among the women — and particularly on developing a "proto-feminist" patterning of the *entrapment* of the women. They are caught between two men — distorted mirror images, even though so different — who want to win. They are trapped between the domineering, endangering zeal of the district attorney and the cruel and violent domineering of the gangster. The D.A. will do anything, even betray them, to get the women to testify; the gangster will do anything — beat, slash, even kill — to keep them from testifying.

The film reaches for a lot. The result is an uneven, edgy movie unusual for its time.

Its conglomerate of disparate, contradictory elements mix obligatory conventional scenes with other scenes that are unique in tone and quality — strong and tense confrontations that are emotionally full, more personally felt and expressed. Its unexpected playing of conventional narrative patterns and iconography, pitting positive audience expectations against the more intense yet subtle counterpull of ironic denial of those expectations, gives it a discordant quality. But that unsettled, unsettling quality is part of its distinct feel, its surprising and unresolved ironies.

Whether fully understood or not, the film was well received at the time. After it opened in New York, S. Charles Einfeld, then director of publicity and advertising and later a major studio executive, wrote to Jack L. Warner. "When I wrote you the other day," he said, "that we had a smash on our hands with *Marked Woman*, I was pretty certain of what I was saying but I didn't want to go on record and predict any such business as we are doing at the New York Strand."[3] Business out in the rest of the country was not at that New York level, but the picture was a solid success. Its levels of implication, however, were not developed by critics until it was resurrected decades later with several extensive interpretive articles from feminist and post-structuralist points of view. At its release, Greene did respond to its strong unique qualities, but primarily as a special gangster film. "It's been done before, of course," he wrote, "this picture of the feudal hell [of the gangster], but it has never been done better." Sensing this early example of insights that Rossen would develop more fully and deeply, he saw in Eduardo Cianelli's gangster "not only corruption, but the sadness of corruption."[4]

The gangster Johnny Vanning is a fascinating composite of the dominant two types of gangsters seen in the tradition of the genre: the polished Anglo-Saxon businessman type and the earthy, volatile ethnic immigrant. He is icy and sardonic, brutal and explosive, amorally arrogant in his knowledge of and violent use of the power he has won in previous battles. But there are skillful script touches (admittedly limited by the demands of plot) that show his awareness of how precarious his hold on power is. At moments he is seen as fanatically unable to brook any threat of opposition or disobedience, even by the women. He coldly controls others but hotly can lose control of himself and his own emotions. He is a particularly callous and crude version of Rossen's seekers of the constant victory, the power that will satisfy and validate their mistaken sense of their identity.

As the film opens, Vanning is taking over a nightclub that features "hostesses" who perform and dance and drink with clients, and also leave the premises with clients. The substitution of "hostesses" for "whores" is an unfortunate imposition of censorship (and clearly transparent), and denies the use of the actual brothel to visualize that aspect of the degradation of being in "the life"; but whether they are called whores or hostesses, they are degraded and sadistically violated by Vanning and his goons. Further, the substitution of the night club and the parties in the ostentatious penthouse — parties which actually were the upscale part of the real scene of classy call girls — also serves Rossen's Marxist point of view. It provides important visual contrasts in what is also seen as a class struggle: the conflict of the wealthy clients and the successful gangster with the world of the working girls, the working class.

Vanning as a shorthand embodiment of the evils of capitalism is seen in the film's interconnection of money with power and the resulting violation of people. This metaphoric use of the iconic gangster was a regular motif in the left-wing proletarian drama of the thirties, which, in the full bloom of his mid-thirties idealism, Rossen admired. The motif is strongly emphasized throughout the script, especially in projecting Vanning's image of himself as a true businessman. As the new owner (through force) of the Club Intime, he tells the women, "From now on I'm organizing it. When I organize something, I get paid big money — or else." It will be good for all of them if they follow orders. "I've got every nightclub in town sewed up and every girl. You're going to work the way I tell you or you're not going to work." He is going to add a gambling room and improve the performance of the women in bringing in money. The greed of capitalism is given its male chauvinist connection: callously, Vanning immediately decides that one of the women looks too old and will not be good for business. "Kind of old, ain't you? I need young dames here. The kind men go for in a hurry." He fires her on the spot; but when one of the women, their leader Mary (Bette Davis), defends her, he relents. Vanning appears to be interested in Mary, who stands up to him.

At least on the surface, Vanning has the lifestyle of the corporate executive that he sees himself to be. He is clearly an *arriviste*, pushing his "new look" to the borders of good taste and beyond. He has all the accoutrements of the gangster figure, but they are carried to an ostentatious extreme: his slick suit, his ever-present white silk scarf, his new chic club, his pretentious penthouse and its vast terrace and dominating view of the city below, his high-powered, obsequious lawyer.

In the course of Rossen's work, these iconic images of the fruits of money — capitalism — work on two levels. These things of the characters' world have meaning for them within the drama of the narrative, for their desires, needs, plans. But these things are also active metaphors for the inner life, a reflection of the turbulence of this inner life in which money is often an illusory counter of the self and its definition and fulfillment — as well as a reflection of consequence in choice and action that result from seeking it. Like Vanning, Rossen's seekers need more than the money and all that comes with it. Deeper, more jagged and entangled in the welter of motives, is the drive for power, the need to overcome, gain control and even get even. They need to fill the void within themselves with this illusory defining of themselves, with the false symbols of identity, of self. They are a lonely lot, these misguided and self-deceiving searchers afflicted with a typically American loneliness seen in so many significant American novels and plays. It is a dogged isolation and emptiness, however surrounded and accompanied they are.

As "business" is conducted at Vanning's club, the girls are seen as acquiescing in the system. Or else. They become complicit in getting as much money out of what they call "the chumps" as possible. The contrast between the women as working class (though corrupted) and the bosses and clients as upper class is evoked visually throughout the film — in settings, décor, costumes, plot and dialogue. For example, juxtaposed between two sequences at the ornate club we see that all five women live in one crowded apartment — not seedy or tawdry, but plain and furnished without any personal taste or joy, and, as far as we can see, with no windows, no view whatsoever. Later the apartment is juxtaposed with the penthouse of Vanning, its vast view and its destructive allure. As the women leave the bright glamour of the club after work in their long evening gowns, the camera first travels with them from the side but views them only from the waist down, focusing on the long expensive gowns and the high heels clacking on the sidewalk. They turn up the front steps of their apartment building, now in full shot, as the milkman, their everyday life, comes out the door and down the steps. The "girls," dead-tired, walk through dark, gray streets; Vanning is chauffeured in his limousine.

The crux of the plot is set when one of a group of "big-spenders" has paid for his losses with a bad check and is murdered. The police find Mary's name and phone number on a business card in his pocket.

She and the other women are caught in a trap of violation and betrayal that is triangular.[5] First, there is the surrounding force of the social and economic system in corrupting the individual. Even Mary, for all her courage and assertion of independence, still is seen as limited by the false consciousness engendered in her by the system. She sees her only way out from the trap of the economic system in terms of money:

> We've all tried this twelve-and-a-half-a-week stuff. It's no good. Living in furnished rooms. Walking to work. Going hungry a couple of days a week so you can have some clothes to put on your back. I've had enough of that for the rest of my life. So have you. ... I know all the angles. And I think I'm smart enough to keep one step ahead of them until I get enough to pack it all in and live on easy street the rest of my life. I know how to beat this racket.

Then there is the lawless, obsessive violator — Vanning. As is the case with a number of Rossen's later characters, the accumulation of money and its trappings is ultimately just the fuel for the deeper, driving need to dominate and control — the need for power. When later he has been arrested and is in jail, the veneer of his cool self-image cracks. His lawyer tells him he *must* make a deal. This infuriates him: he, *Vanning*, doesn't make deals!

> VANNING: You think I care for money? All I care about is to make people do what I tell them.
> GORDON: You're crazy, Johnny.
> VANNING: Maybe I am. Maybe I ain't. I just know one thing. I ain't gonna let no five crummy dames put the skids under me now. Get the word to those dames. If they talk, sure as my name's Johnny Vanning. I'll get 'em.

And the third vector of force pressing in on the women derives from the zeal of the assistant district attorney (Humphrey Bogart) in carrying out the law. For the D.A.'s strategy to work, the women must testify — even if it puts them in jeopardy. Moreover, in addition, for one aspect of his trial strategy he must expose them as (implied) prostitutes, even though they will then be pilloried in the press and even in their hometown newspapers. Vanning's violations of the women are selfish and intentional, brutal and violent; the D.A.'s are social and unintentional, and, in the abstract, sense socially justified for winning the case against an evil man, for justice.

The strategy of D.A. David Graham focuses on Mary. He threatens to indict her as a co-conspirator in the murder if she doesn't testify against Vanning. Vanning, meanwhile, is working out *his* strategy, and he and his sleek, polished attorney concoct an elaborate plan to corrupt the law — and the nature of testimony — by force and money.

In the central structural parallel, Graham has put Mary in jail and won't let her out unless she testifies. Vanning won't bail her out unless she "plays ball." His emissary to her goes further by threatening her with the fate of Audrey Fleming, who she knows was found floating in the river. Frightened, she goes along with Vanning's plan. Following this plan, she does, in fact, testify, and thus satisfies Graham. But Vanning's lawyer exposes her, makes her admit to their concocted story that she had "entertained" clients beyond the rules of the club and that Vanning had threatened to fire her. She is not only shamed, but her motives for testifying are portrayed as merely revenge-seeking. The truth of her testimony is further portrayed as a self-serving lie by the false testimony of a small-town

Marked Woman (1937), Warner Bros. Mary Dwight Strauber (Bette Davis) and D.A. David Graham (Humphrey Bogart) test each other at the trial of the gangster Johnny Vanning.

sheriff who has been "bought" by Vanning. He testifies that the two men she pointed out as the killers had been in his own jail the night of the murder. All are acquitted; money and fear have violated both Mary and justice.

Mary's innocent young sister Betty has come to town, and she and Mary have a bitter argument over what Betty thinks is Mary's hypocrisy in trying to tell her how to live. Angry and upset, she defiantly agrees to go to a party at Vanning's penthouse with the flighty Emmy Lou. At the party she first goes along with, and then resists, an aggressive seducer, running up an outdoor stairway to escape him. As she struggles, Vanning comes out onto the terrace. He doesn't know she's Mary's sister, and had set her up with the man. He's furious at her for putting on an act of innocence—who does she think she is? When she tries to protest, he hits her. She falls down the stairs and hits her head. She is dying. As Emmy Lou watches, Vanning tells Charley to get rid of her. Later she's found dead.

As Vanning awaits a second trial, for the murder of Betty, the pattern of the double entrapment is conveyed in the parallel visits of first Graham and then Vanning to the women's apartment. Graham, of course, insists that they testify against Vanning. After the death of her sister, Mary is now willing to agree, but the other women, too afraid of what Vanning can do to them, still refuse. Why should they risk it? They know that another gangster will take Vanning's place.

When Vanning and two goons come to keep them from testifying, the reality of their uncertainty and their fear is powerfully rendered in the excellent early example of the *plan sequence*, the expressive sequence of images in a scene that became a hallmark of Rossen's style. At the start of the scene Vanning confronts the women in the bedroom. The camera first views them all from the side, as in an unequal battleground — the women tense and fearful as they face their enemy. Mary, though, can't control herself and accuses him of killing her sister. He hits her, and she bangs back against a wall. He then herds the other three women into the living room and has Charley and another man stay with Mary in the bedroom. As they start to leave, and the camera turns to follow them, we see Charley move toward Mary and swing a fist at her. In mid-swing we cut with a jolt to a shot back from the living room as the others come in through the door from the bedroom. Vanning closes the door and stands to one side, while another of his boys stands on the other. Gabby drops into a chair along the wall to the left, Florrie onto a chair to the right. The eldest, Estelle, is standing in the center, closest to the camera. The shot is held as we hear a loud thump, and a painting on the wall near the door shakes. The women respond, terrified. As we hear more blows and more screams, we cut to each woman in turn, and then, at the loudest, most anguished scream, to Vanning lighting a cigarette. The scene switches back to the basic longer shot past all of them as the two thugs come through the door and the women rush to the doorway and into the other room, and gasp in horror. As Vanning leaves, he promises them more of the same if they "squeal"— as he defines their testifying. (In *The Hustler*, Bert Gordon's sadistic attitude toward and treatment of women is a more complex parallel to Vanning's. And *squealer*, as we've seen years later, was one of the frequent epithets used to denigrate those who testified in the HUAC hearings.)

Although badly beaten, Mary will testify. She now knows, she says, "If this is what you call living, I don't want any part of it. Always being afraid.... There must be some other way for me to live."

That glimpse of new possibilities, a kind of redemption, however, is undercut by the lasting mark of it all on Mary's face and the final brilliant set of ironic juxtapositions of the film — situational, verbal, visual — that plays against the Marxist ideal of growth of consciousness. The women are imprisoned by the D.A.— it's for their own protection. They look out the window and see one of Vanning's hoodlums waiting out in the street for them. What that might still mean is revealed at the trial. During her testimony, Mary is seen from her left, her face turned slightly to her right. At the climax of her revelations she turns to look directly at Vanning, so that the right side of her face is now to the camera, and we see the reason for that loudest scream: an X cut into her cheek. "That's Johnny's little trademark," she says, "for anyone who double-crosses him." We cut to Vanning, who turns to nod at one of his men in the audience, as he has done several times during the trial. His threat will endure even after he is in prison.

Justice is achieved, but only after Graham, in a clever rhetorical ploy during his summation to the jury, debases the women who have helped him: "Their characters are questionable, their profession unsavory and distasteful. Oh, it's not been difficult to crucify them. But it has been difficult to crucify the truth."

Vanning is convicted. At the top of the courthouse steps, Graham is being praised by the newspapermen: "How about a couple more pictures of our next D.A.?" "What do you mean, D.A.? If he isn't our next governor, he ought to have his head examined."

Thickening, shadowy fog has set in. In contrast to the acclaim for Graham's "triumph," we see the women as a group walk down the steps into the fog and along the street. Each is then seen in close-up, Mary with a tear or two on her cheeks. They are then seen as a group as they walk on, staring straight ahead, their expressions an enigma, emptied yet resolute, but definitely with no joy or triumph at the victory of law and order. We cut to a wider shot as they turn and start to walk down a narrow street. The camera follows after them as they walk, seen from behind in one line across the width of the street, and disappear into the deeper fog. They *are* together, walking with the strength of their friendship (the only kind of solidarity they can really claim as their own) into the uncertainty of the shadows. There will be another Vanning, another Graham.

3

Warner Bros. and the Party — Five Films, Three Years

Rossen joined the Communist Party within a year of arriving in Hollywood. Although he had never alluded to it directly, he had clearly been aware of the Party, its ideals, its members, and, as we have seen, its theories and constructs for drama. In his unpublished statement of 1951, he discusses his motives for joining:

> They were bitter years [the thirties] ... they were filled with frustration and emptied of hope. I was fortunate. My ability to articulate the silent cry that lay in the throats of so many people for so many years gave me success.
> I did not forget.... I joined out of a deep conviction that the party was leading the fight against these forces, both here and abroad, which were trying to smash the forward march of the people toward a fuller, richer and a happier life. And I also felt with as deep a conviction that the answer lay in Socialism.... I wanted people to live with dignity and not as debased and craven creatures, and this search for dignity is the constantly recurring theme of my work, for I have known what it is to live without it.[1]

In 1953 he looked back again at the intellectual atmosphere of the twenties, when he grew up, and then the Depression years of the thirties, feeling that

> it was a period of great cynicism, disillusionment; it was a period in which I think most young men who were interested in ideas accepted the premise that the system of government ... that we had grown up under had failed.... There weren't any more horizons; there weren't any more promises; we had pretty much reached the apex of a pretty materialistic society.... We felt that we were looking — I felt that I was looking — for new horizons, a new kind of society, something I could believe in and become a part of.... You felt that ... the Communist Party was the medium through which this could be effected.... It offered every possible kind of thing to you at that time which could fulfill your sense of idealism ... anything that tends toward the realization of the inner man.[2]

These feelings, beliefs, and hopes, stand, of course, in stark contrast to his later disillusioned belief that "the same reasons why you go into the party are the same reasons which make you go out, which is ultimately the discovery that the idealism that you were looking for, the fighting for the ideas that you want, are just not in the party.... The Communist Party can never be the instrument to get or effect those reasons or make them work."[3]

However, in the thirties and forties he did believe and he did act. But his doubts and his conflicts rose during this same period, with neither side of this discordant mixture fully dominating the other for many years.

In this period the Screen Writers Guild included the most Communists, and the most active, of any of the segments of the Hollywood industry. Known Communists continued to play a major role in the Guild (and sat on its Executive Board) until 1947, when a major shift in the power structure resulted in their defeat. Estimates vary, but the most likely number of Communists in the SWG was between 150 and 200, not necessarily all at the same time. Rossen was most active during the war years. He served as secretary of the 1941–2 slate, was on the Board in 1945, and was chairman of the Hollywood Writers Mobilization, which the Guild initially sponsored.

He had arrived during the heated battles between the studios and the writers over the attempt to unionize and form the Screen Writers Guild. Conservative writers and the studios had created a counter-union organization, the Screen Playwrights. He later recalled:

> The most active people in that fight — it was highly organized and most effective — were ... members of the Communist Party ... in retrospect, the most capable; and, naturally, I was drawn toward these people, both from the point of view of their dedication to what they were doing and from the point of view of their prestige and their standing as screenwriters.[4]

The Communists in the Guild steered it toward regularly supporting and joining campaigns and causes supported by the Party, and Rossen began to take part in these activities. Many of these campaigns were worthy on their own merits, especially in establishing strong labor relations and agreements with the studios. But they were often used by the Party for its own purposes — whether to recruit party members, to shift the organization toward more extreme positions in line with Soviet positions, or to create actions favorable to the Soviets, often while masking or evading truths about Soviet actions.

Among the earliest of the major campaigns he took part in were the actions of the Hollywood Anti-Nazi League. During his first year in the Party, Rossen had joined the League, which had been formed in July of 1936. Earlier, in 1933, following the developing international Comintern line, the Party had initiated the American League Against War and Fascism. The extent of the activities of the Hollywood League reveal the kind of fervor and momentum that belief in the Party and its positions engendered: *Hollywood Now*, a newsletter; two radio shows; meetings; demonstrations; and rallies. A mass meeting at the Shrine Auditorium in 1936, was one of its first major events. Its ostensible topic was "The Menace of Hitler in America," with W.E.B. Dubois as a featured speaker. As was typical, this menace was seen as particularly dangerous because of the fascistic tendencies of capitalist power in America and the need to defend "socialism" from both offenders. Sponsors listed for the event included Robert Rossen. A subsequent rally was held the same month at the Philharmonic Auditorium, with German playwright Ernst Toller and the French novelist Andre Malraux as the chief speakers.[5]

The formation of the Hollywood League coincided with the start of the Spanish Civil War in July of 1936. The League and its controlling Communist members then took an active role in the development of organizations and activities through the period of the war. The defense of the Loyalists against the fascist forces of Francisco Franco was one of the most popular causes that the Party promoted in the thirties. On the surface this was clearly a case of fighting against those forces "which were trying to smash the forward march of the people." The Comintern had defined the ostensible goals of Party-controlled organizations. However, as events in Spain unfolded, the sympathy and passions created tended to obfuscate the reality of the full situation and the end results of the money raised — for example, the increasing Soviet control of the Loyalist cause, with imprisonments, executions, mass oppression and killings of "dissidents." During the Civil War, Rossen, along with a wide spectrum of liberals and Party stalwarts, had taken part in the formation of the Motion Picture Artists Committee to Aid Republican Spain, which was formed as a subsidiary of the Anti-Nazi League. As it turned out, he was joined in this activity, as well as others, by his friend and political protégé John Garfield. Both were among many who sent telegrams to President Roosevelt in March of 1938 urging him to demand that France open her borders to allow the Loyalists to purchase and receive supplies. To raise money for such supplies (supplied by the Soviets and others, clandestinely), the group sponsored a myriad of events: a revue called *Sticks and Stones*, which included satires on both foreign and domestic "fascists"; presentations of films such as Ernest Hemingway and Joris Ivens' documentary *The Spanish Earth* (in the summer of 1937); a fund-raiser for exhibitions of Pablo Picasso's Guernica; various dinners and cause parties; and the formation of the usual splinter group offshoots, such as the Freedom of the Screen Committee. One of the most rousing series of events involved the French writer and Loyalist supporter Andre Malraux and the then famous Loyalist known as La Pasionaria, the woman who had, it was reported, at a bleak moment during the Fascist siege of Madrid stood with raised fist and shouted "Non Passaron!" At several auditoriums in Los Angeles the audiences rose and answered her performance of her now famous act. One writer commented on the ladies in fur coats and jewelry standing with upraised fists, shouting, "Non Passaron!"[6]

These ideological crusades continued to shape the beliefs and the "temperament" of Rossen. They filtered through into his way of developing studio projects, where on the studio production line of the genre and headline business the motto was: when it works, do it again. After the good public reception (and press) for *Marked Woman*, Lou Edelman proposed Robert Rossen and Lloyd Bacon for another translation of current headline interests. In *Racket Busters* (1938), the crusading district attorney seeks to break the hold of gangsters not on prostitutes but on labor unions, which they have controlled and corrupted. This time Leonardo Bercovici was assigned to assist the busy Rossen in the writing. A fellow Party member, Bercovici was a long-time friend of Rossen. In a later interview he told about working on a play with Rossen in New York before Rossen left for Hollywood. He followed soon after. He was in Mexico in the fifties when Rossen was shooting *The Brave Bulls*, and in that same interview he commented about Rossen's severe tension at that time over the pending Congressional investigations.[7]

The original script that resulted from Rossen's interest in challenging the boundaries of the system's demands and protocols (and its genres) probably went too far in developing a more directly proletarian protest drama in combination with a fast-paced, fact-based crime genre film. In turn, the cogs of the studio turned unfavorably. The script was reduced and the production rushed through in hopes of capitalizing on the success of *Marked Woman*. Even more damaging, the subsequent film was then cut to a mere 71 minutes — an excessive application of the fast-paced Warners style — when the studio grew less sanguine about the possible audience appeal of its union-left slant.

Despite this far-too-typical meddling and control, Rossen always looked back on his days at Warners with satisfaction in the advantages provided by the system. As he told Henry Burton in 1962:

> It was a hell of a good outfit. Writers had a good "deal." They didn't just shove subjects at you. Within reason, you had your pick of what went through the story department. Hal Wallis, who was head of production, had respect for writers and didn't force unsuitable screenplay chores on them. There's always a certain amount of discipline, of course, there has to be, but to the extent there was a free hand, and it was considerable, I had it. Also, for the most part, I worked with directors rather than producers. There was no messing around at Warners. You sat down at the typewriter and got out a script for a picture that had to be on the screen in six weeks![8]

In the case of *Racket Busters*, the released product is only a strong hint of what might have been; however, it does still reflect Rossen's political idealism in the glow of his first immersion in Communist Party crusades. It is his most direct use of the structure of the central thirties social protest drama. Within the gangster narrative he combined his personal interest in a character's need to define oneself more authentically with the protest drama emphasis on the need for raising individual and group consciousness so as to stand up to corruption and betrayal. Even truncated, it is a surprisingly direct application of the Left's political and literary ideology in a major studio release. On its release in early 1938, the *Daily Worker* praised its strong pro-union stance and its emphasis on proletarian solidarity.

Overall, in the abstract, it sets up a variation on the structural pattern of *Marked Women*. This time Humphrey Bogart is (more comfortably) the tough-talking racketeer Martin, who is controlling and corrupting a labor union. In an odd bit of casting, the crusading D.A. is played by Allen Jenkins, the rough-voiced offbeat actor who is usually the good-natured friend of the protagonist. The D.A. wants to get the union's drivers to stand up and testify against Martin. In this variation, the innovation is to focus on the working class, the truck drivers, caught in the pressures of the Great Depression (a Rossen montage captures newspaper headlines, unemployed workers, tawdry street market stalls and wagons). And—like the marked women—the men are caught between the forces of law and order and the mob. But this time there is no moral ambiguity, no implied parallel between an abusive zealousness on both sides of the law. The D.A. is right. The men are fearful and apathetic, and need to change. When they stand up and act together, justice will be done, and rightly so.

Again, a winking shorthand is used instead of the real terminology, and it is turned into a thematic plot point. Seemingly to avoid any trouble with the actual, and actually dangerous, Teamsters Union (who had power and influence in the motion picture industry, and a connection to gangland), the cooperative of the drivers is an "Association" not affiliated with a "Union." And so in the moral turn at the climax the men agree to join a real and uncorrupted *union*.

The moral leader of the group is Pop (Walter Abel), an old-time driver. The moral focus of the film, however, is on the young driver Denny (George Brent), a minor version of Rossen's unformed young man of unfocused energy and insecure self. He's quick with his fists but slow to see the need for socially conscious, collective action. As Pop says about him, "If he could think as straight as he hits, he'd be terrific." Amid the plot emphasis on the topical newsworthy material of racketeers and the crusading D.A., the moral arc of the film traces the raising of Denny's consciousness to act in social ("revolutionary") protest and inspire others to do the same. (It is a more proletarian and unmitigated parallel to the narrative arc of Mary in *Marked Woman*.) The mob has moved in on the drivers, setting up the Association and demanding they produce a phony strike to intimidate and pressure the owners. When Pop protests, the goons start to beat him. Denny comes to his aid, but afterwards he still goes his own, isolated way. His wife is pregnant; he has a family to take care of. When the D.A. moves in on the group to get them to help secure an indictment against the mob boss (even to *testify*), Denny, along with the others, hesitates and evades.

As the mob pressure on the men accelerates, the iconography of the scenes is typical: Bogart in fedora and overcoat (collar up), backed by his phalanx of goons in fedoras and overcoats (collars down); the sudden burst of a beating; the glances, eyes averted, as the men retreat and comply. But Pop moves against their physical, visual retreating. He moves against their apathy, their silence about what is evil. He protests, exhorts the men to join in, and gives evidence to the D.A. And so he is killed. Meanwhile (as in *Marked Woman*), the D.A. has locked up Denny, threatening him with prison for withholding evidence. After Pop is killed, Denny reaches his moment of recognition. When Martin initiates the strike, Denny finally acts, exhorting the men, "We've got to stick together." It is another variation on the ubiquitous ideological mantra of the times ("miner no can get by self"; "no man alone ain't got no chance") — implying the necessary solidarity of more than mere group activity. The structure and motifs of Elia Kazan and Budd Schulberg's *On the Waterfront* not only develop a similar subject and plot line of mob domination and corruption, but also the central motif of raising consciousness of an individual and then an apathetic group (and includes many of the iconographic details of this Rossen script).

In the affirming rush (and rushed) momentum of the last sequence, the men go back to work and will go on to testify. Even the bosses cooperate, and Martin is captured and convicted.

Rossen's next two films, both released in 1939, make an interesting and meaningful contrast in the use of the gangster genre and its broader version in the young-tough-guy-from-the-slums pattern. With significant differences, both show Rossen's interest in unformed young men of energy and natural force, and their responses to society's pressures upon them — starring two men who are icons for that image, John Garfield and James Cagney. The first, *Dust Be My Destiny* (released October 1939), with Garfield, is a lesser film and version of later developments in Rossen's work. The second, *The Roaring Twenties* (November 1939), is the epitome of gangster films of the thirties, a final tribute to that stage of the genre. Both reflect Rossen's ability to work within the hierarchical studio system and yet continue to develop his own ideas and interests.

At this point Rossen was "King of the Lot" for tough-guy films with a certain moral depth and complexity. He could capture the surface of the life and also get at some of the depths, as much as the system would bear. With *Dust Be My Destiny*, adapted from a minor novel by Jerome Odlum and directed by the workmanlike Lewis Seiler, the title promised more depth than the finished product actually had. Nonetheless, the character of John Garfield does have that innate energy, that raw, untutored force of key characters in Rossen's further films — and the Garfield persona in *his* best films. But here his gritty harshness is softened, his inner goodness too apparent. He is not the dramatic, elusive, even threatening enigma of his best roles.

Joe Bell (Garfield) has indeed been wronged by the social and legal system. He is repeatedly treated by people and the law as though he were a petty gangster, but he is actually not one. He's just a tough guy from the slums who's denied by the forces of society a way to express himself and define his true self. The ironies of justice wrongly applied are insistently banged into place, and eventually reversed too easily. A zealous and prejudiced sheriff gets him convicted of trespassing and sentenced to a prison farm. The farm supervisor is cruel and unfair—especially toward Joe when he becomes jealous of his daughter's interest in him. The cruelty brings explosions of the darkness in Joe back to the surface. But to counter that there is the lightening in the budding love between him and the daughter Mabel (Priscilla Lane).

When they try to get away, her father discovers them. In a fight Joe knocks the supervisor down and he hits his head. He dies. So now they are fugitives on the road, running toward a new life somewhere. Two contrasting scenes during their wandering suggest the film's uneasy mixture of a Hollywood left-wing sentimentality on the one hand, and an inventive, truly realistic capturing of the ambiguities in people on the other. In an example of the former, the common man is blatantly sweet. Broke and hungry, out in the streets early one morning, the couple come upon that symbol of normal family life, the milkman. They ask for a bottle of milk, and the milkman readily hands one over.

Dust Be My Destiny (1939), Warner Bros. Joe Bell (John Garfield) and Mabel Alden (Priscilla Lane), on the run and attempting to lead a normal life, are accosted by a small-town sheriff.

And he remarks, as they drink and nod in agreement, that in a better world things like milk would be free for everyone.

In the contrasting example, the difficulty of making a good life in a hard world, even among good family people, is dramatized credibly and with a convincing bitter irony. Penniless, the couple are seen as a great gimmick by a local publicity agent: poor young lovers given a helping hand by a local theater. Such real hometown kindness will be great for business! He offers them money to be married on stage with an audience. They do want to get married and do need the money. They get the money — after expenses are deducted! — and they do get married by a real parson. But they are used and shamed. They are dressed in loose fitting, laughable clothes, and *are* laughed at by the common people of the town when they walk on stage. During the ceremony the audience hoots and hollers, shouting comments — "Speak up, speak louder! Kiss her, kiss her! C'mon, kiss her again!" — all with surrounding laughter and a visual sequence of harsh cuts that capture the careless mockery and pain of their violation and humiliation. It is a fine sequence, but its well-wrought, bitter ironies are not borne out in the softer ironies that follow.

After Joe finds work, a plot coincidence leads to his exposure as a wanted criminal. Rather than run again, and encouraged by his new wife (the saving morality of women), he decides to go back to face the law. It was, after all, self-defense and an accident. She is sure they'll understand. They have to.

The weakest and softest of the ironies was forced upon the film's conclusion by the studio. Rossen refused to write it, and it was written and shot without him. As filmed, the girl's father, it was discovered, had died of a heart attack, not from the blows struck by Joe or the rock. Dickens-like, all is right with the world — though still with some skepticism about society shown by Joe. Rossen wanted the final impact of society's unjust power to be felt via the killing of both of the young people by a posse. It would be the ultimate violation and betrayal — gunning him down as though he were really a gangster when he is totally innocent. One proposed variation, and one Rossen would have accepted, had only Joe killed. The studio, however, had just suffered financially with Fritz Lang's *You Only Live Once*, in which the unjustly hunted Henry Fonda and Sylvia Sidney are killed (although in a more complicated and ambiguous situation), and so refused to use his ending.

A battle over the ending was the first of a number of fights Rossen was to have over the control of movies he wrote, and especially those he directed. His comments about this ranged from resigned to combative. One of the latter:

> It's the combat there has always been between the creators and producers or all those people who work in the studios. They are frustrated people, who dare address themselves to a writer telling him what he is to write. They act the same way toward the director, who has the right to a first editing — the "director's cut" — which means nothing, because they can reedit the film after that to show how it should have been done. But they know nothing, these people. If the film has success, they profit by it; if not, they attribute the failure to the director. There's no rhyme or reason for it. They are idiots.[9]

This time, however, the combat was not all that meaningful. Neither version went beyond convention. There was the studio's glaringly, sentimentally positive Hollywood convention on the one side, while on the other stood Rossen's sentimentally negative protest convention, which is not an organic outgrowth of the film's tone, the softness of its narrative, or of its accumulated facts and feelings, but rather a conceptual leap to ideological tragedy.

While the film was less significant than Rossen had hoped, the collaboration with Garfield was not. It was the first of four films they worked on together, in which Garfield did his best early work as an actor, work that defined the screen image he was to build his career upon.

After their earlier acquaintance in New York, the two had met again shortly after Garfield had come to Warner Bros. in 1938 and developed a close relationship. They had much in common, though in some ways it was their differences that set the nature of their relationship. They both grew up on the Lower East Side in the same Rivington neighborhood. They both had done some boxing, but had done more of their fighting in the streets. Both had been drawn to the theater, had similar aggressive personalities, and were energetic, driving, magnetic. But Garfield didn't have Rossen's education or intellectual bent, and he had not developed as much intellectually, politically, or even artistically in terms of theory and understanding. Along with Lewis Milestone and Clifford Odets (who was Garfield's oldest friend and original role model), Rossen became one of those who guided Garfield in his early career decisions and his entry into the political and social circles of the Hollywood Left. Garfield was an eager, greedy student, but by all accounts he never quite mastered the material.

Garfield loved to hang out in the writer's corner of the Warners' commissary, where Rossen and other contract writers would spend more than just their lunch hours. In those days they were required, as employees, to be on the lot for an eight-hour day, and so they used the commissary as their social club, pursuing everything from talk of Stanislavski or Marxism to Pinochle. There was especially a lot of kidding and verbal jousting. Garfield relished the intellectual camaraderie and wanted to soak it all up as quickly as possible. He even loved being the target of much of the kidding. The Epstein twins, who wrote several of his films, had many stories about him. Julie Garfield: "Okay fellas, let's have ourselves a real intellectual discussion." Phil Epstein: "Sounds fine, but who's going to represent *you*?" They loved to catch him in his literary frauds — claiming to have read all of Stendahl, for one — and in his almost Marx Brothers–like malapropisms (*obsolescence* for *absolution*). Rossen is credited with one of the most memorable exchanges. Garfield was complaining about a studio executive who he claimed was a "congenial idiot." Rossen: "The word's *congenital*, Julie. A congenial idiot is what *you* are."[10] In later years, during and after the conflicts in the filming of *Body and Soul*, the close camaraderie faded into a lingering tension between them.

Rossen's next work in this milieu was on *The Roaring Twenties*, starring Jimmy Cagney and Humphrey Bogart (see Chapter 4). While at one point Rossen had championed Garfield for the role of Eddie Bartlett, the Bogart-Cagney pairing in the film was fated. For *A Child Is Born*, his script after *The Roaring Twenties* (released in January 1940), the studio did want Garfield for the male lead, but this time Rossen told him not to take the part. He told him they'd give him first billing to protect their investment, "but the girl has all the lines." When Garfield bowed out, they gave the part to Jeffrey Lynn, the ubiquitous nice guy of the times.[11]

The film is clearly the result of taking on an assignment within the organized procedures of the Hollywood, and particularly Warner Bros., system — and this time with no real joining of heart or mind. With the prompting of Hal Wallis, Rossen accepted the assignment to write *A Child Is Born,* though one might wonder why either one thought he should. It was the third film he wrote in 1939, along with *Dust Be My Destiny* and *The Roaring Twenties*. Directed again by Lloyd Bacon, it has the least personal imprint among his screenplays. It was based on an original play and an earlier screen version of that play.

The injustice of the justice system has hit a married couple. The pregnant wife (Geraldine Fitzgerald) is accused of a murder that she claims was self-defense. We are not shown the event, so there is some mystery left here. A jury, nonetheless, convicts her, and she is sentenced to twenty years in prison. In the meantime, she goes to the hospital to give birth. Her anguished husband (Lynn) is desperately trying to find new evidence on which to overturn the verdict. The legal system remains overbearing—Lynn is not allowed in to see his wife (evidently to forestall the chance of a jail break from the maternity ward!). While he fusses and fumes, we get glimpses of a cross-section of stories of women in the maternity ward—women demeaned, as is his wife, in a male-dominated society. Among them are a woman who is oppressed by having too many babies with a careless husband; and one whose husband didn't want to have a baby and has taken a new partner in their vaudeville act (and likely his bed). The final plot, moral, and melodramatic crisis is based on a sudden discovery by the doctors that they must save either the life of the baby or of the mother. She must choose. In a variety of circumstances, this kind of dilemma of choice and its consequences is a central theme in many of Rossen's subsequent films, though usually not so baldly melodramatic.

Rossen's next film, *Blues in the Night,* fared better at the box office. It was one of three of his scripts to be released in the hectic year of 1941—while the world was exploding all around America and clearly drawing the country into World War II. Released in December 1941 (just after the Japanese attack on Pearl Harbor), it was written after the two other (and more significant) of his screenplays that year. After the political and ideological tensions involved in finessing the implications of *Out of the Fog* and *The Sea Wolf,* writing it must have seemed almost like a holiday.

While somewhat beyond Rossen's usual territory, *Blues in the Night* is closer to the moral and social concerns of the major thrust of his work at Warners. Directed by Anatol Litwak, It focuses on the struggles of a group of young jazz musicians during the Depression and captures the ambiance of their world nicely. In the depths of the Depression, a group of young New Yorkers, clearly Jewish, are struggling to make a living. They are inspired by a part-time law student and would-be clarinetist (Elia Kazan!) to start a jazz band, despite his mother's admonitions not to throw his life away (shades of Ma in *Body and Soul*). While in jail (never mind why), they hear real blues being sung by a black man in the next cell. *This* is the authentic jazz that they had been yearning to play, and so (somewhat improbably) they set out on an odyssey through the South to find the real soul of jazz (and, the social theme implies, of America). Their trip, partly on box cars (*à la* the "boys on the road" movies), is conveyed in part by a series of Rossen-specialty montages, mainly of glimpses (not often seen in films at this time) of the lives of blacks in the segregated society of the South. (The montage sequences were edited by future director Don Siegel.) These images are a harsh counterpoint (a commentary on racial injustice and prejudice) to the young musicians' dream of a harmonious black and white society, but they do include images of the blacks' enduring positive spirit (William Faulkner: "Dilsey: They endure.") and the soulful sounds of their music.

But the quest for this holy grail of a musical self-fulfillment is not an easy one. There is the typical cross-section of society's betrayals, but the central moral crisis is created when one's integrity and natural talent come into conflict with the drive toward recognition, money, and success — especially when there is a glamorous woman involved. The male lead (Richard Whorf) — a pianist and composer, the most talented of the group — is lured by the siren song of a singer met along the way (Betty Field). He betrays his friends and his talent and integrity, his better self. He leaves the group with her. His corruption is evidenced, rather incredibly, by a psychological crisis. In the midst of the romance of this new life, he breaks down and cannot play the piano! After he later reaches his crucial moment of recognition, he finds his integrity again and returns to his real calling. In his redemption he plays again — a true blues composition of his own. In contrast, the unwavering moral center of the film is a young woman, a good blues singer — Priscilla Lane again — who this time is finally able to influence the man in her life (Whorf) to reach for his better self. And she finds a truer sense of herself as a separate, free-standing person, one not dependent on being someone's "girl."

4

Ode to an Era — *The Roaring Twenties*

Released at the thirties decade's end, *The Roaring Twenties* was conceived as a kind of historical epic, a looking back at what seemed to be a dying age — the era of the gangster and the society that produced him, even idolized him, and then fought and defeated him. It is also a recapitulation of the conventions of the gangster genre in films, a summing up, even a eulogy for a passing era — in both the movies and the country. It is critical of yet sympathetic toward its central figure, Eddie Bartlett, as embodied by James Cagney, already in his prime as the iconic figure in the world of tough guy films.

Among its many attributes, *The Roaring Twenties* is a prime example of the workings of the studio system — the fruitful (if often painful), frustrating and cruel combination of levels of contribution and control, of joint group efforts and individual creativity.

It began as a promotion, a "pitch," by journalist and sometime producer Mark Hellinger. In a brief brochure — with no plot or characters indicated — he outlined the scheme of a film (which he called *The World Moves On*) that "covers a period of twenty years — from 1919, directly after the World War, until 1939, when the picture is released." It would be, he wrote, "the story of an era," dealing with Prohibition, the Depression, and, of course, emphasizing "Crime does not pay." Several writers tried their hands at a treatment. It was Jerry Wald who turned the proposal in the direction of a workable project.[1] Wald was by all accounts the model for the driving, manipulative, scheming protagonist of Budd Schulberg's novel *What Makes Sammy Run*, as Schulberg had observed him through these very years. Wald was at the turning point of his career, poised for his big move, his rise to the top. He was at this point a writer of a special sort and a producer, whether he was credited as such or not — basically an early version of a "packager." He went on to become a major independent producer and sometime studio executive. At the time of this project, he and his then partner Richard Macaulay were practically an independent production company. From 1935 to the production of *The Roaring Twenties* in 1939, Wald claimed writing credits on *eighteen* movies, the last ten with Macauley as a partner. There were four in 1938 alone, and then five more after the "writing" of *The Roaring Twenties* script.

They had a production line — Wald picking up on a produceable idea, sharpening

4. Ode to an Era—The Roaring Twenties

it, selling it, organizing, working to some degree or other with writers (who were sometimes credited but often not), and always making sure *he* added it to his burgeoning list of screen credits, as he saw himself mainly as the producer he wanted to be. Their projects ranged from quickie light comedies and romances to a variety of showbiz and musical formats. Seven were musicals, mainly with elaborate production numbers by Busby Berkeley. But not one of their previous movies had been a gangster film or tough-guy movie, and Wald saw this gangster project as a big, decade-ending, career-building picture.

And so Wald turned to Rossen, with *his* background, experience, and developing reputation for this sort of film, to provide the realistic (and mythic), solid gangster-world flesh to the bare bones of the concepts already defined. Rossen would build the narrative details and structure for the film (building, in turn, on the materials they had inherited). Indicative of his central role: John Garfield was slated to team up with Priscilla Lane for a second time, his role to be the streetwise good guy in contrast to the gangster roles for Jimmy Cagney and Humphrey Bogart. Rossen beefed up the role for his friend; but then he was told that Garfield was out and Jeffrey Lynn in, and so Rossen had to rewrite the part to fit the milder-mannered, straight good-guy persona of Lynn. He was the first to tell Garfield of the change. (Garfield then balked at a new assignment and was put on suspension.)[2] Even though Rossen was working with as high-powered a Hollywood combo as there was, and fighting with them all along the way, the film has a strong and distinct continuity with the central matters and methods of his personal pictures. Rossen, too, saw the project as a major opportunity, his biggest film so far, and so, undoubtedly not without a fight, accepted third billing in the shared credit for the screenplay that was the normal routine for Wald. It's indicative of the acknowledgment of his role in the production of this film that when he next worked with Wald and Macauley on *Out of the Fog*, he received top billing, though he still had to share the screenplay credit with them

The producer was Hal Wallis, arguably the most effective and important producer on the Warners lot. He was not merely an official producer on his films, he was the active, controlling, and *creative* constant and final authority—even when working on several productions (at various stages) at once. It was he, for example, who made the significant analyses and crucial decisions that shaped the final version of *Casablanca* from among the many versions, variations, and contributors.

Two notes that he wrote to director Raoul Walsh during the shooting of *The Roaring Twenties* exemplify his working style, his close interaction with the filmmakers, his close scrutiny of daily rushes, and his precise attention to detail. On July 20, 1939, he wrote:

> However, I don't like your camera setups; those straight-on two-shots and individual close-ups are going to get monotonous and make for choppy cutting....Why don't you shoot over the shoulders of Cagney and Lynn up at the judge. Get a little composition in the thing and a little grouping. So that we don't have to cut from one big closeup to another and just have a series of portraits on the screen with people speaking the lines.

It was a lesson that Rossen took to heart, an approach he developed with more and more finesse, intensity, and meaningfulness throughout his career. On August 20, regarding the magnificent final sequence, a version of which they had just viewed, Wallis wrote: "We want to retake the finish of the picture on the church steps along the lines discussed in the projection room today." He lists a number of alternatives, including shooting it all twice—with people in the background and not—and to get the best build-up to the final line as written, "He used to be a big shot."[3]

The basis for that sequence was in the screenplay, but when you add in the contributions of the producer and the major director Walsh, the cooperative process that is filmmaking at its best is clearly at work here. And yet we see in the final cooperative product the consistent elements of a Rossen job, whether screenplay or total production: the dynamics of direct confrontation in scenes, the telling use of details of the milieu, of setting and décor, the arc of character development and change, and especially the structuring toward betrayal and possible redemption or not.

Walsh, as a director, was noted for his sense of pace and directness, the unadorned, straightforward naturalness of imagery and performance that eschewed any flaunting of style. It came almost to the point, however, of losing the valuable impact and contribution of creative or even effective visual imagery. And Walsh often ignored the shots indicated in the screenplay. Wallis was to push him on this during the making of several subsequent films as well.[4]

On the other hand, Walsh's versatility, and openness to the energy and strength inherent in all forms of dramatic material, is seen in his work in many film types and genres, but especially in the pictures that revealed his own instinctive rapport with materials involving strong male types and themes — from tough guys to cowboys, military men to western gunslingers. His *oeuvre* is a showcase of the best aspects of commercial filmmaking, as well as the amazing rigor and efficiency of the studio system. One can see why he rushed: eighteen films from 1930 through 1942 thirteen from 1945 through 1949; ten from 1951 through 1953. *The Roaring Twenties* initiated a series of movies generally more notable (and more focused on his basic interests and instincts) than the films he had made earlier. A cross-section of these include *Dark Command, They Drive by Night, High Sierra, The Strawberry Blonde, Manpower, They Died with Their Boots On, Gentleman Jim,* and *White Heat.*

The Roaring Twenties recounts and retraces in its own structure the traditional mythic narrative of the gangster: the rise from poverty; the battles for power and success; the accumulation of the trappings, and women, of the wealthy; the betrayals and murderous violations; the inevitable fall. Yet here, with a Rossen final turn in the cycle, comes a kind of redemption. It is like a last hurrah, both damning and nostalgic. Yet it is also a fulcrum point in the development of the crime film genre, a prefiguring of a new direction, a new kind of central figure: the basically good, left-over-from-another-era tragic protagonist, out to do one last job, even for a positive reason, in such significant films as *High Sierra, The Asphalt Jungle, The Killers,* and *Criss-Cross*—films which critic Jack Shadoian has aptly described as "resonant myths of defeat that echoed with heroic positive reverberations." These, in turn, can be seen as leading to the mode of the *film noir* in crime films of the forties and fifties, and then the neo-gangster revisions in later decades.

Despite the title, the movie spans the period from just before World War I to the Depression days of the mid-thirties. Rossen interlaces nine montage sequences (his most extensive use of this device) with the dramatic action, using kaleidoscopic images and a pontifical voice-over narration in the fashion of the then-popular *March of Time* series. In *The Roaring Twenties* the montages not only present the stages of the historical periods that are the context for the stages of the story; they also, in both images and language, emphasize central thematic points. Some are historical, with emphasis on society's influences and collusion in producing the gangsters, showing unemployment, prohibition, and hero worship in the press. Others are political, with repeated emphasis in images and words (picked up in dialogue in the story as well) on the gangster as a logical extension of, and symbol for business in a world of haves and have-nots, a capitalist world based on money:

> The forces of the underworld who best know how to operate outside the law are moving in on a new source of revenue. [images of money flowing, changing hands]
>
> Liquor is the password in this army, the magic password that spells the dollar sign.... [The bootlegger becomes] an adventurous hero ... who cares nothing about tomorrow just as long as money is easy today. Bootlegging has grown from small individual efforts to big business in building huge coalitions and combines; the chase after huge profits is followed closely by their inevitable partners, corruption, violence and murder [images of the new Tommy Guns and a montage of shootings and explosions].
>
> Murder is parceled out in wholesale lots. [Images of money, stocks, ticker tape and then the Stock Market Crash of 1929, paralleling the crash that we see of the central character, Eddie.]

In developing this correlation of the gangster and business, Rossen dramatizes with more complexity the further correlation of this drive for money with a will to power, the need and drive for self-assertion and domination. The two central characters, Eddie Bartlett (Cagney) and George (Bogart) represent two variations on this will for power. Eddie is the human, moral and emotional center of the film, George a reflection of his violent dark side. George is all evil and ego, but Eddie is a mixed human being, driven and driving, domineering and controlling, violent when he needs to be, double-crossing only those he thinks deserve to be double-crossed. Still, he is loyal to his friends, generous and good-natured, blending an unquenched boyishness with his growing obsession with power. He's *Cagney*, embodied in the fast, peppy talk and prodding hand gestures, the impish smile sliding into a tight-lipped sneer, the nimble dancer's steps, the I-dare-you stance of balled-up fists and rocking on the balls of the feet.

Back from the war, Eddie Bartlett is a fine early example of one of Rossen's unformed young seekers seen significantly in later films — Willie Stark, Charley Davis, Fast Eddie Felson. In an interview in *Show* magazine, Rossen explained why his favorite Shakespeare play was *Macbeth* in terms that apply to his typical protagonists, his searchers for their true selves. In *Macbeth* he found a "dramatization of the ambiguity of the human condition," with Macbeth, like contemporary man, "reaching for the symbols of his identity, rather than the reality, destroying yet finding himself in the tragic process." Seeking and choosing these illusory symbols of the self, Rossen's searchers reach for power in all its forms — whether through the desire for success, for status and wealth, violence and domination, conquest of continents, or love twisted into violation.

On several occasions Rossen commented on the connection between power and identity, of people seeking to define and assert their identity through seeking power. In an article in *Films in Review* in 1962 he told Henry Burton:

> In our time, and by "our time" I mean the past 250 years, from just before the French and American Revolutions, there has been an increasing obsession with power, or "identity," which is a substitute for it. The novels of Stendahl are full of it. The characters in my films have a drive for power. And it usually does end in defeat, even historically, either because the character has burned all his bridges behind him and left a bloody trail in his wake, or because he has lost his energy.[5]

Crucial as well in this statement is the reference to *energy*. It is this that is vital to the positive aspects of his central characters. It is a drive, a life force that is a positive power, but is also the source of the destructive nature of the power, the loss or distortion of the vital energy, the nourishing of its illusory substitutes, often promoted by society or seen as the only alternative under the force of society's pressures.

As Rossen commented on this latter aspect in an article based on an interview:

> The element common to many of my films is the desire for success, ambition, which is an important element in American life. It is an important element, and becomes increasingly important in what is known as Western Civilization.... Modern industrial society creates certain highly competitive things, which are often emotional, and tends I think to keep reducing the stature and dignity of the individual more and more. It presses him, if he is trying to maintain that dignity, to strike out against society and to get on top of that society.[6]

Yes, Eddie might — just might — have ended up owning the garage he'd dreamed of if only society had not betrayed him. If they had given him his job back, as promised, and had not thrown him in jail for being the naïve and innocent carrier of a package of bootleg booze. As he tells his cabbie friend Danny, "I *am* tired, Danny, tired of being pushed around, having doors slammed in my face. Tired of being just another guy back from France." But for all the pressures of society, it is made clear, too, that he follows his own bent, his own nature. His energy and dreams are turned, would probably inevitably have turned, to making the easy money, to taking insistent, overbearing control. Even when he's kidded about being a sucker over the girl he loves, he can't take it, and smears the cigar in the mouth of the night club boss all over his face.

For Eddie it all becomes just business, practiced the way the rules of the world seem to demand. Everything is allowed. When his lawyer protests some double-dealing, he tells him, "Cheating, sure, if you get caught, but you don't get caught if you take care of the right people, and this is big business, very big business." As his bootlegging business expands, he can't stop buying more and more cabs — at one point there are 2,000 — that serve as cover for the illegal liquor business. For him they are his connection to respectable big business. As is the stock market that he can't stop investing in.

It is the bigness that counts, the dominating presence. Even though his wardrobe changes with his rise to the top, his goal and desire remain the same. He is true to his sense of himself, however self-deceiving and destructive, yet strangely honorable, that sense may be. He is never shown enjoying his money — is not shown with the usual glamorous "dame," as George is. Money is the mark, the counter, of his sense of identity. He uses it to please the innocent young singer Jean (Lane) who had written him during the war when she was a child, and who is his nostalgic tie to a life of love and family that might have been. She is a rather naïve and static version of the moral, and usually artistic, woman who might bring redemption to one of Rossen's seekers. Eddie uses his money and power to arrange for her first job singing, pays to have a club full of people applaud her (mediocre) first performance, and supports the classy new night club she then sings in. But still he must assert his power: "You'll take a hundred cases and like it!" he tells the boss of the club. He buys her expensive gifts. When he shows off a crystal radio set that he bought for her, he says, "Ought to be good, paid a lot of money for it." "I suppose that makes sense," she says. "That makes anything good."

The price of his money and power is more double-crosses, more violence, and more betrayals, starting with the double-cross of bootlegging czar Nick Brown and the hijacking of his shipments. As they then do battle, Brown kills Eddie's dearest old friend Danny (see Shorty's end in *Body and Soul*). In retaliation, Eddie prepares to go after Brown.

Seeing a chance to take over, George betrays Eddie and calls Brown to tell him Eddie is coming. Eddie gets suspicious and manages to kill Brown anyway, shooting him through the glass of a restaurant's swinging kitchen door.

For Eddie it is finally all futile. Vanity, vanity, saith the preacher — and in the gangster life — all is vanity. The success is hollow, not sweet. Brutal irony reigns. Jean cannot accept his way of life, even though he has promised her he would retire soon. She marries the nice guy Lloyd, who has been Eddie's friend and lawyer. Prohibition ends. Eddie is destroyed by his reaching for respectability in the stock market, his dream of being a big capitalist. When the market, the world of respectable business, crashes, he loses all, coming up $200,000 short for playing recklessly on margin. He sells the cab business to George for the money and hocks the jewelry he had bought for Jean.

In fate's last turn of the wheel, Eddie is a broken man, defeated by a changing world he can't control, while George, somehow, is now an even bigger gangster chieftain, complete with classy modern penthouse, tuxedoes for him and his boys, and women. Drab and disheveled, Eddie can still fulfill one last noble act with the goodness that has somehow endured within him, with all that he might have been if he had been able to find his truest self. It is Jean, the girl-woman, now a mother, who leads him to his redemption as a human being. He still loves her, still wants to care for her, and take care of her. And so for her he performs his one last good deed. Lloyd, now in the D.A.'s office, is out to indict George, and so George has threatened Jean's child. She turns to down-and-out, but underneath it all still tried-and-true Eddie for help. As Graham Greene commented in his review, "Ruined and stubbly, Eddie is still the man to rub out a heel."[7] He faces George in his penthouse and tries to make a deal with him — "People like me and you, George, we don't fit anymore" — but it ends in the inevitable shootout. Threatened, Eddie shoots and kills George, but as he is chased out into the street, he is shot.

The last sequence is beautifully orchestrated. It is humanly and emotionally satisfying — a telling, rhythmic pattern of shots and the restrained, allusive poetics of sharply honed street talk. From the side, the camera follows Eddie running, being hit and falling. He gets up, bumps into a mailbox, and sprawls in the street. Behind him cops pull up and stop the shooter. Eddie gets up. The camera pans, following him as he starts to stagger up the broad cement steps of a church — the final visual irony underplayed. He stops and leans against a side wall.

The camera cuts to Panama (Gladys George), who has always loved Eddie but, loyally, has accepted being his true best friend. She has come, too late, to stop him. She is running to him, yelling, "Eddie!"

The scene cuts back to Eddie, as he stumbles up a step or two in the deep snow at the side of the steps, and then, the camera panning with him, moves out into the center. As the camera moves in closer on him, he stands tall one last time, then collapses onto the snowy steps. Panama runs into this long-held shot, kneels and holds him, one hand tender on his face. A Cop comes into the shot.

"He's dead," she says.

"Who is this guy?"

Cut to Panama, seen past Eddie's head, she above him, hand on his cheek. "This is Eddie Bartlett."

"And how are you hooked up with him?"

"I've never figured that out."

58 Part One : The Writer — Craft, Idealism and Ideology

The Roaring Twenties (1939), Warner Bros. On the church steps, Eddie Bartlett (Jimmy Cagney), the dying one-time gangster, is cradled in the arms of Panama (Gladys George), his truest friend.

Cut to the cop standing above them, asking society's last question: "What was his business?" Back to the original pattern, with her holding Eddie, Pieta-like: "He used to be a big shot."

After that wonderful last line — tender and rueful, yet damning of the system of false values Eddie lived (and died) by — the camera pulls back, and they are centered at the base of the high bank of snowy steps. Fade out.

The effective and affecting visual imagery of the death of Eddie Bartlett underscores the fact that his sad fate has more poignancy than the similar fall of other gangster chieftains in the movies of the period. For Eddie was more than just "a big shot." The uniqueness of his character in the course of the thirties genre is the paradox of his nature. Underneath the feisty, arrogant, callous surface of power, he was still a *naïf*, unworldly in many ways — a Gatsby with an image of his Daisy, Jean, still untarnished. He had made the wrong choice of himself and followed it out through a destructive path, acting finally upon his better self in the dying that was inevitable one way or the other. While in contrast, his betraying partner George had stayed unrelenting and power hungry, a violator to the end.

Of the film, Otis Ferguson said, "Somebody — the director, the writer or both — did some very fine things to keep this story human." And of the Cagney role and performance, Ferguson commented that he is "all crust and speed and sap on the surface," but that underneath there is a "quick generosity and hidden sweetness, straight, anti-fraud, native humor and feckless drive." These are characteristics that can be found in tragic form in the fully drawn young men in the films of Rossen's major period.

5

The Party Line and the Writer — Two Warner Films in a Shifting Political World

Robert Rossen's next two screenplays, *Out of the Fog* and *The Sea Wolf*, starred John Garfield — in contrasting roles. In these two films the sadistic power of the corrupt and domineering antagonists (Garfield in the first, Edward G. Robinson in the second) take on an additional coloration beyond the implications in Rossen's previous films. In their contexts and significant details they contain allusions to dictators, particularly the Nazis and Adolf Hitler (but not, of course, Josef Stalin). And yet despite the history that was in bloody progress at the time, these allusions are left ambiguous, veiled and intermittent, with the level of meaning often only slyly implied. For these two films were written and produced within a political world and its conflicts, and especially the positions and edicts of the Communist Party, which created a more direct influence (and, in this case, pressure) during their writing than during the work on Rossen's previous screenplays. Here it was not just ideology and influence; it was organized politics.

In writing the two screenplays during this period, Rossen was faced with tensions that were different than the usual pressures of work within the studio hierarchy. There was a major shift in the Party line, with its immediate reverberations and constant activities among the Hollywood Reds; but there were also his own conflicted attitudes about Party manipulations and indoctrination, what he later called the Party's constant *rationales*.

As the world began to go to war, Jerry Wald wanted to add a prestige film, a literary film with a "serious" message, to his resume of accomplishments. It happened to have a genre motif, a gangster (in a very different mode) and a basis in a left-wing play of the thirties (political — but in a different mode). And so Wald and Richard Macaulay turned to Rossen again. The unusual (and highly unWald-like) film that resulted, *Out of the Fog*, was a translation of a talky but poetic allegorical stage play into viable, dynamic cinematic terms. It was directed again by Anatol Litwak, a director with a strong sense of the dramatic nuances of expressive black and white photography — but an erratic career.

Litvak's work in the thirties included varied big-city/crime films such as *The Amazing Dr. Clitterhouse, Castle on the Hudson,* and *City for Conquest.* His completed projects accelerated in the early forties, then declined. After the war he directed several strong dramas—*The Long Night, Sorry Wrong Number,* and *The Snake Pit*. But then he worked only intermittently. Later projects like *Anastasia, The Journey,* and *Night of the Generals* were in his best dramatic vein, but, inexplicably, in 1964 he began to direct *A Shot in the Dark* in the successful Peter Sellars–Inspector Clouseau series, only to be replaced by Blake Edwards.

As Rossen worked on the two films, and as the decade turned, history intruded — particularly the Party rationales about the Pact of August of 1939 signed between Germany and the Soviet Union. In September the Germans invaded Poland, and then so did the Soviets, as well as invading Finland and conquering the three Baltic States. Instantly the pronouncements of the Party and its adherents changed. Despite these invasions, the Comintern announced its "struggle against war."[1] Anti-fascism was out; peace was in. The Hollywood Left film community was buzzing with all the usual activities of its crusades, this time for peace. And so now it was the American Peace Mobilization — spawning many replicas and offshoots, including the Mother's Day Peace Council, songs such as "Let God Save the King/The Yanks Are Not Coming," and the usual run of lectures and rallies.[2] At a rally at the Shrine Auditorium, screenwriter Dalton Trumbo gave a keynote speech called "America Declares Peace," and at another even called for action to defeat the proposals for a lend-lease program to send aid to Britain in its fight against the Nazis.[3]

Rossen's script for *Out of the Fog* reflects this swirl of pressures, but nonetheless reflects his own temperament, and his own bridling at pressures imposed by Left or Right (and management itself). The script is a compromise — as had been the stage version that Irwin Shaw had amended (under Party pressure) because of the Pact. The film does maintain the play's final emphasis on the gangster as the corrupting essence of business (which is, of course, typical of Rossen's own themes). But even though Rossen definitely reduced the possible emphasis on allusions to the Nazis, it still contains some phrases and speeches that allow the general public to recognize the connections to anti-fascism. The implications are there, but would have been more direct, emphatic, and numerous if not for the Pact — and Rossen's continuing, though conflicted, acceptance of the Party's *rationales* for its twists and turns of policy.

An example of ambiguous dialogue that can be seen reflecting terminology on both sides of the Pact's dividing line is the emphasis on peace in this speech and the implication of who people like Goff might be — capitalist *manqué* or fascist in a gangster's overcoat: "If you want peace and gentleness, you got to take violence out of the hands of the people like Goff and you got to take it in your own hands and use it like a club. Then, maybe, on the other side of the violence there will be peace and gentleness." It's not that different from the call to action against the union-corrupting racketeers in *Racket Busters*— but in the context of the crucial events of its times, it carries an implication that can be perceived as a veiled call to a type of action far beyond that.

Then history confounded interpretations of the film even further. After delays, *Out of the Fog* was released on June 12, 1941. Shortly thereafter, on June 22, 1941, the Germans invaded Russia. If the film had been written and produced after that, the anti–Nazi implications would certainly have been stronger. Literally overnight the Party line changed. Anti-fascism and war were in. The Party-controlled American Peace Mobilization had on June 21 inaugurated a "National Peace Week." When the Germans invaded on June 22, the event was canceled and the "Perpetual Peace Vigil" in front of the White House was abruptly disbanded. The American Peace Mobilization then changed its name (and consequent actions) to the American People's Mobilization. By June 28 the CPUSA had published its new campaign: "The People's Program of Struggle for the Defeat of Hitler and Hitlerism."[4]

In 1942, following the new Comintern line, a new and strident point of emphasis for the campaign of the Hollywood Left was the call for an immediate opening of a second front on the European continent to aid the Soviet Union.[5] One of the largest rallies of this campaign was held at Madison Square Garden on July 22, 1942, with the keynote statement (stretching both logic and fact) being "Support the President, Rally for a Second Front Now." A featured speaker at the rally was Charles (Charlie) Chaplin.[6]

With the change in the Party's position after Germany invaded Russia, it was then more acceptable for discussion in the Party press of the implications of the metaphor and allusions of the film as cleverly referring to both capitalists and Nazis.

Out of the Fog is by no means all politics, however. It is a small-scale chamber piece — so different in tone and scope than *The Roaring Twenties* — a whimsical and openly sentimental (for some, *too* sentimental), gently humorous fable. It prompts Rossen to a new stage of transition in expressing his integral themes: money and power, the search for identity, and the inner struggle between integrity, trust, and betrayal. These concerns are here acted out within a new human context — the possibility, the endurance of goodness and love in the face of evil. It is a goodness and love that sometimes must be turned into action against evil — even, when necessary, violent action. Here the traditional impact of the destructive economic value system is on a cross-section of the common, gentle people as they are confronted by, and indeed invaded by, the oppressive gangster — for both the pleasures of money and the pleasures of power over others.

The representatives of the good people, in this case an older generation, are Jonah Goodwin (Thomas Mitchell) and Olaf Johnson (John Qualen), sweet but passive dreamers. Storekeepers, they go out in their small boat to fish in the night in the backwaters just off the streets of Brooklyn, but they dream of buying, with their life savings, a real fishing boat to fish for marlin under the warm sun in the Gulf Stream waters off the coast of Cuba. They must be roused from their passive dreams, but the dynamic, volatile moral center of the film, the volatile unformed seeker, this time is a young woman, Stella Goodwin (Ida Lupino), Jonah's daughter. Her dreams are more practical, her impatience with the quiet life driving her to rebel and opening her to the lure of power and illusory symbols of her self. She feels empty and craves the excitement and money of the big world out there. She wants to break with her solid "nice-guy" boyfriend George Watkins (Eddie Albert), an antiques dealer. She rages at him:

> It's just that I'm so fed up with things. Every day just like the other. Get up at seven. The phone company. Wrong number. I'll try them again. Come home at night — same old — I just can't take it anymore, George, I just can't take it!

Out of the shadows on a dark waterfront street steps her seducer, the devil in a black wool overcoat, the false, dangerous prophet with the promise of a life of new excitement — Harold Goff (Garfield). Goff is a petty gangster (not a mob boss) who preys on the small-time fisherman (not the longshoremen) on the waterfront and their daughters. He has a wickedly genial smile that turns to hard stone quickly when he's crossed; he enjoys verbal and physical domination, and the power of seduction, as much as he enjoys the five dollars or the hundred dollars, or the young women, he always seems to get. The act of winning is even a greater pleasure — and a stronger need — than the prize. For Goff an act of betrayal of trust and goodness is innate, as regular as breathing.

His first seduction of Stella is a good example of how the cinematic blocking of a sequence of shots not only breaks up dramatically the stage-drama speeches, but also captures in visual terms the shifting dynamics of the confrontation between the two people in the scene. Goff and Stella are on a street. He offers her a cigarette and a light. We watch her start to walk away, and the camera cuts to him moving toward her and close behind her; seen from the front, his face is past and slightly above her head. A closer shot from the side shows her facing away from him but turning her head now as she listens to his blandishments. The scene then cuts back to the shot of him behind her, her face half turned, listening now as he says, "You can rot in Brooklyn for the rest of your life without meeting anyone except that boyfriend of yours, what's his name, George?" The camera switches to the side shot as she softens, then cuts to the shot toward him behind her as he says, "And you're not the type to rot, sister." She starts to walk away again, but slowly; he follows into a two-shot that faces them. The film cuts to a closer, more intimate and intimidating shot past her in half-profile, toward him, as he invites her to meet him. In close-up, she wavers. The camera shifts to a new angle (for the kill) as she takes a step or two, but again he comes close behind her, smirking now, cock-sure he's got her. The camera reverses to seeing past him, in control, to her as she stops, starts to turn, and walks off. He turns to fuller profile, smiling. She's hooked.

Goff alternates seduction and oppression. He forces Jonah and Olaf to pay him five dollars a week for "protection"— though he is sorry that he has had to use violence: "I regret to do business this way." He makes them sign a loan contract to cover the payments. After they sign he offers, "Have a cigar. It's been a fine week. Twelve new customers."

As he begins to date Stella, Jonah is worried about her, and she reveals how Goff has already solidified her false sense of what is valuable for her, what her false sense of herself is: "He's an exciting man, Pop. Why, he's been all over the country.... I want to see people in the subway and say, 'I'm not like them. I'm not like those people in a subway, I'm different. I've got what they haven't got.'"

In the domestic plainness of the family living room a struggle between the three men for the soul of Stella is quietly but tensely conducted. It is captured beautifully in patterns that can be usefully defined by the theoretic term *plan sequence*, as especially developed in the theories of the influential French critic Andre Bazin.

There is no indication that Rossen directly knew of the writing and theories of Andre Bazin. However, focusing on the implications of *plan sequence* and what Bazin termed *mise en scène* is both an accurate description of Rossen's intentions and procedures and a useful way to define and delineate them. There is, first of all, Rossen's sense of the use of what Bazin calls *décor*, of objects and settings. For the theorist, these physical surfaces of life take on a kind of life, resonating with the life of the people who inhabit them: abstracting out of the "concrete integral" to provide "the outward revelation of an interior destiny." But *mise en scène*, in Bazin's writings, is more than what is "put into the scene." It is what is done with all that is in the scene, including the human presence and the space of the scene. The essential corollary to this resonance of objects is the use of space itself, space made meaningful and resonant — the very space in which the characters live, with which they interact physically and emotionally, in which, in shifting patterns, they interact with others.[7]

At Warners the emphasis was on getting in the solid details of the fast-paced, hard-hitting life depicted in their films — the details that drew in the audience who lived within the world of some of the details, or who would love to live in the world presented by other details. This emphasis gave Rossen the bedrock, the creative impetus, for developing a more personal use of the details. In Rossen's version of *mise en scène* the characters are solidly moored in defined iconographic settings. People interact within the physical environment around them, which both has influenced and reflects their needs and desires. Meanings are thus drawn out of the objects of the physical world. Characters interact emotionally, but also interact *visually,* in space, with each other and with the physical environment that surrounds them. Their individual movements and gestures, and the shifting patterns of their physical relationships, reflect their emotional responses, intensities, and changes. For Rossen these shifting patterns of equilibrium — of space, décor, and people — were often the visual correlatives of harmony or domination, love or betrayal.

It is these shifting patterns that can be orchestrated through a scene into a *plan sequence* of shots that can build the dramatic moments and narrative points of the scene, as well as its implications. Thus it can capture the more intangible human dimension while maintaining the feel of the moment as it is.

In the family living room this kind of orchestration of the images dramatizes the stages of the struggle, even more than does the limited dialogue (reduced from the dialogue in the play). Jonah is getting ready to leave, but Goff interrupts with his arrival, flourishing a corsage for Stella. The basic wide shot is from across the room, a sofa at center on the far wall, the stairway to the bedrooms to the left, the front door to the right. Goff crosses to the left from the doorway and drops down on the sofa. Next comes a closer shot of Goff lounging on the couch and ostentatiously putting his feet up on an arm of the sofa, with Jonah standing awkwardly to the left. The scene returns to the basic wide shot as George comes in the front door and crosses the room, trying to ignore Goff and intent on moving toward the stairs. But Goff gets up and cuts in as the camera pans left with George. Goff moves first to the base of the stairs, corsage displayed, bragging about the cost of it.

The tension is increased and the pace of shots accelerates. The sequence cuts to a shot past Goff toward George, who tells him to leave her alone. As the camera looks past George to Goff, the latter says, "She's free, white, and twenty-one." Cut to George as he steps closer. Cut to Goff past George as Goff starts to push George, who grabs his arm. The next shot shows Stella coming down the stairs. The camera pans with her as she comes down to them and is now seen in a significant pattern between them.

The scene goes back to the basic shot from across the room. There is a slight pan as she moves from them toward the right side of the room and somewhat forward toward the camera, where Pop is standing. A slightly closer variation on the angle of the basic shot follows Goff as he too moves forward and to the right toward them. George is left at the rear, separated from them — and her. "I'm a fast man with a dollar," Goff says, handing her the corsage.

The scene returns back to the fuller basic shot, which is held to the end of the sequence. George moves to the group of the three of them, saying, "Stella, I've got to talk to you." But Stella moves away from him, to the right, and the camera pans with her as she walks to the front door, Goff following after her. They leave. Jonah and George are left standing in the room.

Out of the Fog (1941), Warner Bros. Small-time gangster Harold Goff (John Garfield) enjoys toying with Stella Goodwin (Ida Lupino) as he courts her, while her regular-guy boyfriend George Watkins (Eddie Albert) looks on.

At a café, Stella tells Goff that Jonah has offered to give her his savings — $165 — so that she can go away without Goff. Goff offers to take her to Cuba and promises to marry her. And then Goff uses what she's told him to demand the $165. Without meaning to, she's betrayed them, has abetted Goff's tyranny over them. They refuse, and get the friendly neighborhood cop to take Goff in to night court. But in a satiric mocking of justice, Goff produces the loan document, and the case is dismissed.

Justice has failed them. On a dark street, Goff takes his revenge on Jonah. As he beats him with a rubber hose, Goff is saying, half laughing, "Yes, purely a business venture." Jonah begins to wonder if you've got to be hard, tough inside like Goff.

The resolution of Jonah's new consciousness of the need to stand up to tyranny, however minor or monumental, to not remain silent in the face of violations of humanity, takes place in the steam room of a Turkish bath. This discussion with Olaf, definitely honed to allude to the situation in Europe, is intercut, and ironically counterpointed, with the comic ravings of a Russian shop owner who's been forced into bankruptcy, betrayed by the unjust legalities of the business system. "I sweat," Propotkin roars, "and the profit system comes right out of my pores. They push you, they push you. They take everything from you. They strip you. Naked. And what do *you* do?"

At that moment Jonah is saying, "We're getting old.... We must take up a stand ... before we're pushed right off the earth."

Then, while Jonah is telling Olaf how Goff hit him so hard, Propotkin is yelling, "Harder, harder!" as the attendant massages his back.

As they decide they must kill Goff before he goes any further, the play's long monologue by Jonah is condensed, revised for some emphatic repetitions, and broken into a dramatic interchange between the two of them:

> OLAF (seen past Jonah in profile): All my life I have wanted peace and gentleness. Violence, leave it to men like Goff.
>
> JONAH (seen past the profile of Olaf): All my life I too, Olaf, have wanted peace and gentleness, but can you convince airplanes with bombs and men with guns in their pockets?

The broader implication is clear as he starts to tell Olaf his plan, while Propotkin shouts, "I'm surprised the Pitkin Company left me my teeth!"

To carry out their plan they talk Goff into taking him in their boat to one of his customers. To attract Goff's attention, Jonah stalls the motor, and has to keep repeating the password that they have arranged — "It's the carburetor float" — because Olaf, behind Goff, can't get himself to hit him with an iron pipe. The scene is built comically, with Goff, exasperated, finally shouting, "Okay, it's the carburetor float! *I* think it's the carburetor float! Now do something about it!" He turns and sees Olaf, pipe raised, and they all begin to struggle. Goff fires a shot and pushes them both down, but the boat rocks and tips, and he falls overboard and goes under. He can't swim. "Thanks, God, for stepping in," Jonah says.

The comical and accidental treatment of Goff's death softens the moral dilemma posed by the play. For in the play they are more directly responsible and have to accept their "dirty hands." In the play, when Goff turns to Olaf, Goff raises the gun and Jonah jumps on his back as he fires. Olaf then does hit Goff with the iron pipe, and they throw him overboard. Thematically, one might say that the version in the film still has a significant implication, and maybe a more realistic one, showing that for the good gentle people it is not that easy to be a fighter for the common good. Commercially, however, it is not too likely to be seen and accepted (especially by the Jerry Walds of the industry) as a good ploy to have two nice old men directly kill someone.

Back on shore, all are reconciled — father and daughter, Stella and George, the two men and their $165. As Jonah and Stella embrace, he tells her it's fine to be "an ordinary person.... One thing ordinary people can do just as good as anybody, they can love each other like millionaires." At the close the camera follows them walking off into their waterfront neighborhood, walking home together, as they leave the empty and hurtful dreams that money can buy behind them on the dock.

Responding to the basic sweetness in Shaw's play, Rossen here expresses for the first time — though in far simpler, less hard-earned, and less painful (even tragic) terms than in his later films — the possibility of rebirth and growth to something more than the raised consciousness of progressive or revolutionary action. They rise to a consciousness, instead, of tenderness and connection, of compassion.

The unusual film received mixed notices, and its sad, wry humor garnered scant attention. Anthony Bower in *The Nation*, among others, found it to be an over-symbolic failure, but John Mosher in *The New Yorker* praised it as "one case where a good play makes a good movie."

Meanwhile, *The Sea Wolf* had been released before *Out of the Fog*, on March 26, 1941. It also had been written during the Pact. It too had been tap-dancing around the crucial implications, but from the start there was a difference. The well-known and meaningful novel by Jack London had no gangster, though on the screen Captain Wolf Larsen embodied some of his characteristics. Larsen is, rather, an obsessive version of the destructive potential in a Nietzschean "Superman," the will to power gone mad through resentment and rebellion against the world. And so possible perceptions of him as an embodiment, as well, of the mad will to power of Hitlerian fascism could not be avoided, given the basic material. Still, direct allusions to current politics and events were kept carefully ambiguous.

The notices for *The Sea Wolf* were stronger than for *Out of the Fog*. John Springer in *Films in Review* called it "the best of the many versions of Jack London's book." And its relevance to the threatening aggression in the world was apparent to all but the most loyal Party members and press. John Mosher labeled the ship's captain, Wolf Larsen, a "Hitlerian egomaniac," and many agreed. But beyond the relevance to the turbulent times, Larsen's character has a more timeless significance, representing the kind of tragic and destructive distortion of human energy and power, and the resulting violation of others, that Rossen saw as so important in Macbeth.

The first concepts for the production originated in 1937. Paul Muni, who had been an early victim of society's injustices in *I Am a Fugitive from the Chain Gang*, but who had gone on to more portentous (and somewhat pretentious) roles in "serious" biographical and historical films, was an early choice for the role of Larsen. Displaying his sense of his own importance, Muni, however, wrote his agent that he didn't think "Rafael Sabattini, Sidney Howard, or Eugene O'Neill ... would be interested in writing a screenplay from that story." But if they could get one of them to do so, "I am willing to okay it as my next picture."[8] The choice of Robinson — more energetic, more demonic in his performance — proved more appropriate. And his ties to and emanations of the gangster persona (see, for example, *Little Caesar*) proved particularly appropriate for Rossen's approach to the narrative, characters, and themes.

Another casting decision, along with Rossen's intervention, became even more integral to Rossen's structuring of the material. In what would seem to be the result of contractual matters and studio use of contract players, Producer Hal Wallis had offered the role of George Leach to the totally inappropriate George Raft. Raft wired Wallis on October 23, 1940, "I want to work but this is just a little better than a bit." In one of his infrequent faulty moves, Wallis wired back that it was a great part and he wanted him to do it. Fortunately, Raft refused.[9] Rossen then proposed Garfield. Garfield had wanted to play the part of the reserved, alienated intellectual, Van Leyden, who is the original focus point as tragic hero and eventual challenge to Wolf Larsen's brutality. To promote Garfield, Rossen built up the part of the ex-con seaman Leach, a more suitable role for Garfield's temperament and image.[10] Garfield and Wallis agreed to that casting. The change of emphasis allowed Rossen to develop Leach as a typical Rossen protagonist. As he begins the erratic struggle to find his authentic self, Leach grows to become the forceful leader of the Resistance against the Gestapo-like Larsen and his henchmen. In a central thirties narrative structure, it is the growth of consciousness of the Garfield proletarian that, in turn, leads the intellectual, Van Leyden, to redeem himself by a final noble act of sacrifice.

On the shadowy, menacingly cluttered jungle of Wolf Larsen's ship — echoing constantly with creaking and whining timbers and machinery — there are no gangsters, no struggle for money and its trophies. On board *The Ghost*, the struggle is rooted more deeply in human nature — the struggle of elemental will, power, and strength (in Tennyson's phrase, of "ragged tooth and claw"). It is a more brutal version of a world in which, as Stella had said, the strong take the weak — if they'll let them. Jack London's Nietzschean-influenced microcosm of the survival of the fittest — where God is Dead, and meaning and morality must be shaped by human will — can, as we have noted, be adapted to promote allusions to the need to take action against Fascist brutality, seen in a far more vicious form in the Nazi-like fanaticism of Larsen than in the petty violations of Goff. Whatever the nature of injustice and oppression, the alienated, the down-trodden and pushed-around (Garfield as George Leach and Ida Lupino as Ruth Webster) must re-join the human community ("No man alone...") and take a stand, or not survive — as must the aloof and distanced intellectual, the writer Humphrey Van Leyden (Alexander Knox).

In the opening sequence of the film, Ruth and Van Leyden are almost killed in a ferry boat crash, but are saved and brought aboard *The Ghost*— and now trapped. Leach has signed on but is rebellious from the start, though not with any purpose or sense of community, In one encounter he throws a marlin spike at Larsen, and is subsequently beaten by Larsen's goons and dragged below to be beaten some more.

Larsen regularly torments the ship's doctor, an alcoholic with severe tremors, who suffers most of all because he realizes what he has become, what he has let Larsen and the booze make of him, and how he cannot seem to do anything about it. But after he successfully saves Ruth's life with a blood transfusion, he asks Larsen to have the men show him some respect. Larsen, however, betrays his dearly regained honor and sincerity. He gathers the men, tells them to show the doctor some respect, and mockingly asks him if that was "satisfactory, *Doctor* Prescott?" Larsen then kicks him down the steps, and the doctor falls to the deck below. Larsen leads the laughter as the men push Prescott around, tearing off his neat suitcoat and tie. He climbs the rigging to get away, higher and higher, as the laughter grows. "There's a price no man will pay for living," he shouts and leaps into the sea. But before he takes his own life, the doctor exposes Larsen's secret: That he won't put into any port because his own brother and *his* ship are out to destroy him. And he fears him!

Larsen is more than a symbol of brutal tyranny, whether Fascist Master Race or Nietzschean Superman. His character is well-wrought and well-acted by Robinson as a tortured, driven human being. In the psychological and ethical pattern of Rossen's work, he is the most extreme example of the man who must seek to define his identity, and his destiny, in destructive and self-destructive terms. He is a man of some intellectual brilliance who hides his mind, his philosophic and literary interests, even a certain abstracted sensitivity, from the world. He chooses — is only able — to show and act out a brutal defiance in his violent need to control a world that seems to defy his every dream and desire, and, indeed, does frighten him. Physically, his body is betraying him. His seizures are increasing in frequency and severity; his temporary sieges of partial blindness are more frequent. Finally they become total and permanent. But his anguished thrashing about has deeper roots, is driven by demons of deep-seated resentment, as suggested by the broader French term *resentiment*. He has been cheated out of his rightful place by his brother, by the

5. The Party Line and the Writer—Two Warner Films in a Shifting Political World 69

The Sea Wolf (1941), Warner Bros. Wolf Larsen, dictatorial captain of *The Ghost* (Edward G. Robinson), quietly begins his domination of George Leach (John Garfield) and Ruth Webster (Ida Lupino).

world. All he has is his ship, his "Hell ship," and here he can rule in the only way he knows. Like Ahab in Melville's *Moby Dick*, he will revenge himself on his own White Whale, the torment of his life itself, betraying all in a world that has betrayed him.

Van Leyden understands him. In several scenes Larsen confides in him. He tells him he lives by his favorite passage in Milton's *Paradise Lost*:

> To reign is worth ambition, though in Hell.
> Better to reign in hell than serve in Heaven.

Why, maybe, he suggests, Van Leyden can even write a book about him. So they'll understand how he's risen in his own way: "I'll choose my death, like I chose my life." It is only strength that justifies existence, "The fact that it is my will and my will alone that rules here"—just as one of his attacks hits him and he is staggered by its severity. He cries out that the pressures "on my brain are driving me crazy." Suddenly he realizes he is totally blind. "Don't tell them, don't tell them," he begs. He grabs onto Van Leyden and holds him there until he can begin to see again. Pitying him, Van Leyden holds him.

In a later scene in Larsen's stateroom, after the plot to overthrow Larsen has begun and he has survived their first attempt, his mood shifts rapidly and violently under the pressure of his physical attacks and the threat to his absolute power. He asks Van Leyden to give him the names of the ringleaders, and Van Leyden refuses. Larsen turns to Cooky (Barry Fitzgerald), who is his lackey, his court jester, to get him all the information he can. Cooky accepts, and Larsen turns to mocking him: "Sterling character, isn't he? That's his profession, being a stool pigeon. Cooking is only a hobby."

The "stool pigeon" motif takes one more unexpected turn — on one more cruel, aggressive whim of Larsen's. Cooky has exposed the mutiny plot and given him a list of names — he has named names. Addressing the crew, Larsen tells them he has all the names and knows the plan. But to show his generosity and good faith, he tears up the list. He promises the crew that they will be able to successfully steal precious seal skins from other ships, including his brother's. In the one focus on money in the narrative, he manipulates the crowd by promising that they will all share the profits. "You'll each have enough to keep you for the rest of your lives!" They cheer. And then he turns on Cooky, with a strange prophetic irony in view of the Hollywood history that is to follow. "You have an informer in your midst," announces Larsen. "There's nothing I detest more than an informer." And then, in his way informing himself, he names Cooky as the informer, betraying the man who was following his orders to betray others.

"Get that Squealer!" he shouts. And they chase Cooky as Larsen laughs. They throw him overboard, with a rope attached. Before they can pull him up, a shark attacks him. He's alive but badly hurt.

Leach has organized a small group to fight against Larsen. He and Ruth have allowed an openness, a tenderness to break down their defenses after she has found him in a passageway below decks, beaten up. She offers to help. He wants no help, just to be left alone. She stays. He says he's sorry, he just can't get over wanting revenge.

As they smoke and talk quietly — the shadows seeming gentler now, protective — he tells her, "You got to fight, you can't quit, tomorrow I'll be on my feet."

She feels it's no use. "Tomorrow will be like today, and the day before. They'll always beat you up again and you know it."

He insists (it is the same motif as Jonah's, as many a character's in left-wing drama): "There's something in me that tells me I've got to keep on fighting. Tells me there is something for people like us.... Men like Larsen can't keep grinding us down cause we're nobodies. That ain't true, we're somebodies."

Leach and his small band attack, but after seeming to triumph, they are beaten. This time the latent humanity in the debased and dehumanized crew is not revived. There is no upsurge of collective action. Larsen rallies the crew, this degraded proletariat, to his side. They now betray Leach — and themselves — and Leach is locked up below.

As the final action unfolds, the major development of a sense of communal commitment, the need for solidarity, is in Van Leyden, the intellectual. After Van Leyden comes upon Larsen collapsed in a passageway, he tells them Larsen is now blind, helps in getting provisions, and leaves with them in a small boat. But Larsen has filled their cans of water with vinegar — as their discovery is intercut with shots of the madly blind captain holding ferociously to the wheel of *The Ghost*, desperately holding his world, Hell that it is, intact.

The ship of Larsen's brother comes upon *The Ghost* and begins firing. Larsen flees into a fog bank. As the men panic, Cooky gets even and betrays Larsen. He's blind, he tells the crew, he's *blind*!

The small boat is drifting in the fog also. They encounter *The Ghost*, which is now truly a ghost ship—all in a shambles, wreckage strewn and twisted. It is sinking, with Larsen the only one left on board. They go aboard to get supplies. Blind as he is, Larsen is able to lock Leach in a cabin below decks. Van Leyden goes off to find Larsen and get the key. In alternating shots, Leach and Ruth are seen on each side of the door of the cabin, their faces closer and closer, more open and intimate, though blocked by the wood between them. He tells her to leave without him. But she refuses: "Not without you. ... You live, I live. You die, I die."

In Larsen's stateroom there is a final battle of wills. Van Leyden taunts Larsen. "This is the true death of the Superman," he mocks, "a pitiful, dismal, pathetic finish." Larsen fires at him, manages to hit him. He locks them in the cabin. Van Leyden tells him he missed. Sacrificing any chance for himself, he promises to stay and go down with Larsen and the ship if he'll give him the key to the other cabin. He gets the key, passes it under the door to Ruth, and dies. Larsen realizes he's been tricked.

On deck, the others are escaping as the ship begins to sink more quickly. In the final image, Leach and Ruth, together in the small boat, sail toward an island seen in the distance.

For all of its occasional histrionics and Hollywood movie moments, *The Sea Wolf* is a strong, provocatively strange, and notable film. Beyond the ideological conflicts over the Pact, its deeper ideological structure portrays the working class, "the People," caught in, and escaping from, a shadowy, oppressive world, a jagged, tangled and twisted society. Under the accomplished direction of Michael Curtiz, it offers a more atmospheric and haunting use of décor and lighting than was the case in the production of Rossen's previous scripts. For Rossen, it was a valuable further lesson and development in using visual imagery for the conveying and heightening of moods and emotions, for externalizing the inner lives of characters and their place in a world that threatens and oppresses them.

6

The War and Post-War Worlds on Film — Three with Lewis Milestone

Edge of Darkness was written during 1942, after Pearl Harbor and the U.S. had entered the war, and not released until January 1943. After the hectic writing period as the decades changed, the pace of Robert Rossen's production had slowed. No Rossen-penned movie saw release in 1942. Part of the gap was due to timing and intra-studio bureaucracy. Part, however, was due to his increased activity within the Communist Party. For a part of 1942 he was particularly busy with the organization and development of the Hollywood Writers Mobilization, and then into 1943 he was working on its climactic event, the Writers Conference at U.C.L.A. in October of that year. Yet through this same active period, paradoxically, the tensions were building for him within the Party over its demands for his time and unthinking loyalty.

Edge of Darkness was his tenth filmed screenplay for Warner Bros. and the first of three films written for the noted veteran director Lewis Milestone over a period of four years—interrupted by a temporary move to New York City. The three films with Milestone were directly affected by, and involved with, the history and politics of the times— and with the positions of the Communist Party and Rossen's troubled relationship with them. In this Milestone trilogy we can see a significant movement, a shifting of theme and emotion—and of the film structures that embody them. In *Edge of Darkness*, written during the early stages of World War II, the growth of solidarity is developed in direct heroic rebellion against the cruel evils of Nazi fascism. In *A Walk in the Sun*, made later in the war, the comradeship is of a different kind—a quiet, almost unheroic solidarity developed in the dignity and courage and stamina of soldiers doing the day to day job of fighting a war against the forces of an enemy often not even seen shooting at you as you shoot at them. And then within the new intense conflicts and discordant beliefs of the postwar period, in *The Strange Love of Martha Ivers* there is a striking return to the alienation and destruction wrought by the misshapen force of capitalism. Here is the return of the deadly mix of money and power that can destroy love, family, and people— but this time without the iconic figure of the gangster, and this time with a greater emphasis on psychological damage and violation, on betrayal.

In 1942, *Edge of Darkness* was based on events in the news, and prompted by the surge of patriotism and loyalty at the start of America's new role in the war. This time there were no tensions, and no personal or political conflicts. All was unity. This national enthusiasm and idealism for the war effort was now full-heartedly supported by the Communist Party. Those who rise up in the film are not unlike the resistance fighters, usually implied Communists, seen in films located in France, or part of the heroic Russian proletariat. The structure for most of these resistance films builds to typical growth of solidarity and final communal action against oppression. In the Lillian Hellman–Milestone *The North Star* (produced in 1943 and released in November), the farm workers of a Russian village begin to work together to fight the increasing brutality of the Nazis. When the men, to escape execution, go up into the hills to join the partisans, the women, in solidarity, band together and (to an accompanying score by Aaron Copland) join in the fight against the Germans. *Song of Russia* (released February 1944) was written by fellow Communists and best friends Paul Jarrico and Richard Collins (who a few years later became deep enemies after Collins testified). In it an American musician (*à la* thirties intellectual) is caught in the maelstrom of the Nazis' invasion of Russia. He falls in love with a young Russian peasant woman and, consciousness raised, joins in a "people's" uprising against the Nazis.

In Rossen's film, and the other films of inspiration and encouragement during the difficult early period of the war, the narrative structures and motifs of the basic left-wing social dramas of the thirties serve as the usable matrix. This story of Norwegian resistance fighters uses the materials and structures of the kind of Proletariat dramas we've been seeing enclosed within the trappings of various commercial genres and popular culture materials. This time there are no Vannings or Goffs, no Wolf Larsens — just the unmasked, undisguised face of pure Nazi brutality, torture, and murder. Nonetheless, in the stand against this unfiltered oppression we still see the raising of consciousness of individuals to a true sense of self and progressive action. We see the transforming of a downtrodden and indecisive people into a force for collective action — solidarity displayed in visual imagery as well as plot action and dialogue.

The film opens in a small Norwegian fishing village on scenes of death and devastation — of townspeople and German soldiers alike. The body of the film is a flashback that explains the mystery and takes us beyond it. Gunnar (Errol Flynn) — the head of the local fisherman's union — is the frustrated leader of the underground resistance group who have been waiting for two years for arms and a plan of action to be delivered by the British. Karen (Ann Sheridan), is active with him, but in the narrative structure her family is the negative force that must be changed. Her father, the town doctor (Walter Huston), is a thoughtful, cautious, and reasonable appeaser. He disapproves of Karen's actions and just wants to be left alone. Her mother (Ruth Gordon) is a rather foolish innocent, a denier of reality. Even worse, her uncle, who owns the town's main business, the cannery, is a greedy and conniving capitalist, a betrayer of his people, who sees that it's good for business to collaborate — indeed, develop partnerships — with the Germans. (He's played by Charles Dingle with the same smug, insistent tone he brought so effectively to his similar role as Bette Davis' domineering small-town capitalist brother in *The Little Foxes*, 1941.) He is a man, he says, who deals in facts, business facts. For him, it's "all business" (as the gambler Roberts will say in *Body and Soul*). "It's men like us who are the real patriots of Norway."

The uncle has sent for Johan, Karen's brother, to come home to work in his expanding business. Johan, a weak and wavering young man, has himself betrayed his people by collaborating with the Germans while a student in Oslo. When the German Commandant wants the uncle to spy on the people, he recruits Johan, who, afraid the Germans will kill him, complies.

The impetus for the final battle — initiated by the community spontaneously, without waiting for the signal from the British — is triggered by the Nazis' treatment of the town's sage, the retired schoolmaster. The scene that depicts this crucial turning point is a masterful development of visual imagery and patterns to convey the momentum and passion of coming together in solidarity. (It is a type of patterned imagery, of a propagandic *plan sequence*, initiated by Eisenstein in such Soviet films as *Battleship Potemkin*, and Pudovkin in, for example, *Mother*.)

The first act of the uprising is in the village square as the Nazis attempt to make an example of the schoolmaster. In its combination of action and visual imagery, the build-up to the act of solidarity of the townspeople is an effective application of the patterns of left-wing theater and Soviet films to the fight against the Nazis. The Nazis march in and form a square as the schoolmaster's possessions are brought into the center, books and papers torn and tossed away. The people in tight ranks march in, with Karen and Gunnar leading. The people form a circle around the square of soldiers. The schoolmaster is dragged into the center, through the crowd, pulled by a rope around his waist. Gasoline is poured. Women are seen pushing up to the front rank of the crowd. Gunnar gives the order to do nothing yet and wait for the day. The camera pans along the faces of the Germans, intercut with shots of the word being spread — wait for the day. The fire is started and the people push forward, but are stopped by a solid line of prodding bayonets. The schoolmaster is pulled backwards and falls, and passes out. The town bell begins to ring; it is the signal. The pastor pushes through the crowd and the loosening line of soldiers, picks up the schoolmaster, and starts to sing. All join in singing loud and strong and together, as the pastor carries the schoolmaster off and, en masse, the people march out after them. The doctor and his wife, at the fringes, hesitate, then walk forward to join the masses in their march. They are now all people who will not remain silent in inaction; they are testifying by risking their lives to stand up against that which they think is wrong and should be stopped.

That night, while dying, the schoolmaster passes on to the others the oft-repeated mantra of the idealistic ideology of the period: "The individual can't stand alone like a rock. Even a rock can be crushed."

Karen is taken by the Germans and beaten, possibly raped, before she is returned. After a heated meeting, the leaders decide to delay a response. But her father, the man of inaction, takes uncontrollable, undisciplined violent action. He beats a passing German with his cane, hitting him again and again, killing him. The Germans will execute all the town leaders in retribution. While the leaders are digging their mass grave in a straight-line trench, they stop when they hear singing. The people are marching down the street — toward us — with guns at the ready. The rebellion has begun.

Rapid cutting follows the rebellion as it spreads to other locations, images always stressing the group solidarity of the people. One must say, however, that the images that so stirringly capture their courageous solidarity seem to be at the expense of any intelligent strategy on their part. For they continue to march head on into one gun emplacement after another. Still, while taking great losses, they are inflicting great losses — all the bodies seen at the beginning of the film.

When the Germans make their final stand at the Inn, they set up machine guns in the woods to the side to create a devastating crossfire. The people are about to charge straight on, right into the crossfire, but Jonah has repented and is redeemed. From an upstairs window of the inn he shouts at them that it's a trap. The Germans shoot him.

In an epilogue, survivors, now a true band of underground fighters, are walking through the woods. The doctor slips; Gunnar and Karen pick him up, hold him up.

"It's all right," he says, "I can walk alone."

"You don't have to." Arm in arm, they walk into the woods. The fight will go on.

The film has more complexity of character, motive, and the dilemmas of action than others of the genre or period. Nevertheless, within the fervent patriotic climate of the time, and with the filmmakers' personal background and ideology regarding the ideal of standing up to fascism, it does not shape the bitter ironies of Rossen's best work. There was no irony in war-time, no full examination of the painful ambiguities of acting against evil at the cost of sacrificing so many people. Honor, courage, community, and noble patriotism were displayed, but no liberation was achieved until organized armies did the job (as the men will do in *A Walk in the Sun*—without swelling passion, but with determination and endurance and much sacrifice).

The emphasis on solidarity, and the unity of all factions, in the film parallels not only Rossen's relationship with the Party at this time but also the Party's relationship to liberal and even national goals and campaigns. The Hollywood Writers Mobilization — for which Rossen was chairman — was among the Party's most successful campaigns of building alliances with liberals and liberal groups, while controlling the event (or attempting to) and promoting Party programs and strategies. Usually the extremity of the Party agenda destroyed those alliances, but in this war-time instance it worked out for all concerned.

In effect, the Communists, mainly from the Screen Writers Guild, controlled the Board — and the organization, development, and conduct — of the Mobilization. Nevertheless, many who were active in the Mobilization had no connection to the Communist Party or its interests, or even any inkling of its involvement, let alone its control. During the years of this shared activity, the Communists averaged about 40 percent of the members of the Mobilization Steering Committee, and were by far the most active members. Rossen was elected chairman by a unanimous vote, while other Party members assumed key positions.[1] The major public event, the Writers Conference, was held at UCLA in October 1943 and was attended by over a thousand people. It had broadly-based interest and participation, including UCLA faculty and the support of the University of California president, Robert Gordon Sproul.

While promoting war-time unity, patriotic war-time activities to help win the war, and idealistic war-time goals for writers and intellectuals, the Mobilization used that unity to promote positions dear to the heart of the CPUSA. For example, controlled by Party members, the program featured a strong doctrinaire approach, particularly stressing the writer's function in the *postwar* world. As Hollywood Party leader John Howard Lawson insisted at an initial steering committee session, the promotion of the writer's "social function" was "a matter of elementary duty and terrible urgency" in the coming postwar fight between liberalism and reaction. At another planning meeting, committee member and

Communist Allan Scott called for an emphasis at the conference on the "unconscious fascism" that threatened the nation in the postwar period. In support of Scott, Rossen stressed the need to foster awareness of the way that the forces of reaction were attacking the Office of War Information because they claimed it was run by radicals, referring particularly to attacks made by Congressman Martin Dies and his committee.[2]

At the Writers Conference there were small-group panels as well as general meetings and addresses. As Rossen later told HUAC, "We [the Communist participants] met quite regularly in terms of fraction meetings and discussed the whole program of the Writers' Congress, at first in a general sense and later on a kind of detailed sense, in terms of what was to go into the various panels, in terms of the editing of the presentation of the thing." One result of this "editing" was the selection of panel topics and the selection of Party members as chairmen of the panels: e.g., Minority Groups — Ring Lardner, Jr.; American Scene — Robert Rossen; Feature Film — Richard Collins; Nature of the Enemy — John Wexley; Problems of the Press — Melvin Levy; Pan-American Affairs — Louis Solomon; Training Films — Bernard Vorhaus.[3]

For Rossen's major speech at a general session of the conference he spoke on "An Approach to Characters." The speech was subsequently published in *The New Masses* as "New Characters for the Screen" in its January 18, 1944, issue. The speech was a forward-looking call for using the opportunities created by the ideals of the war effort to, in turn, create "responsible films" (i.e., socially responsible) that would present "strong, positive characters" who could stand up to corruption and oppression in society and help effect social change. In light of all that happened in the following years, one of his key terms, used in an optimistic passage in his address, had an ironic foreshadowing:

> We are still afraid of being betrayed, and that fear goes deep. We've been sick, and this has reflected itself in everything that we've written in the last twenty years. Our stories have been stories of frustration, of defeat.... Well, the average man isn't afraid of being betrayed. He doesn't think it can happen anymore.[4]

This optimism and belief in an individual's successful stand against unspecified forms of betrayal was soon overcome by events in his personal life and the world around him. Early in 1944, the next turn of events at the HWM added to Rossen's growing sense that he needed to reclaim his time and himself, to try to sort out his ideals, beliefs, and conflicts. When his term as HWM chairman was about to expire, he was approached by Lawson, whom he termed "the persuader," with the Party's position. Since Earl Browder's war-time Popular Front strategy was working so well, the Party wanted to capitalize on that momentum and attract "more people ... to strengthen the Party." And so it had been "decided at that time it was important that a man who was not a member of the Communist Party be chairman of the organization as part of the move to broaden the popular front." He was, therefore, to bow out gracefully.[5]

It was indicative of his conflicted relationship to the Party at this time that despite the conflict over his chairmanship of the HWM, and his qualms, as he put it much later, of being "used," he was still involved in Party matters in 1943 and into 1944. He even worked with Lawson in actions to curtail freedom of speech — in the best interests of the Party. In one instance, an Italian film historian, Gatano Salvameni, was scheduled to address an HWM seminar being held at the Hollywood Women's Club. However, in a prior speech Salvameni had, to the Party's surprise, been critical of Stalin, the Italian Communist Party and its leaders, and of CPUSA leaders. His address at the HWM seminar was canceled. To stem press criticism, Lawson asked Rossen to use his goodwill with the Hollywood and local press corps, especially an influential radio commentator, to insist that the cancellation had nothing to do with his anti–Communist statements, and that no freedom of speech was being impaired![6]

In March of 1944 Rossen again worked with Lawson to aid in the suppression of free speech that the Party did not agree with. Ulrich Bell, an independent political idealist, had come to Hollywood to promote the program of his organization, the Free World Association. In a full-page ad in the Hollywood *Daily Variety*, he presented his 10-point policy for pursuing world peace at the end of the war. Unfortunately, his program differed from the Party's position on postwar peace on at least one major point: To achieve peace, his principles asserted, the world needed to disavow both communism and fascism. At meetings held in Hollywood, Lawson and Rossen organized opposition to this point and called for its elimination, but the 10 points remained unchanged.[7]

In the face of Party pressures and these unsettling conflicts in his own mind and beliefs, Rossen decided to move to New York with his wife Sue and their three children, and get away and think things through. Later in 1944 they moved. "In other words," he was to tell the congressional committee in 1953, "I was ready at that point to start away, to start to move away, from the party, definitely. I had tried to do it by moving away from Hollywood in 1944. I had done nothing for a year. I was very disturbed by a great many things that were going on in the party, and my own work."[8]

On the broader Hollywood political front, in 1944 producers had joined with sympathetic filmmakers to form the Motion Picture Alliance for the Preservation of American Ideals. In its "Statement of Principles" the group declared, "We refuse to permit the effort of Communist, Fascist, and other totalitarian-minded groups to pervert the powerful medium into an instrument for the dissemination of un–American ideals and beliefs." Its main, indeed only real, concern was "Communist ... groups." After the war it became the leading anti–Communist force during the investigation and blacklist period.

Edge of Darkness had been Rossen's last script under contract for Warner Bros. When he returned from New York, he was now free. Working with Milestone again would be a pleasant experience and a valuable stage in moving toward his first job of directing. About the collaboration with Milestone, Rossen said, "There was just no separation between us at all. We agreed 100 percent on the approach to that film."

Milestone's own career had had an auspicious beginning. In 1930, in the early sound film *All Quiet on the Western Front*, he transformed Erich Maria Remarque's novel into quietly dramatic scenes and poetic images that make an unforced and compassionate cry for peace. The sad yet unsentimental irony of its final image is one of the most influential moments in film history. As the enemy fire dies down, Paul (Lew Ayres) reaches for a butterfly amid the web of barbed wire. He is shot and killed, while a radio voice announces, "All Quiet on the Western Front." Through the thirties, Milestone went on to make a number of major movies of rather amazing diversity: Howard Hughes' iconic film of comradeship and wartime bravery, *Hell's Angels*; the fast-paced, tough-talking comedy *The Front Page*; the melodramatic saga of Sadie Thompson in *Rain*; the musical *Anything Goes*; the somber, touching adaptation of the John Steinbeck novel and play *Of Mice and Men*; and the unique protest drama *Hallelujah, I'm a Bum*.

During World War II (and at the height of his association with left-wing causes), his work with Lillian Hellman on *The North Star* was a project full of animosity, as

Hellman complained about his revising her screenplay during production and even threatened to give back her fee. (She didn't.) After the war, several of his serious films were considered dated and even plodding, such as *Les Miserables* and the commercially disastrous *Arch of Triumph*, with Ingrid Bergman. Still, he continued his workmanlike diversity: *The Red Pony* (from the Steinbeck novelette); the rousing patriotic *Halls of Montezuma*; the strong men-at-war film *Pork Chop Hill*; and, surprisingly the light-hearted romp *Oceans 11*. It ended badly. In 1962 and 1963 he was replaced after starting to direct *Mutiny on the Bounty* (with Marlon Brando) and *PT-109* (the John Kennedy story).

While there is no evidence or indication of his membership in the CPUSA, he was a regular and faithful presence in left-wing Hollywood circles. One of the original Nineteen to be subpoenaed by the House Un-American Activities Committee, he was never called to testify, in 1947 or in subsequent years. For Rossen, he was a friend and sympathetic mentor, passing on his store of lore and craft of directing movies to the younger man, who was preparing for his own debut as a director in 1947.

The unusual, daring narrative structure of *A Walk in the Sun* (from the novel by Harry Brown) is the direct opposite of *Edge of Darkness*. *Edge* was tightly plotted to dramatize its suspense, its twists and turns, and its stirring, building momentum of its final confrontation with blatant evil; *Walk* is episodic, looser — a *walk* — with a lingering, threatening sense of danger and sudden outbursts of violence. With that episodic structure, it is much like the way it was in the plodding and deadly routines of the war, yet raised to a more lyrical level of quiet tribute. Especially with the ambiance created by the continuing use of a folk ballad, it seems more than just a tribute to the fighting men, but a celebration, in the midst of pain and loss, of the basic goodness of the People, the Common Man. At about that same time, Aaron Copland had written his lovely and stirring "Tribute to the Common Man." The film's reaching to forge a poetry of the folk, of the people, has some of the same impulse behind it as a literary work of the period that reaches for a lyrical folk poetry, James Agee's *Let Us Now Praise Famous Men*, which is not about famous men at all, but rather the dignity and surviving grace of the down and out, those who the unseeing might consider merely "losers." Like Agee's book, the film praises not the special heroics, but the patient, even weary, heroism of the G.I.s. Day by day, mile by mile, country by country they marched and waited, fought — and died (much in the style and mood of the life of the G.I. Joes in the wartime cartoons of Bill Mauldin and dispatches of Ernie Pyle).

It was an approach that some found inventive and appropriate, moving and meaningful; others found it pretentious and false. In *The Nation*, James Agee thought it "an embarrassing movie. The dialogue seems as unreal as it is expert. Most of the characters are as unreal and literary as the dialogue." For Parker Tyler, however, "Most impressive it is that *A Walk in the Sun* uniquely reveals the degree to which a group of five soldiers, relaxing on back and elbows, can draw together as a unit, a kind of thinking, complex animal with five voices, replying to each other as in a litany; the tangential quality of the remarks, the oblique, fanciful way in which each remark is taken up by another speaker, this process creates a form completely defining the kind of human community this fortuitous little group is." And in *The New Yorker*, John McCarten felt that "the film manages to sum up a good deal more of the sight and smell of war than has been evident for a long time." While praising much of the "excellent talk," McCarten did object to one of the film's mannerisms: the repetition of sayings such as "That's the way it is — sure as little apples that's it" as identifying motifs for various characters, just as physical mannerisms, such as chomping on an apple and cutting a notch in a rifle, were also repeated.

While there is a camaraderie of shared danger and trust, of helping each other through it all, there is a different emphasis and tone than in the usual meanings of ideological collective action in the works of the Left. *A Walk in the Sun* develops no great change of consciousness or change of character, no courageous sacrifice to make amends for moral failure. Its acts of courage, its sacrifices, are a part of doing the job, or even the result of a random act of destruction. It has no betrayals, only some human weaknesses under pressure, some mistakes. It, too, however, does comply with the bedrock requirement of the war-film genre: there is a climactic assault and its casualties, though it is shorter and has less declamatory punctuation of heroics than others.

This concept produces the film's unique achievement in capturing the everyday life of a community of men at war and celebrating their endurance and courage; but it also results in the film's weaknesses. Without any dramatized confrontations or direct conflicts with evil, whether in the enemy or within the platoon, it risks being sentimentally good-natured in its depiction of, and empathy with, the men. Its structural emphasis on periods of walking and waiting suddenly interrupted by the violence that is always out there is a strong and realistic contribution to the depiction of the nature of war. These episodes of calm immerse us in their lives, but filling them creates some problems. The drama in these sequences is developed through tensions in the leaders of the platoon. The depiction of the rest of the men in these episodes, however, has less drama and an excess of folksy street poetry. The repartee, the wise-cracks, the favorite sayings, help to identify the individuals, but primarily they are shown as a way of coping with what seems to the men as an endless repetition of foot-slogging and dying, whether a defensive irony that can try to hold off the reality of lurking death or just a way of filling the time. Early on, the troubled Sgt. Porter balks at a light-hearted remark: "What's so funny about Cassino? We lost a lot of good men there." Sgt. Tyne answers, "What do you want us to do, cry about it?" "That's a lot of cocky chatter." "Would it make you feel better if we told you we had the jitters?" "Yeah, it would." "Well, we got 'em."

Wise-cracking and philosophizing, they bitch and gripe to keep on going, joke to keep from crying. Still, the repetitions can become cloying and routine.

As in the novel, the men ironically mutter, "Nobody dies," and trudge on to another fight and another death. (We see here the original impetus for the reversal in Charley Davis' defiant last line in *Body and Soul*, "Everybody dies!")

The musical ballad sets the tone and themes over the opening credits.

> It was just a little walk
> In the warm Italian sun.
> But it wasn't an easy thing...
> They took a little walk in the sun.

The ballad returns throughout the film, repeating key phrases, and commenting on situations and actions, sometimes interspersed with dialogue.

The tension of the platoon's landing at Anzio is captured in an excellent opening sequence, combining lighting, shot compositions, editing, and dialogue. The men are faces, lit in the darkness of the night on the landing craft. Their helmets, their clothing, the equipment on the craft, the night, all are an enclosing darkness out of which they emerge as faces, individuals, men. On the landing craft a number of the motifs, verbal and dramatic, are established. Windy (John Ireland in his first role) is composing a letter to his sister in his head. He becomes the narrator throughout. Here he sets the tone, as he comments on the firing from the land: "A few of the natives have evidently noticed us. They're setting up a bit of a reception. Fireworks." Someone comments on a shell that comes close, "When a shell's looking for a guy, it don't whine. It snarls." The platoon scout, Archimbeau, answers, "You guys kill me, you just kill me." He tells his story about how years from now they'll be fighting the battle of Tibet. The brand-new lieutenant sticks his head up too high and is suddenly shot. "Maybe he'll die," somebody says. "Nobody dies," says another. "Nobody dies," mutters Windy in close-up. The lieutenant does die, and Sgt. Halverson takes over. After they land, he is killed, and Sgt. Porter, already seen as troubled, then takes over, as the platoon is separated from the main force, isolated.

Throughout the film, scenes of talk and waiting are interrupted by an attack. At one point they hear planes and run for the woods. Two men are hit — one is wounded in the leg and one killed. Next come shots of digging a grave, and of men sitting and walking.

> Some of them were just good Joes
> Who'll never see the sunrise again,
> Poor boys, never see the sun rise again.

The internal tension focuses on the accelerating breakdown of Sgt. Porter. Articulated with particular insight, his collapse is deftly shown as a combination of accumulated battle fatigue, undefined and unfaced fear, and the special pressures of being responsible for others. It is orchestrated with quiet power in several scenes of taut, tightening emotion. Of particular note is the refinement here of Rossen's typical *mise en scène*, the placement and patterning of characters within a setting, and in shifting physical relationships to each other — here generally with a basic shot, held and then returned to again and again to intensify a scene and enforce the connection between characters in it. In one scene, a foreshadowing of his further collapse, Porter, seated in a foxhole, suddenly bawls out Windy, who is standing above him. Windy turns and walks out of the shot. Cut to Sgt. Tyne watching the altercation. Cut back to the original angle, but wider, as Tyne walks into the shot and says to Windy, "What's eating him?" "Don't you know?" Still within the shot, Tyne turns and goes to Porter, as Windy watches. Porter says, "I don't like the responsibility." "You're stuck with it."

In the woods, while the men wait yet again, what was expected, inevitable, still is a shock when it does come; and the responsibility passes to Tyne, who has been the calm bedrock of the group, reasonable and sympathetic from the start. Porter is sitting, back against a tree, balled fists up against his face. He has made a dangerous mistake. Tyne walks into the shot, looks down at him, then sits facing him, also leaning against a tree, his back to us, staring at Porter. We move in to a slighter closer version of the basic shot, still past Tyne as Porter lifts his head from his hands, meets Tyne's gaze, then looks down. Cut to close-up of Tyne, concerned. The scene shifts back to the basic shot past Tyne to Porter, who says, "Thanks Bill." Cut to close-up of Tyne. "Nothing, you just didn't think of it, that's all." Moving back to the basic shot, Porter, with an odd, disturbed smile, responds, "Yeah, didn't think of it."

The tension and import are then held in abeyance as the film cuts to a delaying semi-comic, semi-philosophic interlude. In a shot held throughout this sequence of dia-

6. The War and Post-War Worlds on Film—Three with Lewis Milestone

A Walk in the Sun (1946), Twentieth Century–Fox. Sergeant Tyne (Dana Andrews) attempts to settle a problem with a troubled Sergeant Ward (Lloyd Bridges) during one of the quiet times between outbursts of violence.

logue, Sgt. Ward is in the foreground, sitting, with two men past him and Windy lying out to the left, head up on a fallen tree trunk. Ward, who is a farmer, talks of apples, his favorite crop, and soil. The soil that drips from his hand, he says, "is old and tired and worn out." He talks of his wife and apples and then again the soil, hurt by its condition, "Aah, soil's no good." There is a pause, and then the camera cuts to a closer shot, angled past Ward to Windy, who sits up and makes the thematic point of the scene—and the figurative connection to Porter and the platoon's walk in the sun: "Maybe too many soldiers been walking on it. They've been walking on it for a long time. That's what always happens to a country when soldiers walk on it."

The scene returns to the original basic shot, with Porter's fists to his face again as Tyne says, "Time we were moving, Eddie." The camera moves in slightly to the closer variation as Porter looks up over his fists, eyes wide. A close-up of Tyne shows he is worried. The camera shifts back toward Porter, who hesitates, then says, "Call Ward, will you?" Tyne turns and calls him. Cut to Ward, getting up, then back to the basic shot as Ward walks into it and sits next to Porter. The shot is held through the climax of the scene, intensifying their interaction, their sharing of the pain that Porter feels, that *they* know they might one day feel. Porter tells them, "Ward, I can't go on. Tyne's taking over." "It's okay with me," says Ward, adding further words of necessary assurance. Suddenly, Porter gets up on his knees, chatters wildly about needing to lie down, then throws himself forward onto the ground on a diagonal between Tyne and Ward. The camera stays on him as he starts to cry, face pressed against the dirt, the tired and worn out dirt. Ward says, "Poor Eddie. Poor Country." Picking up some dirt and dropping it from his hand, he adds, "Poor dirt."

As they begin to walk off, leaving Porter behind, Windy stops and looks down at Porter. He kneels and in close-up says:

> You're crying, Porter. You're crying because you're wounded. You don't have to be bleeding to be wounded. You just had one battle too many. You've built yourself a foxhole — up there — and nothing in the world can make you come out of it. Go on, keep crying, Porter, we understand.

Cut to Porter crying, face pressed straight down against the weary dirt.

They do reach the farmhouse and bridge that are their assignment, mount a conventional attack on the farmhouse, and blow up the bridge. As the victors finally leap in triumph, out through windows of the conquered farmhouse, we can see bodies strewn on the ground, some still moving.

The scene cuts to Windy, outside, lighting a cigarette; then shifts back to some men, wounded, crawling on the ground; then up to the sun directly overhead; then to Windy's watch: twelve noon. Writing to his sister one last time: "We just blew up a bridge and took a farmhouse. It was easy. Terribly easy."

But then over his ironic words we hear (unfortunately) the melody of the lusty "Caissons Go Rolling Along." This ending is strangely hurried, evasive, and disappointing. The film is suddenly drained of its true emotions. The men's reality is turned into the settled history of victory. For by the time of the film's release in January, 1946, in the America of the film's audience, the war was over — and so, it was decided, in the rosy dawn of a peaceful world, we must be proud and affirm. (Johnny Mercer caught the tenor of the times in the lyrics of a popular song, "Accentuate the Positive.") And so the film's musical ballad comes up, devoid of feeling this time, while several of the central figures come out the door and down the steps of the farmhouse, almost as if they are making their curtain calls or taking their turn in a patriotic pageant, each doing his particular thing one last time. There are no shots of the dead, no images of helping or soothing the wounded, no images of comradeship and compassion, no real pride or bone- and soul-aching weariness. The men — and the viewers — are cheated of their final moments. In fact, the men disappear, and the last images of the film are only the words of the ballad being sung, right down to the affirmation of its final words, "It's where men fight to be free."

James Agee nicely caught the violation of this forced ending: "At the end, with their farmhouse captured, various featured players are shown completing the gags which tag their characters — chomping an apple, notching a rifle, and so on — while, so far as the camera lets you know, their wounded comrades are still writhing unattended in the dooryard."[9]

By the time the film had been released, the humane optimism, even in the face of the brutality of war, seemed to be quickly fading before the rise of the international tensions that would become the Cold War, the subsequent intensity of anti-communism, and the conflicts within the Communist Party itself (and within wavering members like Robert Rossen). It seemed to be a time of betrayal of all the harmony and idealism of the wartime period — a time of moral chaos in one's inner life and in one's world. In Hollywood, any remaining remnant of the wartime unity that had led to maintaining an alliance between liberals and Communists was shattered by the studio strikes of 1945–6. They quickly turned violent, and increasingly and politically divisive. They became potent propaganda fuel for the burgeoning power of the Right to break, once and for all, the Communist Party in Hollywood. Even Ben Margolis, later the leading attorney for the Nineteen and the Ten, saw the danger: "The strike nourished the Motion Picture Alliance and made it more powerful. The Alliance was largely responsible for what Congress did. It was a stimulant to HUAC."[10]

Long-time radical union activist Herbert J. (Herb) Sorrell had brought together a new coalition of workers in some of the industry trades to combat the ruling IATSE. The purpose of the CSU strike that Sorrell declared in March 1945 was, in legal terms, jurisdictional — over who should be allowed to represent workers in the industry. But it became political warfare. The producers and the Alliance supported the IATSE. The leftist liberals supported the CSU, but then began to defect as the Communist Party took over support of the strike. Ironically (though typically), for the few months that the war was still on, the Party opposed the strike within the Comintern's wartime policy of a united front against the Germans. On April 19 a *People's World* headline proclaimed: "FOR NATIONAL UNITY — END THE STRIKE." Then the war ended and the hard line began. The Party now favored strikes — any and all strikes.[11]

By October the strike had turned vicious. Warners had been chosen for a mass picket line; the picket line was more a daily march and demonstration, with many rushing in to take to the streets. On the 8th, violence (and arrests) erupted on the streets outside Warner Bros. Autos were overturned, a variety of missiles were hurled, and batons were swung by the sheriff's riot squad. Both sides hurled accusations as wildly as the bricks and rocks.[12]

After the NLRB ruled in favor of the CSU on the technical, jurisdictional issue, the producers stalled. And so in 1946 Sorrell again took the CSU out on strike. This time pickets were set up at eight studios, at which some fifty movies were in various stages of production. At Columbia 1,500 strikers practically laid siege to the studio. When it all became violent again, *Time* magazine, with its inimitable dramatic bias, reported that strikers "scattered tacks in the path of movie stars' automobiles, threw coffee in the faces of picket-line crossers, [and] stoned bus-loads of AF of L workers convoyed through the their jeering, milling ranks." It did not report the baton-swinging and the excessive number of arrests.[13]

While the strike dragged on, support began to dwindle, and criticism of Sorrell's intransigence increased. The CSU held on and on, lost, then struck again, until they and other "progressive" unions in Hollywood were destroyed.

Responses on the Right set the tone for what was to follow. For Roy Brewer, the devastation of the strikes showed "the capacity of the Communists to destroy things.... Things will not grow naturally with the Communists in the picture.... I don't mind opposition — I like opposition — because sometimes I'm wrong, but I don't want a guy telling me something that he isn't, especially when he's attached to an organization that's trying to destroy the world." For Ronald Reagan, chief author of the "Screen Actors Guild Report to the Motion Picture Industry" on the strike, "The conclusion [was] that certain of the leaders of the CSU do not want the strike settled." An eventual referendum by mail received the strong endorsement of the membership. But the real point was more than the strike: It was the SAG's turn toward a strong anti–Communist position. Three months later Reagan was elected president of the Screen Actors Guild.[14]

A series of disputes over the strike were but one of the sources of tension and growing personal hostilities that led to the final battle for control of the Screen Writers Guild in the period leading up to the first HUAC hearings in the Fall of 1947. By the Guild election in November 1947, an all–Guild slate of liberals and moderates had routed the Communists from the Board of Directors. For the first time, no Communists or non–Party radicals were elected to the Board.[15]

In the spring of 1946 a second Party meeting concerning Albert Maltz, this time more of an inquisition, was one more push toward Rossen's still wavering final exit from the Party. In February 1946 Maltz had published an article in *The New Masses* proposing greater Party allowance for the free play of creativity in writers of the Left.[16] A flurry of denunciations in the Party press began, and two long, vituperative meetings of attack were held in Hollywood, with key Party functionaries even making the trip out from New York to be in attendance.[17] Maltz recanted, affirming his loyalty and admitting his bourgeois mistakes in a subsequent article. Later he gave a series of speeches attacking the government for its suppression of freedom of speech. Rossen was present for at least one of the meetings about Maltz's article.[18]

These tensions, building within himself and beginning to develop in the world around him, permeate Rossen' prescient screenplay for *The Strange Loves of Martha Ivers*, so different in mood and attitude, even though it was being written while *Walk* was in production. Filming on *Ivers* was completed on December 7, 1945, and it was released in July of 1946, only six months after *Walk*'s delayed release. Nevertheless, it was part of a different world, a world with new conflicts. It goes beyond the affirmations of the period of postwar euphoria to evoke a sense of the alienation, corruption, and violation still generated by the destructive values of contemporary society. As Manny Farber, one of the most insightful and thoughtful critics of the period, put it, the film depicts "modern life as a jungle."

This bitter and cynical final collaboration of Rossen and Milestone nonetheless still contains another, although different, mixing of affirmation with evil, with destruction and death. This mixture is a central aspect of the film, but to a degree it creates an imbalance in the structuring of the narrative. The loner Sam's conflict with the evil empire of Martha and her husband Walter is a main element of the plot. However, the amount of screen time devoted to developing the good people (Sam and the needy wanderer Toni that he begins to care for) detracts from the full development of the film's most interesting and insightful material and its theme — Martha and her strange love and driven, destructive, revengeful need for power. Developed and released on a very short production schedule, and with commercial length demands, it is fascinating and provocative, but still makes one wish it could have been made, and refined, with the control and thorough development of Rossen's later films. Even with the imbalance and unsettled focus of the whole, Farber felt its strength and impact, its raw and uneven power: "The chaotic scenes are written with unusual ability, boil and seethe as movie scenes rarely do." John McCarten said it "has the efficiency of a hangman's knot."

As Rossen returns to the forces of a world of money and power, its corruptions and oppressions, he dramatizes the corruption of capitalist power *within* the central character. Not only in the conflict of social classes, not only in the public violations and betrayals that result, but corruption comes in the intimate, interpersonal violations and the betrayal of one's self—the betrayal of love itself or even the ability or freedom to love. Here the woman, Martha Ivers (Barbara Stanwyck), is the force of evil, too hardened into what she is to ever change, too frozen into her view of the world, her need to use money as the fuel for her domination and revenge. For she, too, has been a victim of the misuse of power over her, and so revenge is a new obsessive and distorting element of motivation in the quest for power. This time the unformed seeker, Sam Masterson (Van Heflin), is no longer so youthful, though he's still unsettled. A veteran, an itinerant and this time a non-capitalist gambler, he seems content in his footloose wandering. Though self assured, he is still too aimless, still seeking, still needing something more, something not yet defined—even if he doesn't yet quite know it. He is no moral crusader, undergoes no deep change of consciousness, but he does change from not caring about much of anything as long as he is left alone to taking a personal stand—partly as revenge but partly out of a new sense of defining himself, of caring for more than himself.

And so for the first time in this sequence of films, two contrasting kinds of love, two contrasting ways of loving, are seen as the embodiment of and parallel to two ways of living. It is two kinds of defining the self, chosen by (or forced upon) the central characters: driven and possessing, using—and generating death; free and nurturing, sharing—and generating life. In all of his subsequent films (though present with less emphasis in *Alexander the Great* and *They Came to Cordura*) this parallel, this interaction between kinds of loving and kinds of living in the world, will be an increasingly central and complex aspect of the drama and themes.

In *Strange Love*, Martha knows and uses love only within her deformed sense of her self and the world as she perceives it. Her relationship with her husband, Walter O'Neil (Kirk Douglas) is shaped by her need for possession, for revenge. It leads to violation and betrayal, which he accepts out of his own false dream of childhood love, his own lust for power, his self-hatred and guilt, which leads him to drinking until he can abdicate control of his life. In *his* youth, Sam had run away from the town of the Ivers, the power of the Ivers, and his boyhood love of Martha. But he still harbors the boy in love with her within himself, though has not allowed any love to penetrate his free-form wandering. Returning now to Iverstown by happenstance, he stumbles upon the possibility of loving and caring for someone, but he knows that, once he has arrived, he has returned to Martha as well, still drawn to her power.

In *Ivers* Rossen is in tune with what was becoming a looser form of genre, the *film noir*, but he goes beyond the conventions of that developing genre. *Ivers* is not really a crime film, as are most of the central examples of the movement, genre, tendency, style (et al.) of films that presented a more dour, doomed view of life and society than the standard Hollywood fare. But it does overlap and merge with that genre and its conventional patterns in some interesting ways. Sam bears some resemblance to the usual *noir* hero who would like to do something good or at least not do something evil, but who is seduced—or not—by the woman into not doing the former and doing the latter. Martha is certainly a *femme fatale*, but she is much more the central power figure, like the men in crime films and *film noir*, rather then the auxiliary attraction, the siren that lures men onto the rocks of greed. She shares some of the characteristics of Stanwyck as Phyllis in *Double Indemnity*, but writ large, bigger than life, with wider vistas and bolder dreams. Martha is not merely a scheming, put-upon housewife willing to do anything to get out from her trap and get the money, along with *her* Walter. And in her twisted way she is still more human; she does love, would like to love, has always loved Sam — though fate has kept them apart until it is too late for her to realize that love in a way that is not destructive.

The film has some of the mood of *noir* bitterness, foreboding, and fated doom, but its use of typical *noir* shadows and sharp contrasts of black and white is more limited than in the major films of the genre. Its use of these strong contrasts in lighting and tone is, however, one aspect of its employment of setting, décor, and lighting as a visual correlative of the thematic contrast between the upper class and the working class, the two ways of living and loving. On the one side of the divide is the mansion of Martha, along with its bright extravagance and its gloomy, threatening shadows; the romantically lit, classy nightclub where Sam and Martha dance and kiss; the dark hilltop lovers lane, the site of their romantic return to their youth, as he is tempted again by her world. And on the other side stands the plain, seemingly petty but solid world of Sam and Toni: commonplace hotel rooms; unpretentious bars and restaurants; bus stations; and police stations — all evenly, quietly lit, the everyday working class world.

The tenor of a *noir* mood is heightened by the music of Miklos Rozsa, whose scores helped shape the brooding, doomed romanticism of a number of the films of the period, including *Double Indemnity, The Lost Weekend, The Killers, Brute Force, Naked City, The Asphalt Jungle*, and Alfred Hitchcock's *Spellbound*.

Overall, though, the film is more concerned with defining the causes of its betrayals and failed loves, with developing the interlaced web of consequences on all the characters than in the usual *film noir*. Those who betray may be evil, but even they have a complex of motives, often unfaced (and in the produced film not fully delineated), for their actions, as do those who are tempted to betray. As Jean Renoir, one of Rossen's favorite directors, said in *The Rules of the Game*, "Everybody has his reasons."

In a prologue, the teenage Martha fights with her domineering aunt, hits her with her own cane, and kills her. Martha had been caught returning from a date with Sam, who has run away. Walter, who is living in the mansion, sees it all. His father, Mr. O'Neill, is Mrs. Ivers' business advisor and the tutor for the two of them. He takes over the situation — he and Walter will support her story that an intruder did it and ran away. But there is a price to pay. As the years have passed, O'Neill has used the accidental death as a means of controlling her, profiting from her and her fear. He has taken over her life, just as her aunt had done, and controls the Ivers' fortune. To solidify his reign and advance the career of his son, he has promoted a marriage between Martha and Walter. Walter has always loved Martha, but he knows she doesn't really love him. Martha's motives are complex. She is revenging herself on the two of them by her infidelities, her dominating and tormenting of Walter; but in a half-recognized way the revenge is on herself for what she knows she has become. And, as Sam will discover, her ultimate complicity and nagging guilt — the motives for which are revealed as contradictory as the story develops — is over the scheme to prosecute and convict a vagrant for the murder of Mrs. Ivers, while Walter is a young prosecuting attorney. The vagrant is executed. Their continued success is assured. The family business prospers and grows; the Ivers own and control much of the town. O'Neill has died, and now Martha is in control. Walter is weak, yet in that weakness (not unlike Johan in *Edge of Darkness*) he has collaborated in his father's domination of Martha, has accepted and misused the power his being elected district attorney has given him. He betrays the people and their trust in the law. There is much guilt to carry around and live with. And each one uses it to damage the other.

Almost twenty years later, Sam has returned, and the past explodes into the present. Scenes alternate between Sam and Toni and Martha and Walter, and then the two worlds come together and clash.

Sam's world has a new awakening. Wandering around his old hometown, he meets Toni (Lizabeth Scott). She is the female version of the down-and-out, lonely wanderer — aimless as Sam, but without his self assurance and the strength to go on going it alone. She has too often been betrayed by men and life. Sam is taken with her, opened by her to some other part of himself. She allows herself some sweet, smiling hope.

In the first of a series of contrasts, in the imposing, oppressive mansion, Martha finds Walter drunk as usual. In this drunken moment of buried truth, he faces his guilt over what they've done, what he's done as the public prosecutor in convicting the innocent vagrant. "What's done is done," she says. "He was a criminal. If he hadn't hanged for that, he'd hang for something else." They are in a tight two-shot, she in profile, staring down at him, standing over him. He wants her to live up to her bargain, be a wife to him. He stands, grabs her and kisses her. "Tell me, Martha, what should I do about my love for you — why I don't just abandon all of this." She pulls back and stares at him coldly. The scene cuts to close-ups of each, then past her as she watches him leave in defeat. Again.

In the small, plain, cluttered room at the hotel Toni is happy: she'll stay. Sam tells her she's "really a picture." She tells him she has just got out of jail and is on probation. When he comes out after showering, she is asleep on the bed. He smiles.

But in the morning the law of Iverstown has stepped in. While at the bus station to cash in her ticket, Toni has been rousted for violating her probation. Sam has seen Walter's re-election posters, and goes straight to the top to get her out of jail. At Walter's office he meets Martha. She is pleased, but he does not stay.

He and Martha begin to meet, first at the mansion. At this point her motives seem mixed. She still believes she wants him because she loves him as she did when she was young. But she and Walter are both suspicious of him, afraid of what he knows and why he has come back. Is it blackmail? Showing him her old room, she says, "We're not kids now." "No, no time for dreams." "There's only one dream, Sam," she says, moving to him. "And it came true. You're here now."

But when he pulls away and starts to leave, she flares up, her voice now hard and demanding, "What do you want? Answer me!" He retorts, "You sound like I have to. You sound like your aunt used to do."

For Martha, any possible reawakening of a youthful, innocent love can't be separated from her need to use love to protect her position and power, even to possess him as one more of the possessions she has fought for. For Martha, the conflicting ways of loving — if they can be called that — are inextricably wrapped together. It is a fascinating but difficult ambiguity of motives to represent, and Rossen is not fully successful in delineating them. Likewise with Sam's. He *is* drawn to her, to the old dreams, and to the excitement of her intensity now. And to the money? Is he wavering, unsure, or just the cool gambler playing his cards close to his vest?

Walter's motives are clearer. He is fearful and jealous. He is fearful that Sam will expose their past. He is jealous of Sam and afraid he will take Martha from him — and his position of public power from him. He uses the law to intimidate Toni in the same way Graham threatened Mary in *Marked Woman*. He will see that she serves her full five-year term for grand theft unless she cooperates. This time it is to trick Sam. Frightened, she agrees. At a restaurant she and Sam are interrupted by a man who claims Toni is his wife. Rather too easily, Sam seems to believe him: "Brother, you can have her, in spades." When he leaves the restaurant, they beat him up, throw him in a car, and dump him on the road out of town.

Sam's action are now equivocal — and not convincingly so. Back in town, he accepts Toni's explanation, forgives her, then turns angry: "I don't like to be pushed around. I don't like anybody I like to be pushed around. I don't like *anybody* to be pushed around." He threatens Walter, investigates and finds the story of the prosecution of the vagrant. But then he agrees to meet Martha again, scheming yet also drawn back despite his resolve. At her factory she tells him how she has benefited the town. He tells her he wants half of it all. Is he just testing her, taunting her to get even, tempted to reach for some easy money, or...? What he really wants, why he is doing it, is left ambiguous (or is merely poorly developed).

Back at the hotel he is once again content, but he still seems to be thinking of blackmail. "Toni, you bring me luck. I'm gonna wear you like a charm." They kiss and are happy. While she's showing him a new outfit she bought, Martha comes in, wanting to talk. Toni goes back to her room. Foreshadowing the kind of shot sequence that Rossen was to continue to use with great effectiveness, the visual patterns of the scene develop Sam's wavering emotions and loyalties. As Toni starts to leave, Martha is to the right, near the door. As Toni goes out and Sam moves to the door after her, Martha moves forward to our right and out of the shot. Sam turns. The scene cuts to Martha at a dresser, a whiskey bottle standing on it, looking toward him, waiting. A pause. He walks into the shot and to her, and possibly to what she can offer him. In what is now a medium two-shot, he starts to pour them a drink.

The Strange Love of Martha Ivers (1946), Paramount Pictures. The re-kindling of a love affair of the past between Martha Ivers (Barbara Stanwyck) and Sam Masterson (Van Heflin) turns into a power struggle upon his return to Iverstown after many years (collection of the Margaret Herrick Library).

They go dancing and then park above the city. "It's real, very real. Owning it gives you a sense of power." But she now admits her regrets — and even weakness — and wishes he had stopped her that night. "I wasn't there, Martha," he says. And she realizes he didn't know. Panicked, she starts to beat on him. He grabs her. They kiss. "Sam, help me, help me."

She tells him her version of what happened. She wanted to tell the truth, but she was crazy with fear. "They used that fear well. To even increase it, they made me part of another crime. My testifying sent an innocent man to the gallows. And they used that to make me marry Walter.... Please stay." He kisses her again.

The scene switches to Toni waiting at the hotel room window as they pull up below in Martha's convertible. In the room, Sam tells Toni he's not sure what he wants to do. She's going to leave but wants him to leave with her. "I can't — at least not just yet." He's torn between them, but the realization of that conflict on the screen is not complete.

The final confrontation occurs in a darkened room of the mansion in which are Martha, Sam and Walter, who's drunk as usual. Martha and Walter go at each other in front of Sam — all the hatred of their long power struggle released by his presence. Walter tells him about all of her lovers, but Sam remains different, "all of them rolled into one." "How long do you expect her to go on paying off?" Sam asks Walter. "Forever," he answers.

Yelling at each other, threatening each other with Walter's gun, Martha and Walter reveal more than they should. Feeling a new strength, Walter tells Sam she's insane and will murder one of them someday! Walter starts to leave, staggering; at the door he turns — his voice different, quiet now — and admits how he is sick inside, not just drunk. "Martha, help me." He goes out, and with a loud thump he falls down the stairs.

"Now, Sam," Martha says, standing close, hands on his arms, "do it now. Set me free, set both of us free — oh, Sam, it can be so easy." Her expression is wild, crazy in anticipation. He turns, goes out, brings Walter back and drops him in a chair.

"I thought you loved me." "I thought I did too." "Now you hate me." "Now I'm sorry for you.... You're sick ... don't know the difference between right and wrong."

She responds to his words with a righteous, revealing outburst, an excited justifying of her way of living that is her own condemnation:

> What am I guilty of? What were their lives compared to me? Neither one of them had any right to live. A mean hateful old woman who'd never done anything for anybody! Look what I've done with what she's left me. I've given to charity, to schools, hospitals, given thousands of people work — and what was he, a thief, a drunk who'd have died in the gutter anyway!

But sensing Sam is now standing strong against her, she threatens him with the gun — it will be self defense. Sam realizes what a mistake he has made in holding on to some lure of a past love. He now knows where his life really is, and turns away and leaves. She doesn't shoot.

Martha goes to the window to watch him leave the grounds of the mansion. Walter follows and stands behind her, slightly to her side. It is their final bitter "liebestod." Their mutual confessions and protestations are strangely tinged with an unbreakable self-deceit, a hope that they know is false. Their drift into an inevitable, undeclared suicide, with Walter's gun, is a sharply orchestrated sequence of shots as they are seen through the window, framed — trapped — in the shadowy darkened light of Martha's mansion, of her life.

In the final contrast, in clear, smiling sunlight, Sam and Toni drive from Iverstown along the road to the west, to the new territory ahead. They choose to make a new life, and to love. Though for Sam, purpose still may be too definite and complete, but at least he has a focus, a center, in caring for someone.

For those living and working in the Hollywood of that territory ahead in the west, the choices would not be so easy, and the times ahead would not prove to be so sunny or clear.

PART TWO

*The Director —
Success, Doubt and Disillusion*

In our profession everything is only a matter of experience. Good or bad, experiences always leave traces; it is they that inspire us. —ROBERT ROSSEN

7

The Writer Becomes Director — *Johnny O'Clock*

For Robert Rossen and others on the Left in Hollywood, these were hectic years of decisions and indecisions, intensifying pressures and conflicts, meetings and shifting allegiances. And yet the turmoil that was fragmenting his life of political idealism oddly seemed to re-fuel the momentum of his film production.

By the time shooting on *The Strange Love of Martha Ivers* was completed on December 7, 1945, he had begun to do some work on a screenplay for *The Treasure of Sierra Madre*, hoping to be able to direct it. When John Huston got the director's job, Rossen bowed out. He then turned to the job of writing *Johnny O'Clock*, and by the time *Ivers* was released in July of 1946, he was at work directing *Johnny O'Clock*. Shooting was completed in September 1946, but the film was not released until March 27, 1947. By then he was already at work directing *Body and Soul*, and shooting on that film was completed in April, only one month after the opening of *Johnny O'Clock*. Two months after that, in May of 1947, the political threat accelerated. The House Committee on Un-American Activities conducted its first closed hearings in Hollywood. By October 1947, the "Unfriendly Nineteen" (including Rossen and Lewis Milestone) were in Washington, and the first Ten (plus Bertolt Brecht) were called to testify. That was, of course, only the beginning; yet through the first years of this time of turmoil, Rossen was strikingly productive — in works created and in a new major career created. Five films that he worked on in one way or another were released in the two-and-a-half years between March 1947 and November 1949. By his final film of this period, *All the King's Men*, he was wearing three hats — as producer, writer, and director.

The opportunity to direct came about through Dick Powell and a court battle. The case in court was a typical altercation with Harry Cohn — the domineering, volatile, and often crass but creatively insightful head of Columbia Pictures. This time his fight was with the equally hot-headed director and sometime close friend Charles Vidor. Powell was riding the crest of a comeback that had begun with his portrayal of a tough private-eye in *Murder, My Sweet*—a reversal of his earlier and faded image as a cheerful, smiling (and often singing), young leading man. For some fifteen years Powell had been busy in forty-three movies as an always young, fresh-faced actor and singer in many musicals, from *42nd Street* and *Gold Diggers of 1933* to the (adulterated) screen version of the leftish *Meet the People* in 1944, and in sentimental dramas such as *It Happened Tomorrow* and *Shipmates Forever*. But by 1944 this career had begun to pale. In 1945 Powell changed his image with two strong tough-guy performances in *Murder, My Sweet* (from the Raymond Chandler novel *Farewell, My Lovely*, directed by Edward Dmytryk) and *Cornered* (also directed by Dmytryk). He also went on to do a successful radio show as a brash, hard-nosed private eye. The film *Johnny O'Clock* was set to capitalize on his new hard-boiled image, but he and Cohn (always a hands-on studio head) were not satisfied with the early attempts to fashion a screenplay from the story they had bought. Cohn knew and appreciated Rossen's work for Warner Bros. and Milestone, and brought him in to make a fresh start. Both Cohn and Powell were pleased with the result.

In the meantime, Vidor had sued Cohn to be released from his contract with Cohn and Columbia, claiming, among other things, that Cohn had regularly insulted and abused him. When there were conflicts, he further claimed, Cohn had "punished" him with the assignment to direct a minor film, *Johnny O'Clock*. In a lively court battle Cohn fought back, claiming Vidor merely wanted to make a more lucrative deal elsewhere — with Warner Bros. (he was married to Jack Warner's daughter). Cohn brought witnesses to show that he called everybody things like "son of a bitch," and that it didn't mean anything.[1]

So *Johnny O'Clock*, ready for production, had no director. Powell, knowing Rossen's expertise in the gambler-gangster milieu, and admiring the script he had produced from the weak material, insisted that the screenwriter was the only one who could get the movie done right. Rossen made his case to Cohn; Cohn was impressed, acquiesced, and went back to exchanging insults with Vidor in the courtroom.

Cohn was impressed with the finished product as well — a good, workmanlike job that rescued a "programmer" that now had some class and would make a little money. As was typical of Cohn, when he had not been crossed, he was loyal. He spread the word. When John Garfield was interested in using Rossen on *Body and Soul* just after *Johnny O'Clock* was completed, Charles Einfield, president of Enterprise Pictures, asked Cohn if he could view a print of the Powell film. As Cohn told the story, he replied, "Fuck you. I never saw any film by Rossen; I took a chance on him. Why shouldn't you?" He later told Rossen that he would have shown Einfeld the movie if he had to, but that after he told him what a good job Rossen had done, he didn't have to.[2]

Johnny O'Clock is a standard crime entertainment (gambler-gangster subdivision) adapted from a story by Milton Holmes. Though limited by the basic murder mystery plot (which he does not seem very interested in), Rossen does build strong characterizations and relationships. And it contains a touch of the moral themes that were to become part of the repertoire of his usual concerns and motifs. Here, however, the two aspects — mystery plot with characters, and moral themes — do not blend harmoniously. Critics responded only to the surface of the expected mystery plot, not to the interest in psychological probing of the main characters. In response to the movie's best scene (between Guido Marchettis and his wife), Shirley O'Hara in *The New Republic* saw only that "sadism is rarely given such a play." Bosley Crowther, focusing only on the plot, found its obvious pattern "relieves it of any great suspense." His level of attention is indicated in the final sentence of his brief review: "A great deal of drinking and smoking is done by all concerned." On the popular *Lux Radio Theater*, on May 12, 1947, Powell and Lee J. Cobb reprised their roles in a live broadcast.

7. The Writer Becomes Director—Johnny O'Clock

While it served mainly—and nicely—as a practice run (or, in Rossen terms, a warm-up bout) for his career as a director, *Johnny O'Clock* established his valuable and close relationship with Harry Cohn at Columbia Pictures, and with expert cinematographer Burnett Guffey, then at the beginning of a notable career. In working on it, Rossen used what he was good at, what he had used before, and used it well. Still, even though it breaks no new ground, it glitters with some of Rossen's sharpest, character-revealing wise-guy-and-gal talk; some strong individual scenes of intense confrontations; and, working closely with Guffey, intense visual patterns to develop these confrontations. His screenplays had often indicated this kind of visual patterning; now he could actively develop the patterns on the set as a director working with an excellent cinematographer.

Johnny Powell is the wise-cracking manager, the "*junior* partner," in a classy gambling casino run by mob boss Guido Marchettis (Thomas Gomez). The brains behind Marchettis' muscle, Johnny is a cynical rogue gambler who, as he likes to say, never gambles. "A gambler's a guy who takes chances," and Johnny doesn't take chances. He prides himself on keeping his cool, keeps himself fancy free, and likes to make the quick, smart retort. But in the major character arc of the film, Johnny, who lives for himself in a dog-eat-dog world, slowly and almost grudgingly recognizes there *is* more than that in the world.

The relationship he develops with Nancy (Evelyn Keyes) is one of a representative cross-section of man-woman relationships in the narrative—minor variations of the pattern established in *Ivers*, in which the nature of love (if you can call it that) relationships parallels the moral (or immoral) actions of the men (or women). Nancy's innocent sister Harriet is tormented, toyed with, and thrown away by the bad cop Blayden. Blayden betrays the law; for his share of the profits he is willing to get rid of competitor gamblers by killing them. He finally is eager to betray Johnny for a bigger share of the profits.

Nelle, the glamorous prize wife of the volatile, unscrupulous Marchettis, is the false allure of the world of money and power. Unfaithful and greedy, she drinks too much as Marchettis flaunts her in front of his boys, controlling her as he does them.

Nancy, sassy and smart-mouthed herself, is also proud of her ability to go it alone, but she discovers in herself feelings she had long rejected, and faces her own selfishness. Though not the typical good woman, she breaks through the amoral armor of Johnny to release some inklings of decency, his better self, that hadn't died within him, despite all of his attempts to kill them.

These varieties of love provide one arc of the moral structure. The other, and major, driver of the meaningful character relationships involves the power struggles, double dealings, and betrayals among the gangsters and their corrupt partners in the legal system—the exploiting, amoral world of money. Conflicts in the two arcs come together in the actions of the boss, Marchettis. From the beginnings of the plot to its climactic events, Marchettis is a definite descendant of Johnny Vanning—domineering and possessive, yet uneasy in his power, needing to control and win at any cost. He has the vast ostentatious penthouse apartment (French doors leading out to the terrace, the latest sleek furniture, elaborate scrollwork and fretwork curling and curving in scalloped-edged shapes on walls and around alcoves). The apartment's imposing stairway has a flowing scalloped railing pattern to match; and yet along one wall of the living room there are ungainly stacks of file boxes, and leaning against the wall are paintings that he has bought. But he is much more of a fully drawn, emotionally troubled and driven character than Vanning. He, significantly, is uneasy in his marriage, for all his bravado. The more insecure and jealous he feels, and the more he then becomes fearful and even self-hating, the more he must dominate. He must get even for all slights, real or imagined. He is one interesting variation within the long line of gangster-gambler violators in Rossen's films — men who, more and more, begin to seem something like Hollywood studio bosses in their relationships with the hired help, the people who really make the movies.

Despite their long relationship, Marchettis is willing to at least consider pushing Johnny aside for a new partnership with the rogue cop Blayden. Or so Blayden taunts Johnny: "That's the way it's gonna be — the greaseball and me." "Wanna bet?" retorts Johnny.

As the crime plot develops, however, Blayden disappears and is found dead, floating in the river. Harriet is found dead in her apartment, the gas turned on. But an autopsy reveals her "suicide" as faked; she had been poisoned. Inspector Koch (Lee J. Cobb), calm and polite and thoughtful (though a bit of a cigar-chomping klutz), begins to investigate and becomes suspicious of Johnny.

Meanwhile, on the character front, the impending, intertwined conflict with Marchettis on the "love" and power front has been initiated in a sequence of scenes with sharp verbal and visual irony. Nelle (Ellen Drew) had had a love affair with Johnny, but she had betrayed him for money and married Marchettis. Unsatisfied with what she now has, she wants Johnny back, too. She gives Johnny a special watch with an inscription on the back: "To my darling with unending love." He doesn't want it, but she won't take it back. He gives it to Harriet, the romantically naïve hatcheck girl (Nina Foch in quite a different mode than her later assertive portrayals), with a note to give it back to Nelle.

Marchettis has just come back from a vacation in Mexico. He proudly displays a watch that Nelle had given him, specially made, he says, to celebrate his return. It is the same as the watch she gave Johnny — but with no inscription.

In one scene Guido's possessiveness definitely turns into an unsettling, dangerous jealousy, and the unspoken tensions mount. They are all in the apartment, along with a group of gamblers who have come to town for a major poker game (one of them, Turk, is Jeff Chandler in an early minor role). In the first sequence in this scene, Nelle, quite drunk, mocks Guido in front of these men about a drawing he has bought and keeps bragging about. She has bet on a race, which is on the radio as Johnny enters and comes down the stairs. He stops, leaning back against a chair to the left. Nelle is in the center, looking up at him, leaning back over the arm of a sofa, smiling in welcome. The scene cut to him, cool; then to her, giving a welcoming toss of her head, her eyes fixed on him, as the camera pans to see Guido against the back wall watching and noticing.

A bit later Johnny is sitting with the gamblers at a card table, with Nelle standing to his left, leaning in close, a drink in her hand. Guido walks to them, to Johnny's right — so that Johnny is caught between them — and puts a hand on Johnny's shoulder. Guido talks about old times together and says to Johnny, "That's why I know I'll never have to worry about you." Nelle puts a hand on Johnny's other shoulder, starts to laugh, chokes on some ice, coughs, and spills her drink. In a cut to a wider shot, she crosses behind the two of them and asks one of the boys for another drink; but her glass falls to the floor as she passes it to him, scattering ice. Guido turns and vents his anger on the cowering fellow, bellowing, "You punch-drunk idiot," and starting to swing at him.

"Let him alone," Johnny says.

"He works for me!"

Johnny O'Clock (1947), Columbia Pictures. Johnny O'Clock (Dick Powell) and Nancy Hobson (Evelyn Keyes) get to know each other as she visits the gambling club where her murdered sister worked.

"Then put a ring in his nose."
Nelle says it's her fault and rushes out to the terrace.

In the climactic sequence of this expertly articulated scene, Guido follows her out, and they argue. "You ever let go of anything?" she asks? "When I'm through with it," he answers. A shot that is held to the end of the sequence has the camera out past the terrace rail, looking past him toward her. She turns and walks away, and he follows. She turns, now seen from the side. In a two-shot pattern, he grabs her arms. She is quieter now, seductive, and turns and leans back against the terrace rail, her back now to the camera. Guido moves closer, his face seen above her hair, half-desirous, half-angry. He grabs her arms again, then his face loosens to a slight smile as he leans in further and kisses her. She then walks past him out of the shot—leaving him alone again.

In the contrasting love (or developing love) relationship, Harriet's sister Nancy has come back from a stint with a touring stage company. When she and Johnny meet, there is an immediate connection—revealed by glances that are no longer hard-as-nails as they go though the lighting-of-her-cigarette ritual, which is repeated twice more later. She admits she feels guilty about leaving innocent Harriet alone. "Nancy Hobbs on the road to face her future. Out of my way everybody." And all she is now is fourth-girl-from-the-left in a traveling girl show!

When she can't leave town because a heavy storm has grounded all planes, they go to his apartment, where they reveal their awakening feelings, their fresh openness with each other. The dialogue is half-wise, half-tender, expertly crafted but familiar, building to their first kiss. The scene dissolves into a shot of him coming into the room with his tux on, ready for work, and they are now lovers. She wants it to be straight from the start. "Let's make the words mean what they say. If it's gonna be for laughs, it's okay, but I want to be in on the joke from the start." He sits on the sofa with her and can at least say "I want you to stick around."

From here on Johnny goes back and forth between cool and warm, hard-faced and softening, with her. It is true to his character — ice melts slowly — and the alternations are tied to circumstances and pressures upon him. But they still can't avoid an artificial sense — of character notations rather than fully felt revelations.

Koch has found some clues but is not yet sure what to make of them. He calls in both Johnny and Guido for questioning. He shows them the jewel case he found in Harriet's purse and hands the watch to Guido, who turns it over and reads the inscription. Koch shows the note, knowing it's Johnny's handwriting. "Yeah, she gave me the watch." The camera is on Johnny and Guido, with Johnny standing in back of the sitting Guido, who is tightening with the proof of what he really knew all along. But Guido does not turn around. The camera cuts to Koch watching them. Neither is willing to tell him anything, though Johnny has found a Mexican coin in Harriet's apartment and knows what it means.

Knowing what must now happen, Johnny wants Nancy to leave town; he's his totally cold, unrevealing self when he takes her to the airport. As he is driving from the airport — after dropping off Nancy — he's fired on by a passing car. He crashes but is not hurt badly. He has been betrayed by Charley, an ex-con whom he befriended. Nancy, who was watching, rushes to him. He insists that she leave, but she refuses to let go; she knows it's real between them. "With me," he says, "it's trouble and grief. In capital letters. You got someplace to go — *go*!" She answers, "No place to go." He pulls her close, and they embrace.

The final contrasting, conflicted power struggle between Guido and Nelle is developed both with convincing force and nuanced ambiguity. It has a raw emotional intensity not found in the rest of the film. The scenes built on his jealousy and her taunting of him move into another dimension of feeling, becoming the strongest and most affecting in the film. In the climactic scene between them, Guido, furious at her betrayal, attacks her, dominates her. Yet his force is full of self-loathing, a fear of his own inferiority that her betrayal has stirred. It's more than possession. He knows he loves her, feels it almost as a weakness, a betrayal of his best interests that expose him and makes him vulnerable. She is defiant, yet she surrenders. She's being strategic, yes, but she has to be, as she is driven by her own insatiable needs.

In the noir-shadowed bedroom, Nelle is lying on the bed asleep. Guido wakes her. In a medium shot of the two of them (from a slightly high angle), he grabs her and twists her down on the bed (facing the camera), hands on her throat. A close shot, downward, reveals her panicked face; then the camera cuts to his face, twisted in grief and hate, as he talks of how easy it would be to kill her. "This is Guido Marchettis saying this. Your husband, the *greaseball*." The scene shifts back to the original medium shot, with him still holding her down, hands still on her throat. "That's what you thought all the time, didn't you? Take him, he don't count, who is he? *Greaseball!*" The scene cuts to a closer shot on her face in the light, looking past his dark hair and shoulder, and then shifts back to his face. "That's what you been thinking ever since I met you." Cut to a wider shot that shows him releasing her and, with a final shove, moving away from the bed.

She protests that there is nothing between her and Johnny. Now from her angle, we see him sit on a plush bedstool near the bed, his back to her. She gets up and starts to go to him. In more light we see them now from the side as she comes to him, kneels before him, pleading. No! He wants her to get out! Putting her head on his lap, she says, "Anything you say, anything you want." Tentatively, he pats her head.

In building to the climax of the plot, all the strands are integrated into a nicely wrought web: the good love and the bad love, the jealousy, the betrayals and greed, the mystery of the murders (the latter not really much in doubt). Johnny is caught between the gangster and the law, and between his conflicting selves.

Johnny threatens Charley, and Charley admits that he "traded [him] for someone who could do him more good." But Charley finally admits also he was afraid and had to betray. He saw them kill Blayden because he had gone too far, had become too dangerous. Guido couldn't risk having him around anymore. The girl knew what had happened, so they had to kill her too. But Charley hadn't seen that.

Johnny had not previously told Nancy what he knew. When he does, she's stunned, feels sick, but then wants justice. She urges him to go to the police. But he's back to steel and personal justice, personal justification. He'll make Guido pay for what he's done when the time comes, but first he wants the money he's owed. They argue, and Johnny tells her he knows what he's doing, that he's no fool. "We're going to have everything," he promises. "No, you're no fool," she answers. "You're smart. My sister's been murdered, but Johnny O'Clock's no fool."

Johnny insists he'll get Guido, "in my way, in my time. And I'll get away with it." She shouts at him, and he slaps her. He's immediately sorry, and knows that he wants her. But he *will* go after his money, however crazy she thinks he is.

While not as finely drawn or meaningful a character as Rossen's major protagonists, Johnny does share with them an over-reaching obsessiveness. He can't let go, and is carried away by what he thinks he needs to do — or even what he thinks is right and just.

At the club, Koch and the police are there, and he waits outside with Nancy. Inside, in the room with the safe, as Nelle watches, Guido seems willing to give Johnny the money — as long as he goes away and stays away. But after Johnny takes what he thinks is his share and starts to leave, he passes Nelle near the doorway. Her look triggers Guido's jealousy. Guido takes out his gun and tells Johnny to turn around because he doesn't want to shoot him in the back. Johnny keeps standing with his back to them — the gap between them unbridgeable.

"What do you win if you shoot?"
"My wife. I saw it in her eyes. It's not over, she'll go after you."
"Twenty years down the drain."
"Nothing between us but cash."
"Now a dame."
"My wife, *mine!*"

Johnny turns and starts to retrieve his gun from under his jacket. Guido shoots once; Johnny fires and fires, a close-up on the gun capturing the final fury. Guido is dead and

Johnny wounded. And Nelle wants him to take her with him. He pushes past her and goes out of the room.

Koch has come in to find Johnny. He picks up a packet of money from the floor and sees a blood stain.

Nancy has also come into the club. She finds Johnny in the big gambling room and tells him he needs a doctor.

"Don't need anybody."

"You need me."

"Nobody now. Just me alone."

"You're not alone."

It's the old refrain, but personal this time — a matter of love, not collective action.

Johnny doesn't trust Koch and wants to hold him hostage so he can escape. "All my life this guy's been chasing me." But this time Nancy doesn't plead; she mocks him, and he accepts her truth — and love — and throws down the gun.

One on each side of him, Nelle and Koch help him out the door. *Johnny O'Clock* may be, as Harry Cohn thought, just a nicely done "programmer," but that's a lovely last shot as we watch them go out from the shadows of the casino into the street. Johnny is not caught between them, he is seen *helped* between them. Almost two decades later, after many years of both troubles and fulfillment, Rossen, in the last shot of his career, will have Vincent come up to the door of the mental hospital and, seen between the psychiatrist and the social worker, say, "Help me."

During these same earlier, busy years, Rossen worked on two films over which he did not have final control (or much final impact). At the request of Hal Wallis, he did a rewrite on *Desert Fury*, which was much re-hashed afterwards. *Desert Fury* is a good example of the studio system gone awry. Though populated by casino owners, gamblers, racketeers, and crooked cops, and replete with multiple betrayals, it is more rampant melodrama than true crime film. It was originally intended as a major release (it has a big-name cast) but after many delays the production continued to go through many stages of disagreements and disputes, long after Rossen's participation ended. It ended up at a much-reduced (and much plot-damaged) 96 minutes. It was not released until September 25, 1947, two months before the release of *Body and Soul*.

A similar pattern of delays, disputes and drastic editing befell *The Undercover Man*. To jump ahead in our chronology: After the completion of *Body and Soul* and its opening to positive reviews and strong business, Rossen went back to Columbia Pictures to work as a producer on *The Undercover Man*—reestablishing his important connection to Harry Cohn. Cohn wanted to capitalize on the current publicity given Internal Revenue agents in helping the FBI obtain convictions of gangsters. He had bought an article by Frank J. Wilson entitled "Undercover Man: He Trapped Capone," and Cohn wanted to update the story into the forties. Cohn was not satisfied with its development; he removed the original producer, and late in 1947 he asked Rossen to step in and act as producer for the first time.[3] Indicative of the unsettled nature of the period's investigative politics, Rossen's inclusion in the original 19 for the first hearings did not deter the fiercely independent Cohn. Other studio heads and producers were already being more cautious — or zealous. Rossen established Robert Rossen Productions, and the job served as good practice for his subsequent films. He was also able to work again with cinematographer Burnett Guffey; their collaboration was later to prove valuable in the filming of *All the King's Men*.

Rossen's work was in the early stages of the production — coordinating and giving some unified shape to the efforts of at least three screenwriters.

An anti-racketeer melodrama, *The Undercover Man* was directed by Joseph H. Lewis, who was frustrated by, and resentful of, the constant changes and shifting lines of command. Lewis was a significant stylist in the *noir* mode, both in using expressive, even expressionistic, lighting and camera angles, and in developing bizarre, even excessive, portrayals of the characters. He used iconic L.A. locations as settings, such as Union Station, Angel's Flight, and the Grand Central Market. His work in the genre included *My Name Is Julia Ross, So Dark the Night, A Lady Without Passport, Gun Crazy, The Big Combo,* and *A Lawless Street*. In *The Undercover Man* he could use some of the expressive tones in Guffey's cinematography, but he was mainly caught in untangling the elaborate plot turns and Cohn's insistence on the semi-documentary approach that was also fashionable at the time, as in the successful *The Naked City*.

Although Rossen was credited only as producer on a film already given its basic structure, the elements of the plot-heavy narrative have interesting ties to the central motifs of his films, though with excessive instances and variations. Central are the issues of the corruption of the legal system, and of testifying and its consequences — which was, of course, a nagging, prodding real-life concern at this time. Treasury agents Glenn Ford and James Whitmore need to develop a case of tax evasion as a means of obtaining some kind of conviction for a mob czar, an up-to-date Al Capone–like figure. They find it difficult to find people who will cooperate, and especially testify — who will not remain silent even against a totally evil gangster. People are beaten and killed. Others are afraid. So the agents go underground to penetrate the mob itself and discover not only the dirty depths of the underworld, but the corruption of the police and city officials.

Ford's character wonders if the human cost of it is worth it, but, after some anguishing, decides to go on with the job. He forces the lawyer of the mob boss to testify, threatening him with a jail term for his complicity in the tax evasion scheme. And so the lawyer testifies — and, as an example to others, is murdered for "squealing." It is a situation rife with provocative ironies. But here, mainly carried out by other hands, there are just too many instances piled on. Finally, in the overkill script, Ford must still expose and incriminate several *jurors* who have been bought off by the mob! Though well-meant thematically, it was all too much to begin with, much less when given only 85 truncated minutes of film.

By the time shooting on the film had been completed in April of 1948, Rossen was already preparing to work on *All the King's Men*. But *Undercover Man* was not released until a year later, on April 20, 1949 — at the final stages of the rigorous (though not nearly so harmful) editing of *All the King's Men*. In the midst of the turmoil, Rossen had achieved the kind of control over his work that he had sought, that he had fought for while directing *Body and Soul*.

8

The Battle and the Myth, Personal and Political — *Body and Soul*

Body and Soul was completed in April of 1947 and released in November of 1947 — before Robert Rossen's work as producer on *Undercover Man*. It marked a significant turning point in his career; it is at the core of his deepest interests, the kind of moral — and, by implication, political — conflicts that were central to both his life and films. He did not write the original screenplay, but the work he did on it — including important and controversial revisions of the screenplay — make it the first in the sequence of major films in the canon of his work (counter to much that has been promulgated about the film, its production, and its "authorship"). It was also, however, the film that was most directly involved with, and affected by, his membership in the Communist Party. In the making of *Body and Soul*, the battle for the control over his work was not with studio moguls but with fellow members of the Party. These were conflicts between Rossen (whose own inner qualms about the Party had not been settled by his sojourn in New York) and John Garfield, Bob Roberts, and Abraham Polonsky. The consequences of this battle continued to reverberate for decades, even more than half a century afterwards, long after Rossen had died.

Garfield had formed a business partnership with Bob Roberts, who was more directly involved with the Hollywood CP than Garfield ever was. By the start of 1947 their company, Roberts Productions, had made a deal to affiliate with a new, Left-oriented financing and releasing company, Enterprise Pictures. And what better way to start, Garfield thought, than a boxing film. Several possibilities fell through, including a biographical film about the Jewish boxer Barney Ross.

Ever since Garfield had been denied the chance to play the lead in the Group Theater's production of Clifford Odets' proletarian boxing play *Golden Boy* in 1937, he had wanted to act in a picture about a boxer up from the slums who is corrupted by the lure of money and success — not that far off, he knew, from the trajectory of his own life. In the original Group Theater production, Luther Adler, who was active in the Communist inner circle within the Group, had been given the part. Garfield's frustration was then compounded by the fact that the smooth, conventionally handsome William Holden got the part in the 1939 screen version. In *Golden Boy* Odets has Joe Bonaparte give up the violin to become a boxer, as he is corrupted to betray art, love and family. Odets later acknowledged that he had been influenced by an Edna Ferber short story, "Humoresque," about a ruthless up-from-the-streets violinist. So in the forties, in the movie *Humoresque*, Odets went back to the original version of the short story, and Garfield was pleased to play the character in his original form as a violinist (but with the rough vigor of a boxer). And then he got to play the boxer he hadn't been able to play in *Golden Boy* when they made *Body and Soul*. Finally, in 1951, at thirty-nine, Garfield did get to play Joe Bonaparte for seven weeks in a Broadway revival of *Golden Boy*. It was his final performance before the frantic, harried last days of his life in the spring of 1952.

The script that was developed by Abraham Polonsky was an echo of Odets' play, reshaped for Garfield's screen persona (as that had basically been shaped in his movies with Rossen). Charley Davis betrays the love and life of his artist wife Peg and his family, and chooses the same devil's (capitalist's) trove that Joe Bonaparte did.

At this early point in his Hollywood career, Polonsky had seen only one of his scripts reach the production stage, and that had been so changed by others that he himself hardly recognized it. As it turned out, *Golden Earrings*, an exotic costume romance with Marlene Dietrich, was not released until *after Body and Soul*. But Polonsky was already an active force in the Hollywood branch of the Communist Party. As the FBI was told in 1951, "Polonsky was one of the real CP leaders in Hollywood.... From that time [his arrival], Polonsky was always a leader in the CP and one of the few men who could successfully challenge the views of John Howard Lawson on any particular issue."[1]

Even at the start of his career he believed only in *his* version of the script for *Body and Soul*, every word of it — and his ideological thematic construct for it. His prominence and active role in the Party, coupled with his own forceful assertion of his righteousness, whether political or artistic, gave him more power on the set, more "clout," than his neophyte screenwriting career would normally have warranted. Garfield, as was his wont, was in awe of Polonsky's erudite Marxist and aesthetic pontificating, and his Party prominence. Anxious, as well, over his first independent production, Garfield was torn between his newly discovered heroic genius and his old mentor Rossen. When Polonsky consistently and insistently asserted his demands, Garfield thus vacillated, often deferring to Polonsky and to Roberts. Polonsky acted out the domineering role he was accustomed to playing within the Party, especially since he was opposing the reputedly renegade Rossen. Shortly after the release of *Body and Soul*, for one example, he led the fight to get the Screen Writers Guild to support the Hollywood Ten. When it was defeated, he told screenwriter Stanley Roberts that he would continue the fight, even if it wrecked the SWG. "If need be, we will wreck twenty to achieve what we want."[2]

Influential for the dogma regarding Polonsky's iconic stature are the writings by Paul Buhle, a New Left activist and ideologue, and the most prolific hagiographer of the Hollywood Left and their works. A central aspect of Buhle's approach to Polonsky's work is his repeated — and exaggerated — definition of Polonsky's central role in the development of film noir. In this context, two of Polonsky's scripts — for *Body and Soul* and *Force of Evil* — can be placed within the circle of *film noir*. But the two films are really only on the periphery of the collage of tone, style and theme that in any meaningful sense is *film noir*. In one central aspect of the two films (and most others written by Polonsky), the central character grows in consciousness, in progressive social clarity, and lives to face and/or fight another day; whereas in the basic trajectory of *noir* narrative he cannot escape his defeat and doom. The two films are certainly not in the center of the style or movement; moreover, they are by no means the most significant or influential examples of it. In fact, the closest the two Polonsky scripts come to noir substance and tenor is the visual imagery that Rossen "imposed" on the original script. There is very little resemblance to the look or attitude of a true *noir* in the banal imagery of *Force of Evil*. As critic and historian Raymond Durgnant commented about the film and Polonsky's typical method, "Further, instead of breaking down complexity into images, Joe explains his thoughts (and nearly everyone else's), Doris hers, Leo and Leo's wife theirs, and so on, in conversation."[3]

Nevertheless, on the limited basis of these two films — and, importantly, with the total absence of Robert Rossen from the discussion — Buhle places Polonsky in the forefront, seemingly making him the leader of the movement, noting "the *noir* master's imprint on the crime film and the *noir* mood." Extending the claim in *Blacklisted*, he labels *Force of Evil* part of the deservedly most famous films of the Hollywood left, and along with Polonsky's two scripted pre-blacklisted films, *Body and Soul* and *I Can Get It for You Wholesale*, part of the classic trilogy of *Noir's Marxist master*"[4] [emphasis added].

Indicative of the spread of these unexamined assumptions and appropriated phraseology in the mass media, the *New York Times* obituary for Polonsky picked up on and further promulgated the phrase, "an early master of Hollywood *film noir*." Again following Buhle, the *Times* went on to refer to *Body and Soul* as Polonsky's film.[5]

The acerbic critic John Simon sees this kind of distortion of fact and value as part of a broader pattern: "It took blacklisting to make them important ... [thus] Polonsky became an auteur, so that his current return to film is being celebrated as if it were a major artistic, even historic event. But *Willie Boy* [*Tell Them Willie Boy Is Here*], despite its minor virtues, remains a mediocre film, trying hard to imbue its clipped statements and portentous gesture with existential and symbolic significance, and not succeeding very well."[6]

In the campaign of the Left, *Body and Soul* becomes totally a creation of Polonsky. In *Radical Hollywood*, for one example, it is stated that "Abraham Polonsky's 1940s films *Body and Soul* (1947) and *Force of Evil* (1948) quite simply embody the highest achievement of the American Left in cinema before the onset of repression." In Buhle's entry on *Body and Soul* in the encyclopedic *Blacklisted*, he begins, "One of Polonsky's two master works of this period...." In the subsequent paragraphs he does not even mention Rossen.[7]

And Polonsky, in his interview in *Tender Comrades*, says, "*Body and Soul* turned out to be a tremendous success. My script is the fundamental reason it turned out the way it did, although it was a wonderful job James Wong Howe did."[8]

The basis of the adversarial fervor in Polonsky's conduct during the production and remembrance of the conflicts over the film is reflected in the grandiose party-line ideology that he attached to the alleged meaning of his version of *Body and Soul*, as he repeated in several books and interviews. He saw the film as a fable (his aesthetic terminology suggesting the way of capturing a pattern of life beyond an individual instance), but "not a fable about Charley Davis; it is a fable of the working class." And it would be "crazy" to kill off "the proletariat." For in his grandiose conception of the theme, Charley "discovers a moral and (in the broader sense) political need to rejoin the working class, regardless of the personal price." And so, as Buhle (with characteristic political coloring) paraphrases Polonsky's concept to an even more bloated and dated degree of ideological bombast, what Polonsky had in mind for the ending was "a knockout blow for the working class's enemies, with Garfield the proletariat's symbolic representative, during the last moment when a sweeping labor victory over postwar capitalism could still be imagined."[9] It was the "last moment," apparently, because of the fascistic hardening of the capitalist cold war and the injustice of Walter Reuther starting to ban the Communist-led unions and their leaders from the C.I.O. And all this with Charley, the rich, immoral prize fighter, as a representative and symbol of the pure labor movement and a valid dramatic vehicle for this apocalyptic working class fancy!

The result was a constant battle between Rossen, the experienced screenwriter who had worked with diverse directors and directed a film himself, and Polonsky, with one produced script to his credit, over Rossen's actions to modify and adapt the script in line with his expertise and his vision *as director*. In *Tender Comrades*, Polonsky said, "No one co-directs with Robert Rossen. You keep trying to prevent him from spoiling the picture, and writers hardly ever win those fights. We [*sic*] made Rossen promise that he wouldn't change a line on the screenplay, and then we found out he was handing out pages on the set, anyway. That was his character."

In *Radical Hollywood*, Buhle generalizes from a statement by one person, Polonsky, to the all-encompassing term "co-workers": "Rossen struck *coworkers* [emphasis added] as personally competitive almost to the point of mania."[10]

It was a conflict that produced tension in Rossen's relationship with Garfield (who was driven, by then, by the tensions and contradictions in his own life). And with greater significance, it produced one of the most influential and oft-repeated myths within the ethos of untarnished heroes and tainted betrayers of the era. In this mythic formula, the value and importance of Polonsky's limited work and career is exaggerated — and *Body and Soul* spoken of as *his* film; while the vilification about Rossen over the film has been filtered through academic and critical circles, contributing to the spread of the conventional wisdom not only about Rossen's career but also about his character.

An exchange between Buhle and Polonsky:

BUHLE: "People say ... that when Rossen didn't make the cut as one of the Ten he was outraged. He thought that he was the great Hollywood Communist artist.
POLONSKY: You wouldn't want to be on a desert island with Rossen, because if the two of you didn't have any food, he might want to have you for lunch tomorrow.
    He was talented like Elia Kazan was talented, but like Kazan he also had a rotten character. In the end they both became stool pigeons. I figured all along that Rossen couldn't be trusted, but no one asked me.[11]

There was, as it did turn out, an impartial observer of the course of events in the making of the film. Robert Aldrich, who went on to become one of the important directors of the postwar era, was there on the set during the entire shooting schedule. He has quite a different version of the story — of who actually did the destructive interfering.

At the time, Aldrich was working for Enterprise in several capacities, and on *Body and Soul* was the production manager and assistant director. He had two major points of emphasis in his impressions of what happened during the production. In later interviews and reminiscences he iterated and reiterated that he had "reservations concerning *Polonsky's* [emphasis added] interference on the set."[12] As he emphasized on another occasion, Aldrich felt that it was Polonsky's actions that were extreme and not productive: "Abraham Polonsky, although he'd written a marvelous script, really interfered too much."[13]

In addition, in his emphasis on Rossen's effective work on the film, Aldrich remembered that Rossen and the cinematographer James Wong Howe hit it off from the start. Rossen, he recalled, had strong ideas about what he wanted. He and Howe worked out each scene meticulously, adjusting dialogue, movements, and patterns in relation to camera angles, movements, and techniques. He encouraged Howe to try, again and again if necessary, whatever he could to get the visual effects that Rossen wanted. Their concern for every detail and their experiments did push the film over budget, which caused Aldrich some trouble; but he felt that the results of Rossen's experimenting "worked beautifully" and produced the only financial success Enterprise had: "It had one hit and nine disasters. The hit was *Body and Soul*."[14]

Rossen's close work with Howe was one way of carrying his basic realization as a director: "When I myself controlled my productions, I made my best films."[15]

Despite these conflicts, it is important and striking to note that there were significant similarities in both Rossen and Polonsky's concepts and approach to the film. Both were influenced by the same left-wing theater backgrounds. Polonsky's original screenplay embodied the structures, aims and motifs — including the ideologically prominent sense of betrayal driven by capitalist greed — of the social and protest drama of the thirties that had also shaped Rossen's dramas to this point. Furthermore, the screenplay used the themes and iconography, the character patterns and interactions, that had already been dramatized in some of Rossen's scripts throughout the thirties and forties. The kind of poetry of the streets that both were fond of and good at reproducing, and the concrete details of the material, were derived from the environment in which Rossen, Polonsky and Garfield had grown up — as well as in the plays that Clifford Odets had created out of his experiences in this same environment.

Charley Davis (Garfield) has grown up in a poor neighborhood on the east side of New York, a neighborhood where Jews mixed with other ethnic and religious groups, and learned the customs and mores — just and unjust, useful and destructive — of America. They all knew the boxing clubs, the pool halls, the candy stores — like the one Charley's parents own — which became the social centers of the neighborhood for youngsters and often the breeding ground for recruits for gambling and other rackets.

Rossen later said about directing Garfield in the film:

> I knew Garfield ten — no, more than that — fifteen years before. We used to meet on the Intervale Avenue Subway station, and I knew him as an actor. I didn't have to direct him in certain parts of the film. All I had to say was yes or no, because he totally understood it....
> I have generally worked with actors whose own personality, joined to that of my character, could give a good result. But I chose those actors often in a purely instinctive way, because of what one can read in their eyes — which the audience will read as I do, even if it is not really there. I think John Garfield was excellent in *Body and Soul*. He is of course an experienced actor, but he was better there than anywhere else. That is because the setting in which he was to play was not unknown to him. It was a part of New York, a life, that he knew and that he understood without even thinking about it. It was no trouble, he found it from within himself without seeking. When a take had to be redone, he knew why quite as well as I. It was a question of understanding.[16]

Rossen also felt that Garfield understood the importance of making changes, of responding to the moment, and the setting — of spontaneity — while filming a script. He emphasized this in commenting on efficient studio directors like Sidney Lumet:

> Lumet will always do a good picture, but never a great one. He lacks the one thing: spontaneity. Everything is too laid out, too well planned.... Anybody who likes to work in studios

likes to work in them because you cannot improvise.... When you ... go on location in a real setting everything around you leads you into another idea. You can go down looking for this and you find that. You've got to have the guts to have this spontaneous quality of getting it right away, changing it when you have to.[17]

Rossen had learned from, and admired, the approach of Lewis Milestone. Like all the major directors that Rossen admired, director Milestone left his personal imprint visually and dramatically on his films — in contrast to the efficient but impersonal studio directors whom Rossen had worked with earlier in the thirties. Milestone's method was to work closely, and demandingly, with writers, making daily changes in response to the palpable realities of day to day shooting.

Spontaneous responding to the immediacy of a scene or sequence, a setting or environment, during production was one of the ways in which Rossen's direction (and script modifications, though he received no screen credit) turned Polonsky's verbally oriented and directly didactic script into a more richly human, visually realized drama. The modulations in the intensity of scenes; the vibrant, evocative images; and the rhythms of the pace represent a development and deepening of the central narrative patterns of Rossen's earlier films — especially those with Garfield. The absolutist terms of the economic allegory are re-shaped during the production to express his continuing concerns about people, not merely ideology. The emotional impact, the vital core of energy, however misplaced, is captured so palpably in the raw, believable power of the quintessential performance by Garfield, and, as well, in the strength and dignity, and the deep well of love and care underneath, in the performance of Anne Revere as Ma. Within the visual imagery and rhythms, the physical and emotional choreography of the intense yet precisely shaped scenes of confrontation, the actors' fulfillment of the characters emerges beyond the script's motifs and icons of the drama of the Left. The characters become more fully felt and realized *people,* who in turn can be understood as meaningful figures in the carpet of social and moral themes beyond any ideological (or even sport film) formulas.

While *Body and Soul* received the plaudits of the press and has been popular ever since, neither its central themes nor its relationship to the rest of Rossen's work have been fully recognized. Communist critic Joseph North, however, did propose that a Role of Honor be established, and that Robert Rossen should be placed on it for *Body and Soul* and *They Won't Forget.* In *The New Yorker,* John McCarten complained that it "takes an awfully long time to get to its fight scenes." *Newsweek* found it only "an outstanding prizefight picture." In the *New York Times,* Bosley Crowther did praise its power and the sense of humanity that it achieved, but he still saw it as a fight film: "Robert Rossen has directed it with such an honest regard for human feelings and with such a searching and seeing camera, that any possible resemblance to other fight yarns, living or dead, may be gratefully allowed.... [It] hits the all-time high in throat-catching fight films." *Time* seemed to sense what was going on: "Its stout socially conscious sentiments [have been] turned into an universal moral" (though the reviewer failed to explain either the sentiments or the moral). James Agee praised its "quick satirical observation, a sense of meanness to match the meanness of the worlds they are showing, a correct assumption of cynical knowledge in the audience which relieves them of the now almost universal practice of drawing diagrams for the retarded." He found it "almost continuously interesting and exhilarating while I watched it." However, Agee also emphasized that the *script* itself, "which gets very bitter and discreetly leftist about commercialism in prizefighting, is really nothing much, I suppose, when you get right down to it." But even Agee, the most notable critic of his time, did not watch it fully and openly enough to really "get right down to it," failing to note the film's dramatization and visualization of the themes that become so central in Rossen's films—power and success, needs and motives, betrayals and redemption.

The evil side of the narrative equation in *Body and Soul* is the basic gangster-gambler, Roberts, in the tradition of the Left theater of the thirties, as capitalist corrupter and violator. He is not developed much beyond the symbolic stereotype except for having a smoother, slicker—and non-ethnic—ambiance than in the thirties plays and movies. Besides the stress on his complete dedication to making money, there are some hints of the underlying need for power and domination that is the driving force in Rossen's more developed versions of this character (compare, for example, Bert Gordon in *The Hustler* or the gangster-like Willie Stark in *All the King's Men*).

But the central narrative thrust is the moral testing of the young man from the slums with the characteristic *élan* of the protagonists of Rossen's films and a skill, an art, a gift (boxing) that he betrays, as he betrays the better part of himself and those around him. He has, Peg tells him, the natural "fearful symmetry" of the powerful tiger in William Blake's poem "Tiger, Tiger, Burning Bright." We follow his rise from the tight confines of the cigar store of his parents, the family life centered on a plain, cluttered kitchen, to the coldly fashionable expanse of a luxurious apartment, a center for crowded, empty parties and aggressive business deals. The more Charley is surrounded by hangers-on, the more, like so many Rossen protagonists, he is alone.

Charley buys the gambler's values: "I just want to be a success.... You know, every man for himself." But in the business of boxing he encounters the very economic corruption and violation that had originally trapped him. He, too, becomes, in the words of his best friend Shorty, "a money-machine." He lets Roberts own all of him, body and soul. He breaks with his family and with Shorty—whose death he indirectly causes. In the thematic pattern we've seen developing in Rossen's films, Charley turns against true and fulfilling love, faithful and sharing personal relationships. Peg is the too perfect and patient artist, the woman of both beauty and soul. She understands him, but, with firm morality, will not go along with him down this false path. In working with Lili Palmer, Rossen draws out more anger, pain, and resentment in the character than was originally scripted. Charley turns to the unfaithful lure, the fur-draped body, of glamorous Alice, the false prize of economic success, a follower herself of easy money and all it can buy. In his entourage he does keep one connection to decency—the black sparring partner Ben, whose title he had taken and whose eventual death he is also indirectly responsible for.

The circle of betrayal that results is extensive and intricate. It is, however, given a final significant reconfiguration by a final kind of "betrayal" that, ironically, is positive and moral and truly fulfilling. Charley betrays his gift; he betrays Ma and his family; he betrays Shorty; he betrays Peg; and, unknowingly, he betrays Ben (and believes he did). Alice betrays Quinn (and later subtly betrays Charley); Quinn betrays Charley and Shorty; and Quinn betrays Ben. Ben's manager, Arnold, is forced to betray Ben. At the championship fight between Ben and Charley, Roberts betrays Ben, as well as Charley and Arnold. He betrays Shorty. He betrays—uses and manipulates—Charley and even his money all along. At the climax, Roberts betrays Charley even when the "fix" is on. The ironic, positive final turn is taken when Charley "betrays" Roberts, but this time he is really acting for what is right and against what is wrong.

The structure of the film is circular. It begins on the eve of the crucial championship fight. This substantial opening segment is then followed by a flashback to the beginnings and the rise of Charley in the central section of the film. In the third section we are back in the present — the night of the fight. The opening section itself has three sequences and three settings: Charley's crisis of conscience at the training camp and the contrast of the two warring sides of himself; the family kitchen and the moral, loving world of Ma and Peg; and the nightclub and arena, and the greedy, corrupting world of Roberts and Alice.

Unable to sleep, Charley returns to the old neighborhood, to Ma's apartment and Peg and Ma. The elements of the *mise en scène*, the sequence of images, are a notable example of Rossen's best work. The tensions and emotions, the interplay of morals and needs and feelings, in the scene are conveyed not only through dialogue but through decor, camera angles, spatial patterns, gestures, movements, and changing patterns of physical relationships of characters in the shots. It is the kind of emotive and expressive use of visual images that, along with a dynamic pulse — an energy of pace and portrayal — is *not* found in Polonsky's subsequent (and consistently over-praised) film *Force of Evil*.

In the visual patterns of the scene in *Body and Soul*, Ma is standing at the kitchen table in the center of the kitchen, mooring her universe. Past her, we see Charley come in the back door and walk to her. "Hello Ma," he says, and she puts down the cup, the sign of her contained nurturing life, that she has been drying. It misses the table, and the camera cuts to the cup now cracked on the floor. She bends down into the shot to pick it up. Still in the same shot, Charley moves forward and kneels next to her, seen past the slant of the edge of the table. Always the mother, she warns, with implied significance, "Careful, Charley, you'll cut yourself." Their heads are close as they start to rise, and the shot continues as the camera tilts up with them, looking past the horizontal spread of the table top and its checked table cloth. The camera moves in slowly to the two of them as they stand, close to each other; but she turns away and walks out of the shot. A mother's rebuke. He stands alone.

The scene cuts to her turning from the sink and walking back and past him to sit at the table. Cut to her sitting and to him standing past her, behind her. Without looking at him, her back to him, she demands, "What do you want, Charley?"

"Ben died.... Today. I couldn't sleep, Ma. I thought maybe I..."

"Peg's sleeping here, Charley."

There is a room behind the kitchen, the upper half of its wall windowed. Now it is Peg's room. Charley goes into it, touches her nightgown, a hair brush he had given her. Ma stands, hard and disapproving, in the doorway to Peg's room as he says, "I couldn't stand it up there, Ma, after they took Ben away. I couldn't sleep. So I came down. I had to find a place where I could lie down. Well, you know, Ma, you have to find a place.... I didn't mean all those things I said to Peg, you know that." With its repetitions, it is a trademark Polonsky speech. But Rossen does not merely stay on Charley as he speaks (as Polonsky would do with Joe in *Force of Evil*). He breaks it down into a dramatic interchange of images and movements. We first see Charley with Peg's things, past Ma's disapproving back. He then walks to her, toward us. Then, reversed, past his shoulder and profile, we see her face, first turned from him, then facing him, glaring at him. "What's the matter, Ma, don't you want me here?"

When Peg (Lilli Palmer) comes into the kitchen with some groceries, she almost moves to Charley, then goes to her room and slams the door. Through the window-wall we see her throw herself on the bed in the shadows. He rushes into the room after her, and, tightly shot within the room, he lifts her into his arms and kisses her. The camera cuts to viewing them past Ma's profile, her face tight and disapproving, unforgiving. Peg pulls away, drops onto the bed and turns away as she says, "Go away, Charley, go away." Rossen uses only two other words (rather than Polonsky's dialogue) in this beautifully realized sequence in her room. Twice Charley says, "Peg."

Charley leaves and goes directly to Alice, who is singing, without much response or much skill, in a half-empty nightclub; it is the kind of job that Charley, through Roberts, had secured for her. (In *The Roaring Twenties* Eddie had gotten Jean her first job that way, but she went on to develop her own career as a singer.) "C'mon, Alice, let's go," Charley says. "Okay, Champ," she replies.

The scene shifts to the day and night of the fight. In his dressing room, Charley is upset about the death of Ben, the black former champion. Roberts had forced him to fight Charley, even though he had brain damage, and he hadn't told Charley the "fix" was on. "Everybody dies," Roberts tells Charley. "Ben, Shorty, even you." The fix is on, he now tells Charley — he will throw the fight and make a lot of money. Despite all the money he's made already, Charley is still in debt to Roberts. In clever phrases that (possibly too insistently) emphasize the corrupting force of business — and money — Roberts goes on to encourage and intimidate him:

> The books are all balanced. The bets are in. You bet your purse against yourself. You got to be business-like, Charley.
> The numbers are in. You get your money and we're squared away. You know the way the betting is.
> Everything is addition and subtraction, the rest is conversation.

Roberts delivers one final volley as he leaves: "The smart money is against it, and you're smart. You gotta be business-like, Charley, and business men got to keep their agreement."

In the central flashback we go back to Charley's beginnings and then return to the present in the central section of the film. Through "all the years," money, money, money has been the obsessive core of Charley's drive for success — to be the champ and get all that goes with it. But beyond the continual verbal, visual and plot references to money, we are shown Charley's resentment as well, his need to get even, to show them that he can be somebody — not just by winning fights, but by winning his place in the world, defining himself by his money. But the money is never enough; it does not bring him the freedom it promised. In the investment he's made, the more he gains, the more he loses.

Early on he meets the possibilities of love and connection with another — Peg. A young cultured artist, she makes some money by working as a model. She meets Charley when, clad in a bathing suit and a banner, she is Miss Iroquois Democratic Club at a political rally where Charley receives an award for winning his first amateur bout. She's taken by his boyish spunk and openness, and the softer eagerness under the tough-guy surface. When she asks him if he likes fighting, he says, "I just want to be a success." But as Charley begins his forced march to the top, he violates the possibility of love developing between them, thinking he can have it all.

When Pop is killed in the explosion when mobsters throw a bomb into the speakeasy next to the family's candy store, the two sides of Charley are shown in two contrasting scenes — contrasting not only in words, but in the visual images and rhythms, and in the gestures of the performances that capture in concrete correlatives the warring elements within him. In one long-held shot, almost wordless, Charley kneels in half-profile and removes a piece of a wall of the store from his father's chest. Ma comes in and kneels, facing the camera, her hands on Pop's chest, looking down at his face. Charley is at a lower level and looking up at her throughout. She looks at Charley and then down, hands still on Pop's chest. She looks away to the side and back, and starts to cry just a little. She starts to bend closer over Pop, as her hands now clench on his chest, then buries her face on his chest as she cries. Charley now reaches out and rubs her back. "Don't cry, Ma," he says as she lets out a loud sob. "Don't cry."

In the contrasting scene, a social worker has come to the apartment, asking questions of Ma and Charley. The camera cuts between group shots and an accelerating pattern of close-ups of each as Charley, proud and upset, finally says, "We don't want any help!" In close-up, he says to Shorty, who's been present, "Shorty, get me that fight." Charley and Ma cross to the door as the social worker leaves. At the door, in a waist-high two-shot, they exchange volleys: "I want money, you understand?" "No, no." "I want money — money, money." "I forbid, I forbid — it's better to buy a gun and shoot yourself." "You need money to buy a gun." He goes out the door and slams it behind him. The camera stays on Ma — left behind, she fears, for good.

Charley rises through a series of bouts and, over Shorty's protest, signs with Roberts. "Nobody fights the championship for anything unless Roberts gets cut in, you know that. He's the dough, he's real estate, everything. Business." Shorty is not convinced: "They'll be cutting you to pieces, Charley." But Charley retorts, "There'll be more for everybody.... I'll be champ and I'll give the orders. I'll say what and when."

Scenes in Charley's ostentatious new apartment further illustrate Rossen's developing mastery of *mise en scène*. The apartment becomes the physical measure of his changes, full of the symbols of his new life and the false "counters" of his identity. It becomes the battleground for the moral fight over the changes in his life, and the betrayal and defeat of friend, family, lover and love. It is the emblem of his Faustian "deal" with the gambler-devil.

He has just come back from a first triumphant road tour with Roberts in control — after one hard year of moving up in class. Peg kisses his scars. "You get something every time," he says, as we see his face past her in profile. She tries, is still willing, to understand him. "But it's worth it," he continues. "As long as you win. Look [gesturing around the apartment]— lots of money, lots of clothes, everything." Like a kid with a new toy, he shows off a prize possession (a rather blatant symbol, which, however, will be used dramatically later). He presses a button, and a section of the wall with one of her paintings hanging on it revolves, a liquor bar taking its place. He goes out to get something. Shorty warns her to get married soon.

"Have I got a rival?"

"Yeah, money. You know what Charley is, what they're making him. A money machine."

Charley comes back, showing off another overcoat. "How do you like this coat?" he beams.

Before the championship fight with Ben there is one more scene of conflict in

Charley's apartment when all are there. Again the patterns created portray the power — and betrayal — relationships of the people. Roberts has stayed behind the scenes, is meeting Charley for the first time. In the basic shot for this sequence Roberts is standing to the left, with Charley in the middle, Ma to the rear and to the right, Peg also at the right (sitting on the arm of the sofa), and Shorty in the lower right corner sitting on the sofa — the low man in the pecking order. The bar is open behind them — Peg's painting forgotten.

Charley is showing off the apartment; he goes off to the right, to the windows. The scene cuts to the camera facing Shorty, with Peg to his left, as he challenges Roberts, wanting to know what kind of deal he's made. The scene switches back to the basic angle, but closer — and without Shorty. As Charley comes back into the center, Roberts says, pointing down, "Who did you say this was?" "My friend," answers Charley. "For how much?" Roberts says. Shorty rises up into the shot, challenging Roberts and standing in front of Charley, as Roberts' bodyguard comes in behind Roberts. Shorty says, "Ten percent." And Roberts says, "Evening, friend." Shorty starts to go off to the right, stops next to Charley, takes his arm and says, "Remember what I told you about your arm, Charley." Charley answers, "I told you it was my arm, didn't I?" while swatting off his hand. As Shorty passes Ma, the camera cuts to a close-up of her. She looks at Charley, looks *to* Charley to do something. She knows what it means when he doesn't — and is afraid. The scene goes back to the basic shot, and at the right we see Shorty going into another room and Ma turning and following him out — pushed out of Charley's life.

The camera pans to the left, leaving Peg (still at the right) out of the shot as Roberts says, "Well, can we talk?" He tells Charley the new terms: he takes 50 percent. As they talk about who gets what, the camera focuses on them, back and forth, close to each other. Roberts promises the championship fight right away, and Charley agrees. He will have to pay Shorty out of his share, but he doesn't want him to know. As they shake hands, Peg says, "And what about me?" As Charley turns, the new angle places her behind them and between them. "What percent do I get?" she asks.

From another angle, from behind Peg's back, Charley is nearer to her, but Roberts is between them. He sends Charley to get his mother, to say goodnight to her. Charley goes to get her. Ignoring Peg, Roberts crosses to the left, and the camera pans with him to the doorway as Ma comes back in. Roberts moves closer, still to the left; Charley is in the middle, between him and Ma; and then Shorty is back in the doorway to the other room. Roberts tells Ma, "You're a lucky woman to have a boy like Charley. He's going to make a lot of money for everybody. No more candy store for you." Ma, stern-faced, is not impressed. Cut to Peg now leaning against the bar, looking skeptical and troubled. In a closer shot of the other four, Roberts gives Charley an envelope stuffed with money. As he starts to leave, he takes Charley by the arm and the camera pans with them, showing just the two of them as they stop and Roberts "advises" him to concentrate on the fight — and postpone the wedding. Cut to Peg and then back to Roberts, who says, "Goodnight, Charley's girl." He picks up her fur coat and says, "Remember, after mink comes sable." He leaves. The camera cuts to Peg, who abruptly walks out of the shot. The camera then reveals Charley in the middle of the room, holding the envelope of money, with Ma and Shorty seen back by the door of the inner room. Charley takes the money out and looks at it, as we see Peg enter the shot back in the upper right corner and sit at the piano, separated from him.

8. The Battle and the Myth, Personal and Political—Body and Soul

The future is set. The scene shifts to the big workout bag in the sunlight at the outdoor ring. And then arrives an image that foreshadows the lure of glamour and sex, the empty satisfaction that comes with the new territory of money and success. Down past Charley's shoulder, as his hands hit the bag, we see the legs of Alice—soon to be his new prize possession. The camera reveals her, in a tight sweater, looking at him. He knocks the bag from its rope. They talk. She flirts, he buys. Quinn, who is his fight manager, has been watching them. Alice is *his*, he tells her. He's given her everything! He threatens that she'd better back off.

The next scene shows the fight, with Alice screaming, "Kill 'em, Charley, kill 'em!" Charley batters Ben, who finally goes down, sprawling flat on his face. Charley has won, but the victory has raised the stakes—and the cost—of his gamble with success, of the tilting equation between what is won and what is lost.

In Ben's dressing room after the fight Charley comes in, wanting to help with the still unconscious Ben. Roberts tells him everything will be all right and he should go to the victory party. Charley leaves. Ben's manager, Arnold, accuses Roberts of double-crossing them and almost killing Ben. "You promised to have Davis take it easy; maybe he'll die." "Everybody dies," responds Roberts. Shorty is present and tells Roberts he doesn't want to be partners with him, that he and Charley are out. Roberts tells Shorty that he's no partner and has only been receiving handouts from Charley. Roberts leaves, saying, "Send me the hospital bill."

At the victory celebration Shorty won't join the hilarity. Even though Roberts is there, he finally tells Charley and Peg what he's heard. He tells Charley that for people like Roberts, Charley is "not just a kid who can fight, he's money, and people want money so bad they make it stink and they make you stink." Shorty rushes outside. Roberts nods, and his goon follows. Peg rushes after them, but she is too late. She has to watch as the goon catches Shorty, pushes him down some steps toward a basement, and (rather improbably) beats him up. Charley comes out and, fists swinging toward the camera, vents his anger (and in some way his own guilt and self-hate), pounding relentlessly on the goon, again and again, until he's pulled away. In the confusion, Shorty, dazed and dizzy, wanders into the street and is hit by a speeding taxi and killed.

In a contrasting, quietly modulated, tenderly sad and humanly doomed scene at the steps leading up to Peg's building, Peg tells Charley she can't go on. "You've got to get out." Under a light but surrounded by shadows, he is in profile, looking up at her standing above him on the stairs. "What can I do—go back to the candy store? It was an accident." "Only the dying," she says. "Nothing else. It was all inevitable. You must quit." She sits next to him, and he promises he'll take care of Ben. "We'll do fine, I'll make the money." She quietly, almost tearfully, shakes her head. "I can't start again," he says, "from what, with what?" The camera cuts to a close-up of her: "It's nothing to argue, Charley. I can't live this way." He pleads, but she insists, "I can't marry you. That'll mean marrying him." In a wider shot, the camera stays on Charley as she gets up and goes up the stairs and into the building. A close-up of his face, torn but stubborn, growing resolute, shows Charley start to get up, and the shot blurs into a dissolve.

Instantly we are hit with a barrage of images, a montage (similar to those in the earlier Rossen films) of the headlong momentum of the elements of the life and self that Charley has chosen, that he—being who he is and his life what it is—believed he *had* to choose. Years race by, out of control. The momentum of the montage not only condenses the years and the hectic quality of Charley's life, it conveys the treadmill he's on — or the unstoppable whirling merry-go-round — as he's swept along, out of control, by what he thought he wanted. There is a desperation to it, an emptiness (a Marxist alienation).

The final betrayal of himself, his authentic self, takes place in a dressing room at the gym. Roberts collects his "markers" and makes him pay for all he has squandered — money, time, life — and all he *owes*. As Roberts says, "The dough rolling in, the dough rolling out." So he *will* fight the tough challenger Marlowe and he *will* throw the fight. "Fifteen rounds to a decision." Charley protests that he won't "take a dive." Quinn tells him, "A fact's a fact, Charley. You need the money." Roberts gives Charley sixty grand to bet against himself. At two to one.

In an ironic celebration of the signing of the big bout, there is a wild, disjointed scene of a drunken party at Charley's apartment. The party scene captures, primarily with visual images, the corruption of Charley, the losses his victories have won. The room is mobbed. In the foreground a woman is lifted up, hugged, and starts dancing on a table. Men kneel, playing craps. Charley is alone on the dark terrace. Inside, a drunk weaves through the crowd, goes up to the bar, and presses the button. The bar revolves and Peg's painting, a rather rueful self-portrait, swings out. The drunk is assessing it when Charley pushes through the crowd, pushes him down, and revolves the painting back out of sight, out of this mess. He goes to punch the drunk, but is stopped and takes a drink instead. The morning after, the room is a shambles. The camera pans over glasses and garbage strewn about, chairs tipped over, a drunk asleep on a sofa, and pictures lop-sided on the wall. As the camera pans, Charley walks in at the rear and surveys the dregs of his life. In the left foreground a drunk is asleep in a chair, Peg's painting leaning against his chest. Charley turns off a table lamp, walks forward, and thinks of his money. Cut to a bust shot as he finds the wad, takes it out, looks at it, and puts it back. Cut back to the basic shot as he walks forward again, and sees the portrait. He takes it, stares at it, swings and knocks a glass off of a table, and walks out with the painting.

Charley goes to Peg. There is a scene of muted tenderness, a quiet sense of slowly, grudgingly, fearfully and then openly letting out feelings that have been blocked for a long time, of trying to return to what they had. (The rhythm and tone of the editing here make a meaningful contrast to the editing at the end of the next big scene.) He can finally tell her that what he wants is her. "Here I am Charley," she says. He's unsure of himself, exposed: "Peg, I'm scared, so low down. I had to see, I wondered, I had to find out once and for all, I had to know. And we won't be broke. I got sixty grand — and more to come..." She stops him. "Don't tell me what you can buy, you've got nothing to buy." She just wants him to be what he was, wants it to be the way it was. She's excited now and gives herself over to giddy words of hope. Then she turns pensive: "Do you know what it's like to love and be alone?" They kiss. He needs rest and sleeps at last. When he wakes, she's left a note. She has taken the money and gone to Ma's.

It will not be that easy; the battle must still be fought. Recognitions are not that easily maintained, the way out to that new direction not that easy to find or to take. In a beautifully orchestrated scene, one of the finest in the film, the adroit and emotional patterning of visual images, the gestures and movements of performance, and the relationship to meaningful setting keep the scene dramatic and human, keep the significant dialogue from being too overt, operatic, or didactic.

The scene is a significant example of Rossen's instinctive combining of the encompassing patterns of classical *mise en scène*—in Bazin's terms, to "transfer to the screen the continuum of reality without chopping the world up into little fragments"—with the forceful editing of a sequence of shots as found in the hard-hitting Warners style (and as was later central in the revival of Soviet montage-oriented style in the work and theory of Jean-Luc Godard).[18] In this way he sought to maintain in his own work the integrity of the scene and its continuity he admired in the films of Jean Renoir, conscious of the value of allowing the life to be seen and experienced, and yet to express his own temperament of dramatic intensity with more accelerated editing, especially as scenes reach their climax.

The scene begins with joy and domestic love at the stove in the bright kitchen of Ma's apartment. Peg is helping Ma cook breakfast, Charley's breakfast. Ma's face is bright in the bright kitchen, smiling for what may be the first time in the movie. She kisses Peg on the cheek. The camera cuts to a shot facing Charley as he finishes shaving in the room off of the kitchen. Peg comes in to give him a taste. In a two-shot, side by side, they are playful. Peg tells him Ma is in love—with *them*. But Charley is still thinking, he wants the money—to bet. No, she says, still playful, if you lose the fight we lose the money too. She turns as she hears someone come into the kitchen and doesn't see the look on Charley's face that we get to see—troubled, torn, trapped.

The rest of the scene is played out in a series of shots at the round dining table—the secure, stable center of the kitchen (itself the center and mooring of family and love). Shimon, from the market, has brought the groceries. In an establishing shot, he comes forward, past the table, as Charley comes in at the rear and Peg follows. Shimon crosses back and gives a bag to Ma. They talk about the excitement in the neighborhood about Charley's fight—his *last* fight, Ma, now sitting at the table, is so happy to say. Shimon gives her a taste of some grapes. Peg is behind them at the stove. All is well, as it has always been. But we see them from the side past Charley. In the reverse shot, he puts on a good face as they toast his last fight. Shimon is leaving, telling them everyone in the neighborhood is betting on Charley. In the foreground Ma says, "People shouldn't bet." Cut to Shimon, with Peg, at the door: "No, Mrs. Davis, it isn't the money. It's a way of showing we are proud." A close-up of Charley shows him looking inward, isolated.

Knowing what they don't know, and not knowing how to tell them, he can't stand still. We watch him walk around the table and pass them as Peg sits next to Ma. Like a tiger prowling, burning but not bright, he walks to the left foreground, isolated, the table now coming between him and them—*all* of it coming between him and them. "Tell 'em not to bet on me," he says. Ma says it's like Shimon said, it's to honor him. They're eating grapes as he is tormented. Peg takes it playfully and kids him about how she told him betting was no good. Now he agrees.

In reverse angle, we see him from behind them, between them, caught between them but still separated from them by the kitchen table. He can't hold it in anymore. "I'm all mobbed up, tied hand and foot, down to my last buck. Do you think I want to end up like Ben? Punchy, with a blood clot on my brain waiting to die any day—or with a bullet in my back in some alley?" The scene cuts to Ma in close-up and holds on her through his answer to her question "What do you mean bullet?" "Don't you understand, the fight's fixed!" "Fixed, what does it mean, fixed?" The camera moves to Charley, swallowing, looking down, and holds on him through the next interchange: "It means ... I'm throwing the fight." He tries to justify it: "It's all arranged, it's a racket anyway. That's why I want to bet the sixty grand. You get it, Peg, don't you?" She answers, "I get it."

But they *don't* get it. The camera focuses on them, shifts back to him as he says, quiet and bitter, "Well, what do you want me to do?" Staring hard at them, he demands, "What are you looking at?" With the camera back on Peg and Ma, his mother says, sadly, "Then you don't understand what Shimon said." Charley explodes, not only justifying now, but hurt, attacking, resenting their righteousness. Nobody ever looks out for him! The camera again looks past them to him, standing between them, as if they are judging him, as he thinks they are, as indeed they are:

> You're all so high and mighty. You wouldn't ever have that dirty candy store if it wasn't for me. You wouldn't have a dime, the clothes on your back. It's my money, isn't it? You were in such a big hurry to slap it in the bank.... I take the beatings, and you take the dough. Like all the rest of them!

In close-up, Peg doesn't answer. Cut to Charley: "Give me back the sixty grand!" The camera then focuses on Peg and Ma as Peg gets up, then switches to a medium shot past the back of Charley's head as she comes closer, then reveals her face in close-up, furious. Her speech, which could have seemed operatic, is made dramatic and physical, palpable in their shared pain as the words interact with her slapping him and with the dynamics of strongly edited cuts back and forth to each of them, past the other's head. The intensity of emotions and their release at its peak in the pattern of close-ups is beyond all of her usual poise and restraint. "I'm like the rest of them? So you want your money back? Well, take it back..." Slap, forehand, backhand. Cut. Slaps. Cut. Slaps. Cut. Slaps. Cut. Cut. "...and everything else you've given me. Here, what everybody gives you. The long years of happiness. The promises broken, the lonely nights..." The last edit reveals his face, sad and defeated, lost, as she pulls back and leaves the shot, and we hear her begin to sob.

The flashback concludes with the training at the camp and the death of Ben, who Charley has had working for him. With more and more pressure on his brain, Ben has been losing control. Up in the ring he is railing against Roberts, shadow boxing. He trips and hits his head when he falls.

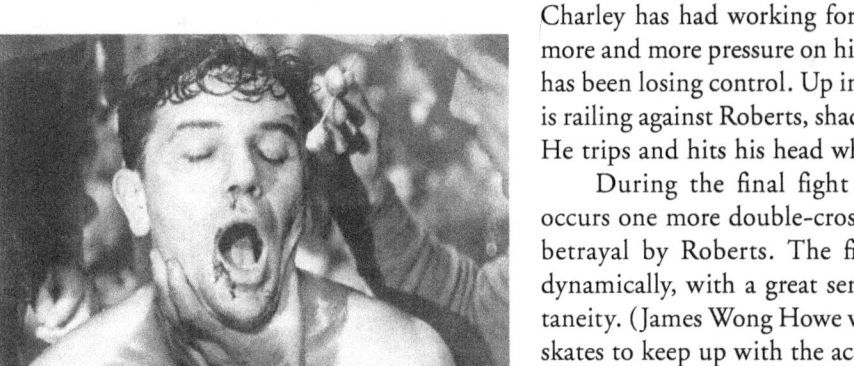

Body and Soul (1947), Enterprise–United Artists. Charley Davis (John Garfield) is battered and betrayed in the championship bout that has been "fixed" for him to lose — before he rebels and goes on to win (collection of the Margaret Herrick Library).

During the final fight itself there occurs one more double-cross, one more betrayal by Roberts. The fight is shot dynamically, with a great sense of spontaneity. (James Wong Howe was on roller skates to keep up with the action, shooting with an eyemo, a hand-held newsreel camera.) There's a lot of holding on and sparring through twelve rounds. The fix is on: fifteen rounds to a decision. But then Quinn, in Charley's corner, gets the nod from Roberts and nods to Marlowe. Knock him out; it's better for business — just as they had done with Ben. In round thirteen Marlowe pounds Charley brutally, knocking him down three times. He's half-carried to his corner. "You sold me out, you rat," he manages to tell Quinn. "Sold out like Ben." In round fourteen he holds on, is knocked down again, holds himself up on the ropes, but then begins to hit Marlowe, and hits him some more. Between rounds, he hisses, "I'm gonna kill 'em." The auditorium is hushed at the start of round fifteen as he stalks Marlowe, who is clearly confused and worried. After several brutal exchanges, Charley pounds away at Marlowe, at all of them. The referee has to stop him as Marlowe sags to the floor.

As Charley is coming down the aisle toward us, victorious, Roberts confronts him. "What makes you think you can get away with this?"

"What are you gonna do, kill me?" Charley retorts. And with a bitter smile, this time *he* says, "Everybody dies!"

That last turn of the film's betrayals — Charley's assertion of independence and his victory — carries a prophetic irony for the political and moral controversies that were to follow. The significant ironic foreshadowing is certainly not something Polonsky would have intended. For what is seen from Roberts' point of view as a double-cross, a betrayal, is obviously from Charley's point of view — and ours — a positive moral act. He is no longer remaining "silent" in the face of oppressive, violating, and consistently betraying evil, capitalist or not. He is standing up to it. With his fists and his courage, he can be seen as finding a kind of redemption in testifying, in his way, against what he knows is wrong, for what he thinks is right — even if he can't exactly define it.

A month after the film was completed, the House Un-American Activities Committee held closed hearings in Hollywood. By the time of the picture's release in November 1947, the first full hearings of HUAC had been held in Washington. The hearings did not affect the distribution and commercial success of the film. However, testifying or not — and all of the complexities, the paradoxes of its morality, of what constitutes betrayal — had taken center stage in the lives of many in Hollywood. These paradoxes would remain a painful moral issue and wound for some until their deaths — and even for long after.

9

Conflicts and Consequences — The First Hearings, 1947

The actual arrival of the subpoenas for the hearings of the House Un-American Activities Committee was a seismic shock but, like the impact of a hurricane that you knew was inevitably on its way, not a surprise. Nineteen were issued, counting the oddity of one for the visiting German playwright Bertold Brecht, and including one for Robert Rossen. Many had thought there would be more. As it turned out, the Committee finally scheduled only ten (plus Brecht), though, in solidarity, all nineteen did go to Washington. The shock at first produced a vibrant solidarity among the liberals, the Left, the Communists in Hollywood — replete with the usual ritual of cause parties, meetings, conferences, rallies, press releases, media appearances, and a well-publicized caravan to Washington, D.C. The harmony, almost a fighting euphoria, soon turned to dissonance.

During the hearings the performances and statements of the ten Hollywood people who refused to testify (often with great flourishes) were vociferously disruptive and combative. They were on the attack — against politics in America and against the House Un-American Activities Committee — while protesting that they and American ideals were being attacked. Their individual testimonies (and subsequent campaigns of protest), however, had a striking uniformity in addressing a consistent pattern of themes.

It was, indeed, an organized strategy, devised and developed and refined in what was practically a screenplay for the performances of the Ten at the hearings — right down to dress rehearsals at the Shoreham Hotel in Washington. The architects of the plan were Ben Margolis and Charles Katz, both of whom had previously (and subsequently) participated in many cases and campaigns for the Party and Party members. Katz commented after the hearings that they agreed from the start that "we wanted to destroy the committee, and it was an objective that seemed realistic at the time." Margolis discussed this real goal, the Party's goal, and the basis of his strategy in a letter to Robert Kenney: "We shall undoubtedly receive many setbacks. Only by proper utilization of each stage of the proceedings, and of setbacks themselves, can a case like ours achieve the necessary public support.... Then the public can understand what the fight is about.... The presentation of these issues will advance our objectives even though the court rules against us." These "objectives" were the point, not the best defense for the witnesses. For the "stages" of *their* losses, the witnesses' losses, can be utilized to advance the Party's objectives, its positions and policies, in the eyes of the public. In a speech at the Civil Rights Congress celebration of the Nineteen, Margolis defined the purposes of the strategy further: "What the Supreme Court does depends to a large extent on the political climate of the country." Their job was to expose HUAC as an "enemy of the people" to produce the proper climate. As Ted Morgan cogently commented on the result in *Reds*, "Margolis turned the hearings into a show trial abounding in disruption and confrontation.... The Ten didn't realize that they were thrown to the wolves to improve the Party's image."[1]

Bartley Crum served as legal consultant for some of the Nineteen, but he was present at only a few meetings — mainly toward the end of the process. He stated that he had wanted Edward Dmytryk and Adrian Scott to testify, but that any such attempt was blocked by the unanimity rule that had been established. Dmytryk later testified that "people like Herbert Biberman" advocated prepared positions from the start, such as this so-called "unanimity rule" that was euphemistically proclaimed as showing how everyone agreed, but that, Dmytryk pointed out, actually was a means of control: Any individual's action must have the unanimous consent of the group. He had agreed that they would "pool our attorneys but we [he and Adrian Scott] went into it without realizing that the thing was carefully planned by a certain number."[2]

One of the meetings of the Nineteen was held at the home of Rossen. At one point of this evening, Rossen, once again upset at the insistence on discipline, came out of the room in which they were meeting and told his wife Sue, "We apparently just can't tell the truth." The strategy of the group's counsels, he told her, was "to protect the Communist Party."[3] He did attend some further meetings but began to go his own way, kept his own counsel. He was clearly caught between two forces that at that time he believed infringed on his ideals, his independence, and his freedom of thought. After the hearings, he continued to support protests against the Committee and defend the rights of those already being blacklisted. For a time he continued, as well, his wavering, fluctuating relationship of activity and conflicts with the Party. He left no record of how he would have testified if he had been called into the hearing chamber. While he did privately voice his disapproval of the Ten's strategy and performance, he did not want to turn against them and so made no public comments.

One example of the tactics that had been worked out for the Ten's performance at the hearings was refusing to testify by saying you are testifying, and being confrontational and combative at the same time:

> The climactic John Howard Lawson variant on this I-am-answering tactic:
>
> CHAIRMAN: ...Now, do you care to answer the question?
> LAWSON: You are using the old technique, which was used in Hitler's Germany in order to create a scare here —
>
> A shouting match ensued. After *seven* fragmentary exchanges:
>
> CHAIRMAN: That is not the question. That is not the question. The question is, Have you ever been a member of the Communist Party?
> LAWSON: I am framing my answer in the only way in which any American citizen can frame his answer to a question which absolutely invades his rights.[4]

Herbert Biberman's brief testimony was marked by the same interrupting, fragmented give and take of this tactic as he carried out the planned theme of attacking the Committee for destroying democratic principles:

BIBERMAN: It has become very clear to me that the real purpose of this investigation —
CHAIRMAN (pounding gavel): That is not an answer to the question —
BIBERMAN: — is to drive a wedge —
CHAIRMAN (pounding gavel): That is not the question —
BIBERMAN: — into the component parts —
CHAIRMAN (pounding gavel): Not the question —
BIBERMAN: — of the Motion Picture Industry.
CHAIRMAN (pounding gavel): Ask him the next question.
BIBERMAN: And by defending my constitutional rights here, I am defending —
CHAIRMAN (pounding gavel): Go ahead and ask him the next question.
BIBERMAN: — the right not only of ourselves —
STRIPLING: Are you a member —
BIBERMAN: — but of the producers and of the American people.
STRIPLING: — of the Communist Party?

In his written statement, Biberman went further:

> It is not force or violence this committee is investigating, but earnest, unceasing citizenship. This committee is on the course of overthrowing, not Karl Marx, but the constitutional way of American Life.
> It is because I am an active citizen that I am here ... because I committed the sin of devoting ten years to energetic advocacy of my faith in the American people under our Bill of Rights. I believe the American people will not give up the holy struggle for a peaceful world, will not be bullied into an hysterical war.[5]

The association of the Committee with Nazi Germany was regularly introduced as part of the tactic of attacking the Committee for its infringement on freedom of speech. Definitive of the position were statements by John Howard Lawson, including: "[This Committee] is serving more powerful forces. Those forces are trying to introduce fascism in this country.... I will never permit what I write and think to be subject to the orders of self-appointed dictators, ambitious politicians, thought-control gestapos, or any other form of censorship."[6] At times, this strategy was connected to a number of the speeches that claimed that the hearings were the result of what was becoming rampant anti–Semitism in America.

Samuel Ornitz, always so intensely concerned about matters that he felt affected the Jews, was the most emotional and accusatory in his written statement:

> I refer to this evil because it has been responsible for the systematic and ruthless slaughter of six million of my people.... It may be redundant to repeat that anti–Semitism and anti–Communism were the number one poison weapon used by Hitler...
> For when Constitutional guarantees are over-ridden, the Jew is the first one to suffer ... but only the first one. As soon as the Jew is crushed, the others get it....
> Nor did this evil die with Hitler.[7]

The climax of the litany of protests in defense of freedom of expression erupted, with the beautifully placed "beat" of a well-wrought screenplay, at the close of the testimony of Dalton Trumbo — as one might have expected from this most loquacious imaginatively oratorical, and theatrical of witnesses. As his friend and fellow Party member Paul Jarrico remembered, he was "the most original, the most flamboyant, the most unique of all the characters I knew on the left.... He was a fabulous bullshitter."[8]

This theatrical climax came after a series of the usual exchanges over whether he was answering questions or not. Trumbo then orchestrated a reversal of roles when asked what was called the $64 question — "Are you now or have you ever been..." His gloss was to complain instead that the Committee's chief investigator, Robert Stripling, had illegally shown a Party membership card to the press. And then Trumbo asked, "Is that true?"

> STRIPLING: That is not true.
> CHAIRMAN: You are not asking the questions.
> TRUMBO: I was.
> CHAIRMAN: The chief investigator is.

The Chairman finally gave up.

> CHAIRMAN: Excuse the witness (pounding the gavel). Impossible.
> TRUMBO (shouting as he is led from the witness chair): This is the beginning —
> CHAIRMAN (pounding the gavel): Just a minute —
> TRUMBO: — of the American concentration camp!⁹

While this specter of concentration camps in America was being raised at the hearings, millions were being sent to the real concentration — and death — camps in Russia and its satellites. By August of 1945, 1,545,000 former Russian POWs and 2.5 million alleged "Russians" were taken from the occupied zones and sent to various levels of concentration camps in Russia. These postwar repatriates were added to the 1.5 million deportations that Laventri Beria supervised during the war. Of these, the NKVD reported that 375,000 had died; others estimate more than 500,000 died through executions, and transport to or detention in the camps.[10]

Also at the close of the war, another two million people were deported from their home areas *within* Russia on the basis of ethnic and political classifications that allegedly threatened the security of the nation. All in all, close to six million people passed through the various prisons and types of camps within two years of the end of the war. In the year of the hearings alone, 1947, 380,000 people were sentenced to camps. By the hearings of 1953, 1.3 million had been sentenced.[11]

In 1953 there were more prisoners in the Gulag network of concentration camps than ever before: 2,561,351. (It should be noted that Gulag totals at any given time are based on those still recorded as living *after* hundreds of thousands had died.) There were nearly as many people in "special exile" villages. In the harshest regions of the country there were 210,000 in new "special" camps for political suspects. One million two hundred thousand Germans living in the Soviet Union were deported to camps.

Throughout Eastern Europe, and under Soviet control, an estimated 1 million "Titoists," "Trotskyists," and other enemies of the people were killed in purges, deportations, executions, and imprisonments. The briefest of samplings of these imprisonments: In Hungary, in the years after the war, supported by Soviet troops, 600,000 out of a population of nine million were moved from their homes, some deported to other countries, some sent to newly constructed "labor camps." In East Germany, 240,000 were imprisoned in special camps in the first five years of Communist rule. Ninety-five thousand were still in camps in 1950.[12]

After the Ten's performance at the hearings (which ignored this reality), screenwriter Philip Dunne, one of the most active of their original liberal supporters, was appalled. He commented, "They'd come up with this cockamamie idea of saying I'm trying to answer the question in my own words, and then delivering a diatribe against the committee."[13] Dunne realized that their belligerent, ideologically extreme strategy — during the hearings and after — would cause liberals who had supported them to pull back, and alliances to fade and disappear. The tone and the premise had been set for the battle lines, the moral extremism, and the tragedies in the struggles ahead in the years of the blacklist.

After only a few of these displays, liberal producer Dore Schary, who was to take over as head of MGM in 1951, agreed: "I suggested to Scott, Dmytryk, and Katz that I believed that they could keep the majority of public opinion on their side by avoiding the histrionics of those members of the Ten who had preceded them to the stand." Later, liberal journalist Richard Rovere acidly remarked, "The investigators and the investigated have seemed richly to deserve each other." Dorothy Healey, for years the leader of the Communist Party in Los Angeles, saw it more philosophically, and in a sense morally: "I don't know, though, I do think in retrospect that it would have been better for — what? Morale or solidarity, I guess — if individuals who had been put on the spot had identified themselves politically."[14]

Dunne believed that the strategies and activities of the Hollywood Reds had important political repercussions throughout the country:

> It was primarily their conformity to the twists and turns in the party line dictated by the exigencies of Soviet foreign policy and their tacit support of repression in the Soviet Union itself that provided McCarthy, Nixon [and the others] with enough credibility to destroy the reputations and livelihoods of Communists and non–Communists alike."[15]

Another early active supporter, John Huston, also decried the loss of public sympathy for the witnesses and for the principle behind their defense:

> You felt your skin crawl and your stomach turn. I disapproved of what was being done to the Ten, but I also disapproved of their response. They had lost a chance to defend a most important principle.... Before the spectacle, the attitude of the press had been extremely sympathetic. Now it changed.[16]

Not only had the press changed, but liberals began backing off. They should not have, but they could no longer join in the kind of extreme displays that had destroyed, one after the other, all attempts for a unified front in Hollywood for over a decade. There was a mutual failure — rather not an effective unified alliance of liberals and radicals — to combat the increasing power and momentum of the Right in the years between hearings.

In addition to the loss of any effective protest campaign, there was a destructive impact on individuals in Hollywood and in other centers of the world of entertainment. In his memoir, *Take Two*, Dunne summed up his appraisal of the consequences of the whole spectrum of the strategies and what lay behind them:

> Those who joined the Communist Party, and faithfully followed its twisting line, cannot escape their share of responsibility for the broken careers and bankruptcies, the ruin of reputations, the sleepless nights and heartaches the many had to endure because of the [selfish] folly of the few.[17]

Schary was "convinced," even later, "that if the Ten had taken the course I suggested, the disaster that followed the hearings would not have taken place, despite Hedda Hopper, Westbrook Pegler, and the Motion Picture Alliance for the Preservation of American Ideals, which was the wordy title dreamed up by strong right-wing opposition in Hollywood."[18]

Schary may well have been too naïve. However, even though testifying would not have saved the jobs of the Ten et al., a different, more honest (and more moral?) strategy might well have changed the climate of public and media opinion about Hollywood to the point of inhibiting the actions of the producers, giving at least some of them some basis and even courage on which to stand up to the pressures of the Right and allowing a freer range of options and consequences for others caught up in whatever process would have then developed.

At any rate, in 1947 the producers had certainly been handed their rationale, and their excuse, by the performance of the Ten. They were given the basis for a public relations justification to once and for all — or so it must have seemed — put an end to the decades of battles with the disruptive Communists and their defenders. On November 25, 1947, after a conference at the Waldorf Astoria Hotel in New York City, the members of the Association of Motion Picture Producers issued "the Waldorf Statement." There were four paragraphs of definition and explanation.

The producers announced that because "their *actions* [emphasis added] have been a disservice to their employers and have impaired their usefulness to the industry," the producers "will forthwith discharge or suspend without compensation" the Ten until they are acquitted of contempt or testify under oath that they are not members of the Communist Party. And more importantly, the producers felt it possible to go further without any danger of public disapproval and with the further justification of Federal policies and definitions: "We will not knowingly employ a Communist or a member of any party or group which advocates the overthrow of the Government of the United States by force or by illegal or unconstitutional methods." The statement did concede that "there is the danger of hurting innocent people ... we will invite the Hollywood talent guilds to work with us to eliminate any subversives, to protect the innocent, and to safeguard free speech and a free screen whenever threatened."[19]

There is a certain irony behind one of the tangential motives for the Waldorf Statement. A group headed by lawyer Mendel Silberberg wrote the statement. Silberberg was a prominent member of the Jewish community in Los Angeles, and a confidante and adviser for many of the Jewish movie producers and magnates. In an earlier meeting with Dunne, Silberberg had expressed his fear that once a blacklist started, the Jews would suffer. After the hearings, Silberberg, however, was still worried about the negative impact of the performance of the Ten (and their Jewish members) at the hearings and what continuing performances would bring. And so at the Waldorf conference he decided on what he deemed the best way to mitigate the damage to the industry — and the Jews. He drafted the statement for the Association. As Neal Gabler wrote, "No one in Hollywood was more conscious of the image of Jews in the public mind. No one was more keenly aware of the practical consequences of the Hollywood Jews seeming to harbor Communists. No one more accurately represented the Hollywood Jews' fears and hopes."[20]

The rueful irony creeps in when the Jews testifying at the hearings so strongly and vehemently insisted on introducing the "Jewish Question" themselves in their emphasis on the alleged anti–Semitic nature of the hearings, the Committee, and America. Later, in 1953, Rossen was to turn that claim around by introducing the Party's destructive hypocrisy about the Soviet Union's anti–Semitism as one of his underlying motives for testifying.

In the fifties, Schary commented on how he had been dismayed by the producer group's action and statement. While they proclaimed their protection of the innocent and free speech, they were really signaling and implementing the opposite.[21] Whether in principle, in anger, in selfishness, or in fear, they had succumbed to the pressures of right-wing zealots. For all their own motives — individual and collective, principled and invidious — the producers, for all intents and purposes, created the blacklist. It was a term, and an implication of fearful and greedy betrayal, that they never accepted (at least publicly).

Through this ideological turbulence, Rossen tried erratically — and in some ways psychologically evasively — to define his break with the Party. The record is not clear, nor are his statements, as to any exact date that he defied the Party and finally irreparably left it. His recollections tend to focus on his taking part from then on only in meetings and activities relating to the HUAC investigation and its legal and professional consequences — both before and after the first hearings. The first of these meetings was held immediately after the issuance of the subpoenas, when the group met with the four lawyers who would become the core of the legal team. Much off the Party's activities in Hollywood through this period — and everybody's chief personal concerns — had to do with the hearings. So Rossen's emphasis does not seem to rule out any continuing vacillations in his relations with the Party while he was still participating in some of its activities. In one instance he took part in a meeting in October 1947, sponsored by the left-wing National Lawyers Guild, to create a campaign to define HUAC as an agency of dictatorial, if not fascistic, "thought control"[22] (in line with the strategy of the Ten at the hearings and in the campaigns that followed).

Following these first hearings — when the initial group of Nineteen were still thought of as a unit and further hearings were thought to be imminent — Rossen attended a number of events and meetings. One was a reception in honor of the Hollywood Nineteen held on November 2 and sponsored by the Civil Rights Congress. Rossen, one of the original Nineteen, was one of the 18 signers of a petition to the House of Representatives to overrule the Committee's citations. Similarly, after the Ten were convicted, he was later one of the signers of the *amicus curiae* brief submitted to the Supreme Court on behalf of John Howard Lawson (as the test case) and the others.[23]

On Thanksgiving Day of 1947, Robert Rossen and most of the Nineteen were among the large crowd having their turkey and trimmings in the pleasant courtyard of the El Patio Theater in Hollywood before they all went into the auditorium for speeches, auctions and a further round of enthusiastic fundraising. They were attending "A Thanksgiving Meeting with the Ten," one of a number of fundraising functions attended by a broad political spectrum of supporters of the Ten's proclaimed defense of freedom of speech and the Constitution. There was, for example, "Election Night with the Ten," at Hugo Butler's home. And for those in the inner circles there was the very expensive fund- and spirits-raising party "New Years Eve with the Hollywood Ten" at Lucey's Restaurant.[24]

In more large-scale activities, on October 15 the Progressive Citizens of America held a fundraising rally at the Shrine Auditorium, staged dramatically by director Joseph Losey (soon to depart for England, never to return). On November 16 they organized a larger rally at Gilmore Stadium. HICCASP continued the money-raising meetings and rallies it had started after the subpoenas were delivered. The liberals in the original support group, the Committee for the First Amendment, held meetings with studio officials. They announced a project of ten radio broadcasts and a speakers bureau. But it was indicative of the short-lived nature of this unity that the discussions with studio officials went nowhere; and after a program entitled "Hollywood Fights Back" on October 26, the radio broadcasts and the speakers bureau disappeared.[25]

Several attempts were made to have individuals influence their guilds to defend the Ten. At the Screen Directors Guild meeting of December 1, 1947, Rossen himself rose to speak. He was continuing to take part in strategy meetings and fundraising activities into 1948; but because of his inner conflicts about his continued connection to the Party and his monumental job of work on *All the King's Men*, his participation dwindled. At that December meeting in 1947, however, he proposed a Guild protest against the "firing" (as he put it) of director Edward Dmytryk. It is not clear if he was acting out of personal concern for, and a sense of affinity with, Dmytryk, or as a spokesman for the Nineteen and the Party. According to the *Hollywood Reporter*, he was actually booed. The members then passed a resolution requiring all Guild officers to sign the Taft-Hartley "non–Communist" affidavit.[26] Dmytryk served a prison sentence of almost a year for contempt of Congress, along with the others of the Hollywood Ten. The eleventh person actually called to appear before the Committee, Brecht, had "testified"—tersely, enigmatically, ironically—and then left the country. After Dmytryk's prison term, he broke with the Party and testified in 1951.

Even as late as 1949, the Ten and others did consider Rossen connected enough to convene a nighttime meeting and confront him about the lack of correctness of the ideological stance and content of *All the King's Men* (see Chapter 12). And it is again indicative of the shifting, even confused, debates going on within his own mind and heart that he agreed to attend the meeting. It may well be symbolic, even symptomatic, of his attitude at the time that for a while he took part in that vindictive thought-control session. Then he got up and walked out. Infuriating and demeaning as that meeting was, it proved far easier, and far less painful, to walk out of that room than to walk out of the Party and leave behind one's life in the Communist Party in Hollywood.

10

Power and Betrayal, Personal and Public—*All the King's Men*

In November of 1949 the first panel on the screen shows:

> Columbia Pictures
> Presents
> ROBERT ROSSEN'S
> PRODUCTION
> Of

And on the second panel:

> ALL THE
> KING'S MEN

It was a marker, an emblem, of Rossen's new power in the industry, the new stage of his career, of how far he had come in his own search for independence and control of his films. It is, however, misleading in a way, for it does not show the new tensions that had hit him and the industry while he was working on the film. This proud assertion gave no hint of the threats to that newfound power, the tortuous political and moral dilemmas that had already been generated and would intensify, with damaging consequences, in the years ahead.

The blacklisting of hundreds was not to begin until 1951 when the second extensive round of hearings was held. In the meantime, however, there were contracts that were not offered or not renewed, projects not assigned, private letters and meetings and other forms of quiet accommodation. As the years went by, many, including Rossen, anxiously waited for the other Congressional cleated boot to drop, and debated with each other (and with themselves) what to do when it did.

Some, like Rossen, were also fretfully debating in their minds and hearts what to do with their relationship—their broken romance—with the Communist Party. There were now new tensions and contradictions, disagreements and disillusionments with the Party and its pattern of betrayals, in opposition to the government's crackdown on Communism. Many felt loyalty toward those in Hollywood under duress, but experienced conflicts with the stalwart Reds who many felt were actually helping to fuel the vendetta of the Right by the continuing extremity of their attacks on the Committee—and, by extension, America.

In the midst of this public and, for him, inner turmoil, Rossen found his creative way—his calling, his *métier*—by going beyond the confusions and conflicts in his political life. Professionally, his path amidst this political, economic, moral, and emotional turmoil was clearer than most, at least for the time being, and more secure due to his strong connection to Harry Cohn. Still, early in 1948, when Cohn and Rossen turned to thoughts of their next movie, the realities of the time did intrude on Cohn's Hollywood, as they began to do with more and more regularity. Several years before, when Cohn had been advised by legal counsel to "get rid of that Commie John Howard Lawson," he had refused. Now even he knew the times had changed, though he continued to go his own renegade way as much as he could. By some accounts he was known to urge compliance with some of the formalities (whether truthfully or not was beside the point). Cohn and Rossen reached a *modus vivendi*. Rossen would write a private letter to Cohn attesting to the fact that he was not at that date a member of the Communist Party. Rossen did, but what he meant or what the literal truth at that point was remains as conflicted as his feelings about and dealings with the Party at the time.[1]

The result was *All the King's Men*. Rossen had been attracted by the Robert Penn Warren novel and its central character, Willie Stark, so clearly a Rossen character (let alone a spirit much like himself and his new mentor, Harry Cohn). He had thought of purchasing the rights himself, but when the novel won the Pulitzer Prize early in 1948, the price was beyond him. He urged Cohn to buy the rights. Others at Columbia agreed it would be a fine prestige picture, and Cohn agreed to buy it, envisioning (rightly, as it turned out) a prestigious major award winner. He agreed, as well, not only that Rossen would write and direct it, but that under the terms of their releasing agreement Rossen would also act as producer. This was one of the earliest instances of that kind of complete, three-way control by a Hollywood filmmaker (complete, of course, within the parameters of Hollywood at the time, and those set by one of its choicest moguls, Harry Cohn).[2]

All the King's Men became Rossen's way of responding to, and (sadly, painfully) commenting on, the world of politics and all its avid proclaimers, proclamations, corruptions and betrayals. The film is a fascinating mixture, with the intellectually controlled skepticism of Warren's novel transformed into Rossen's more volatile, jagged, emotionally open, and personally felt cynicism, culminating in disillusionment and anger at the loss of what one could believe in, could give one's idealism to.

As Rossen said years later in talking about his last film, *Lilith*, what he likes to do "when I adapt a book that I like is to render the spirit of it rather then letter."[3] In commenting on the film adaptation of his book *All the King's Men*, novelist Robert Penn Warren agreed: "I think that is an extraordinarily good movie. I can praise it, because it seems to me that when a movie is made from a novel, the novel is merely raw material, the movie is a new creation, and the novelist can properly attract neither praise nor blame for it. The movie, as a matter of fact, does not "mean" what I think my book meant. It is Bob's movie."[4]

It was a monumental task, something to invest one's self in deeply, both practically and creatively. But in the summer of 1948, as Rossen began work on adapting Warren's novel, which he admired, he did try to get as much of it—too much of it, he soon realized—as he could into a long, sprawling screenplay.

After some ten drafts and frequent consultations with Warren, Rossen found his way into the life that was in the novel; and he found the key to the style for his film in the films of the movement of Italian Neo-Realism, which he saw as "very close in spirit" to what he wanted to achieve. And so he discarded much of the screenplay he had been laboring on and creatively rewrote his own script.

In his later interview in the French film journal *Cahiers du Cinema*, Rossen expressed his admiration for the Italian movement: "*Open City, The Bicycle Thief*, and so on, marked me deeply, and I even thought, when I became a director, that was the true way of making films." It was a matter of style — episodic, character-focused, loosely structured, like life itself, naturalistic, even raw, in look and performance. But it was also a matter of vision: "It seemed to me that the whole Hollywood system was condemned if people did not finally decide to look at life with a clear gaze, with a cold eye. Which does not exclude emotion, sensibility. It means only that life represented must be as we see it and not as we wish it to be. We have to say what is out of joint in our time."[5] He felt in tune not only with the aims of the Neo-Realists in dealing with the lives of common people, but with many of their techniques and approaches. Their use of natural locations, natural lighting, and ordinary people was important to him. But in personal ways, even more important for his approach to the day to day working on films, was their value of improvising, of responding to settings and people, even to events that develop over the course of making a movie — re-working and re-working a script as one filmed (in stark contrast to the procedures of the directors Rossen had worked with within the Warners system).

As production began, Rossen began to respond freely to the immediacy of the moment on location — mainly in Stockton, California — changing and developing the script as filming progressed, using natural light and all kinds of weather conditions. He used many non-actors and marshaled thousands of people in crowd scenes, shooting with four cameras, often when the extras were unawares. In creating the particularly powerful yet naturalistic impact of the film's scenes he also created, as it turned out, rather stalwart problems of editing.

Before going on location and discovering these decisive moments, Rossen had submitted his "final" draft to the Columbia executives in charge of the production. When the daily rushes were viewed back at the studio, there was consternation — this was not the script or the polished look that was expected. Harry Cohn was informed. He passed on their "notes" to Rossen, who sent back an angry telegram.

Cohn telephoned him. As he later liked to tell the story, Cohn said, "So what you're saying is, 'Go fuck yourself!'"

"You're goddamned right!"

"So, okay, what the hell, do the picture."[6]

Columbia's executives in New York had opposed the casting of Broderick Crawford, who had been playing in Westerns, as Willie Stark, but again Cohn went with Rossen's instincts. Of course, it didn't hurt that Crawford was willing to take a cut in salary. As was Rossen.

Rossen was sure of Crawford from his first test, and liked to tell the story that he let him go on with his powerful reading even though the camera had run out of film. In choosing and working with an actor, he favored "actors whose own personality, joined to that of my character, could give a good result. But I chose those actors often in a purely instinctive way, because of what one can read in their eyes—which the audience will read as I do, even if it is not really there.... With Broderick Crawford it was the same thing."[7]

Cohn believed in Rossen's talent—for making a good picture and making some money with it—but also felt an affinity between them. Cohn saw him as a protégé cut from the same cloth as himself. Not only did Cohn see similarities in Rossen's brusque, outspoken manner, but also in his attitude toward life—the outsider fighting back. As studio executive William Graf defined him, Cohn "liked to be considered a tough guy, the guy who was a ball breaker." But Cohn also liked a tussle; he dominated and attacked, but he liked a response, a rebuttal, even a counter-attack. He and Rossen were like two Lower East-Siders—two guys punching each other on the arm, testing, enjoying. Novelist-screenwriter Daniel Fuchs worked for Cohn on several movies. He saw Cohn as always suspicious and defensive under the famous bluster, whether garrulous or foul-mouthed. Whatever success and power he had achieved, he still was resentful, Fuchs felt, and saw himself as an underdog fighting against the "Wasp" hierarchy.[8] Cohn needed, like Rossen, to fight every step of the way.

One bitter fight Rossen had over *All the Kings Men* was with his Communist Party comrades. While the film was in production, some members knew about it, had discussed it with Rossen, and had read parts or versions of the script. The meeting that took place early in 1949 was influenced by a hard-line cultural *Zhdanovism* (also called *Zhdanovschina*) that had been instituted by the Party's Cominform (successor to the Comintern) as a world-wide campaign in the burgeoning Cold War. In response to the perceived needs of the Soviet Union in the developing Cold War between the Soviets and the Western nations, Andre Zhdanov (and his staff) defined the active role that art must take in defending the rights of the people—and, of course, the interest of the Soviet Union. Zhdanov was an influential member of the Soviet Central Committee at that time, a long-time culture commissar, and an active force in the international political control of the Communist Parties of the world. He first enunciated this position about art and its principles, and the need to enforce them, at a so-called "Peace" conference in Poland in September 1947. In the speech he applied the terms of the ideology and strategies of the Cold War to the realm of culture and the need to define and control the arts' participation in the conflict with "the ruthless expansionist drive of American big business." Throughout the Soviet-controlled areas of Europe, and under the auspices of the strong Communist Party in Italy, there were major conferences prescribing the necessary steps to be taken to apply "Zhdanovism" to all the arts, including film, so that all artists would act on the basic principle that what was of central importance was that a work must serve to "educate the people and arm them ideologically."[9]

In America, the Zhdanov campaign, the Party line, as often was the case, was promoted and brought down to local levels by V.J. Jerome. In the American Communist Party, Jerome was a rather amorphous figure, a man who wore many hats. He was ostensibly the culture czar, and from the mid–1930s on had attempted, not always successfully, to enforce the Party's interests and strategies among the Hollywood filmmakers. Through this period his chief conduit in Hollywood and loyal aide in maintaining discipline was John Howard Lawson. Lawson was the fervent, abrasive enforcer of Party lines among the Hollywood CPUSA members and their close followers. Dorothy Healey, the long-time leader of the Communist Party of Los Angeles County, felt that he "was a tragic figure. He was a man of talent and ability but he was struggling so hard to prove he was not a petty-bourgeois intellectual."[10]

Late in life, in his memoir *Being Red*, Howard Fast struck a wry note in his criticism of what he called Lawson's "puritanical lunacy." His anger dissipated by the years, he recounted a favorite Party members' anecdote regarding Lawson's repeated and insistent critiques of the "anti-human lust for brutality" of Fast's novel (and subsequently movie) *Spartacus*. At various social events Lawson even demanded that his reluctant listeners consider calling for Fast's expulsion from the Party. In response, Fast recalled, "certain people put up signs in their homes: THERE WILL BE NO DISCUSSION OF SPARTACUS HERE TONIGHT."[11]

It was Lawson who chaired the session and set the tone for the "discussion" of Rossen's film. While the chief complaints directly followed the terms of the Zhdanov directives, the levels of vituperation and emotion went beyond ideological niceties — even before the earthquake impact of Rossen's testifying.

The Rossen tribunal was held at the home of Albert Maltz. In 1946 he had been the object of equally vituperative attacks in two nighttime meetings — over his call for more creative freedom for writers in an article he had published, not a film. By the end of the long second session he had recanted. Despite what he had gone through, or maybe because of it, Maltz was ardent in his attacks on Rossen at the new meeting. But as Edward Dmytryk, who was at the meeting as one of the original Ten, remembered, he was outdone by others:

> *Censure* is too flabby a word. Rossen's *excoriation* took place during a meeting for the Ten held at Maltz's home. Thoroughly bewildered, he was, for the better part of the evening, pilloried by Lawson and those two acid-tongued specialists in the Party's disciplinary procedures, [Herbert] Biberman and [Alvah] Bessie, three men who, lumped together, had not one-tenth of Bob's talent....
>
> Bob did his best to fight back, but he was outnumbered, and there was no meeting ground. Eventually, he had more than enough. "Stick the whole Party up your ass!" he said and walked out of the house. And out of the Party.[12]

It is part of the film's strength and value that it does violate (not by any conscious intention) the narrow definition of what a political film should be, as advocated by Zhdanov. From the perspective of Zhadonvism, Rossen's film did not have the proper emphasis upon and "analysis" of the economic structures that should have been seen as the underlying causes of the corruption of Willie Stark's state government. Willie's violations were too personal, too unconnected to these basic capitalist structures. This plodding analysis did not allow for Rossen's more sophisticated development of Willy as *embodying* these capitalist evils, as dramatized by many details in the film. For another "flaw," *the people* were passive, complicit in their own enslavement. There was no proletarian uprising. And worst of all, that was part of a general lack of *positive* elements, the absence of *positive* proletarian heroes. The only positive action is taken (and at the last minute) by two weak bourgeois intellectuals! (See also my discussion of Zhdanovism in Chapter 19.)

When filming was completed, once again Cohn responded to Rossen's urging, and to strong preview results, and opened the picture before the end of the year (November 1949) so as to make it eligible for the Academy Awards. Rossen paid for some advertising himself, one *Hollywood Reporter* ad citing an award from the New York University Center for Research proclaiming it "one of the decade's most distinguished films in the field of human relations." The strategy was well warranted. *All The King's Men* received the widest acclaim of any of Rossen's films, as well as some 30 awards. Among these were the New York Film Critics award for Best Picture, though Best Director went to Carol Reed for *The Fallen Idol* (Crawford won that award for Best Actor); the Screen Directors Guild award for Best Direction; the Foreign Language Press Film Critics Circle award for Best Film, Best Screenwriting, Best Direction, and Best Production; and the *Look* Achievement Award for Best Screenwriting. The film also received seven Academy Award nominations. The *Los Angeles Daily News* said it "rates all the Oscars for the year." Crawford again won for Best Actor, Mercedes McCambridge for Best Supporting Actress. Al Clark and Robert Parrish lost the Best Editing award to the boxing movie *Champion*, while Burnett Guffey's technically innovative and artistically impressive photography had been unfairly denied a nomination. Rossen lost both Best Screenplay and Best Director to Joseph Mankiewicz for the sentimental *A Letter to Three Wives*, but won for Best Picture of 1949. Cohn, who didn't like Oscar ceremonies anyway, said it was Rossen's show and stayed home. Jimmy Cagney presented the Oscar to Rossen, who said, in what may be the shortest acceptance speech in memory, "It's been a long evening. I just can't talk."

Life called it "the most exciting film to come out of Hollywood this year." *Newsweek* praised its "considerable distinction and singular dramatic force," and commented, "Crawford gives a performance that matches the story's powerfully crude eloquence and force." *Daily Variety* said he "delivers one of the most dynamic character studies the screen has ever glimpsed." John McCarten in *The New Yorker* found that it "didn't lose its nerve when dealing with the facts of American politics and faced up to Lord Acton's conclusion about the corrupting influence of power."

Bosley Crowther in the *New York Times* felt Crawford "concentrates tremendous energy into every delineation" of his character, though he found Rossen had achieved "much less success" with the other characterizations. The film, he found, has "a quality of turbulence and vitality that is the one [impression] it most fully demonstrates ... it has a superb pictorialism which perpetually crackles and explodes ... [and] bears witness to the boundless potential of the screen."[13]

The film extends, expands, and develops meaningful variations on Rossen's consistent themes: how personal betrayals, the forsaking and loss of one's true self, have public and political consequences, and how this personal corruption and the corruption of the power structure of society are linked and interact in a destructive embrace. The typical Rossen hero is split between two men. Jack Burden (John Ireland, who also serves as a voiceover narrator, as he did in *A Walk in the Sun*) is the rootless intellectual who comes from but has rebelled against the entrenched money class. But he has found no viable alternative for his personal or public life. Cold, frozen, and alienated, he gives himself to the promise of the idealistic dream posed by the power of Willie Stark — whatever the consequences.

Willie (Crawford) rises from the mass of the beaten-down and dispossessed. One of Rossen's key symbolic figures — the young man of unfocused vitality and power — he finds his true calling, his gift, in rousing and working for the common people, the "hicks" like himself. But lured and overwhelmed by the illusory trappings of political power — as the material fruits of power feed his own inner needs, his pleasure in domination and control — he is corrupted. (Lord Acton: "Power tends to corrupt; absolute power corrupts absolutely.") Within the film's complex web of betrayals, Willie betrays his own gift —

his *élan*—and himself, as he betrays his ideals, his family, the People, and individuals, who he uses and misuses. In seeking the counters, the symbols of their identity, both Willie and Jack choose the illusory and the destructive. But it is the intellectual Jack Burden, who has not himself been immune to betrayal, who comes to the saving moral recognition—the beginnings of redemption—that is typical of Rossen's endings. It is the political man of action, Willie Stark, whose betrayals are beyond atonement and who is destroyed.

Just two months before his death, in the last major interview he granted, Rossen was still analyzing the contradictions, the complexities of the will to power of men like Willie Stark:

> The drive toward power never permits itself to be naked and always needs a rationale, whether it's the rationale of a schizophrenic or the rationale of a Willie Stark. It needs it because it cannot face the fact that need for power becomes primarily a subjective need. We like to think, as Lyndon Johnson likes to think—I am positive he thinks this way—that his tremendous power or his drive toward power is for the good of the many....
>
> You see, I think it's natural for people to want power, but then I think you have to decide what you mean by power. Is it the power to move people or, say, the power to create things? You see the problem? Power is such a complex kind of subject, because you see there are certain things in power that are very human and very right and very neat—the power, let's say, of a girl singer to get on the stage and hold an audience by sheer force of her personality or voice. That's power at a given moment and a given time, but that power is a good power, that power is a creative power, that power is an expression of human personality which is primarily what we are all after and don't have now—and why we are so buggered.[14]

A new and distinctive aspect of Willie's corruption of his personal power and that of the state is that he acts not against, but within the power structure of the state, the political system that is already corrupt, and then corrupts it further—with consequences for the broad public entity. But there is a more complex paradox here in his use of power, in the connection between personal and public corruption. Unlike the gangsters and gamblers, the symbolic capitalists, who are totally destructive and evil, and unlike those like Charley who betray what is their own ideal and the good within themselves totally, Willie continues to believe, in some part of his consciousness and spirit, in the idealism of his original cause. He has taken power away from the moneyed class and their minions who have oppressed and violated the people. He still believes that he is carrying out his good works for the people—and that justifies the means he takes to stay in power. He produces tangible results—hospitals, highways, schools and universities, stadiums—but at the cost of stolen funds and payoffs, fraud and intimidation, injuries and deaths.

In commenting some years later, in 1965, Rossen had another perspective on this paradox of good and evil in Willie's pursuit of power. Out of the interaction between the environment he comes from as a "redneck" and his own character, his nature, "came his antagonism, or his hostility ... that the answer for him, which he could find in any character relationship he had, was the desire for power and the deep belief that if he had power, he could then do things that would help people."[15] It is a courageous political film, the most powerful of its time in its direct critique of the corruption of the political system for selfish ends—an assertion of independence in the face of pressures toward conformity and compliance. It is also a prophetic political film in its dramatization of the manipulation of the public—and the truth—by the self-serving synergy in the combination of politicians and the media.

It is also a personal film. It not only filters the conflicts of the novel through the prism of Rossen's continuing concerns — identity, environment, power, betrayal, et al.— it reveals a more personal identification and involvement. Its view of morality and politics reflects conflicts within the filmmaker. In many ways, Rossen *is* Willie Stark and his driving energy, even his aggressiveness, as Rossen is attracted to and yet wary of Willie's need for power, its lures and its destructiveness. Willie's embodiment in Broderick Crawford carries physical and personality echoes of both Rossen and Harry Cohn. In talking about his choice of Crawford for the role, Rossen said that although Crawford had no background for "the role and the atmosphere, there was in him a psychological reaction before the world that was perfect for this role; to be able to dominate the other, to have a great power over him, to use it. He knew how to render it, and I was persuaded of that before filming." Willie is also Cohn in manner and style, even in the ruthlessness that is only a part of the Cohn personality. But Willie is, in a broader sense, Hollywood Bosses and the crusading Congressmen and political power figures within the industry. Rossen is also Jack Burden, the writer doing Willie's dirty work, even as he recognizes his destructiveness — the artist caught in the system, or the Party, and his own needs, trapped in the confusions of his own dilemma.

The manipulation of the People and truth is the here and now of the time of the investigators and investigations in Hollywood (and elsewhere) — of the time of righteous and destructive crusades of both the Right and the Left. On an ideological level, it is the reflection of the manipulations of zealots and true believers of the Left — within Rossen's own growing sense of doubt and rejection of world Communism and the American Communist Party.

Like the power figures in both the Soviet Union and America, Willie, for his own purposes, conducts secret investigations into the personal lives of people. His political opponents, for their own purposes, conduct a blatantly public investigation of him, a hearing on a grand scale, a "Moscow Trial," an impeachment. All those around him, those affected by him, are caught in the dilemma of choosing to acquiesce to his power and corruption or act — in one way or another to "testify" or not. One, Judge Stanton, is even driven to suicide. Jack Burden, the alienated idealist, is caught between turning against Willie or continuing to act on his instructions, his party line, even as he knows that Willie is betraying the very ideals he believed Willie could make a reality.

As he shot the film, Rossen applied to his work many of the principles of the Neorealist films he had seen. He not only used natural light and settings and the people who actually lived in them, he particularly worked freely and spontaneously, using the speed and skill of Burnett Guffey in capturing the immediacy of decisive moments as they occurred, planned or not. Rossen adapted the script as he himself responded to what he said "was the moment of truth, the moment when things reveal themselves as they are. They open out in virtue of a situation that creates a moment of emotion."

Rossen's experimental approach to the film produced a volume of footage and disparate collection of scenes that created an imposing problem in the editing, the shaping of the footage shot. Rossen always saw editing as an integral part of his approach to filmmaking:

> I have always, since I began, attached much importance to editing.... I always think about the editing when I shoot, for it is the second part of the writing of the film. Cinema is in fact a way of writing on the same ground as the other, except that it is with the film that one

must write.... It happens that one writes a scene that, in the scenario, seems right and that, when one sees the film, does not become an integral part of the whole. It is the same scene, and yet it has no longer the significance that you wanted; it has not enough impact. Then you take that scene, you set it at different places in the sequence of the film, and it comes alive. Never could you have foreseen that while writing, not even while shooting. The scene takes its meaning at a precise point that one could not have assigned to it before.[16]

The editing process on *All the King's Men* tackled problems that were practical as well as artistic, and the practical circumstance proved to be a serendipitous opening to the solution of the artistic problem. The first edit, by Rossen and Al Clark, was not satisfying for a preview audience or for Rossen. He brought in Robert Parrish, who saw the crux of the problem as maintaining the picture's excitement and freedom while reducing its length and creating a more structured order that was appropriate for it and its meanings. It was, he felt, like taking the freeform shooting and editing of the final fight sequence in *Body and Soul* and carrying it through an entire movie. After further editing and another disappointing preview, Rossen had Parrish view *The Roaring Twenties*. After viewing it, Parrish saw what Rossen meant. "It seemed to me," he later recounted, "to be a film of impressions more than a film of conventional step-by-step scenes, dissolves, fades, etc. But it worked."

They recut the picture to develop the impact of these "impressions"—scenes pared down to a strong center, building to it and then moving on. But the effective structure was more than that. It combined this focus on shorter scenes with dramatic climaxes (often with fast, sharp editing within the scene) with scenes that developed more slowly and with carefully orchestrated *plan sequences* of imagery. As in earlier Rossen films, montages of images and sounds condense time and events while building momentum and impact. Rossen actually re-shot some scenes, especially for Mercedes McCambridge, and built what Parrish felt "was actually like a 106-minute [later 109-minute] montage. On reflection I see that it was cut in the way that many pictures are cut today, where dramatic effect is more important than conventional continuity."[17]

Whatever the practical reasons for the editing, for Rossen the problem was more than a matter of quantity. He wanted to achieve that focused emotional intensity that he always sought. He wanted to blend the dramatic pace and momentum, the intensity of individual scenes, the impact and energy of personal interactions with the open, naturalistic flow of action in the Neo-realist manner. The result is an increase in Rossen's emphasis on editing, but an editing that maintains his use of an orchestrated *mise en scène* and a greater artistry in developing dramatized metaphors in his visual images—the implications of spatial relationships between people, and between people and their settings, the concrete correlative of their environment.

At the end of the hectic process of production and editing, Rossen still had strong reservations about the extensive cutting necessary to reduce the length of the film to meet the demands of the studio chieftains in New York. He had to make the kind of compromise that he felt to be a surrender. That disturbed him for the rest of his career, whatever degree of independence he was able to achieve. He told *Newsweek* that despite his freedom in shooting the film, he did not have the power to control what became known as the "final cut." Using their contractual "final cut," the studio still trimmed *All the King's Men* much further than Rossen wanted, cutting possibly close to an hour of material. Rossen was able to work on that final cut, but the personal relationships that parallel the political corruption still bore the brunt of the cutting. Nonetheless, he felt (at least later) that the interaction is still there. He told *Films in Review,* "Among other things it stresses the impact of the social environment on character—something I have in all my pictures—or, at least, in all the good ones."[18]

In the first section of the film, the exciting, and already ironic, pattern of three election campaigns—their events, people, and visual imagery—creates the first shaping of Willie's political and social environment. It is an environment which both nurtures and controls him, which he then surmounts in his idealistic crusade. But it is a crusade that carries within itself the seeds of its corrupted form as *his* personal empire, his world of naked power.

Willie's first campaign, dull and plodding, is to fight the corruption of the political machine in his home town. Even at this level the bosses (whom he'll later control) threaten him, but he stands up to them, runs, and loses. As years pass, in the first montage of the film, he is studying with his wife, Lucy, becoming a lawyer and leading the fight to investigate the collapse of a school fire escape due to faulty, illegally money-saving construction. It's election time again, this time a race for governor, and the political boss, Duffy, and the boys are afraid that the governor they control is "losing the hick vote" to his opponent in his reelection campaign. They need a candidate to draw votes from the opponent. "Find a dummy," says Sadie (Mercedes McCambridge), their cynical political operator. Duffy knows one and sends Sadie to get Willie to run and to manage his campaign.

In his second campaign, Willie is telling them the truth, but in dull abstractions and statistics—and with the same dull response. Jack Burden (John Ireland) is covering his campaign and realizes that "it's a frame." While the three of them are drinking in Willie's hotel room, Sadie taunts Willie and tells him the truth. Willie understands (more than he realizes): "I wanted it. I wanted it so badly I stayed up nights thinking about it. A man wants something so badly he gets mixed up in knowing what he wants. It's something inside of you."

Willie's discovery of his power, his transformation, and the first signals of what he really wants so badly—his need to feed his ego—are built in a beautiful sequence at a country fairground rally the next day, a positive celebration of the People. Hung over and still half-drunk, Willie is sitting like an overgrown boy on a children's swing, swaying as two little girls stare at him. He waves them away. Jack pours more whiskey in his coffee cup. Later, up on the stage, along with Duffy and his henchmen, Willie can't focus. He sways, then suddenly throws away his speech. With intensity and accelerating momentum, it now flows from him, as the camera cuts between his energized face and the responding faces of the People, his people, individuals and groups, families.

"There's no need for my telling you what the state needs. You are the state and you know what you need...." And he tells them the story of a hick just like them, himself, who was being used to manipulate them: "Well, those fellows in the striped pants (pointing at Duffy), they saw the hick and they took him in." Seen in a series of rapid cuts, Duffy starts the band, trying to drown out Willie, who continues, now shouting, the crowd roaring back. As Willie continues, Duffy tells his goons to get up there and stop him, but Duffy's "goon" Sugar Boy, gun drawn, defends Willie and halts the goons. "Now listen to me, you hicks. Yeah, you're hicks, too, and they fooled you a thousand times, just like they fooled me.... But I'm on my own now and I'm out for blood."

The camera moves in on Willie's face, fiery, passionate, but with the sudden thrill

All the King's Men (1949), Columbia Pictures. Willie Stark (Broderick Crawford), along with his son Tom (John Derek), is stopped by sheriffs during an early idealistic (and losing) campaign, while a still uncommitted Jack Burden (John Ireland) looks on between them.

of the power of his own voice. "Listen to me, you hicks!" he shouts as the scene shifts into a montage of the new campaign: Willie inflamed, wild and raging in close-ups; crowds cheering and jeering; Jack Burden typing his stories; Sadie watching, awed and caught up in the power of it, of Willie — both giving themselves to him.

> Listen to me and lift up your eyes and look at God's blessed and unflyblown truth [cut to the rapt crowd].... And this is the truth. You're a hick. And nobody ever helped a hick but a hick himself.

The cheers erupt, but he silences them, already in total control: "All right, listen to me, listen to me..."

Willie loses in a tight election, but as Jack says in voiceover, "He had lost the election, but he had won the state ... and he knew it ... and the people knew it."

The change in Willie's life and himself and the start of his third campaign for governor are conveyed in a typical set of Rossen montages (as Jack, now Willie's chief assistant, narrates) that are interspersed with several scenes of focused, illustrative "impressions" of what Willie is becoming. The montages contrast rallies for the People with the building of his empire. Jack: "He spent a lot of money doing it ... an awful lot of money.... I was beginning to wonder where he got it from." A montage displays a check for $7,000 dollars and Willie's hand taking it; another for $5,000, with Willie's face superimposed; another for $3,500, a poster of Willie's face superimposed. "There were rumors throughout the state that Willie was making deals with all kinds of people ... strange deals ... for Willie Stark." A montage shows crowds having fun at a fairgrounds, with Willie's poster superimposed; then fireworks exploding and the crowd cheering.

For Willie, getting money, or even the things it can buy, is not what drives him. Money is the lever for obtaining the power that excites him. To get the money to help him win, he will collaborate with anybody. But in his case, reaching for the money does not give others the power over him — as it did for Charley and others. He maintains his dominance, even over those he has taken money from, even though he must make compromises with them and with the political bosses whom he can now control — but really only until *they* can get the power to betray him.

The structure of the narrative sets up a parallel between Willie's public and personal life. The power of his public charisma and the beginnings of his betrayal of his ideals — his belief that he can do good even though he has to break a few eggs (to make his revolutionary omelet) — is paralleled by the beginnings of his betrayals of individuals and family, and his luring of others to do the same.

Jack's mother, whose family has lost their fortune, has married again, accepting arrogant domination for the security of new wealth. Jack has rebelled and returns only occasionally to the genteel isolation of the family on Burden's Island. During the campaign, Jack returns to the island, this time with Willie, who wants their help. It is an intricately woven scene that establishes the web of confused and unfaced motivations that will lead them all to one form or another of corruption and betrayal. McEvoy is quiet and noncommittal, but it is implied that he believes deals can be made. Anne Stanton is beautiful and sheltered, like the island. She and Jack grew up together, have almost been, uncertainly and indecisively, in love — or not. She is thrilled by Willie's talk, which mixes idealism with a frank realism that is new to her, and she is already drawn to his personal magnetism. She will become his lover, and her new surge of passion, innocent as it is, will contribute to his betrayal of Lucy and his family. It will eventually lead her, unwittingly, to a further and destructive violation. Her brother Adam is an idealistic doctor who is skeptical of Willie's arrogantly displayed realism, his claim that good comes out of bad: "That's what good comes out of. Because you can't make it out of anything else. You didn't know that, did you?" It is not merely showmanship; he does believe it, and will act upon it. Adam does wonder about Willie's promise of a new hospital; later he will accept his offer to be the administrator, only to be betrayed and make his own severe retribution. The lofty idealist Judge Stanton accepts Willie's promise of giving him complete power as his attorney general. Willie makes the offer only to get the publicity of the esteemed Judge's support. Willie's betrayal of that promise will lead to further violations and the main crisis that intertwines the public and personal worlds of Willie. And Jack? He is already deep within the web.

At Willie's inauguration, in a dynamic series of shots, we see that the beginning is also the beginning of the end. The camera reveals faces of the crowd, his *People*, in the square below the Capitol, looking up, chanting, "We want Willie, we want Willie!" Cut to a shot from behind Willie as he walks out and looks down at them, then close-ups of people cheering. Cut to a shot past torches and waving arms, up at Willie on the balcony — and hanging behind him is a giant banner of his face. The sequence then shifts to a three-shot of Jack, Anne, and Adam in the crowd, Anne smiling and thrilled. The camera moves closer in on Willie and the banner behind him as he starts to speak — caught up himself in the exhilaration not only of achieving power and the people's acclaim, but of getting his due, paying *them*, the defeated politicos, back for all that they kept from him, took from him. Shots from the side reveal searchlights probing the sky before the scene shifts back to the crowd, farmers looking up at Willie, a torch flaming between them. Willie tells them, "This much I swear to you. These things you shall have. I'm going to build a hospital.... And it is the right of the people that they shall not be deprived of hope." Willie waves to the cheering crowd. In the three-shot, Anne turns to Jack, "Does he mean it, Jack? Does he?" Adam says, "That's his bribe," and walks out of the shot.

A montage captures the burst of building and law-making, the surging of ego and power: bulldozers and cranes, girders of power plants, a dam; cops roughing up citizens, Willie with show girls, with his black book of everybody's secrets. (Jack's voiceover: "Willie's little black book was a record of sin and corruption. And me, Jack Burden? I kept the book and added up the accounts.") Further images show Willie dancing with Anne at a charity ball, and Willie's signature, bold and big, on the sign marking the site of the "Governor Stark Hospital."

And then come the beginnings of betrayal on the personal level. Willie's flagrant infidelities infuriate Sadie: "After all I've done for him — now he's two-timing me!" A brief scene — an essence, an impression — between Anne and Willie in the Capital Lobby shows she is upset that he hadn't met her as planned. Sadie rushes Willie to a meeting.

In counterpoint, there is now a troubling, publicity-threatening scandal of corruption in the political ranks, the trickle down of greed to the petty and ugly dirty dealings of subordinate officials. State Auditor Pillsbury's problem is that he got caught, as Willie says, with "his hand in the pork barrel." Willie's problem is to keep the scandal from hurting him, Willie Stark. In a faceless hotel room he mocks Pillsbury, then has him sign his resignation due to ill health; but he will not use it unless he has to. Instead, he uses the black book and the telephone to keep people in line: "What have we got on Hopkins, Jack?" And then on the phone: "You've got a mortgage coming due on that place of yours in about five weeks, haven't you? You'd like it renewed, wouldn't you?"

After Pillsbury, Sadie and Duffy leave, and the moral crisis is reached. Judge Stanton has been present and wants to prosecute Pillsbury. Willie refuses. His overall strategy is more important. Jack stands between them, partially blocked, partially trapped in his own inner debate. As Willie says, "Judge, you talk like Pillsbury was ... was human. He isn't. He's a thing. You don't prosecute an adding machine if the spring gets busted and makes a mistake. You fix it." Judge Stanton insists; he will present his resignation in the morning. He walks to the door, and Jack, almost impulsively, crosses and meets him at the door. The judge wants Jack to leave with him, to admit his mistake in believing in Willie. Willie walks into the shot, now demanding attention, control. The shot is tighter now, close in on the three of them, more intense, the stakes higher. Jack is now deeper in the shot than Willie, between the two of them, at the point of an upside-down V, impaled between them, unable to stop it or choose, as Willie attacks the judge and justifies his actions. "I'll tell you what you are," says Willie. "You're scared.... You don't want to get your hands dirty. You want to pick up the marbles — but you don't want to get your hands dirty. Look at my whole program, Judge. How do you think I put that across?"

The judge starts to leave and says, "Are you coming with me, Jack?" Willie turns to look at Jack, who is frozen in place. The judge leaves, and business as usual goes on.

Judge Stanton has promised to drop out of politics, but he breaks his promise and leaks the scandal to the press. Willie beats back the protests, but he is afraid the judge's move was just the beginning. He wants Jack to investigate and dig up some dirt on the judge. Jack is straining to hold onto what he believes, to what he has given himself to, to what he's using to make sense of himself. He starts to investigate. He and Anne argue with Adam over whether Willie will really do good. Jack even uses the old cliché, "You can't make an omelet without cracking eggs." He fights with Sadie, who is even more desperately torn, more intimately betrayed, by Willie's unfaithfulness than he is. She claims Willie is planning to ditch Jack. "He'll ditch everybody in the world because that's what Willie wants. Nobody in the world but him." As they shout at each other, out of control, Jack suddenly slaps her, hard.

The start of the final crisis rises from an auto accident involving Willie's adopted son, Tom. Drunk, Tom lost control of his speeding car and crashed into a field. Both he and his girlfriend Helene have been found unconscious, but only she is seriously hurt and near death.

In the strong but subtle scene that follows, her father, Mr. Hale, comes to the Governor's Mansion to demand justice. The reception hall is spacious, with a broad, royal staircase curving up to the second floor. It is the ornate display of excessive power. The gang are all there, even Lucy. Hale insists that Tom was drunk. On his "throne," drinking constantly, Willie denies it, citing the police report. Tom joins them, though he feels dizzy, and admits he was drunk. Willie still tries to intimidate and even bribe Hale, but in an emotional speech Hale now defies him: "I believed in you ... I followed you ... and I fought for you. Well, the words are still good. But you're not." He stands. "And I don't believe you ever were." He walks away, and Willie, nodding, sends Sugar Boy (who is now always at his side, his most loyal and devoted follower) to follow him.

Lucy goes upstairs, and Willie goes to follow. "Lucy! Lucy!" he calls and staggers. On the stairs, he falls, and Jack helps him up. "I'd like Anne to see you now," Jack says.

The girl dies; her father disappears; and opposition mounts. The more he's pressured, the more Willie appears to be the brutal echo of Rossen's gangsters. Like Vanning in *Marked Woman*, he can brook no denial. (Vanning: "You think I care for money? All I care about is to make people do what I tell them.") In what may be his cruelest, most blindly, compulsively selfish act, Willie demands that Tom, still troubled by headaches, play in the "Big Game." Tom is injured in the football game in Willie Stark Stadium and ends up paralyzed for life. As the headlines tell us, "STARK BEGINS RE-ELECTION CAMPAIGN," even Tom in a wheelchair can be useful, as can the family Willie has deserted but now returns to, with reporters and photographers in tow. The false domestic idyll is interrupted. Over the radio they hear that Hale has been found beaten to death! Willie and his entourage abruptly leave.

The film's climactic section builds momentum as proceedings for impeachment are started against the governor. Willie fights back every way he knows. He even brings Tom and Lucy back to the Governor's Mansion and to all of his speeches to his People—the dear family standing together against injustice.

A magnificent montage propels the clashing elements of his campaign: Willie exhorts the folks that "It's not me they're after, it's you!" Willie manipulates the folks—"Tell the boys to get the hicks out. Bring 'em in from the sticks, empty the pool halls. Turn 'em out. Turn the yokels out." Excited crowds are turned out; "WIN WITH WILLIE" signs are passed out, and sign-carriers are directed from the top of a bus. Police break up opposition crowds, and thugs beat people up in doorways. Willie intimidates and bribes senators. But it still comes down to Judge Stanton.

Jack has found the dirt, even on Judge Stanton. Even he has been corrupted — back in the distant past. Jack's new disillusionment over the Judge has torn him apart even more, and left him stuck in cynical, defeated indecision. He fights against Anne's defense of Willie but can't stand Adam's stance of purity. As if it will somehow assuage his pain over what he's found, Jack gives Anne the documents he's got on the judge. "Give them to him, Anne. Change the picture of the world that Adam has in his head, just like our picture of it has been changed."

Jack has made his compromise. He will go with Willie to Burden's Landing to face the judge; he will not show Willie the documents if the judge will agree to cooperate. Once again the *plan sequence* of images conveys not only the powerful impact of the climactic drama in the scene in Judge Stanton's study, but also the more subtle flux of the emotional dynamics among the three of them.

Willie wants to know if the Judge is behind the impeachment proceedings. The judge admits he is, and says that now Willie can leave. Instead, Willie pours himself a drink and sits. As he begins his intimidation — his prosecution — of the judge, there is a sequence of reversals of two shots: Willie in profile, looking up, smirking, dominating even though he is sitting, while Sugar stands close behind, protecting; and a two-shot of the judge and Jack as the judge responds, the judge just behind Jack's shoulder so that Jack has to keep looking back at him and then forward at Willie, as if caught watching a deadly tennis match. "Do you remember a man named Littlepaugh?" Willie begins. Jack interrupts, "How did you find out?" But Willie demands to know how the judge got his first big job as counsel for the Fortune Electric Company.

When he hands the judge the documents (which Anne had given him), the camera cuts to a wide shot — the four of them in profile. The judge examines the papers. Cut to Willie sitting as he says, "You know, Judge, dirt's a funny thing. Some of it rubs off on everybody. How *did* you get the job, Judge? Blackmail?"

Cut to a shot of the judge and Jack. The judge looks away from Jack, even as he addresses him. Jack can hardly look at him. In sorrow and guilt, the judge remembers, "I swear I never even remembered his name. Isn't that remarkable, Jack?"

As Willie continues to pressure, demanding that the judge call it all off or be exposed, the camera shifts back to the wide shot of all four of them (which is now held to the end of the scene). The judge refuses to answer, turns his back to the camera, and starts to walk out. He crosses behind Jack and faces Willie. Looking at Willie and then at Jack, he says, "Ever since then I ... I've done my duty. I ... I'm responsible for many good things. [He looks down at the papers.] But I also did this."

Willie stands, jutting up close to him: "How about my answer?" For a moment the judge is pinned closely between Jack and Willie, with Sugar hovering, threatening, behind Willie. "You'll have it in the morning." And with dignity he walks back to the door to guide them out, bidding them goodnight. As they start to leave, Willie and Sugar go out the door first. In the foreground, Jack hesitates, then walks to the door, stops, and looks at the judge but doesn't speak. Through the doorway we see Willie waiting in the hall.

Jack turns and follows Willie out into the hall. The judge closes the door and walks forward toward the camera, away from them and into his own thoughts.

In the hall, Anne and Adam arrive. As Jack again demands to know how Willie found out, they hear a shot. Judge Stanton has killed himself. His principles can't let him collaborate with Willie; his dignity—his pride?—can't let him face the exposure of the human fact that at one time his need and his greed had led him to betrayal and violation.

As the long day and night of the impeachment trial begins, Anne comes to Jack's hotel room and breaks into sobs. She covers her face with her hands, but he pulls her hands away and pulls her to him. "No, I want to see you cry." She needs him to help her find Adam. Adam had been furious at her—but at himself too—and had slapped her and gone off. And Willie has left her. He's going back to Lucy; he needs to. "Oh, Jack—help me, please, please. Adam's all I've got left now. Oh, Jack, if you ever loved me..."

"If I ever loved you." Silence as he looks at her, then, "I'll go find Adam."

But he can't. There's an impeachment going on. The final sequence is one of the finest Rossen has put together (with much post-production editing). It takes place in two segments—day and then a dissolve into night and victory (and defeat). But it is all one pulsing, exciting, yet painful symbol and symptom of the People manipulated by corrupting power, their government itself, into an unthinking mass, a herd. It shapes a concluding ironic counterpoint to Willie's passionate and idealistic speech to the hicks at the beginning of his crusade.

Busses pull up and disgorge the People as they join the throngs pressing as close as they can get to the Capitol, up to the line of state troopers caging them in. They are victims of the demagogic manipulation, but eager accomplices in their own captivity. Shots capture them moving, milling about, individual faces rapt and excited, looking up, in families and groups. As they wave their "We Want Willie" signs in an ironic reprise of Willie's first campaigns, the band plays with a strong, heavy drumbeat. Jack is seen walking among them, and then up to the steps of the Capitol, looking for Adam. The loudspeaker blares: "All right now. Everybody ... that means *everybody* ... let's let Willie know we're here! All together—WE WANT WILLIE. WE WANT WILLIE." The people pick up the chant, the drum beats, and the troopers struggle to hold firm against the excited press of the mob straining to get as close as possible. Inside the chamber we hear the chant. Willie goes to the window and waves, eliciting cheers.

Later in the day, the crowd remains. The loudspeaker: "Attention, please.... This is a special announcement from Willie Stark to you people out there. He doesn't want any of you to leave.... He wants you to stay in front of the state Capitol until the fight is over.... Stay where you are! Stay where you are!" And the camera pans up to the engraved plaque above the entrance: THE PEOPLE'S WILL IS THE LAW OF THE STATE—GOVERNOR STARK. The People cheer.

As we dissolve into night, the crowd is quiet, expectant, and then explodes in triumph as the loudspeaker announces: "Willie Stark has won!" Willie comes out to the top of the steps to give his victory speech. How much of it can he still believe? Is the demagogue, the dictator, the commissar still a true believer himself? Does he still hold to the righteousness of his cause? "Remember, it's not I who have won, but you. Your will is my strength, and your need is my justice, and I shall live in your right and your will..."

As he finishes, he sees Jack and puts his arm around him. He sees Adam coming toward him, and goes to greet him when Adam shoots him. Sugar shoots and kills Adam. Then, loving and loyal to the last, Sugar kneels and cradles Willie in his arms (as Panama does Eddie on the church steps in *The Roaring Twenties*). "D-does it hurt m-much, boss? D-d-does it hurt much?"

Sadie and Duffy look on, silent. Anne stands apart, despondent, guilty. But Jack cannot leave it that way. Nor can Rossen. The tradition, the idealism, the hope demand some growth of consciousness, some possibility of change and redemption. "We've got to go on living," Jack tells Anne. "How?" He insists — he must insist to save himself as well as her: "So that Adam's death has meaning, so that it wasn't wasted.... Look at those people.... Look at them! They still believe in him. And we've got to make them see Willie the way Adam saw him, or there's no meaning in anything ... anything."

For Jack there may be — must be — a change. For Willie there can be none. For Willie, even as he is dying, there is only power, *his* power: "It could have been the whole world, Willie Stark. The whole world ... Willie Stark. Why did he do it to me ... Willie Stark? Why?"

To his dying end, Willie the demagogue and dictator is an echo, amplified and political, of gangster icons of the thirties. Now, however, he not only represents the false allure and dangers of money, but even more emphatically the corruption of the seeker of power beyond the money. His drive for control and domination is overweening, insatiable. Seeing the whole world in himself, he violates others and destroys himself in the process. But for Willie — as for the Josefs, the Adolphs, the Maos of the world — there is the manipulation of the power of idealism to affect, corrupt, and destroy others in vast universes of numbers. But there is, further, the power of the people, the common folk or the minions in the hierarchies, those who are the believers, who have their own needs and greeds, all wanting as much of it all as is possible for themselves, even as the chains are tightened around them.

11

A Time of Tests, Trials and Fears — *The Brave Bulls*

The second series of Congressional hearings were not to begin until 1951, yet its portents were already painfully unsettling the lives of those in the Hollywood Communist world or at its nearest fringes, and even those they had only influenced.

This world of unease, of a pressure beyond one's control, of fear and a kind of trembling of soul, casts its shadow on Rossen's next film, *The Brave Bulls*. In it, the loss of self, the corruption and betrayal of one's gift, takes a strikingly different form for the matador Juan Bello. What is new is *fear*. Juan Bello is a matador who cannot control his fear, who cannot control his career in the world of the *business* of bullfighting. It is a world ripe with the many ambiguous forms of betrayal, even that of betraying one's self.

Rossen made the movie at a moment of his own paradoxes of control and success. He had the support of Columbia boss Harry Cohn, and had even been asked to do a (usable) favor for Cohn in taking on (uncredited) some of the producer tasks for the 1950 movie *No Sad Songs for Me* when Sam Woods suddenly died. Buddy Adler was the credited producer, while Rudolph Maté directed.

But as the international crisis and tensions, the seemingly imminent dangers of the Cold War, intensified, in Hollywood in 1950 it was a time of trials and moral tests. The Soviets had the Atomic Bomb. Television displayed glimpses of construction of bomb shelters in suburban backyards and bomb drills in schools. Horror movies carried allusions to A-bomb destruction. The Soviet's blockade of Berlin had lasted for many months and lingered longer in most minds. A new terror had spread through Eastern Europe, spawning government takeovers, purges, trials, deportations, labor camps, and executions. Strong actions were needed, and taken, to prevent Communist takeovers in Greece and Turkey. The Marshall Plan and Truman Doctrine were hailed in the West, and vilified in the East and in international Communist circles. The Korean War had begun; it was not ended quickly, as had been hoped. China had fallen to the Communists, and there was much right-wing demanding of who lost China. In the winter of 1950 the Korean War escalated dangerously with the entrance of the Chinese, and with sudden devastating impact on American troops just below the Chinese border, all graphically depicted on television.

All this exacerbated fears of Communism, at home and abroad, and encouraged more aggressive anti–Communist actions and feelings within the country, where internal events had also contributed to this momentum. The Hiss and Rosenberg espionage cases, the Klaus Fuchs international spy case, and other revelations of espionage in the U.S. raised the public awareness of, and hostility toward, Communists. Right-wing organizations and demagogues, and a wide segment of the press, especially the Hearst newspapers, heightened, manipulated, and promoted the hostility and fears of the public with insistent ranting about Communist threats and dangers. The public furor was fed, of course, by the wilder claims and "investigations" of Senator Joseph McCarthy in the several years after his Wheeling, West Virginia, speech early in 1950. His distorting crusade was given exaggerated emphasis and prominence in the Hearst press — as it has been, conversely, by many historians, especially on the Left, and popular histories, documentaries, and films ever since. However, it played only a minor role in any actual effective and realistic actions against Communist propaganda and infiltration. Truman's Loyalty Program had broader consequences and was hotly debated at the time. As was the McCarren Internal Security Act of 1950. The McCarren Act expanded legislation that had been instituted several years earlier. It called for all "Communist-Action" and "Communist-Front" organizations to register with the Attorney General, and for officers of those organizations to do so if the organization did not comply. Much earlier than that, convictions of Communist Party leaders were obtained under the Smith Act. Organized labor, led by Walter Reuther, also took strong steps against Communist influence at this time, calling for reforms and expelling a number of Communist-controlled unions.

In Hollywood the power balance in the guilds had shifted against the Communists. Ronald Reagan was President of the Screen Actors Guild, and the all–Guild slate had wrested control from the Communist bloc in the Screen Writers Guild. The conservative Motion Picture Alliance for the Preservation of American Ideas, and its action arm the Motion Picture Industry Council, both basically under the direction of Roy Brewer, wanted to prove that the movie industry was not being "soft on Communism."

Communist Party members — including those among the original Hollywood Ten, others among the original Nineteen, others already facing an erratic and uneven form of blacklisting, others who feared subpoenas — began to consider and act out emigration. Mexico was the closest and easiest (and most inexpensive) option. Rossen was among the first to go to Mexico with his family.

Although Rossen began actual shooting *The Brave Bulls* in Mexico in the spring of 1950, in 1949 he had already begun development on the film, adapted from the popular novel by Tom Lea. In the novel Rossen had seen the potential for the dramatization of his basic themes and concerns, and echoes of the current real-life dilemmas of himself and others; but filming it in Mexico also enabled him to avoid or at least delay the next subpoena. Harry Cohn agreed with Rossen's estimate of the strength of the book. Bullfighting pictures were then still popular — *Blood and Sand*, *The Bullfighter and the Lady*, *The Sun Also Rises* were among the major versions. Cohn also agreed on the value of the location shooting, mainly to replicate the kind of authenticity that had been achieved, and praised, in *All the King's Men*. Cohn was also aware of, and accepted, Rossen's personal reasons for shooting in Mexico. He again also wanted Rossen to produce (with his own production company) as well as direct the picture.

Busy with *No Sad Songs for Me* and the complicated preparations for filming in Mexico, Rossen had assigned the screenplay to John Bright, who had been a colleague during the early Warners days, but with whom he had never actually worked before. Bright's screenwriting career had started auspiciously with co-writing credits on some of the iconic early thirties films in the Warners style—*Blonde Crazy, The Public Enemy, Smart Money, The Crowd Roars*—as well as the image-setting Mae West picture *She Done Him Wrong* (with Cary Grant). But though he had worked regularly after that for some time, *The Brave Bulls* was his first movie of any note for many years.

As was his regular method of working, Rossen worked closely with Bright on the screenplay and continued to adapt material and scenes as the production got underway. But he took no screenplay credit.

While working long and draining hours on the many demanding aspects of producing a film in a foreign country, Rossen had the assistance of a number of people in the Mexican movie industry, particularly the Tello brothers, Antonio and Luis. As film editor, he used Henry Batista, who had worked in both Mexico and the United States. Floyd Crosby and James Wong Howe were the cinematographers. Howe, who had shot the acclaimed fight scenes in *Body and Soul*, was used principally for what Rossen called "special-effect work" for the bullfighting scenes. Crosby, who did, in Rossen's memory, 80 percent of the work, had an unusual career. His debut was back in 1931 with the Academy Award–winning art film *Tabu*, directed by Robert Flaherty; but after that he had worked sporadically until doing *The Brave Bulls* and then Carl Foreman's *High Noon* in sequence. But after those two meaningful films, for the next fifteen years he became an efficiency expert. He worked on *seventy* movies, most of them Westerns, thrillers, and horror and science films, all, as would be expected, on small budgets and short production schedules. In that period he ranged from *The Old Man and the Sea* (a rare, for him, serious film) to *Beach Blanket Bingo* and *How to Stuff a Wild Bikini*, with some worthy Westerns in between.

Unlike the others who moved to Mexico in those years, Rossen was able to combine that forced expatriation with production of a film that took place in Mexico. Yet he could not escape the still looming threat to his newfound control and independence in his career. There is an unease in the film—not only in its plot and emotions, but in a certain haste and unevenness, in the telling and ordering of the material. Moments and sequences of visual and dramatic power and skill sit alongside other moments not as carefully refined and shaped as in his other films. It seems as if Rossen feels in himself the pressures on the matador Luis Bello, the uncontrollable contradictions—to get the job done right, with style and honor, and yet get it done now, before it is too late.

Even with its new exotic subject—bullfighting—and foreign setting, in its way the story of Luis Bello is shaped as another of Rossen's metaphor for the young man of potential grace and an innate gift who seeks and accepts, who may be *forced* to accept, the illusory (and destructive) symbols of the self. And, in striking form, it is a personal metaphor of the artist, the filmmaker, who is also working in a climate of fear, who cannot control his career in the world of the *business* of making movies—with its controlling studio bosses and its crusading political forces, its lures of money and success, its susceptibility to all of the ambiguous and shadowy forms of betrayal.

The fear that overwhelms Luis Bello may be a new element in the demanding inner life of a Rossen protagonist. It is, however, still a part of a welter of forces, both within him and in his environment, that lead him to the violation of his talent, the collapse of his energy and pride, his fall from grace. Unlike Willie, Charley Davis or Eddie Bartlett, Luis hurts no one but himself. And unlike them (and Fast Eddie Felson in *The Hustler*), he doesn't violate himself by winning in the wrong way, but by *losing*. But like them, he is influenced by and caught up in the world of winning — of making money, needing and wanting money.

The cruel and controlling power of money is developed as a central force and theme to a much greater degree in the film than in the novel. It is not only the money men, the bosses and owners, who make the sport (the art) of bullfighting a corrupt business. The betrayals wrought by money work on many levels, and have many and varied guises and disguises: Raoul, Luis' long-time friend and manager who controls Luis' money and lives on the money Luis can make; Luis' family and entourage who live, quite well, on his funding and always want more; the glamorous woman whom Luis loves; the fates and losses of the matadors, many penniless and defeated, that he knows and reveres.

It is not only the others who betray Luis through money; he betrays himself. Luis, too, spends his money, and so always needs more money. He lives beyond the bounds of the dedicated matador, with his sleek convertible, large, luxurious home in the city, house in the country, servants, parties and tours of the clubs and restaurants. He looks impeccable in his celebrity's wardrobe and movie star's sunglasses.

But these false external counters of the self are used for more than an indication of the pressure of society, the corruption of its values. The film is a further and tentative exploration of the mysteries of the internal life, the mysterious workings, purposes and cross-purposes, of the self. It is a direction that Rossen's most mature work would follow. We can note that at this time the Italian Neo-realists who he admired had also begun to move in this direction. Describing his intentions for his films in the fifties, Roberto Rossellini had talked of his attempts to "discover a new and solid base for constructing and representing man as he is — in the marriage that exists in him between poetry and reality, desire and action, dream and life."[1] In summing up Rossellini's films of this period in terms that can apply to Rossen's first steps in this direction, the critic Peter Bondanella called Rossellini's work "a cinema of psychological introspection and visual symbolism where character and environment served to emphasize the newly established protagonist of modernist cinema, the isolated and alienated individual."[2] A decade later the foremost practitioner of this cinema, Michelangelo Antonioni, talked of conveying, often by indirection and visual metaphor, not only the individual's relationship to society, but "the relation of the individual with himself."[3]

The crucial development of Luis' character in the film is in the connection between the corrupting pressures of money and the onset of his fear. Metaphorically, he is willing to sell his courage as a commodity, his talent as a performance; and so we can accept the symbolic connection between that selling of courage and his loss of it, his new fear. We can accept the way his desperate use of that courage and talent as a commodity corrupts the purity of what he does and even the actual quality of his performance. But the fear that rises in him is also uncontrollable. It has deeper roots than money; it is *there* after all the years of facing the horns and death — all the relentless Sundays at 4 P.M., all the years of seeing others die in front of him. But once the fear has risen, he pushes himself too quickly to return to the ring — and the horns. His own need for money, his anger over the misuse of his money by others, his recognition of the core of emptiness in his life of status and power — these drive him to avoid his fear rather than deal with it properly (even if that were possible), to go on before he is ready and make it all worse. The danger and the risk, the anger and the fear, and the money all get bound up together in his growing despair. But in the narrative, gaps remain in the merging of the two strands of plot and theme—in dramatizing how the corruptions of money both literally and psychologically contribute to his feelings of fear, and how other aspects of his self play their parts.

For the documentary literalness of crowd scenes and bullfighting scenes, Rossen again used a number of eyemos—newsreel cameras—all shooting at once. The documentary treatment of the fights had an odd sidelight, as they were not allowed to film the killing of a bull. "They [The SPCA] are tougher than any censorship group I know ... you fool around with an animal, and boy! ... So I found a couple of really good, important bullfights in the Mexican newsreels, and we found the suits they were wearing and used them as doubles for the actors' costumes, so that when the shot comes for the bull to gore the man—it was a shot of a real goring."[4] They were able to blend the newsreel shots with the documentary quality of their own shooting, using newsreel footage for more of the long-shot fight action than merely the goring or killing. But, unfortunately, the harmony of that combination was too often marred by cutting awkwardly into that documentary and documentary-like footage with head-on close-ups of Luis (Mel Ferrer) staring down at the bull.

In the overall structure of the film, however, there is generally a harmonious combination of Rossen's typical mixing of emphatic editing with *plan sequences*, with their longer-held shots and shifting movements and patterns.

In the first section of the film, at the first *corrida*, the crowd stands and cheers the beauty and risks of Luis' tight passes of the bull. They are hushed as he, poised and focused, goes in for the kill—and is gored. He has been hurt before, but there is something different this time. He cancels his next fight. "I'm tired. I want to go home ... to rest."

But for Luis, family is no haven, no lost center of a secure and righteous world, as it was for Charley Davis. "Everybody asks me for money. You ask for money in my dreams. I pay for everything. With my flesh—the flesh I expose to the bulls while you get ripe with fat." His manager, Raoul Fuentes (Anthony Quinn), has arranged a big fight in Mexico City. Old "Skinny" Salazar is going to be on the card with him. "He's getting old to fight the bulls," Luis says. "He needs the money," Raoul says. "Money," Luis says and looks away.

In his spacious and gracious home, Luis is seen on a second level, overlooking the large living and dining area. In a long-held shot that conveys his loneliness in the midst of his expensive possessions, he goes down the stairs, crosses the room, and sits at a long, rectangular dining table. A servant brings his dinner. An ornate chandelier hangs down into the shot, with luxurious drapings on the wall behind him. None of it is giving him any pleasure.

Raoul comes in and sits at the table. Luis wants to get a fight for his young brother Pepe. "If you want to push him fast, it'll take money for publicity—lots of money." Luis asks, "What happens to all the money I make?"

Raoul is not the greedy and manipulative gambler-promoter Roberts, with no interest save money and power. He has been with Luis from the start and has helped him, shaped him as a man and matador. Raoul believes in his ability and art. But he, like Luis, is a peasant—up from the poor countryside, his slum. For Raoul, it's a tough, ruthless world out there, and so anything goes. He does what he can for Luis, but he is also doing what he can for *Raoul*—even if it means betraying Luis in small ways or in large.

At a nightclub Raoul introduces Luis to Linda de Calderon (Miroslava), blonde, glamorous, sleek, a white fur stole around her lovely shoulders. We next see her being served her breakfast in her equally glamorous bed and bedroom. Where she gets the money for living in the manner to which she is accustomed is never discussed, but it is definitely hinted as somehow coming from the rich men in her life.

Linda is money, but she, too, is a more complex character than merely a false siren of the life money can buy; she is not Charley's Alice. The ambiguity of her personality and motives are nicely articulated by Miroslava, who reveals, but without exaggeration, the full human being under the sleek veneer.

On their first romantic night together, in a softly glowing close-up, she says, "What is it about you? What is it about you?" And she, we believe, believes it. At least right then. At first, Linda and this new chance at love are associated with the presence of the positive spirit of the bulls and matadors, the lore, the art and ritual. It is a glimpse of what bullfighting (filmmaking?) can be when free of the greed, pressures and betrayals of the business. At a farm in the country, Luis is working with a calf as the farmhands cheer. He comes over to Linda and Raoul, and says it feels good to be working again. Raoul says that nobody has his "style."

"Raoul used the wrong word," Linda says. "It's not style, it's grace."

"That's from practice," Luis says, but he's pleased.

But the real world intrudes. At the bull farm they are listening to the broadcast of Luis' major fight in Mexico City. The announcer's voice continues through the sequence as we cut to the bullring — and the jarring contrast to the ideal, now shown in the collapse of Luis Bello, in his betrayal of his art. But it is also the betrayal of him by the crowd (the People) and the media. There is a montage of images of a bull charging, a matador working in close and gracefully, the crowd bursting rhythmically in cheers at each pass, and toreros and their crews watching from behind the barrier. Over it, the announcer: "It is not a sport. It is an art, a ritual, a tragic drama in which the man is supposed to live, but the bull is not. The closer the matador works to the horns and the more style he maintains, the spectator shares with him the experience of defying death with grace."

These noble words are, with bitter irony, turned to their extreme opposites when Luis' skill and nerve fail him. In his fight, Luis does not hold his ground, plant his feet, and work close to the horns. "He is running, ladies and gentlemen, he is running!" The jeering and booing mount as Luis manages a kill, but only while backing off rather than going up and over the horns. He is like a butcher, the announcer says. When "Skinny" Salazar comes out and works in close and fine, they cheer, and the unctuous voice of the announcer proclaims, "This is what they have come to see! That's courage, that's style!" A stream of "Olés" is suddenly choked off as Salazar is gored and dies.

At his home with Raoul, Luis can be cynical about it: "Maybe that's what a bullfighter gets paid for — to give a brave feeling to a man who hasn't got it, [who] has to buy it so he can talk about it."

"Salazar died broke, you know that, don't you?" he says to Raoul.

"Except a big house."

"And a big mortgage."

Raoul says Salazar was good with the bulls, smart with the bulls. Luis replies, "I want to be smart with the money. I spend too much, Raoul. Will you help me? I don't know anything about money, but I need it. Now more than ever."

Later, in the quiet darkness of his house, he finds comfort with Linda. She feels for him, feels with him, but she has to try to understand. "Why do you do it, Luis? How can you go out doing that Sunday after Sunday? Why do you do it, Luis, what for?"

"It's what I do, you know that," he answers. "Luis Bello without bulls, nothing. Going back to nothing."

Her sympathy brings out in him what it was, what it should be. "There is something to it, something great about it sometimes [as Fast Eddie will say about playing pool in *The Hustler*]. I wish I could show it to you then.... I haven't felt it for a long time. I don't know, I try. I wish I could."

She takes him in her arms, and as they embrace — her face seen against his cheek, past his head — we see her tears, tears for herself as well as him. As she says, "Oh, Luis, darling. I wish it could stay like this ... everything could stay away like this. Oh, god, keep everything away." She begins to sob, crying over more than she can tell him. She knows who she is and how she has lived.

The moment cannot last. The crashing, downward spiral accelerates.

To get his mind and body in shape for his next big fight in Mexico City, Luis goes out on the road, but (as seen in montage) he does not fight well. He is not what he wishes himself to be. Linda is staying in his home. Trying as well as she can to hold on to what they have together. She seeks to be his love truly, to be what she wishes she could be.

Linda sits alone at the table in Luis' house — where Luis had been sitting alone — and, again, Raoul comes in. The scene is a turning point in the narrative — and in their lives. It is played in dim, tormented light and developed beautifully in two basic long-held shots that intensify the increasing physical and emotional tensions between them, and within them — the sparring for control, for her release from him. In the first shot, Raoul stands behind her; she does not turn to look at him as they talk, and blows smoke as she holds firm against him. She had not shown up for a date they had made to go to Cuernavaca — how many such dates *had* she shown up for? She says she's not going. A moment of conscience, he mocks. No, a moment of truth. He laughs at her being true.

"Leave me alone, Raoul." It is a plea referring to more than at just that moment. "Leave him alone," he retorts, revealing his split, and competing, concerns — for Luis as a friend, for Luis as a money-maker, and for himself and what he wants for himself.

The camera cuts to the second basic angle as she gets up and walks away from him, toward the camera. He comes after her as she turns to face him. He tells her Luis has "fear" now, and she doesn't understand that. The scene cuts to her as she says, "Yes, I do, I understand very well." Returning to that second basic angle, but somewhat closer as they face off against each other, the camera shows her standing up to him and his power over her. She accuses him of being glad Luis has the "fear" while Luis thinks he is his friend.

"You get things for him," she snaps and turns from him abruptly.

"Pretty things," he says, touching her hair. She walks away, the camera following, and turns back to defy him. "And when you take them away, you say, don't worry, ask Raoul Fuentes, he'll get you anything." A pause. And then, her face in the light, she insists, "This you won't take away."

The shot is held as he comes into it, the shot now from behind his back as he reasserts himself over her. "I don't have to. You'll go away. I know you, Linda. You'll go away like you've always done with all of them." He grabs her by the arms and shakes her as they turn into profile and the shot continues. They are now yelling at each other. She insists Luis believes in her and *can* believe in her; he insists she is bad for Luis. He knows her, has been with Luis too long to let her ruin him when she leaves him.

"At what percent?!" she demands.

"Less than yours.... He won't even be a good matador any longer. Right now he only doubts himself in the ring. Then he'll doubt himself as a man. That's not good for Luis Bello."

"Nor for you!"

"Nor for me!"

He crosses in front of her and forward, toward the camera, and sits. She moves to stand in front of him, above him. It is like she is insisting to herself that she can fight him. She accuses him of liking Luis' fear. "It makes you feel better than him. You've wanted to feel that way for so long now. That's why you won't let me go. Because you know Luis wants me."

The camera cuts to him, revealing all. "What's his is mine."

Back at the original angle of that second basic shot, she stands above him as she slaps him. It is one last struggle against betrayal. He grabs her and pulls her down to the side, toward the camera, and kisses her, his face above hers. She succumbs — to him and to herself. (As Orson Welles said to Rita Hayworth, who couldn't help her unfaithfulness either, in the crazy mirror fun house world at the end of *The Lady from Shanghai*, "One who follows his nature keeps his original nature in the end. But haven't you ever heard of something better to follow?") For all the scene's power and the implications of human weakness, of the intricate web of one's nature and motives, might that final kiss be too neat and easy a plot turn to betrayal?

The Brave Bulls (1951), Columbia Pictures. Luis Bello's friend and manager, Raul Fuentes (Anthony Quinn), and Luis' love, Linda de Calderon (Miroslava), are about to betray the matador.

The destructive impact of this betrayal is beautifully conveyed. When he returns to Mexico City, Luis learns that Raoul has been killed while driving Luis' car back from Cuernavaca, and that Linda has been killed in the car with him. Whatever progress he has made in pulling himself together is shattered. He has given himself to love, and it has betrayed him. He shatters a glass partition in his living room and rushes away.

In the Cantina Mamacita he is the only customer, and he is very drunk. They want him to go. "Go where? I got no place to go. Even smashed up my car. I got no place except the bulls and I'm through with them.... I want it to stay closed. I don't want anybody in here." He takes out his wallet and slams it on the table. "I'll pay for everything. I want it quiet. *Quiet!*" Luis suddenly stands, goes to an upright piano, bangs on the keys. Shouting, "Linda, Linda!" he rushes toward the camera and out of the shot.

He comes running into the next room. The scene in this room, another masterful *plan sequence*, is a mix of wide-angle shots and close-ups of varied tightness as he explodes in lacerating, jagged pain and fury, talking loudly and wildly as he moves and careens one way and then the other. He finds a dark-haired woman and grabs her by the arms. Cut to a close-up of him holding on to her, shaking her as he raves, "Raoul, he was my right arm. My sword. Did they do it to me—I'll never know, but I'll think, I'll think..." He lets her go and moves abruptly out of the shot.

The camera cuts to the wider angle as the dark-haired woman tries to get out of the room. He pulls her back and slams the glass door; the glass shatters. He pulls her to him, then pushes her down into a chair. We see him standing above her, bending close over her head, and then standing up, twisting in the hurt he pours out in his words: "A torero has no fear! ... [Then quietly] I'm afraid, I'm afraid of all the horns. [Weak now, defeated] One of the horns is Linda dead, another is Raoul dead, another is Linda and Raoul together, alive. That's the horn that cuts and tears."

He gets angry again and pulls the woman up, a hand on her throat. In close-up now he starts to kiss her, then pushes her away. In a wider shot he starts to fight the bull and crashes into things as she cowers in the foreground with a table between them. He comes after her, after the bull, up and over the table, and crashes down on the floor.

Later, Pepe and his friends come to get him and lift him off the floor in the wreckage of the room—and his life—and carry him out. "Did he pay?" Pepe asks the owner. He looks at all the money in the wallet she is holding, and adds, "I'll say he paid."

Luis has indeed paid. He has crashed to the depths of his despair over what has been done to him, what he has done to himself, his gift, his dream, and, as Linda had said, his grace. He has hit bottom before he can find his redemption. He finds it out in the countryside where he began, among his people, in the small country bullring of Eladio Gomez, with the brave bulls that Gomez has bought, for the honor of it, for more than he can afford to pay. But no redemption is easily won.

In his first fight of the day his bull is truly noble; he is not. He does not plant his feet, does not hold his ground, does not make his passes while close and tight to the horns. The respect and cheers turn quickly to boos and hoots. Cushions come down on him, and one even hits him in the eye. On this first try for the kill, he is knocked down. When he tries again, in shameful close-up he comes forward with the sword, swerves away, and drops the sword. He gets another and runs again. He withdraws behind the barrier.

Pepe fights beautifully, to the striking contrast of cheers and drum-beat "Olés." And then he is gored in the thigh and carried off.

Luis goes out into the ring, sees Pepe's blood, and picks up his *muleta* and sword, thinking, "It comes as God wants." He makes a good kill, and they love him again.

His final bull is the ugly one—the matching shadow of the paradox of his own nature. They are almost as one as he performs graceful, daring, and close passes. He and the ugly bull are finding their redemption together—in something deeper than their physical actions. Seeming to sense this, the crowd roars in unison. Pepe, not badly hurt, limps out to watch from behind the barricade. When Luis salutes the crowd before the kill, he is thinking, "I dedicate the bull not to you out there, but to what I now know— that a man cannot live in fear."

At the moment of truth, we alternate close-ups alternate showing the face of Luis and the face of the bull. "Only we know," Luis thinks, "they don't. Only we know what it's like to stand here and look at death — right in the eye." Cut to a sequence of images of a noble kill — for both bull and matador.

As the crowd pours out into the ring to be near them, to touch them and their glory, Luis and Pepe embrace. "C'mon, Kid — look at them — look what they're doing, smiling now. The whole world's ours! [But it is a mocking tone, without Willie's all-encompassing ego.] The hell with them." They start to walk. "We'll live forever and both get rich!" ("Nobody dies!"/"Everybody dies!")

They walk out together into the bright sunlight — as the crowd streams with them and down the street — not alone and into the fog like the women in *Marked Woman*, or down dark streets like Charley and Peg in *Body and Soul*.

The film is full of these powerful and moving moments and passages, striking and suggestive images and montages. They capture a painful sense of the collapse of a good man and the stirring rise to regain himself. But the final fight cannot fully escape the conventional neatness of the kind of last-minute victory at the end of a sports film. Overall, the script and its development fall just short of fulfilling the potential of the complexity of motives and emotions that are opened, the connections between the inner life and the forces of the social milieu that can warp one's self — that nagging connection between his fear within and the world out there that is so unfaithful.

The film did receive generally favorable reviews — praising its power and honesty, but finding problems in its characterization. Several emphasized its genre, comparing it favorably as a *bullfighting* movie to *The Bullfighter and the Lady* of the same year. Typically, Bosley Crowther's positive review in the *New York Times* stressed the excellence of its surface qualities, ignoring its metaphor of grace, loss, and redemption, as well as its parallels to the world of the artist, the filmmaker:

> Robert Rossen's brilliant translation [of the book] ... so sweeping in its visual comprehension ... best film on bullfighting yet. In fact, it is not very likely that we will ever see its match in our lifetime.... The ways in which he has used his camera for perceiving sharp and suggestive details ... blood on a man's drawn face after a swift, staggering brush with a charging bull.[5]

As the film was released, many in Hollywood were facing the horns of their own frightening dilemmas. In March of 1951 eight subpoenas were served. By April and May — when the Hollywood Ten were completing their prison terms — dozens of people had been served and began to appear before the Committee. Rossen had hoped to make a second movie in Mexico, but in its early stages that plan dissipated. In mid–April he received his subpoena. He had decided on his strategy. He told Harry Cohn his plan — his way of facing the Committee and his personal dilemma and fears.

Some years before, Cohn, a dedicated gambler, had introduced Rossen to the intricacies of playing the horses on visits to Santa Anita and Hollywood Park. He liked to tell a story, with himself as the butt of the joke, that when Rossen had followed a tip and bet on a twenty-to-one shot, he had asked him, "How much did you bet?"

"Twenty dollars on the nose."

"You're a goddamned idiot," Cohn had told him. But the horse won.

This time Cohn had again told him, "You're an idiot. You all are."[6]

12

The Political and Moral Turmoil of the Blacklist Era — The Hearings, 1951

Facing a trial of one's integrity, sense of self, inner strength, moral insight and courage — as dramatized in *The Brave Bulls* — was part of the life in Hollywood in the years before, during, and after the production of the film. Four years had passed between the first hearings and the hearings in which Robert Rossen and others were called to testify in 1951. The most intense period of the blacklist was about to begin.

The situation that Rossen and the others faced in 1951 had developed not only within the intensifying conflict in the Cold War between the Soviet Union and the West, especially America, but within the battles over Communism in the United States. The particular nature of what they now faced was, as we have seen, also the result of actions in the Hollywood world in those four years and during those first hearings themselves.

Rossen's first test on the horns of this dilemma culminated with his appearance before the Committee in June of 1951. Before his appearance, in an earlier period of uncertainty, he had written a statement that captures vividly the deep anxiety and fearful sense of threat of these years of being caught by forces that you couldn't control, but hoped you could find a way to control. It is a mood and ambience reflected, intentionally or not, in the prevalent *film noir* of the period, as in the apt title of a lesser film, *The Dark Corner*. Rossen's statement is also revealing of the complex thought and strategies involved — of what to reveal and not to reveal, of how to find a middle way to carefully pass through the political, professional, and moral mine field. It is not clear what he had intended to do with the statement (present it when called, submit it to an Op Ed page), but in any event he chose another approach, another strategy. The document, to be sure, has an uneven combination of self-dramatization and obfuscation. There is in it an evasion, conscious or not, of any full decision to break totally with his belief in the movement, not only with the official Party that he had actually finally left for good. It may also well be an evasion of facing or revealing any complicity in the kinds of immorality and betrayal by international Communism that he defined in general terms in his eventual testimony in 1951 (and much more explicitly in 1953). He begins:

> As things look now, my career in the Hollywood film industry appears to be over. It is a career of which I have been and am very proud. I have always been serious about films. I considered them an art form on a level with any other art form and I think I contributed somewhat to the recognition of that idea. The fifteen years that I spent in films, either as writer, have been fruitful and creative ones.... And now, at this time, my career seems to be over.[1]

And it is because some witnesses have alleged he was a member of the Communist Party. "These are not allegations. They are truths. I *once* [emphasis added] was a member of the Communist Party."[2] Rossen goes on to describe the state of the nation and his beliefs for joining (as previously discussed), and states he left the Party in 1946 or 1947. He then presents a series of questions, which he answers, on categories related to membership. He discusses paying dues, attending study classes on "dialectical materialism," meetings at which Marxist principles were applied to current issues, and activities to promote the results of such analyses — all general, rather benign and equivocating. He did not mention any "control" or attempt to control the Screen Writers Guild, for example. "The electives went usually to those candidates who were most active in fighting for the Guild, and we were most active."[3] On the crucial question of why he left, he stresses only a mild central point of "separation"— no outrage, no mention of anything the Party did, of the kinds of reasons for outrage he discusses in 1953. The Party, he says, "did not really understand the American scene, and was not representative of it. In a sense I felt a separation. I felt that the party was facing one way and the American people another." The people wanted some form of capitalism, "a capitalist democracy" whose problems would be solved in other ways than Communism offered.

"I particularly felt this separation in my own creative work." This was not, he claims in the document, because there was ever anybody telling him what to write — not mentioning at least one meeting, two years earlier, over *All The Kings Men* (see Chapter 10). However, he alludes to the fallacy of the Marxist theories that were the basis for such meetings:

> However, I could not make the theory fit the facts nor the people. The people that I wrote about, and they were, for the most part, people that I had known, did not fit the pattern of what they ought to be [in terms of Marxist principles].[4]

Here the only available copy of the manuscript breaks off.

Once started, the new hearings produced a flood of subpoenas and sessions of the Committee on and off through 1952 and into 1953. And the blacklist intensified and spread. In 1955, Adrian Scott provided a summary of the blacklist to that time in an article in the left-wing, and short-lived, *Hollywood Review*. By his count, 214 of what he termed "studio employees" had been blacklisted, including 106 writers, 36 actors, and 11 directors. Later appraisals of the totals vary, and are usually higher, and can't actually be based on any single source. Several estimates place the Screen Actors Guild total at more than one hundred. The totals of Scott, and several others, appear to be based on those who took the Fifth Amendment, which leaves out all those who never appeared and yet were blacklisted. On the other hand, many who were on some lists did go through "rehabilitation," so totals on any of the lists are a complicated problem. HUAC reports had about 325 names by 1954, while the American Legion list had over 300, but not all of those were denied work. On the other hand, there was also a kind of "graylist" of people who became suspect in more random ways — those that were not included in the usual lists but were, for example, named in one of the publications. The most common figure cited for the blacklist is somewhat more than 300.[5]

In this series of hearings, among those who appeared, some testified (and named names), some took the Fifth Amendment, and a few remained vehement and hostile in their protests. Among those who testified fully were Edward Dmytryk (who had gone to prison as one of the Ten convicted of Contempt of Congress), Elia Kazan, Budd Schulberg, Clifford Odets, Lee J. Cobb, Frank Tuttle, Leo Townsend, Isobel Lennart, Roy Huggins, and Martin Berkeley (a former Party member and ardent anti–Communist who named so many that Committee counsel felt it blurred the significance of his testimony).

Among those who did not want to cooperate, the legal fashion for those who were netted and pulled in was to take the Fifth Amendment, which the Ten and their strategy had not found acceptable. "Taking the Fifth" seemed the best way out for almost all those who refused to testify, whether former Communist Party members or those who were caught between. The latter were those who felt — as the pressure from both sides built and the climate of opinion, the either-or moral equation, solidified — that they had no other moral alternative. Barring any other complications, "taking the Fifth" did not lead to a citation for contempt — though of course it led, in most cases, to being blacklisted. There were several degrees of refusal practiced within this strategy. The most innovative of them became known as the "Diminished Fifth" — in which one, with varying time frames, talked about not being a member only in the present tense, or at some time in the past, or at a specific time; otherwise, one invoked the Fifth and, in addition, used it to decline to talk about organizations or other people.

Rossen had told Harry Cohn about his own strategy in playing the "Diminished Fifth." He said that he would admit to having been a Communist since 1937 but was no longer a member of the Party. He would testify about himself only.

What Rossen did do when he testified on June 25 followed a more restricted strategy than he had discussed with Cohn. He thought it would show his cooperation yet more strongly defend his Fifth Amendment right to not state anything that had the possibility of incriminating himself. While obviously evasive, it was the kind of reasonable strategy that might have had a different outcome *if* the words and deeds of the preceding four years had not been so monumentally unreasonable. This was a big *if*. At the hearing, Rossen stated that he was not a member of the Party at that moment but declined to answer questions about whether he had been a member yesterday, last month, last year, or even before he walked in the door. Beyond that common position, however, he carefully avoided any phrasing that implied he had ever been a member. For example, when asked why he withdrew from the Party "as of the time you walked into the room," he insisted, "I did not state that I had ever been a member of the Communist Party." At another point he said, "I didn't state I had withdrawn from anything."[6] The strategy here was based on the opinion (warranted or not) that somehow that would make him less likely to be held in contempt when refusing to discuss anybody else, even to the point of knowing them or not. Repeatedly citing the Fifth and sometimes also the First Amendment, he declined to answer any questions about people or specific events or activities.

On the other hand, he was open to discussing his opposition to the Communist movement in general, although his statements were circumspect and nowhere near the strong, explicit criticism of evil in his testimony of 1953. He stated, "I should like to emphatically state that I am not a member of the Communist Party. I am not sympathetic with it or its aims." Several times he stressed that "there is no question of my loyalty to this country or my opposition to any kind of divided loyalty, especially to the Soviet Union."[7]

When asked, for no clear reason, if he would want his children to ever join the Party, he said, no "...because I don't believe in it.... [It] leads only to one thing ... dictatorship.... It opposes freedom of religion, freedom of speech, and it basically is against the dignity of the human individual.... I believe in the democratic way of life." But when asked by Representative Jackson if "you believe ... the Communist Party is a conspiracy dedicated to the overthrow of other constitutional forms of government," his answer was careful and conditional, revealing his cautious attempt to walk a fine line:

> In my opinion, I would have to agree to the extent that unquestionably the Communist Party of either this country or any other country would be dedicated to imposing upon the other country a Soviet form of government, which in and of itself would mean a new kind of constitution, a new kind of system of government.[8]

The fact that he and others were not indicted for this limited level of testimony shows that some shift of the basic ground, a change in the Committee's assumptions and procedures, had occurred. It was only a beginning, but it was an indication of how there might then have been a different script to follow if the ideological climate had not been so rancorous and heated in the years since 1947.

Rossen and others were not indicted, but most who followed this path were blacklisted. Even Cohn, who found the growing blacklist distasteful (he called it *blackmail*) reluctantly went along with the demand passed on by Nate Spingold, his long-time liaison with the corporate bosses in New York. Those who refused to cooperate with the Committee would have to be fired. Reluctantly, Cohn released Rossen from his contract, as well as other trusted and close employees and colleagues, such as producer Sidney Buchman. Later, Cohn would be heard to say when facing a problem, "I wish Sidney were here."[9]

Shortly after his appearance, Rossen left for Europe. He was never to set foot in Hollywood again. He did not have another movie released in the United States until close to four years later, in March of 1955. By then his whole world had changed.

Painfully disturbing, and more revealing of the desperation felt by many in facing the dilemma of testifying, was the appearance of Rossen's old friend and colleague John Garfield on April 23, 1951. While Garfield was probably not a member of the Party, he had taken part in person, and with his signature and money, in a myriad of Party-controlled activities and organizations, and had been involved with numerous Party members in both business and politics. When he appeared before the Committee he did not want to take the First or Fifth Amendment, but he did not want to incriminate himself or anyone else either. His strategy — or, more accurately, confused and contradictory lack of strategy — was to profess his extreme disapproval of Communism and the Communist Party, but also to attempt to claim his total, and totally unlikely, inability to recall his involvement with anybody who was a Communist or his participation in any of the organizations, meetings, publications and petitions presented to him.

> WOOD: Let me ask you categorically, have you any knowledge of the identity of a single individual who was a member of the Communist Party during the time you were in Hollywood?
> GARFIELD: No, sir.

And later,

> JACKSON: I am still not convinced of the entire accuracy of what you are giving this committee. It is your contention you did not know, during all the time you were in New York affiliated with the Group theater ... you did not know a Communist.
> GARFIELD: That is right.
> JACKSON: And that during the years you were in Hollywood and in close contact with a situation in which a number of Communist cells were operating, with electricians, actors, and every class represented, that during the entire period of time you were in Hollywood you did not know of your own personal knowledge a single member of the Communist Party?
> GARFIELD: That is absolutely correct, because I was not a party member or associated in any shape, way, or form.

After several more exchanges, Jackson concluded, "I must say, Mr. Chairman, in conclusion, that I am still not satisfied."

Nor was anyone else. The *Daily Worker* attacked him for betraying the cause by disowning all he had claimed to believe in. Archer Winsten, in the liberal *New York Post*, said *nobody* could have lived in New York in the thirties and not have known a single Communist. On May 23 *Variety* ran a story quoting unnamed sources saying that not only was HUAC considering re-calling him, but Congressman Jackson was urging an FBI investigation of possible perjury. Friends, both Communists and not, turned on him.[10]

Three months after he testified, Garfield's last movie was released. Despite his intense and appropriately troubled, even desperate, performance, it is, unfortunately, a redundant, clichéd version of his old themes — of what could have been the motto of his own life — *He Ran All the Way*. It was produced by Bob Roberts, directed by Jack Berry, and written by Hugo Butler and Guy Endore (and Dalton Trumbo), from a novel by Sam Ross. All but Ross were among the Communists he had never known. For the next year Garfield felt the next punch was coming soon, and any day now it would be thrown at him. He struggled even more desperately with the dilemma of testifying or not. By all accounts he was beginning a strategic reversal of his previous position through non–Committee channels (including an article in *The Saturday Evening Post*) — based on the premise that he had been "used" by the Communists — when he died of a heart attack in May of 1952.

Despite all these pressures and assaults on their freedom and livelihood, and despite all the efforts on the Left to campaign for the Ten and against the Committee and blacklist — despite all this, the splintering Left still had the time and energy, and the resolute and blinkered idealistic belief in programs espoused by the Party, to campaign with the same old zeal for a number of "causes." Two of the most significant campaigns through these years of the hearings were the interrelated crusades for the third-party presidential campaign of Henry Wallace and the world-wide campaign, once again, for "Peace."

The complicated (and unclear) stages of the relationship of Rossen and the Party during this time can be at least suggested by any relationship of his to activities for these two "causes" and to his participation (as discussed previously) in activities to protest the hearings and blacklist.

When he later testified in 1953, Rossen's statements about the chronology of his final break with the Party seem to be in contradiction with some other information. It is possible that he was attempting to distance himself as much as possible from the Party; however, it is also possible that the seeming contradictions merely indicate the indefinite, ambiguous stages of thinking and action involved in breaking with not only the Party but with long-held beliefs. In 1953, he stated:

> I think I stopped paying dues somewhere around 1946 ... and I honestly think that by 1947 I was out of the Party....
> I believe if I hadn't been subpoenaed in 1947, I would have gone even further from the Party. The subpoena brought me back in the end of 1947 to an activity specifically related to that committee and to the fight of the Hollywood Ten, which you may know was originally the Hollywood Nineteen. I was one of the 19 who were subpoenaed in 1947.
> Whatever meetings I might have attended after that I'm pretty sure were in direct relation to this specific problem, but I know by the end of 1947, somewhere in, around there, I was out — and I was out very, very completely.[11]

In testimony and interviews several people have discussed Rossen's not paying dues, whether as an attack on him or a factual point. Over a period of time (never made particularly clear), this was a matter of concern to the Party, which still considered him member enough to send people to get him to pay his dues.

The spring of 1949 meeting called to criticize Rossen and *All the Kings Men* is a confusing instance. Rossen definitely has stated he was no longer in the Party by that time, but the Party still decided to attack him for his film; and, for whatever reason, he still decided to attend the meeting. Ring Lardner, Jr. was at the meeting. In an interview years later, his comment about the meeting clearly indicated that, at least in his recollection, Rossen was still a member at that time. He commented that "the result of the discussion was to drive Rossen out of the Party."[12] Of course, since Rossen attended, Lardner may have assumed Rossen was not yet "out very, very completely." Such things were not advertised.

The presidential campaign for Henry Wallace in 1948 was the last major crusade on which Rossen was associated with a Party organization. But then, at least for a time, so were many liberals. The Wallace third-party campaign had begun in 1947 and developed in 1948 during the presidential election. Even at this time there were exposes and substantial evidence that the Wallace campaign was initiated by and controlled by the Communist Party. These claims were heatedly denied by the converted and their new idealistic recruits, claiming it, of course, to be nothing more than "Red-baiting." In Hollywood, in March of 1948, most of the Ten and the Nineteen and other Party members (and even now-disenchanted former members) formed the Hollywood Wallace for President Committee. For a time liberals like Huston joined in, but soon drifted then scurried away. Others, like Dunne, opposed the move from the onset. When Huston had solicited his aid, Dunne later said, "I listed my objections to the Wallace candidacy. But he did take it on, and the most prominent members of it were the Hollywood Ten."[13] Rossen was a founding member, along with many others, but he was soon too busy with *All the King's Men* to continue to be active in the campaign. In 1953, while responding to questions about why he left the Party, he provided an indication of the reasons for any continued connection to activities that appealed to his liberal ideals. He commented, "And this doesn't mean, you know, I still don't contribute money to certain things I believe in. For instance, I contributed to the Wallace campaign. Well, I thought it was a pretty good idea to have a third party in this country, and one doesn't go — at least I don't, or I can't, change — to go from being a member of the extreme left to being a member of the extreme right."[14]

The failed Wallace crusade was only one aspect of the new International Communist campaigns for "Peace." This was the Cominform's major international campaign of the period, yet there is no available documentation of Rossen being involved in any of the events or organizations under Communist control in this crusade, or of his discussing it in later testimony or interviews. (For example, there is no reference to him in the Committee's extensive research and documentation of this movement, published as the *Report on the Communist Peace Offensive* in April 1951.) Indeed, the Communists' role and claims in this campaign were typical of the kind of "rationales" and destructive hypocrisies he protested against in his 1953 testimony. In contrast, especially after the collapse of Wallace's bid for the presidency, other Hollywood members of the CPUSA continued to find time to actively pursue the Soviet's version of Peace through other means than the Progressive Party. This influential version of the traditional Soviet campaign coupled the revered ideal of Peace with the new danger and fear of atomic warfare. It consistently associated, and directly correlated, *Peace* with two complementary messages: defense of the "peaceful" policies and actions of the Soviet Union, and attack on the "aggressive" intentions and policies of the United States, including such imperialist aggressions as the Marshall Plan, the Truman Doctrine, NATO, the Berlin Airlift, etc.

The concept was first introduced at the Cominform's inaugural conference in September 1947. It called for a program to "appeal to men of letters, men of art, culture and science" to promote the Soviet foreign policy for "Peace" and "to awaken the people of Europe and the world to the growing danger of a new world war, as a consequence of the ruthless expansionist drive of American big business."[15] The phrasing was a perfect example of the propagandic mask: attack ruthless expansion to draw attention away from ruthless expansion in Eastern Europe. In his 1953 testimony, Rossen was to cite this kind of campaign and its terminology as the kind of false protection of "the masses, the people," while ignoring and evading the consequences for actual individuals. Several further conferences and open letters in international journals developed the elements of the Cominform concepts, particularly emphasizing the role of "intellectuals" of all nations in leading the people in struggle.[16]

The major response of the American Party was the well-publicized and controversial Waldorf Conference for World Peace (in official Cominform terminology, the Cultural and Scientific Conference for Peace). After extensive planning, it was held in March 1949 — for Hollywood Reds, almost exactly halfway between the first congressional hearings of 1947 and the second round in 1951. Many in Hollywood were indeed exhilarated by the call to a new major crusade and joined other CPUSA comrades in support of the event and promotion of its cause. Joseph Losey (who during World War II had staged Rallies for Russian War Relief), Lillian Hellman and John Howard Lawson were on its organizing committee. Hellman and Lawson, along with Clifford Odets and composer Aaron Copland, were among the featured speakers. Copland had recently completed his beautiful score for the film *The Heiress*. Among the organizers, sponsors, signers of invitations, open letters, and calls were what was probably the largest number of Hollywood Leftists ever assembled for a single event, including Albert Maltz, Budd Schulberg, Arthur Miller, E.Y. Harburg, Donald Ogden Stewart, Ring Lardner, Jr., Dalton Trumbo, Clifford Odets, Paul Robeson, Howard Fast, Charles Chaplin, Jules Dassin, Edward Dmytryk, Dorothy Parker, Lester Cole, Martin Ritt, Gale Sondergaard, et al.[17] But without Robert Rossen.

Speeches by Maltz in the Spring and Summer of 1949 highlight, in fervent belief, the Soviet's connection of American "fascism" and the dire danger of war, and the need for Peace. "One is destroyed in order that a thousand will be rendered silent and impotent by fear. Through fear and hysteria Americans are to be forced to give up their rights as free citizens." But in line with the emphasis of the current "Peace" crusade, he regularly tied these fascistic oppressions to warmongering and the need to speak out for peace. At the El Patio Theater in Hollywood, for one example, on May 25, he said:

> Henry Wallace has been called a traitor; and anyone who dare advance the ideas of socialism is called a traitor; and all those who speak for peace today are called traitors by those who seek war. Only *they — they* are the patriots.[18]

After the Waldorf Conference in America, the worldwide Soviet campaign picked up momentum in 1950, starting with the World Peace Conference in Stockholm in March. The Stockholm Conference, it was claimed, was sponsored by the Democratic Committee of the World Congress of Partisans for Peace. In turn, its subsequent Stockholm Peace Initiative, Stockholm Peace Appeal, and Stockholm Peace Petition garnered millions of signers. In the U.S. the CPUSA organized the Sponsoring Committee for the World Peace Appeal. Their chief implementation was the American Peace Crusade, whose office was listed at 1186 Broadway, New York City, the headquarters of the CPUSA. Among their exhortations to the faithful was this official proclamation: "The Communist Party therefore calls on every single one of its members to turn his and her entire activity to this single, gigantic peace effort." The APC spawned hundreds of groups; it obtained more than two million signatures in the U.S. alone for the so-called Stockholm Peace Petition. To promote the Petition, at rallies Pete Seeger performed a re-working of a thirties labor organizing song that he composed:

> Put my name down, brother, where do I sign,
> I'm going to join the fight for peace, right down the line.[19]

With Picasso's Dove of Peace as its symbol, this was arguably the most successful mass public relations campaign ever. Still, while it was broadly noted that there had been 273,470,566 signers of the Petition, little note was made of the fact that 80 percent of the signers — 235,000,000 — were from Communist dominated countries.[20]

With the invasion of South Korea by North Korea in June 1950, much of the anti-war activism turned to the alleged United States aggressions there — once again allowing the Cominform to draw attention away from a whole spectrum of aggressions by the Soviets throughout Central and Eastern Europe. The American Peace Crusade now focused on protesting the U.S. "invasion" of North Korea and justifying the actual invasion of South Korea as a defensive act of "liberation." In its support, the Hollywood Arts, Sciences, and Professions Council distributed a booklet called *The Truth About Korea* through the mailing list of industry guilds and unions and other organizations. Its premise was that the U.S. was the aggressor and had attacked North Korea.[21]

Picasso's contribution to the Stockholm Peace Petition was not his only work dedicated to the anti–American "Peace" crusade. During the Korean War he created a number of paintings and posters, including a devastatingly brutal depiction in 1951 of a phalanx of surrealistic robot-like American soldiers attacking nude innocent women and children in "Man Slaughter in Korea."

In a "Letter to Picasso," Czeslaw Milosz (historian, philosopher, and esteemed veteran of the battles for freedom in Eastern Europe) eloquently summed up the kind of betrayal of truth, morality, and human beings that Picasso, and other artists and intellectuals, committed: "I need hardly tell you what your name, quite appropriately annexed by the Stalinists, has been used to cover up.... In fact your weight added to the balance and deprived of all hope those in the East who did not want to submit to the absurd ... what would have been the consequence of a categorical protest voiced by all of you."[22]

Part Three

The Director — Blacklisting, Rebellion and Isolation

It is because if I look at the world in which we live, if I think about this world of today, I cannot keep from seeing in it a great number of cripples, and I cannot think of them as if it were a matter of contemptibly depraved beings. I want to speak of them with sympathy, to try to understand them. — Robert Rossen

13

What Is Behaving Decently?— Testifying and Silence

In New York City on May 7, 1953, Robert Rossen made what he thought would be the kind of protest called for by Czeslaw Milosz. For more than half a century he has been vilified for it. He appeared before the House Committee on Un-American Activities. He testified about his beliefs and principles, his membership in the Party, and his reasons for leaving the Party and for testifying. He testified as well as to his knowledge of some he knew as members, though he said very little about them. Before he had requested that appearance, he had wrestled with his own conscience in attempting to answer for himself the kind of question posed by Victor Navasky in *Naming Names*. What *is* it to behave decently?

Carey McWilliams recalled intense conversations he had had with Rossen at that time, when the progressive activist and author was editor of *The Nation*:

> I knew and liked Robert Rossen, the director, who was on the next list of those to be summoned after the Hollywood Ten. I spent hours listening to him as he agonized over the decision he had to make, and I was not surprised when he finally decided to testify. Unless he could make films, life had little meaning for him.... Back in 1946, the two of us had served as co-chairmen of a committee which raised more than $20,000 to aid some CIO strikers who were having a rough time of it. So I had reason to know something about his basic social views and sympathies.[1]

In his testimony, Rossen stressed the complicated issue of conscience:

> The decision that I arrived at in 1951 was an individual decision. I wasn't a member of the Communist Party at the time, as I stated. I felt that the position I had taken at the time was a position of what I considered to be a position of individual morality. I felt it was a matter between me and my own conscience.... I did a lot of thinking. I don't think, after 2 years of thinking, that any one individual can ever indulge himself in the luxury of individual morality or pit it against what I feel today very strongly is the security and safety of this Nation....
> This is a government, a democracy, of laws and not men; and the law says that this Congress or this committee of this Congress has a right to inquire into maters affecting the security of this United States of America.[2]

Whatever the political and ideological reasons, there were certainly personal needs and motives behind his reasoning and internal debate that must remain conjectures. Still, several likely possibilities can be cited. For one, Rossen's sincere and intense interest in America, as evidenced in the distinct American flavor of most of his serious work, might well have had two effects. The first can be seen as a growing optimism about the possibilities of the nation, an attitude that would support his change of stance toward the committee, an attitude reflected in this statement from his testimony:

> What this country really can become is still something to be believed in very firmly, very strongly, with great conviction.... I wouldn't like to see young people today believe what I believed in. I wouldn't like to have them feel there is no growth left in this country: there are no horizons; we have reached our apex, and that it's a dead society. It's not a dead society. It's a young society, it's a growing society; it's a healthy society. It needs a lot of corrections of course, and all societies do, but it needs the corrections, and can get the corrections and realize its hope only in terms of the system of government that's been devised.[3]

A second implication of his concern for American subjects is a more personal one. For Rossen, making movies was a passion, a need, a driving force, and two years of inactivity had left him deeply frustrated. With the kind of particularly American subjects he was most interested in, and handled best, he would find it more difficult than had others (like Joseph Losey, Carl Foreman, and Jules Dassin) to work effectively abroad. And one cannot discount, either, within the conflicting pulls of Rossen's character, the need and drive for control, for success, which, as in the case of his characters, seemed essential parts of his own will to power.

The nature of the testimony he was called upon to give provides another mitigating factor. He was asked to comment only on those names already compiled from research and voluminous files, names which had also been mentioned time and time again in the six years of testimony preceding his own final appearance. Even the adamant Victor Navasky had to admit in *Naming Names* that "by the 1950s it [HUAC] went after members and former Party members exclusively, and subpoenaed nobody who had not already been identified as a Communist by at least two sources."[4] Though Navasky still insisted that any further re-naming supplied fuel to the powerful and rabid "free-lance blacklisters" and was still immoral.

The question that Rossen and others had to answer, each in his or her own way, was: How, then, would the refusal to provide this kind of redundant, and by this time inconsequential, testimony be worth the denial of the beliefs and principles he had been struggling to define — and the denial, to be sure, of his making films?

What was unusual in his case was that the moral dilemma he faced was like a personal dramatization of the central issues of many of his films. For in the films the definition and fulfillment of one's identity, or the corruption of one's true self, one's *élan*, one's gift, became more and more intricately entangled with the troubling ambiguities of motives and the paradoxical varieties of betrayal.

Whatever the combination of motives, the decision and the long ordeal before and after had a lasting effect on Rossen and his work. The actress Jean Seberg (after her work with Rossen in *Lilith*) captured this perceptively in a 1966 article:

> He was a very complicated man, agonized even, who continually asked himself questions about himself. Perhaps one must seek out the cause of this anguish in the great McCarthy trauma, in which his world had literally toppled.... Rossen had been on the blacklist for a long time.... I think the moral shock of this affair changed him deeply. He was led to withdraw into himself, to live a little apart with his family, to take things into consideration

more, to examine the secret motivations of people.... His art became more and more personal; it is there perhaps that one must see the reason for commercial failure. He was more attached to symbols, to deep ideas, than to appearances.[5]

Before his own untimely death, Rossen's son Steve recalled how others had seen a change in his father in the years after his testimony, just as he had. To be sure, he was still an inveterate fighter and hustler in a world in which he felt he had to fight and hustle, but he had seemed to others to grow more subdued, with less Lower East Side wise-guy need to savor the battle and flourish the win. He was still unwilling to resign himself to what, and who, assailed him, but it could be said he was moving beyond his view of life through the prism of ideology, and had become more thoughtful and compassionate over what all must face, what all seemed to have to do.

In the harsh political world of 1953, Rossen amplified his view of the Communist Party and its relation to the crises in the world that affected the security of the nation—crises that he believed called for a social as well as individual morality. He emphasized several major issues on which he believed he had to take a stand. Two crucial issues for him were the question of the Jews and the Soviet Union, and the question of freedom, especially freedom of speech, for individuals, communities, and societies.

These were questions that those on the Left, and particularly those who later led the attacks on him, also placed great emphasis on — in both their testimony and many public venues and means throughout the years. The contrast between his position on these significant questions and those of the Hollywood Reds — and in relation to the facts of history, current and past — can help cast a clearer light on the complicated answer to the question posed first by Navasky as central to the moral equation of the time.

Should one testify as to the realities of the world of Communism and thus in most cases also name names? or should one remain silent (often loudly) about these realities and refuse to cooperate with government investigations?

Central to Rossen's thinking and his testimony was the question of the Jews and Communism. Rossen rebelled against what he believed was the destructive duplicity of the Soviets and CPUSA — proclaiming official recognition and support while murdering, repressing, imprisoning, and torturing. The repressions of Jews (along with many, many others) had begun in the thirties, as had the Party's false claims, he testified. In the late thirties, he explained, "the important part of the Nazi-Soviet pact, to me, personally, was the [alleged] fact that it saved over a million Jews from being destroyed by Hitler." He now knew this to be a terrible falsehood, but he said that at the time it was the Party's doctrine, its "rationale," as presented in the Party press.[6]

Rossen had done his homework. In his testimony he provided examples from the Party press that illustrated this consistent duplicity. In one example from a crucial series of articles and editorials in September of 1939 (during the Nazi-Soviet Pact), *The Daily Worker* proclaimed in one editorial, "For National Freedom and World Peace":

> As Hitler's hordes advanced further into Poland, the atrocities against the Jewish people and other minorities exceeded some of fascism's goriest deeds.
> In this situation the Soviet Government sent in the Red Army, an army of liberation, to protect the Ukrainian and White Russian minorities, after the semi-fascist Polish government had ceased to exist and had left them to the ravages of war and fascist enslavement.
> More than a million Jews living in Western Ukraine and Western Belo Russia [i.e., eastern Poland] are now beyond the pale of fascist anti–Semitism.[7]

Rossen cited several other articles that included almost the same phrases. One by Harry Gaines even proclaimed, "Especially the Jewish peoples of the areas liberated by the Red Army will have cause for thanking. No longer will they be persecuted once the Red Army has set them free." However, the *Worker*, he pointed out, did not discuss why the Soviet government had to deport several hundred thousand Poles, including Jews, to Siberia, and also invade the three Baltic States and Finland. "It was always necessary at that time to get a rationale. In other words, practically my whole life in the Party, as I reflect upon it, is one of rationales."[8]

Rossen went on to stress that since the thirties he had seen many more examples of the Soviet's cynical and brutal hypocrisy on "the Jewish question." Recent events, such as the attacks on Jewish intellectuals and doctors, and the defendants in the Slansky trials as *traitors*, had convinced him that Communist claims of supporting minorities were an immoral lie:

> And the Soviet Union was very well aware, knowing Communists as I have — no action is taken without the awareness of the consequences of that action. The Soviet Union knew that by raising the word "Jew" and raising the word "traitor" it was specifically inciting the people of these various countries, which had been hotbeds of anti-Semitism for hundreds of years, to anti-Semitism; and I think the act was done deliberately, and all of the good intentions, the avowed, professed interests of the Soviet Union in Jews as a minority was thrown overboard completely....
>
> And I think that is one of the most evil, immoral, and corrupt acts that has occurred in my lifetime — something I feel very deeply about, very strongly about — and I think if there was any illusion, any more, in terms of the feeling of the Soviet Union toward minorities — I think this act must expose to anybody that this is all an illusion and it has no basis in fact....
>
> To the extent that it [the American Communist Party] supports Soviet policy in this — to the extent that it supports these trials — to the extent that it does not denounce the equation of the word "Jew" to traitor that has been made — to that extent, whether by conscious intent, or whatever it is — to that extent, it must be anti-Semitic.[9]

This testimony clearly is based on the thinking and re-thinking that he had been doing in January 1953 when he brought his thinking on the Jews into focus with the composition of a letter to the *New York Times*. In that letter he wrote:

> For if ever a theme [that "absolute power breeds absolute corruption"] has been completely proven by an action, the official sanction of the incitement to anti-Semitism, contained in the recent purges and trials occurring behind the Iron Curtain, is that action. Of all the cynical and corrupt acts committed in the name of saving the land of socialism, this is the most cynical, the most corrupt, the most immoral.[10]

The actual treatment of Jews was an important, and personally emotional, aspect of his recognizing the vast and destructive spectrum of "the cynical and corrupt acts committed in the name of saving the land of socialism." To understand the basis of his strong feelings, a brief review of a small sampling of these "acts" is a valuable, if brutal, guidebook.

In the world of the Soviet Union, the year of the first hearings, 1947, was the year of the start of the official postwar Soviet campaign of suppression of the Jews. The campaign was not the first instance of anti-Semitism in Russia. Despite the large number of Jews in the Communist movement, actions against Jews were entwined with the terror against the Kulaks in the late twenties and early thirties, and then with the terror and purges of "Trotskyists" et al. in the thirties. The oppression and killing continued with

Vladimir Molotov's further attack on Jews in the Party apparatus in 1939, the execution and deportation of Poles, especially Jews, after the invasion of Poland, and the wholesale deportations during World War II.[11]

After the war, this new major campaign started with the purging of the alleged excess of Jews in the Party *apparat*. Andrei Zhdanov complained it was getting to be "some kind of synagogue." The two major thrusts, however, were against Jewish cultural leaders and Zionists — who were seen as agents of the U.S. Although, for a combination of strategic motives, Stalin had recognized the new state of Israel, his long-nurtured anti–Semitism became obsessive in the late forties and early fifties. During a crisis at the Stalin Automobile Plant, Stalin told Khrushchev, "The good workers at the factory should be given clubs so they can beat the hell out of those Jews at the end of a working day." Two Jewish journalists who had written about the factory were executed for being complicit in an "anti–Soviet Jewish nationalistic sabotage group." Zhdanov's new cultural terror (known as *Zhdanovshchina*) was particularly harsh on Jewish writers, actors, and artists because they were also suspected Zionists. In the Fall of 1947, at the very time of the hearings, Stalin ordered Victor Abakunov, the new chief of security, to join the hunt for "Every Jew [who] is a nationalist and agent of American intelligence." Abakunov's department widened the spread of arrests and torture of Jews. On November 21, 1947, Stalin personally ordered Abakunov to murder the leading Jewish intellectual in Russia, Solomon Mikhoels, who had long acted as chief liaison between the Jewish community and the government. Mikhoels was injected with a poison, battered on the head, and shot. His body and that of his companion were then run over with a truck and left in the snow.[12]

The pogrom continued with more purges, arrests, torture, executions, and a formal Jewish Case prepared for a public show trial. One program was a series of attacks on Jewish intellectuals for being "cosmopolitan." In February 1949, *Pravda* asked, "What vision can a Gurvich or a Yusovsky possibly have of the national character of Russian Soviet man?" At one point Soviet records show 110 Jewish prisoners undergoing interrogation in the Lubianka in a single day. The torturer, V.I. Komarov, later boasted, "I was merciless with them. I tore their souls apart.... I was especially pitiless with (and I hated the most) the Jewish nationalists."[13]

By 1950 the original Jewish Case was closed without a trial, but with no prisoners released and no tortures banned. Instead, proceedings were instituted against the Jewish Anti-Fascist Committee and its leaders, while thousands of Jews were purged from the government and government industries. Leaders of the Committee were imprisoned in 1950, but not brought to trial until 1952. There were 125 sentences — 25 to death "immediately," and 100 to the camps.[14]

In 1950 the first Jewish doctor was arrested, and the final spasm began — the so-called "Doctors' Plot" to assassinate Stalin and other leaders. The doctor, Professor Yakov Etinger, was tortured so intensely that he died. The arrests of doctors continued into 1952, to be joined by new arrests of Jewish poets and former government officials. In one group, thirteen were executed. On September 8 Stalin gave explicit orders to the chief torturer, "Midget" Riumin, to torture the doctors until they had confessed to killing several Soviet officials, including Zhdanov, who had died of natural causes due to extreme alcoholism.

After several years of unreported terror, the Doctors' Plot was finally made public and official with an article in *Pravda* on January 13, 1953, headlined, "Ignoble Spies and

Killers Under the Mask of Professor-Doctors." This set off another wave of anti–Semitism throughout Russia. The final stage — never consummated — was to be a program of "voluntary-compulsory eviction of Jews." New concentration camps were being built for the "evicted" Jews.[15]

By 1951— the year of the second extensive set of hearings in Hollywood — the purge of Jews had spread into the Soviet-controlled states of Eastern Europe. That summer, for example, 14,000 Jews were deported from Budapest, Hungary, to "labor camps" in the provinces. In the purges within the Communist parties of the Soviet bloc countries, many of those purged were Jews in the oft-repeated "struggle against Zionism and Zionists." The most important of these trials was the "Slansky Trial" in Czechoslovakia in 1952 of former Communist leader Rudolph Slansky and his "Trotskyite, Titoist, Zionist terrorist group."[16]

About all of this — what was really happening to the Jews throughout the thirties, during the Pact, during the war, and in the postwar period — the Hollywood Reds remained silent.

During the first hearings, and for years after (for example, in the decades of claims about the espionage trial of Julius and Ethel Rosenberg), what they were not silent about were the alleged evils of the United States in the treatment of Jews or the even worse imminent treatment of Jews. In the hearings themselves, one of the main focus points of the Ten in orchestrating the Party's strategy of attacking, and hopefully dishonoring, the Committee was the Ten's insistent claims of rampant destructive anti–Semitism by the Committee and in America. The position taken by the Ten was that the hearings were a part of a pogrom — an attack on Jews and other minorities in the United States. Adrian Scott was the least hostile and dogmatic of the witnesses. Still, he announced that he had been called among the first Ten for one reason: that his recent film *Crossfire* had been, at least in part, an attack on anti–Semitism and that the ranking members of the Committee were anti–Semitic. (At least one definably was.) Scott's written statement, which he was not allowed to read, was entirely devoted to his and the Nineteen's fight against persecution of minorities, and the Committee's complicity in maintaining and promoting it:

> I wish to speak now about another war. I would like to speak about the "cold war" being waged by the Committee of [sic] Un-American Activities against the Jewish and Negro people....
> The next phase — total war against minorities — needs no elaboration. History has recorded what has happened in Nazi Germany.[17]

Edward Dmytryk, the director of *Crossfire* (Scott was the producer), was already conflicted over his relationship with the Party. In his statement he was less extreme than the others on several of the usual topics, but he began by tying suppression of minorities with suppression of freedoms, and returned to that correlation several times:

> The dark periods in our history have been those in which our freedoms have been suppressed, to however small a degree ... that darkness exists into the present day in the continued suppression of minorities.... Is a Committee member anti–Semitic? He will force the producers to blacklist men who deplore anti–Semitism.[18]

Samuel Ornitz was the most emotional in his claims:

> I wish to address this Committee as a Jew, because one of its leading members is the outstanding anti–Semite in the Congress and revels in this fact.... I refer to this evil because it

has been responsible for the systematic and ruthless slaughter of six million of my people....
It may be redundant to repeat that anti–Semitism and anti–Communism were the number one poison weapon used by Hitler....

For when Constitutional guarantees are over-ridden, the Jew is the first one to suffer ... but only the first one. As soon as the Jew is crushed, the others get it...

Nor did this evil die with Hitler....

I must not fail — nor for one moment falter before the threat of contempt, which word sounds like the short way of saying concentration camp.[19]

However deep and sincere the feelings about the "plight" of Jews in America that underlay his ideological hyperbole, there is something bitterly ironic and painfully sad in this blinded, blinkered passion. Until his death in 1957, this man who was so deeply and actively concerned with the plight of the Jews denied and continued to deny the real destructive attacks on Jews in Soviet Russia and its satellites.

For Party members and their close followers, defenses and lies about the treatment of Jews in Soviet Russia and its satellites extended far beyond the hearings. About the status of Jews in the Soviet Union during the period of the hearings, for example, the indefatigable Dalton Trumbo, in criticizing the arguments of anti–Communist New Liberals during the Cold War, had this to say: "They must equate 6,000,000 Jews burned and gassed and tortured to death in the territories of Nazi Germany with 3,500,000 Jews living in the Soviet Union under the *protection* of laws which ban discrimination of any kind"[20] [emphasis added].

In his 1999 memoir *Being Red*, novelist and sometime screenwriter Howard Fast, several of whose novels were turned into films (including the blacklist-breaking *Spartacus*) was still justifying the Nazi-Soviet Pact of the late thirties, in part because of the Jews. Responding to criticism about the transporting of Jews during those Soviet actions, he granted that, indeed, there was what he called the "movement" of people. However, he proclaimed, "Russia had ... moved three million [*sic!*] Polish Jews and Ukrainian Jews eastward to get them beyond the reach of the Nazis and their death camps."[21]

In contrast, in 1947, at the time of the first hearings, Jacques Pat conducted a thorough survey of sources, records, and interviews. In two articles in the Jewish *Daily Forward*, he documented how 400,000 of the Jews who fled from Poland to the U.S.S.R. to escape the Germans during the time of the Pact *died* during deportation by the Russians to, or incarceration in, concentration and forced labor camps.[22]

Recent events and revelations in the period leading up to his testimony had also convinced Rossen that proclaimed rationales other than those about the Jews, were equally illusory. In the mid-thirties, he said,

Well, values had broken down. This is a real fact. There weren't any values, and the Communist Party seemed to be at a place that had the values. Its people were the most dedicated. It worked the hardest, and it was interested in cultural movements. It was interested in anything you were interested in. Therefore, you felt this was the only place you could possibly go.... It offered every possible kind of thing to you at the time which could fulfill your sense of idealism, and it was a kind of dedication.

But he had learned that "the same reasons why you go into the party are the same reasons which make you go out, which is ultimately the discovery that the idealism that you were looking for, the fighting for the ideas that you want, are just not in the party."[23]

For Rossen, these new reasons in connection with the Jews were part of the broader issue of freedom — the freedom of the individual, whether Communist or not, and of communities to think and to act. He saw that the Party at this time allowed no free thinking, insisting that one accept and follow the Party line, however ludicrous the changes:

> Well, now if anybody wanted any manifestation of the bankruptcy of the Communist Party thinking ... you had the Duclos letter.... Now, suddenly a letter appeared in France by Duclos. The very people that we had been led to believe for years were the paragons of wisdom, the people in whom all Marxism reposed and could answer all the questions now had been wrong for their whole existence in the party.[24]

Even the leader of the American Party, Earl Browder, he pointed out, was now declared a violator, a betrayer of Communist principles, and expelled. (Later, Browder was allowed somewhat of a rehabilitation because of his assistance in Soviet espionage activities.) The iconic Duclos letter to the Communist Party press in Paris in May of 1945 had detailed the vital necessity of positions and principles of a new hard line to be taken against American and capitalist aggression throughout the world. Allegedly written by French Party official Jacques Duclos (though actually written by the Politburo in Moscow), it is generally interpreted as the public signaling of the internal Soviet decision to move to the aggressive stance that initiated the Cold War of the postwar era.

Rossen had felt this bankruptcy of thinking and its repression of individual freedoms on a small scale in the Party's treatment of its members. He remembered the meeting in 1943 over the statements of Albert Maltz as a prime example. Maltz had brought up the question of Party activities taking time away from his development as a writer. He was reprimanded and "told his first function was to be a Communist." At this time in his own life, Rossen had begun to realize that "now at this point the Party is no longer interested in this man as a creative artist. They're interested in his functions or in his functioning as a member of the Communist Party. They're interested in how many meetings he goes to; to how many organizations does he belong."

Rossen realized that the position the Party was to insist on, which Maltz accepted, was that, "Oh, no, now you are a Communist; you will accept Communist Party discipline.... In other words, you now are made into what I consider a cliché word by this time, a party hack, and now the party is now longer interested in your creative development.... You begin to suddenly see you are being used."[25]

These insights and conclusions clearly reflect his memory of the personal attack on his personal freedom as an artist in the inquisition over *All the King's Men* in 1949, but, oddly, he does not directly refer to that event in the course of his testimony. In a letter to the *New York Times* in January of 1953, which he wrote (but did not submit) while thinking deeply about his past, his beliefs, and his present course of action, Rossen did refer to the 1949 meeting. He commented on the response of "certain sections of the extreme left" to *All the King's Men*. "I was told by them," he wrote, "that the leading character of the film would be likened to Stalin and its theme to the Soviet regime, and to this degree, I was fanning the flames of World War III." He goes on: "In the light of history their apprehension was well grounded."[26]

In his testimony Rossen recalled another personal situation that violated his freedom to speak out. After his appearance in 1951— even though he "did not give this committee any names or information"— he was attacked, "both directly and indirectly":

> The fact that I expressed my opposition to communism that time was enough to expose me to many different kinds of criticism in my several years since I have appeared before this committee.

There's a very interesting commentary that just — purely on the issue, I would say, civil rights — the Communist Party was not very willing to espouse that cause purely in terms of disagreeing with them, on a political level. In other words, civil rights did not work at all in terms of Communist policy if you disagreed.[27]

Still, Rossen now felt, there were more devastating infringements on personal freedom than the Party infringing on its Hollywood writers' self-expression. He had begun to realize the basic "lie" of the Party, its basic betrayal of individuals. In one key passage he said:

> I think this was a common thing in my experience in the Party, and naturally you begin to see all of these things in different lights; you begin to get the feeling that, in a sense, where you always felt you were using people, you know, trying to convert them and so forth; you began to suddenly see you were being used; that the Party respect for you, the Party veneration of the masses, which is a wonderful word — its so-called feeling for the masses, for people — somehow or other never really expressed itself in terms of its feeling for the individual. There was quite a separation between the word "masses" and the word "person," and that — it didn't equate itself at all.[28]

He was referring to such consequences for *persons* as these (a minute sampling culled from masses of documentation):

- A conservative consensus estimate puts the total of deaths through all forms of terror within the Soviet Union at 20 million.
- Of those, 7 million occurred through forced collectivization and institutionalized forced famine from the twenties to mid-thirties. Some 5 million of those were in the Ukraine, 2 million of those accused as kulaks, supposed counter-revolutionary bourgeois farm owners and exploiters. There were, in addition, mass deportations from all farm areas: by 1937, 5.7 million households, about 15 million people.
- In 1937-38 alone, under Order 00447 and Order 00485: 1.5 million arrested. Of those 700,000 executed.
- A broader picture of these same years, as determined by former Soviet chief historian Dimitri Volkogonov: "...between 1937 and 1939 from five to five and a half million people had been arrested. Not less than a third of them had been shot, and many of the rest died in the camps."
- At the time of the first hearings, Nikita Khrushchev supervised the expulsion of "harmful elements" in the Ukraine: Almost a million, the great majority sent to the camps.
- In terms of camps: Through the Soviet period, there were an estimated 28,700,000 "forced laborers," including:
    — Gulag network of camps: 8 million passed through by 1940, 18 million by 1953
    — Camps of "Forced labor without incarceration": 700,000
    — Sites in Siberia for "Special Exiles": 6,015,000
    — Deaths in Gulag and Exile Villages: 2,749,163 (This estimate is considered low. It uses various official camp statistics, but cannot account for mass executions or deaths during transport, interrogations, etc.)[29]

An equally small sampling of defenses of the Soviets and of their own complicity in this monumental destruction by those who remained "silent" and condemned those who testified:

- John Howard Lawson: "The only truly conscious anti-fascist force during the war years was the Communist Party."
- Ring Lardner, Jr.: "...the best hope for mankind lay in the Soviets. Only in Russia were massive construction and planning for the future going on." Even though there was some "moral and social *rigidity* [emphasis added] under Stalin's rule."
- Lillian Hellman: "I thought that in the end Russia, having achieved a state socialism, would stop its *infringements* [emphasis added] on personal liberty."
- Jules Dassin: "I don't see that the ideas we tried to present were wrong. And the intentions were, as far as I'm concerned, always pure."
- Albert Maltz: "I felt the Party was the best hope for mankind; that it would be the one force which moved the world toward brotherhood.... It actuated a passion for social justice which cultivated one's own innate passion and decency."
- Dalton Trumbo: "I never believed in the *perfection* [emphasis added] of the Soviet Union.... So I don't feel impelled to penitential cries."[30]
- Abraham Polonsky: "...the best vehicle for bringing about the socialist transformation of society." Even though "...the tendency in social commitment is *uniformity* [emphasis added], as in the United States and in the Soviet Union."
- Walter Bernstein: "...their terrible struggle to build the first socialist state in a world that had tried from the beginning to destroy them."
- Martin Ritt: "[There were] certain *excesses* [emphasis added]. But I don't feel I have anything to be ashamed of.[31]

Eugene Genovese, a Marxist historian and former Communist, has condemned in strong terms this kind of deceitful and evasive righteousness — and its consequences. He has captured indelibly the nature of the betrayal by silence about this destructive discrepancy between Communist ideals and realities: "By admitting nothing, explaining nothing and apologizing for nothing ... in a noble effort to liberate the human race from violence and oppression, we broke all records for mass slaughter.... We have a disquieting number of corpses to account for."[32]

In 1973, the left-wing historian E.P. Thompson was also still romantically defending the value of the "utopian energies within the socialist [sic] tradition." In response, his old friend, the eminent scholar of Marxism Leszek Kolakowski, wrote:

> O blessed Innocence! You and I, we were both active in our respective Communist Parties in the '40s and '50s, which means that, whatever our noble intentions and our charming ignorance (or refusal to get rid of ignorance) were, we supported, within our modest means, a regime based on mass slave labor and police terror of the worst kind in human history.[33]

14

Starting Anew in Europe—*Mambo*

After he testified, Robert Rossen's subsequent work was not "marred by bad conscience"—as Abraham Polonsky insisted many years later. It was deepened by the painful experience of difficult decisions and their consequences. It reflected the scars of hard-earned insight. In the reality of the business of making movies, it took a while, and no little courage and determination, and a good many battles along the way to get to where he wanted to be, what he wanted to do.

After the long internal dilemma and debate, the determined self-assertion, and the trauma of testifying in 1953, Rossen went back to Europe. He did not seek to regain his status by working in America and in Hollywood—as did most of those who testified. The reasons—the motives that he as a filmmaker had begun to develop with increasing complexity in his characters—were undoubtedly complicated. He did not want to engage in—or plunge his family into—the personal conflicts and animosity he would face, and subsequently had to continue to face. He did not want to go back in a position of diminished power to the battles of control in the studio system. He wanted to pursue the development of the epic film that had become his dream and obsession, the story of Alexander the Great, which he wanted to produce in Spain.

He and his family lived in Italy after a short time again in Paris. Others from the Communist and Communist-friendly Left had left Hollywood and were living in Europe at this time, but Rossen did not become part of their groups in France or in Italy.

Ironically, while he continued to work on the preparation of *Alexander*, he found that he had to place himself in a frustrating, and artistically damaging, battle for control, Italian style. He soon signed on to write and direct *Mambo*. It was a start again, a renewal, but it was by no means a fulfillment. Its history and its final form show the price that has to be paid to work again in the business of making movies. During the production he had to fight with even more controlling and intrusive bosses, the co-producers Carlo Ponti and Dino di Laurentiis. It was one of several films di Laurentiis produced for his wife, the noted actress Silvana Mangano.

Despite their meddling, the producers knew and admired Rossen's work. They brought him in to re-write and bring some order to a script that had already been worked on by a phalanx of writers. Three others besides Rossen were finally given screen credit for the screenplay. In directing the constantly changing screenplay, Rossen tried to shape the material to give it both a coherent narrative structure and meaningful thematic implications that would be earned, not just stated. Meanwhile, the others continued to insert their ideas, and demands, via re-re-writes — to make the film commercially sound with spectacle and musical numbers, and especially to make sure that Mangano was kept an untarnished heroine, yet one with enough weaknesses, of course, to keep the plot going. She had become world famous (as an actress and a beautiful body) after her role in the Giuseppe De Santis Neo-realist film *Bitter Rice*. Her beauty had been so prominent in the film that the Italian Communist Party and allied critics complained that too much display of her tightly-sweatered breasts and shapely legs distracted audiences from the film's social message.[1] In her two films before *Mambo*, Mangano had been a downtrodden streetwalker with a heart of gold who becomes a nun in the Neo-realist *Anna*, and a noble, patient, gloriously beautiful, and beautifully displayed, wife and lover in the epic *Ulysses*. Immediately after making *Mambo* she was magnificently tragic, restrained and dignified as a prostitute betrayed into a cruel marriage in the final segment of Vittorio De Sica's four-part compendium *The Gold of Naples*.

In *Mambo* the irony is that the more the producers insisted that her character be kept sympathetic, the more perplexing her blinkered, self-absorbed view of her life became. As Rossen told it later, he tried his *damnedest* to make sense of her character on film, and then had to give in and let it happen. As he remembered, *Mambo* was to be for fun and practice only; but then when he saw some heart in it, some corner of his old territory, "[I] got involved, took it seriously, but it didn't come off." Without control, he found that as written and then re-written, as meddled with during production and then edited and re-edited, he began to feel he "just didn't believe it anymore."[2]

In America the film has slipped from historical or critical view. In Italy it has had more of an historical afterlife — in part because of interest in the careers of Mangano and Vittorio Gassman. But more meaningfully, it has been looked back on by some cadres in the culture wars as an example of the way that Neo-realism remained fresh, and progressed and developed to fit the styles of changing times — widening its focus on the milieus of lower class characters, showing more emphasis on the inner life of characters, combining meaningful drama even with comedy, music, and, in this case, dance.

The film is an interesting collection of paradoxes, of might-have-beens. Released at 110 minutes in Italy in 1953, it soon was edited down for its general release in Europe early in 1954. A 94-minute version, released both late and hurriedly in 1955 in the U.S., is the version available here today. One can only surmise what has been lost in the drastic reduction and re-editing. Yet what remains is provocative and still strong in many ways. Despite his own growing irritation at the process, it was an interesting challenge for Rossen — to combine in a new situation and world, and with music and dance, a surprising number of themes that are recurrent in his films.

While women assume larger roles as Rossen's *oeuvre* develops, Giovanna (Mangano) is the only case of a woman being the protagonist and central consciousness. She is a female version of the unformed young man of a certain *élan* and strength seeking his identity and fulfillment, whether through success, his craft, or love, whether with false or true definitions of those counters and emblems of the self. Her voiceover narration constantly defines her view of things, and this creates one of the provocative yet unresolved problems of the film. She sees herself as always sorely put upon; she comes across as too self-pitying, too self-justifying, too much within herself. There is an interesting sense here of how one's stance toward the world — however it has been shaped and formed — determines one's view of the world; and so that is what the world *is* for you, however accurate or not that is. That could have produced a fascinating character, but to carry out that approach needs more irony in the context of Giovanna's narrations than the film allows, constructs, or clearly intends. She seems mainly to be seen as right, not as a good but *flawed* person.

Giovanna's relationship to her putative calling — dancing — is a crucial example of this blurring of meaning. A former shop-girl, she tries to find a new life in dancing after feeling trapped in her life and her romance — a false kind of love and loving — with a selfish and devious gambler (Gassman). Mangano was a trained dancer early in her career. In her break-through film *Bitter Rice*, her wild and spirited boogie-woogie dance with Gassman had a raw energy and sexuality. But here in *Mambo* her on-stage dancing is formal, too stately and cold, as if missing an internal beat, a real passion. She is never in real harmony with, or convincing about, the Caribbean dance style of the troupe that she is a part of. It's almost as if it were implying a subtle and thematic point about her approach to her dancing career and her life — or at least it would be nice to think so. The choreography for the troupe was by the Jamaican-American Katherine Dunham.

Others — including the dance director and teacher Toni (Shelley Winters) — see her as talented, and she becomes a star, but an empty star. She talks about dancing only as a way out of her former life, a means of achieving some success and even revenge, but also as nothing but exhausting, dull work. Here, abstractly, is a typical Rossen conflict — misusing your talent for the wrong goals. But for that to work we need to see that she takes some joy in it, has some love for it that she then distorts (as is the case for Rossen's usual protagonists). That dimension is missing in the version available.

Rossen has structured the film with an opening that leads to a flashback, which in turn moves past the time of the opening to the conclusion. In that opening, Giovanna is returning to Venice after a year of working with Toni's dance group. Her first words about dancing set the tone, petulant rather than conflicted. She was, she says, retuning home after a year of "hard work" to be a dancing star. She had become "a machine, living without a soul, just as Toni wanted." The others eat together. She is alone.

> I didn't care anymore about dancing or success, yet before I met Toni, I had only one thought in mind — to be somebody. I didn't even know what I wanted to become — to be important, that was enough. [The scene cuts to her old neighborhood — narrow streets, weathered stone building fronts — and follows her walking, as her voiceover leads into the flashback.] I used to live in a poor home among old, tired people, but my dreams kept me young and alive, and I was sure that someday by some miracle I would escape from the dreary surroundings.

The flashback establishes the elements that generated her original choice, and will continue to be the basis of her choices — and moral testing — after her return to Venice. Her empty life is first conveyed in the contrast between the shop of ornate glassware for the wealthy in which she works and the oppressive apartment, with its tiny rooms and typical kitchen, where most of the living and fighting with her father take place. Her father (Eduardo Cianelli, Vanning in *Marked Woman*) is dominating and complaining, as he had been with her mother. When, as usual, he tells her to get married, her resentment toward him is clear: "Yes, there was love," she says, "there was love as long as my mother worked and slaved — there was love as long as you got what you wanted. Now you weep! Why didn't you weep for her when she was alive?"

The possibility of love, and marriage, in her life is Mario (Gassman). Mario is a gambling-house worker, often unemployed, and a minor smuggler of cigarettes on the black market. He's a charismatic scoundrel — handsome and energetic, selfish and childish, immoral and unfaithful. Yet, despite her experience with her father, he has some power over her; she is drawn to him, and gives in to him again and again.

Into her life comes a stately and charming, and rather mysterious, aristocrat. The Count, Enrico (Michael Rennie), has seen her in the glassware shop. He invites her to a costume ball, and a strong sequence captures the excitement and sexuality of their new encounter. It is all overpowering, almost too thrilling for Giovanna — people in ornate masks and glamorous antique costumes, milling crowds and burgeoning noise, the Latin dance group performing among them. Enrico takes off her mask and tells her she is the most beautiful woman there. "You are so alive, so very alive." And she is captivated, entranced, as they walk through the crowd, confetti falling from the balcony, the dancers coming down the stairs. He needs to see someone and leaves her alone. She is drinking too much and wanders, as the film's edits become more hectic, and the dancers and the drummers move through the crowd. She is happy and drunk, and begins to dance with them. We see him watching. She lifts her skirt high, twirling and twirling, the camera dizzy with her, the drumming intense when she suddenly drops to the floor. He goes to her and takes her to the side as the wildness continues around them. "I'll give you anything," he says, "anything you want."

And yet — the scene cuts to the gray morning after on an empty plaza as she walks alone, feeling betrayed and shamed (over what and exactly why is elided). In voiceover she says, "It was daybreak before I could leave, disgusted. I felt the need for revenge. I knew I didn't have the strength to do anything, even to throw myself in the canal."

Toni comes after her to dance in her troupe. She accepts. She will get her revenge and rebel against all of them, all if it. When she tells Mario, he protests that she's being unfaithful; he taught her everything she knows. She answers: "I remember all the lessons, Mario. I'm doing just what you taught me to do — to get ahead — not to care for anything or anyone. Use them, isn't that what you said, Mario? Climb a little higher?" He starts to leaves, but comes back and slaps her. "Something to remember me by."

In voiceover, with shots of Rome, she says, "Toni lifted me out of my unhappy life in Venice and took me to Rome as a pilgrim."

But immediately, over a montage of working with the troupe, we are told that to her it "meant nothing but hard work." Significantly, as the montage develops, and she practices singing as well (as Toni coaches and encourages her), the shots of dance practice culminate in her falling to the floor, exhausted.

About Toni and her dedication to her, she can only complain that Toni is a failed dancer herself who needs someone to put all her lonely life into — "someone to become something that she just couldn't." While this is an interesting appraisal, we are never shown enough interaction between them, or enough about Toni, to put this into a fuller context.

When Giovanna and the troupe return to Venice, the same confusion of attitude is maintained. "I wanted to forget the past," she narrates as the flashback leads her back to Venice and into the present time of the story. A poster announces her as the star of the troupe's performance. A production number — with much cutting that attempts to build excitement — shows her singing and dancing with the troupe as Toni watches; but neither her sense of herself as a dancer or her relationship with Toni is made clear. Backstage there are roses from Enrico, and Mario appears, well dressed, now working at the casino. She rushes to him, smiling. *Why?*

At a party at the casino she agrees to perform, and uses her performance, dancing and singing, to taunt and get some revenge on the two men. (This misuse of her gift is the latent theme, but the destructive irony of it remains unfocused.) As she says in voiceover: "Enrico had wanted to buy me and now I would make him suffer, humiliate him as he had humiliated me. I would even choose Mario to Enrico, poor and unlucky Mario, worthless Mario."

And yet her feelings are apparently more contradictory than that, and her motives blurred in the structuring of the narrative and its continual voiceovers. In Mario's apartment she narrates that she hates it as much as ever, but that "I had deliberately chosen to return. I would degrade myself, merely to spite Enrico." Still, when he touches her, she embraces him tightly — as the screen fades to black and the music swells! And so there seems more to her motive than revenge; he still has the old physical power over her.

The next section gives us some focus on the crucial thematic conflict that had been left loosely unfocussed and undeveloped: dance and Toni vs. Mario and love/revenge (or whatever it is). After a bitter argument between Mario and Toni — while the dancers rehearse on-stage — over what and who is best for Giovanna, Toni abruptly decides that the troupe should leave Venice immediately.

Giovanna refuses to go. Toni tries to convince her: "You're throwing your career away for nothing ... a future that has purpose and meaning."

Giovanna has made her choice, though through what mix of motives is unclear, and the decision is not developed as crucially as it should be. She is betraying Toni, but is she betraying her craft, her skill, her art? For dancing is still not shown to be that important to her; her *resentiment* still rules.

The price of her betrayal is immediately paid — by Toni. As the troupe is preparing to leave on their bus, Giovanna, with Mario, comes to get her bags. She tells Toni she's sorry, nothing more. Distraught, frustrated and hurt, Toni rushes heedlessly into a parking structure to get her car. Running up the ramp, she is hit by a car coming down and killed. The group circles the body, a dancer kneels and touches Toni; she looks at Giovanna, who turns away and, clinging to Mario, walks off. What are we to surmise?

We next see St. Marks Square and its pigeons, and the dock along the Grand Canal for the vaporettos. In the accompanying voiceover there is not a word about Giovanna's response to the death of Toni, her implication in it, or even her self-protective evasion of it. At this point, and in the future, such a crucial event as Toni's death is not shown as having any effect on her at all, showing her flaw — or the script's? Instead we hear: "Defiantly, I stayed with Mario — his fortunes had improved — everyday I went with him to the ferry that took him to work.... One day I saw Enrico — I pretended not to see him."

Enrico wants to marry her; she learns he is a hemophiliac. Mario, fired from the casino, proposes that she marry the Count for his money. He and she can still be lovers, but "he's sick and will die. In a little while we'll be rich and free."

She rebels: "I see what you are!" But in a sequence of shots and voiceovers, she succumbs again to him and her resentment. "At least we had something in common, Mario and I, the same loneliness, the same desperation. The world owed me something."

And so with that mixture of resentment and an unsettled (and unsettling) attraction to Enrico, she marries him — a betrayal of him and his feelings and whatever are hers for him. But it is what Enrico wants — for an interesting and complex set of reasons. She is a beautiful prize for his rich tastes. She is a means of defiance against his formal, masked, dead way of life. She is a means of escaping from the domination of his mother. She can bring him pleasure in the limited time he knows he has to live. And he has learned how to love, for he does, we now see, love her.

But the trap set for Enrico becomes her trap. They live amid the formal trappings of his mother's palacio, and eat in the formal ritual at his mother's table, along with his resentful sister. His mother is dominating, cold and demanding. Yet the prison (captured strongly by Rossen in décor, character patterns and attitudes) — which he admits to her is a prison for himself as well — paradoxically leads to a new openness between them and, through fits and starts, a new understanding within Giovanna.

Enrico admits he hasn't long to live; but he was afraid to tell her, is afraid he will lose her. She is touched, telling him, "I married you, I'm your wife." But she is still torn and needs to feel alive, to go where there is life. She leaves, partly to be honest with him. When she is back with Mario, he insists she go back to the Count — the money is so near! No, she won't, she must get away. But then — in response to what she has been doing and what he is demanding — she experiences a moment of change, of recognition. She sees that she doesn't want to run anymore. She *will* go back, but on her own terms, with her need to find her own kind of freedom.

She goes back to Enrico and tells him they must leave — for his sake now, as well as hers. In contrast to Mario's speech, she shows that for the first time what matters is how someone else feels: "You'll never be a man until you get away from these walls. You say you want to live, then we'll live, but away from here."

Rome is their liberation. Over a sequence of shots in the city that celebrate their new shared feelings of happiness and affection, of her newfound ability to love, she narrates, "I enjoyed seeing Enrico living each moment to the fullest." As we see them dining, enjoying their wine and toasting each other, musicians playing behind them, she continues: "I loved his new joy of life — he was so loving and tender. The past seemed forgotten."

The peak of their idyllic moment is reached in their hotel suite. On the radio they have heard her singing. He wants her to go back to dancing. "I'm here with you," she says. "Don't ever say that again."

She goes out on the terrace, and he follows. We see them in profile, sharing the beauty and the grandeur of Rome that is spread out before them; and in reverse shots past one to the other, we see their newfound closeness. In a nicely phrased speech, Enrico is defining for her, and for us, the connection between one's true calling and one's true loving, one's true way of living one's life and defining oneself. It is the summation of the connection that illuminates a central positive value in Rossen's films.

It is a moment of redemption for her, in the tradition of Greek's drama, a scene of recognition. But it is a limited and morally disappointing one. She still is allowed to show no regrets, no sense of guilt or admission of implication in what her past has produced. The connection that he defines for her has not been made in her life with the dance troupe and Toni, in dancing. Enrico tells her what we want her to be able to tell herself: "You should. It's important to you. It's a wonderful thing to be able to do something really well. Feel that your life has some use. Even more wonderful to be able to share it with as many people as you can. Leave them with a moment of beauty."

But when they have to go back to Venice for his sister's wedding, this does not seem to be enough for her. His mother's house is still cold, artificial, and suffocating; his mother is still hostile, politely tolerating this suspect intruder at a large formal dinner. Suddenly, Giovanna feels that "in that gray palace in Venice, everything was just as before." Once again she must get away and wanders again through the city.

In the climactic sequence, Mario intrudes one last time on her life. The sequence generates her final redemption, but its plot details seem contrived, her emotional and moral turns too frequent. She has wandered along the dock where Enrico's speedboat is moored. Mario is there. Unless she comes back to him, he threatens to go to the Count and tell him "certain things." She threatens back, "If you do, I'll kill you." Enrico has come looking for her and is seen to overhear them. Unaccountably, they agree to let Mario drive them all on a ride in the speedboat, which he will drive on a careening, recklessly speeding, erratic course around the lagoon. The wild ride may suggest the unpredictable danger of Mario, but it dramatizes a pointless threat that Mario may kill them all.

It is dark when they return to the dock. The denouement presents one last melodramatic irony. She reveals her growth, her redemption, and asserts her positive, loving choice. She tells Enrico, "This man means nothing to me. What's important is what we mean to each other—what we both needed all our lives." Mario cannot accept this from her. Infuriated, he insults her *and* Enrico, who starts to walk away from him but turns back. They jostle each other, and they fight. Enrico falls and hits his head; he is bleeding. Mario reveals his selfish, combative sense of the world one last time: "Leave him—it wasn't our fault. It was an accident, he slipped. Just leave him."

Giovanna kneels, holds Enrico in her arms (another of Rossen's Pietas), and speaks to him: "You're here—where else is there for me but here, what else is there for me but you. That's why you must live." But he doesn't.

She is to be his sole heir, but she rejects her inheritance and leaves Venice. "There was left to me only what I had learned through work and a rich but tragic lover. That and my talent as a dancer."

In a theater the dance troupe is rehearsing on stage. Giovanna goes to the stage, passes among them, and goes off backstage to change. They continue to dance.

Her true love, and his death, have brought her to the things of this world that matter to her, but her circling back to her beginning for what she now sees as her way to "peace and happiness" is not fully earned. For from that beginning, her voiceover comments, and her actions regarding dancing and Toni, have been so totally negative that it hardly seems like she is going back to the true vocation that she has misused. Her return may indirectly show her recognition of this, and of her misunderstanding and her misuse of Toni and what she was offering her, but the voiceover and the action of the ending that remain—walking on stage to rejoin the dance (of life?)—is not enough.

It is a redemption, *manqué*. And it is a film *manqué*, not what it might have been with careful, uncut, independent work. And control. Giovanna is a potentially fascinating, complex character, but onscreen her character is unfulfilled in all her contradictions and evasions, weaknesses and strengths. For Rossen, the mixed affair that is the film is a first stop along the way back—not unlike the situation of his own career at this point in his life.

15

Seeking the Power and the Glory — *Alexander the Great*

For Rossen's next film, released in 1956, truly *his* film, there is no name of a studio on the first credits panel. As the film *Alexander the Great* comes on screen, we hear an assertive, echoing drumbeat. A coin with Alexander etched in profile appears center screen, and Richard Burton, Alexander, intones: "It is men who endure toil and dare danger that achieve glorious deeds, and it is a lovely thing to live with courage and to be leaving behind an everlasting renown." Immediately upon the word "renown," on either side of the coin appears:

ROBERT   ROSSEN
Presents

At first glance, Alexander as a protagonist and *Alexander the Great* as a film seem an anomaly in the arching pattern of the films of Robert Rossen. But it does fit in several salient ways. From the start of Rossen's career he had been interested in genres, in using their basic elements and icons and re-shaping them. Here was a new and different genre to use and conquer. But the film is, more than that, a unique version of his basic concerns. An historical epic that takes him far from the twentieth century streets of New York and into undiscovered country, it oddly and meaningfully has very personal connections to the man who grew up on those streets and has been fighting for his place in the world ever since. *Hubris* is the classical term for the kind of grandly over-reaching, often destructive and tragic nature — the combative pride — of someone like Alexander, of his ambitions, his dreams and desires.

It also applies to the dreams and desires and ambitions of the filmmaker who devoted years to making a movie of Alexander's story. As Alexander wanted to conquer the world, Rossen wanted the film about him to make his place in the world — in his case to *re*-establish his place in the film world and mark his comeback with great impact, to beat the bastards with a knockout blow, a grand run of the table. There was a pride and a pleasure in pushing the large-scale production, combining commercial prospects with personal artistic vision, through the system that had besieged him. If it succeeded, he would have the leverage to do his own thing again. In any event, it did not work out that way. Its commercial disappointment and critical disinterest (and, ironically, his own *hubris* in reaching for the territory beyond, like Alexander) set him back several years.

An early production in the new screen format of Cinemascope, the film has not only a vast scope of narrative action, it has a staggering scope of work required for an independent production. In declaring (as Alexander was to do) his independence, Rossen had to work on a broader, more demanding scale than was the case for *All the King's Men* or *The Brave Bulls*: Writing and rewriting; organizing and implementing the myriad of details of production; selecting and directing a large cast of featured players and extras, including 4,000 soldiers from the Spanish army; supervising the immense task of editing—not only once, but twice (for once again the "money people" insisted on extensive cuts in the running time). He was one of the first to use the hills and plains of southeast Spain as a setting. Spaghetti Westerns, which popularized the use of Spanish locations, were to use many of the same sites that Rossen discovered, as did the makers of American Westerns and epic productions like *El Cid*.

While living in Italy, and even while working on *Mambo*, he had begun the struggle to obtain financing and distribution for the film. By the time *Mambo* was in its European release, he was in the early stages of the actual production of *Alexander the Great*, shot over a period of eight months in 1955 after months of re-writing and preparation. He had finally arranged a financing and distribution deal with United Artists, negotiating with the head of U.A., Arthur Krim, whom he had known for some time.

Krim was a consistent "friend" of the Left, though a staunch Democrat. In 1960 he backed Otto Preminger in his decision to announce that Dalton Trumbo was the screenwriter for *Exodus*. While a lawyer in New York, Krim had been friends with theater people of the Left, particularly Elia Kazan, Clifford Odets, and John Garfield. Before he and Robert Benjamin took over U.A. in 1951, he had been head of Eagle-Lion Studios.

As a businessman, Krim was a formidable operator. United Artists had been mismanaged for years under the erratic control of founders Charles Chaplin, Mary Pickford, and others. Krim and Benjamin turned it into a financially efficient and successful organization. Their strategy emphasized financing films directed at the general audience, using known box-office names, rather than the kind of pet projects that U.A. was known for. Still, Krim and Benjamin were willing to back smaller films by artists they believed in. After a long, successful tenure, in 1978 Krim and Benjamin were driven out when Transamerica Corporation took over U.A.; they then founded their own production company, Orion.[1]

Rossen's *Alexander* was to be a crossover project for U.A.—both a film with a personal vision by an artist they believed in and a commercially promising epic with a strong international cast that included Richard Burton (who was paid $100,000), Frederick March, Claire Bloom, Danielle Darrieux, and Stanley Baker. As things were to work out, as they usually do in the movie business, the demands of commercial success outweighed those of artistic vision.

One of the behind-the-camera "stars" who was a major contributor to U.A.'s initial confidence in this crossover approach was the British-Australian cinematographer Robert Krasker. Krasker had worked on Gabriel Pascal's *Caesar and Cleopatra* (at the time, the most expensive film produced in England); Laurence Olivier's blend of art and epic, *Henry V*; and *Romeo and Juliet*. He had also created a magnificent body of work in the beautifully brooding imagery of such significant small-scale, personal vision films as *Brief*

Encounter, Odd Man Out, The Third Man, and *The Quiet American*. Oddly, in later years he mainly applied his expertise and efficiency to working on such large-scale epics as *El Cid, The Fall of the Roman Empire,* and *The Heroes of Telemark*. He was of inestimable value in working with Rossen on mastering the new format of Cinemascope, and on creating the epic grandeur of the scenes of battle and the pomp and circumstance of the world of ruling power. But he was equally important in working to achieve the visual correlatives for the dramatization of the intense personal confrontations of his larger than life and yet ultimately human characters — their corrupting choices of the illusory terms, the counters, of their identity.

Rossen's independence in the production of the film was illusory in one decisive area: money. The distributors, United Artists, controlled the financing and so controlled the final length and form of the film. He was given a free hand during the shooting, or at least allowed it under the circumstances of filming in a distant, hard-to-reach land. In post-production editing, however, he lost that control; the consequences had a significant effect on the final unity and effectiveness of the film that was released, or of some later versions that were edited even further. In an interview Rossen commented: "The only pressures — and I could have withstood them, I suppose, if I had been strong enough at the time — were pressures on cutting the film, on getting it down in size. You see, *Alexander* originally was a three-hour picture. I wanted it done with an intermission. They got very frightened at the length, and they finally wore me down." He learned that to truly fulfill one's vision, "one must have great power for that. One must be able to impose one's will, one's conditions. One must struggle." He did, however, force a compromise of some two hours and twenty minutes, which, ironically, proved rather unwieldy for the film's commercial prospects after all. Years later he continued to insist, "It's a much better picture in three hours than it is in two hours and twenty minutes, precisely for one reason. It unveils the various guilts Alexander felt toward his father much more deeply — for instance, his chase of Darius."[2]

Some of the context of this chase and other key elements of psychology, of personal and political relationships (along with meaningful images and montages, dialogue, portions of scenes and whole sequences), were lost; so that despite its length (141 minutes), *Alexander* never fully succeeds in integrating its spectacles and its serious intentions, whether of theme or of character development. There remain a wealth of striking images that reflect Rossen's usual knack for producing visuals with palpable impact and thematic and emotional allusions. But the film is too often left with declamatory speeches for the statement of its basic psychological and political themes. This is particularly damaging in the truncation of the section at the end on the redemption of Alexander's spirit, and the positive hopes and ideals of Greek civilization that paradoxically could rise from the wreckage of devastating military conquests. Even with the emphasis on scenes of action in the second half of the film, the progress and stages of the many military campaigns are not fully or clearly delineated. Still, with Richard Burton in good form as Alexander, it was a film more human, thoughtful and meaningful than almost any other of its genre. Burton, as a matter of fact, felt that it was originally the best script that he had ever read, but that commercial pressures had forced changes that disrupted its balance, flow, and clarity.

Budgeted at four million dollars, *Alexander* went considerably over, and was not particularly successful at the box office — or with the critics — after it opened on March 29, 1956.

Rossen is fascinated with Alexander; he wants to reveal him on various levels. But beyond the accurate historical and mythic details that he incorporates, Rossen and the film work best at seeing Alexander as a seeker of power, who does believe in the good his power can bring but *needs* that power so strongly that he is blind to the betrayal of the good his power was supposed to achieve. Rossen seemed to feel a personal affinity for the driving power, the striving *hubris*, of Alexander's character. Here was a magnificent version of his unformed young man of power, energy, and will — and the ineffable human stain of corruption and betrayal. Alexander was a young man whose driving power and ambition, whose internal paradoxes of character, whose personal and public betrayals corrupted that which he believed in, corrupted that which he could do best, and betrayed his own dream of leading and inspiring others toward a better world. Alexander was a young man whose passionate and even obsessive over-reaching, his *hubris*, touched Rossen on his own nerve endings. No earthy redneck hick, and so unlike Willie Stark, Alexander nonetheless shares with Willie the power to sway and manipulate, to dominate and control (in Alexander's case, the whole world). They share the power that leads to the corrupt use of their gift and *élan*. Unlike Willie, Alexander attains a growth of consciousness and redemption before he dies. Rossen summed up his interpretation of Alexander:

> A man born before his time, a catalytic agent, he emerged from an era of warring nationalisms to try for the first time in history to get the peoples of Asia and Europe to live together. But he became a destructive force and in the process of destroying other people while attempting to unify them, he destroyed himself.[3]

Early in the film Alexander's tutor Aristotle tells him that his power and glory is the power and glory of Greece, destined and fit to rule the world for its own good. For they are the best, and all others are barbarians. It is their moral duty to conquer them and embrace them — but, Aristotle says, "if necessary destroy them."

This hubristic belief that Macedonia is the better part of Greece, that Greece is the better part of the known world, that it is just and right that Macedonia rule Greece and Greece rule the world, is an accurate representation of the central political and cultural doctrine of the era. The historical Aristotle, among others, based this belief on the power of geography and environment in shaping, defining characteristics of a nation and people. The Greeks occupied the ideal environment between Europe and Asia, and so, he maintained, Greeks were most suited to ruling others. In turn (and all so neatly), the inhabitants of Asia, servile by nature, were well suited to being ruled by Greeks. Herodotus also taught, as summarized by one scholar of the period, that the battle with the Persians was a "contest between the slavery of the barbarian and the liberty of the Greek, between the Oriental autocracy and Hellenistic constitutionalism." Or, as explained in the summary in the *Cambridge Encyclopedia of Ancient History*, this battle was the saving of "Europe, as yet unborn, for freedom, for science, for civilization." Isocrates, writing circa 380 B.C.E., argued that "it is impossible for people raised and governed as they [the Persians] are to have any virtue.... They indulge their bodies in the luxury of their riches. They have souls humiliated and terrified by the monarch." Isocrates contrasted the disciplined, masculine and strong, free nature of the Greeks with the soft, corrupt, effeminate, weak and servile nature of the Easterners.

The extent of the popular expression of these beliefs is exemplified in the wickedly satirical vase paintings of the period. In one example, as Paula Fredriksen describes it, "a heroically nude Greek prepares to sexually assault a terrified Persian. The Greek runs at the Persian, grasping his erect penis in his right hand like a sword. The Persian presents his buttocks, while the caption reads, 'I stand bent over.'" Fredriksen adds that a more colloquial translation might be: "We've really buggered the Persians."[4]

Rossen's thinking and reading and working on the film began at the time he was still debating within himself how to deal with HUAC and the blacklist, and with the Communist Party. As he read and worked, he could see the parallels between this ancient history and his time of living with the consequences of breaking with the Party and its betrayals of his idealism (and, of course, millions of people).

On the level of allusion to the contemporary illusions of Communist ideology, Alexander's quest to unify the people, to conquer and control them for the sake of an abstract future good, parallels that of the leaders of the Soviet Union or the new Communist China or North Korea. It reveals how the realities of human nature, of power and fanatical zeal, lead to the betrayal of those abstract ideals—betrayal on a grand scale. In the film, as in the world of the twentieth century, many people are destroyed for the sake of the People, the Proletariat. Harsh dictatorship is installed, "necessary" measures are taken—no matter how cruel and bloody—all so that the noble "cause" for the People can be fulfilled. When Alexander takes over the army, his first act is a purge to kill the "traitors" within. A shot of a series of crucified men marks his ascendancy to power. As he marches into Persia, more traitors are purged and whole villages are burned because of the threat of alleged disloyal ("Trotskyite"?), treacherous activities. For all their professed noble aims, Alexander and the others are driven by lust for power and glory. For glory, for country, for the illusory ideals of ideology, any act, however cruel and bloody, becomes justifiable.

In the film there is much talk of glory (too much repeated *talk* of glory). It is, however, an accurate representation of the personal ideal of the time of Alexander, the defining banner of the fulfillment of the self for a noble man. In reality, it is the lofty doctrinal cant that, recognized or not, disguises, rationalizes, and justifies its necessary corollary—power.

In his final interview the year before his death, Rossen was again talking about his continuing fascination with the complexities of power and Alexander:

> But then again, if you go back to the era of Alexander, which was not as complex a society, you find the same power motives.... Power for him was a natural and inevitable thing based on his background, but his constructive use of power did not come until the last three or four years of his life. Not until then did he really understand that power could be a constructive weapon.[5]

Power, wrapped and glorified in the grand robes and banners of glory, is Alexander's very birthright. The attainment of that power, and the power struggle necessary to achieve it, is the meat of the first, lengthy section of the film. The struggle is conducted on several interlaced levels. While Philip of Macedonia (Fredric March), Alexander's father, is fighting Athens for control of Greece, Alexander is born. From the start, Phillip's joy is mixed with foreboding and fear. For his wife, Queen Olympia (Danielle Darrieux), Alexander is a "god"—and his fulfillment as the ruler of Greece will be the means of her fulfillment as well in her struggle for power with Philip. Philip fears her treachery, and fears his son and what he knows must be the eventual battle between them to rule Macedonia, Greece, and the world. As he matures, Alexander too knows he must overcome his father to fulfill his destiny. As he is told by Aristotle, Phillip, too, is a barbarian. To rule Greece properly,

Aristotle says, "it will take a man as great as you can be." Such a man, however, must be free of his mother as well.

The pageantry of Philip's presentation of his son to the massed people is counterpointed by the first images of Alexander's mother. She is seen lofty and isolated in heroic profile, leaning against the pillar at the topmost level of a temple, as she looks out onto a valley and rolling hills beyond. Below, crowds mill around Philip as he rides into the city with his troops and dismounts among them. When Olympia joins Philip, she maintains her aloofness; their relationship is cold and hostile—with Alexander a contested prize between them. When Philip walks out to greet the crowd, holding the babe up for the people to see, the cheers rise. Then we see the babe held high past the powerful line of upraised swords of Phillip's guards. The die is cast.

As initiated in this opening section, the complex of Alexander's motives exists on two levels: his political, ideological, nationalistic beliefs and goals; and his familial conflicts with both his father and his mother. Overall, the characterization is made more complete, more interesting, and more modern by showing the influence of his psychological struggle with his father—and emotional tensions with his mother—on his political battle with his father and on his whole crusade to conquer and reform the known world. For example, Rossen described one intersection of the two levels this way: that the complex of "various guilts" and hatreds that he felt toward his father led him to the obsession of "his chase of Darius It is more than the simple chase to kill the Emperor of the Persian Empire. The chase for Darius is tied up with his tremendous fear that as long as a father figure exists in royalty, he has to kill him."

The emphasis on the father-son conflict was based on Rossen's extensive research for the project. It was the first time that he dealt with this relationship as an influence on a protagonist, though there is some implication of an attraction-conflict relationship with a father figure for Jack Burden in *All the King's Men*. In *Alexander*, in addition to developing the influence of this conflict on Alexander's political and military actions, Rossen's structure established another striking point: that the more the son rejects the father and his flaws, the more he becomes his father and assumes his flaws. Philip is not only a rival and a threat to Alexander, he is the very model for the kind of ruthless domination, the relentless need to win at any cost (whether for an ideal or personal vindication or even pleasure), that Alexander is to pursue.

Two narrative strands develop in this opening section of the film: the conflict among Alexander, Phillip, and Olympia for power; and the military conflicts with Athens and suspected traitors to control all of Greece. In parallel scenes, Olympia seeks to enlist Alexander in her fight against Phillip and for her own survival, and Phillip seeks Alexander's help in forcing her into exile. He offers to make Alexander Regent, to rule while his father wages war. A rushed sequence of scenes—transitions and elisions not particularly clear—then develop both the military and personal struggles that lead to the climactic confrontation of Phillip and Alexander, and Alexander's assumption of total power.

As Regent, Alexander is shown subduing the alleged rebellion in the surrounding towns. We see horsemen riding, a town burning, and Alexander telling some town leaders that they will rebuild their town and name it "Alexandropolis" ("Stalingrad"?). Still, Phillip subsequently fires him. Alexander confronts him at his encampment during the war with the Athenians, and Philip relents. He needs Alexander and his popularity now—and needs his approval of his new young love, whom he plans to make his new queen.

In the battle with the Athenians, Alexander saves his father's life. The battle is shot in a helter-skelter manner, with who is who not always made clear — all presumably to suggest the mad chaos of war. Closeups of men's torsos, horses' legs and heads, swords, spears, and shields alternate with close shots of men battering each other. Interspersed are wider shots of disorganized battling and some clearer groups of men and individual fighting. When Phillip is backed up against a rock formation, Alexander rides in, leaps down and saves his father. They look at each other, and Phillip limps off.

That night Phillip is drunk. Shouting, "Phillip the Barbarian! Phillip the Barbarian!" he does a leaping, limping dance among the rocks and bodies in the crevasse and on the slope of a hill, almost doing an awkward jig. While his shouts echo in the canyon, Alexander walks to him and tells him, "You're Phillip of Macedonia. Now Captain General of all Greece." Phillip shouts back, "My Army, my kingdom! My Greece! Phillip the Barbarian!" As his words echo, he walks off among the dead bodies strewn like debris on the hill.

Phillip marries, and strips Olympia of her title. At the drunken wedding feast, Phillip goads Alexander. He will have "a legitimate heir to the throne." Alexander explodes in anger and rushes at him. Phillip draws his knife and starts to attack Alexander but falls. "Look at him, Macedonia," Alexander shouts, "this is the man who is prepared to pass from Europe into Asia, but cannot even pass from one couch to another!" Phillip starts to rise, knife upheld, but collapses.

But he maintains his power. There is an abrupt time shift. A new son is born. Olympia and Alexander have been exiled but then allowed back. His father wants him to lead the fight against Persia. His mother wants him to betray his father.

In a public ceremony, Alexander and Phillip — public allies — walk side by side up the steps of the palace. Alexander sees his closest friend lurking to the side. He understands but does nothing, and so betrays his father for the lure of absolute power. The friend rushes forward and stabs Phillip. Alexander stabs and executes the killer, his friend, on the spot. Phillip is dead. Later, Alexander betrays his friend's honor. He uses his act to strengthen his own rule, and justify purges, with the threat of conspiracy. "My friend was used as a tool by others — in Athens, here — for gold and power. They will be dealt with." The plan to attack Persia will go on — "only the name of the King has changed." At this there are shouts of "Alexander, Alexander!" ("We want Willie! We want Willie!")

Under the new regime, Phillip's new wife, Eurydice, and her child are found dead — killed by cohorts of Olympia but proclaimed as suicide. Memnon, a leading Athenian ally of Phillip's, is exiled; others are executed for treason, massed together and publicly stoned to death. Alexander now has the power he sought — and the greater glory, as well as the ability to kill whomever he wants. He now wants the world.

As Alexander departs for Asia and the battle with Persia, he stands with his mother on the terrace in front of the palace, troops massed below them, lances pointing upward. After he descends to them, mounts, and leads them off, the camera cuts to Olympia watching from above. Her son now has the power. Has she?

The next section, the campaign into Persia and beyond, is presented without solid clarity. It mixes many brief snippets with longer scenes of key battles and personal confrontations, all tied together with speeches and voiceovers, maps, and some informative printed titles about what has happened or is about to happen. There are speeches about bringing harmony, civilization, and culture to the new Greek lands. The proclaimed ideals are ironically belied by a visual litany of marching armies, death and destruction, and burning cities. But the betrayal of the noble goals is blurred by the truncated structure of the narrative that tries to get in so much material and unify abrupt changes in Alexander and others.

A central narrative strand involves Memnon (Peter Cushing), the Athenian who had been exiled and has now gone over to the Persians. And intertwined is the major plot strand involving his wife, Barsine (Claire Bloom). She has been won over by Alexander, believes in his ideals, and has fallen in love with him. She wants Memnon to turn back to Alexander. Only he can bring the "new force and idea" that the world needs. Athens "may be old and corrupt, but still its ideas and glory are worth keeping alive in the hearts of men."

"Whose glory," Memnon demands, "Athens or Alexander?"

"Both, if need be." It is the justification of tyrannies the world over.

But Memnon knows the rest. "I believe he was never out of your mind or your heart, was he?" She doesn't answer.

A montage and several brief scenes trace the success of the campaign and Alexander's growing arrogance and cruelty. Persians are defeated, villages are burned. Athenian Greeks are captured and accused of being traitors. Memnon is murdered. Many are to be sent to work in Macedonian mines (the Gulag?). The entire population of a village is to be sold into slavery. When Alexander approaches a group of captured Athenians, we see that Barsine is among them. For conspiring with Darius of Persia, they are to be held as hostages.

She is appalled by the cruelty she has seen and, for the moment, turns against him. She challenges him, accusing him of "savagery" and betrayal: "And for those who might have come over to you we have had our warning. Against you it must be to the death." They exchange intense stares. He half smiles and turns his head toward his troops, "Yours the victory, yours the spoils." He looks back at her, then walks off as she stares after him.

Nonetheless, love is indefinable, paradoxical; it has its powers and momentum beyond ideology and the ravages of war. The scene shifts to Alexander lying in bed, a sheet partially covering his nude body, bright in the morning sun streaming into the tent. The camera shows Barsine dressing, looking lovingly, satisfied, at him, a quiet smile starting to spread. But then we see a soldier outside the tent throwing a woman down to the ground and walking off. Barsine watches in horror, angry again. Alexander has seen it too. Rising from the bed, he tries to mollify her, but, revealingly, he says the wrong thing, "You will be treated according to your rank."

She runs from the tent, going to the right foreground outside in a shot that will be held to the end of the scene. As they move within it, the camera captures the tempestuous intensity of their connection, his desire for her, for a connection to her closer than any other that he has ever allowed. He goes after her and takes her arm, but she won't turn and look at him. She says, with scathing scorn, "Alexander, conqueror. You sack the city, burn it to the ground, loot and pillage—and take a woman!" He turns her to him. "What did you expect to see?" she asks, hard now against him. "What I saw in your eyes when you first awoke. What I saw in your eyes in Athens." "In Athens I betrayed Memnon with my soul," she says.

Suddenly, under the tension, he seems distracted, taken away, hearing words in his head, mouthing "Alexander." He moves away, the camera panning with him and away from her. She follows and enters the shot, her anger broken, coming back to him emo-

Alexander the Great (1956), United Artists. Alexander (Richard Burton) and Barsine (Claire Bloom) are in one of the tense and shifting moods of their mercurial love affair, reflecting her conflicted obsession with him, and his driven obsession with glory.

tionally. "What do you fear to say that you did not fear to say last night?" she asks. But he cannot return to that intimacy. He is clearly in a semi-trance and mutters, "Thoughts. Stormy. Tossed." Then, louder, "You chose to go. Go! My head turns, it swims."

"Why must you always choose to be alone? Alexander — now look at me." She moves closer. He turns and they look at each other. He does not want her to go; she does not want to. It is his most open, human moment.

Here too the forms and degrees of loving reflect major attitudes and ways of living. Phillip's obsessive ardor for his new young wife parallels the excesses of his rule as he becomes obsessed with defending his power at any cost. Olympia's obsessive love for her son and his glory parallels her zeal in seeking power for him, and for herself, at any cost. Barsine's intense love for Alexander almost penetrates the armor of his obsessive egoism, but even her love shifts erratically as it is embedded in the ideals she believes he represents but may be betraying. Alexander's later symbolic marriage (and rather abstract love) with a young Persian woman will represent not only his redemption, but the ideal of unity and civilization that he has proclaimed as his goal.

The war goes on; the Athenians then *do* betray him. They will not supply their ships. But against all advice, he insists on going on. When told his father would not do that, he explodes, "My father, my father, my father! I am Alexander, not my father!"

But Barsine and the power of his own idealism do have an effect. In one turn of his character he releases his Greek prisoners and hostages. They are free men and must be free to choose — to go home or fight along with him. "I will embrace in my cause any man who believes in it." Barsine is seen watching, pleased. "Greece is where you are ... where you walk, talk, breathe, live."

The defeat of Darius, the King of Persia, goes through several stages (truncated too much, in Rossen's view, in the final editing). In a pitched battle, Darius chooses to retreat after a spear impales the aide on horseback right next to him. Going to Darius' palace, Alexander is kind and gracious, and tells those gathered there that Darius is not dead. Two children go to his side; the eldest daughter, Roxanne, watches intently. Again, Darius is pursued by Alexander, and he is betrayed by his followers, killed and left, bound, on the ornate wagon that is his moveable throne. Alexander finds him, along with a letter that Darius has written him. "Look now at what I was and what I have become.... Take my daughter Roxanne for your wife, so that the seed of Darius and Phillip may be mingled in her and that our worlds may become as one."

After another victory, Alexander carouses like his father, drunk and inflated with his own power, walking and shouting among his followers — not in a muddy, corpse-strewn ravine, but in an ornate palace. He is buoyant and promises them all riches: "Gold, silver, spices, slaves, women — yours!" They cheer him and toast him as he sits on a throne. Barsine is among them and joins in, lifting her glass to him. She (oddly, and without explanation) seems to be pleased, even with this side of him.

The celebrations continue and reach an ironic climax. The time sequence is not clear. In the night, some have started to burn the city below. In daylight Barsine — with quite another shift of mood, a seeming complexity of motive — now grabs a torch and leads the rest to set fire to the palace! This will end it all, she shouts, this will start them on the journey home! But it is Alexander who now rushes to stop the burning. "No, it is my palace, mine, mine, mine!" He goes to confront her, insisting, "It must not be said of Alexander that when he passed only charred ruins remained as his monument." He walks from her as the camera pans with him. Stepping into the shot, she will not let him evade her, but is quieter now, intimate again. "Alexander, let there be an end."

"Why," he says, "so you can hold me chained?" A two-shot reveals their faces, now close, as she gets emotionally closer and opens more tightly closed chambers. "Yes, so I can hold you chained." "Is this the degree of your love?" "My love has no degree." "You fear that I leave you for another woman." Holding his eyes with hers, she says, "No other woman is my rival except your mother. And your frenzied desire to outdo your father."

He pulls away and out of the shot, as he shouts, "I am not Phillip's son. I am the son of God!" In a new shot she stands to the side behind him; he stares straight ahead into his own world. She has lost him to his obsessive dream again. "The world is my domain, and my mission is to rule and rebuild it. We will march to the end of the world." She comes closer, but he doesn't look at her.

In the next section, although Darius is dead, there are more lands and people to conquer, more to destroy. The battles continue, the cruelty and madness, the betrayals peak. In a nighttime encampment he hears his friend Philotas talking against him. When confronted, Philotas protests that he was just telling them what he had overheard, but Alexander has him arrested and tortured. Philotas is seen hanging by his arms from a cross-bar, screaming, pleading. The scene cuts to mud and dead bodies and loud, strong drums juxtaposed with crowded, ornate images of feasting and celebration.

At a drunken feast the final emotional and moral crisis is reached. As Cleitus and Alexander shout at each other, his dearest and most loyal friend is drunk enough to reveal his buried pain and anger: "It is by the blood of Macedonians and their wounds that you have grown so great.... All that have come with you are vanquished.... You cast aside every man who's helped you. Even your father!... You bear me a grudge for saving your life — as you do for any man who can cast a shadow on your glory."

Alexander can bear it no longer. "There is no man alive who can throw a shadow on my glory!" He moves to attack Cleitus but is restrained. Cleitus is led out by others, but he returns. He enters deep in the shot as Alexander is seen in the foreground, his back to Cleitus. Cleitus now resumes his verbal attack, shouting finally that Alexander had even murdered his own father! He turns and starts to leave. Still in the foreground, Alexander turns, throws a spear and hits Cleitus in the back. But the fury of his pride is broken by guilt and grief; the mad dream finally is broken. He rushes to his fallen friend, kneels and holds him in his arms and cries. "Cleitus is dead, and I have killed him." He lays him down and stands. "We will go back."

The historian Ptolemy narrates the montage of brutal images of "the terrible return from India to Babylon." The images are devastating, showing the suffering that is the cost of empty conquest. But the narration, nonetheless, proclaims redemption: "But he even turned this retreat to victory. For within him out of the death of Cleitus a new idea was born — a new understanding, a new driving force — that it was not land that must be conquered, but the hearts of men." The last shots of the final consequences of conquest and ideology show a grave mound with a shield at its foot, a helmet for a headstone, amidst empty, bloody red sand.

There is, however, to be a scene of redemption for Alexander also. The scale of the moral rebirth may be more rhetorical and grandiose, but in it there is the basic Rossen mixture of belief and hard-nosed realism — part political and spiritual idealism, part instinctive commercialism. In more serious terms, the Italian philosopher of the Left, Antonio Gramsci, has commented about socially conscious idealists: how in them "the pessimism of the intelligence is opposed by the optimism of the will."

Immediately the scene shifts to a glorious, sun-drenched, blue-skied image, a romantic, mythic symbol of celebration and redemption, not only of Alexander but of his renewed ideal of one world in harmony, united in peace. It is a daring leap to the realm of myth, a metaphor for the positive legacy of Hellenism, the riches of culture, law, and civilization that the conquests of the Greeks *did* bring to the known world. And it is a lovely moment onscreen of transcendence, of the possibility, at least, of love and harmony in the world.

In the foreground of a shot with deep, deep focus, Alexander and Roxanne in festive costume are being wed. As was the custom, Roxanne is kneeling before him. Behind them, curving in a long arc, are many other couples being wed, even more colorfully arrayed, all the women kneeling before their men, all the couples a blending of Greeks and Persians. One of the priests intones, "Let the children of Alexander, a Greek, and Roxanne, a Persian, be of both worlds and live in one." She rises and they kiss; they walk forward toward the camera, man and wife, and out of the shot.

The shot is held. The priests walk back along the line of the people, the camera traveling back with them. The priests chant, "Let this be true of all Greeks and Persians who are married here this day." As they pass each couple, the woman rises and they kiss.

It might well have been best to stop right there, but with a sound of trumpets there is a wedding feast—and an epilogue of final paradoxes, the intentions unclear. Alexander gives a prayer for them all—full of peace and harmony and hope. He collapses and is laid in state, dying. Barsine, wearing a tiara that looks like a small crown, comes to sit beside him. Is she now a friend, his last confidante, his deep love? He instructs Barsine on the details for his burial: Men must believe "that from the gods I came and to the gods I returned." She holds his hand and agrees, then stands back to let his followers group around him. "To whom do you leave your Empire?" "To—(pause)—the strongest!"

His final words are ambiguous—whether Rossen's skeptical view of the inevitable reemergence of Alexander's belief in power or a reminder of the strength needed to ensure the ideals of peace and harmony—(or, more personally, of the power he believed he needed in Hollywood to be able to control the production of his films). For that, he would have to fight a few more battles.

16

The Road Back—*Island in the Sun* and *They Came to Cordura*

Alexander the Great was not only a business disappointment because its lack of success did not elevate him instantly to a position of power once again in the movie industry, it was a personal disappointment because it did not validate the years of work and dedication, of creative energy and the investment of spirit in his belief in its material and its themes. Still, there was nothing for it but to resume the struggle. He might well have said, as did his Alexander, "We will go back." He returned to American—not, and never, to Hollywood—to re-build his moviemaking strength.

In neither of the next two films did he have the control he sought, and felt he needed, for his best work. The first, *Island in the Sun*, was strictly a job for hire. He was hired on also for *They Came to Cordura*, but it did have material that he believed in, that touched on his continuing thematic concerns—and on the sensitive scars in his personal life.

Ironically, upon its release in June of 1957, *Island in the Sun* had the kind of commercial success that *Alexander the Great* had failed to provide one year earlier. While in Europe he had kept in touch with Darryl F. Zanuck and now accepted his offer to work as a "director-for-hire," not only as a much-needed source of income, but also as a stepping stone in rebuilding his status as a "power player." And it allowed him to work in the Bahamas rather than Hollywood. Working with Zanuck on the movie—for all of its aggravation and disappointment, as it turned out—did prove useful some years later in getting his *Hustler* project on celluloid.

Rossen came on the *Island in the Sun* production as director after the script had been written and re-written (from the novel by Alec Waugh) under the strong hand of Zanuck. Rossen took no screenplay credit, but during filming he did re-work the film—giving some semblance of real life to its glossy material and creating a more coherent narrative out of its loose-knit plaid of four love stories (and a political sub-plot). As he re-shaped the materials, one can detect in the narrative some variations on his thematic interests, especially his increasing emphasis on the varieties of love, both damaging and fulfilling.

Zanuck had chosen the story for the social value he saw in it, but also for its commercial potential, the exploitable impact of its bi-racial love stories. It was his first independent production in partnership with Twentieth Century–Fox after leaving his post as

16. The Road Back—Island in the Sun *and* They Came to Cordura

head of production at the studio. At Fox he had experienced success and received praise for producing *Pinky*, in which solidly white actress Jeanne Crain had played the light black ("negro" at the time) heroine trying to cross the color line. Since then, the industry's production code had been challenged and loosened so that Zanuck could push the boundaries and show audiences some physical contact between actors who were really of different races. At the same time there had been a breakthrough in starring roles for black actors. Chief among these were Harry Belafonte and Dorothy Dandridge, who had been together as the romantic leads in *Bright Road* and *Carmen Jones*.

This time the romance for each of them was to have a white partner.

On its release, *Island* received mixed reviews. Still, the romance of the setting and the supposed daring of the romances, and the public uproar (much of it instigated by racist organizations) over the mixed-race love affairs (mild and even evasive as they were), made it one of the top-grossing films of the year. Zanuck was pleased; his gambit had worked. Some years later, however, Belafonte, as he became more political and more active in civil rights campaigns, decided that it was "a terrible picture based on a terrible best-selling book."

For Rossen it was a useful workshop for the further development of greater rhythm, intricacy, and implication in the use of *mise en scène*, of the *plan sequences* (of images and editing) that were the core of his style, particularly in his approach to the filming of major and climactic scenes and sequences. In *Island*, several of these sequences are among the finest he developed to convey, build, and enhance dramatic emotional confrontations between and among characters—even beyond the value of the written material. He and the distinguished British cinematographer Freddie Young (*Lawrence of Arabia*, *Lord Jim*, *Doctor Zhivago*, et al.) did work beautifully together in using the décor and the setting—the lush energy and romantic allure of the Caribbean island—for more than its beauty.

One aspect of the concepts of Andre Bazin in defining the elements of *mise en scène* is particularly relevant to the recognition and explication of the dynamics of these key sequences in *Island*. In his discussion of *equilibrium*, the metaphoric content of a series of images is seen as derived from more than the implications of the objects, décor, and settings of the scene, "the outward revelation of an interior human destiny." Equally important in its metaphoric qualities is *movement*—of characters and/or camera—and especially the dynamics of changes in the balance, the equilibrium of the physical composition and relationships. These changes produce a new balance, a new stage of equilibrium and connection (whether harmonious or conflicted), paralleling and helping to establish the shift in the psychological balance, the emotional relationship of the characters in the scene.[1] As befitted his own temperament and interest in strong dramatic confrontations, Rossen's approach was to combine the traditional design of a *plan sequence*—the patterns and movements of basic, long-held shots, the movements in and out of equilibrium—with an acceleration of editing to capture the rise in emotions and interactions as dramatic moments and scenes reach their climax.

In *Island in the Sun*—the island is in the Caribbean and a "British Crown Colony"—the four love stories do intertwine to some degree, but not enough for a truly dynamic narrative.

On the island the political leader of the blacks is David Boyeur (Harry Belafonte). In contrast to the whites, he knows exactly who he is, what he wants to do, and what he *should* do for his people. However, even though he is obviously right, and even though the pride that is part of his calm, stern arrogance is valuable and necessary, he is also righteous to a point of rigidity, even, in his own way, obsession. In a film that Rossen controlled, David might have been shown as a valuable and necessary political fighter whose very craft — his political power — even in a good cause did, understandably, take some toll on him as a human being and as a lover. The movie is too righteous about itself (and probably has to be), to allow that kind of meaningful nuance.

This insistence in his politics is paralleled by the same unwavering attitude in his personal life, his interracial "love" affair. Their love exists in quotes. David really cares for Mavis Norman (Joan Fontaine), but he cannot allow it to flower, cannot allow himself to love her (even though he does love her), because she is white and because he has his cause to fight for. But the opportunity is missed to show the painful emotional impact of his dilemma, to let him show he is torn up over this. The two are shown in romantic settings, posed romantically. But they hardly ever touch, and if so, then only briefly. They never kiss. Is this all to be revealing, or merely evasive, of censorship?

Mavis does fight back, does make the claim for love, but always is outdebated, and always acquiesces and accepts. She feels that she is an outsider in the island society, although she has grown up within it. She wants more in her life, but she does not know

Island in the Sun (1957), Twentieth Century–Fox. Mavis Norman (Joan Fontaine), in love with David Boyeur (Harry Belafonte), accompanies him as he visits his people, whose cause is for him the core of his life — and his love.

what, beyond thinking of going to England. She believes she can find herself, define herself, in her love of David, in their going to England together.

The visual correlatives for their climactic final scene convey their tensions and disequilibrium, distancings and closings, separation and loss. The images give tangible life and feeling to the abstract moral and ideological talk of the scene. In a wide-angle shot they are first seen near the edge of a cliff, the sea pounding the shore below, palm trees stretching above. It is his world, the world of his cause and passion; the beauty of it is the beauty of his people, his liberation and his entrapment. Mavis sits on a hard rocky ledge, looking forward. Seen against a blue sky, David stands apart and above her on a higher rock, legs spread, arms tight across his chest.

Through the scene, as they argue, they paradoxically come closer, physically and emotionally, and become more open with each other even as they come to their dead end. They touch more, at least on their arms, than they had in the rest of the movie, but each time they break apart — separate, close, separate.

At the start, after the opening image, the camera shifts to a closer shot in the same pattern as she tells him she wants them to go together to England, to be free of the island and the beauty of its chains. He walks down to her as she turns to face him, both in profile now. He is still above her, one arm leaning on a palm tree. He tells her it will never work. He will never be free there. "My skin is my country." At this he walks away from her, the camera panning with him, and she follows after him. The new angle is maintained through a series of exchanges and movements. He turns back to her and argues that it is different when it is a black woman and a white man. That looks appealing to *them*. "Their wives look sort of dull. But if I were to walk in with you or a girl like you as my wife..." He pauses. Still from the same angle, the shot is now closer to them as she fights to get through to him: "Do you care what stupid and prejudiced people think?"

He moves in closer, leans over her, their faces close, but in taut opposition, his above over hers, superior in his hard certainty. "You've never had to fight stupidity and prejudice. Besides I'd be a fool. It would be inevitable ... that night that we'd forget ourselves and you'd call me a nigger." He walks away and again she follows. He walks away again abruptly, closer to the edge of the cliff, facing away from her. She can't let him go, follows him, and takes his arm. He turns back.

From a different angle, past them we see the waves crashing on the curve of the bay below. He admits he didn't mean it but insists that "here is my world, these are my people and here is where I belong." And here she'd be in his way. "They'd never understand, my own people — they'd feel I betrayed them. I have no choice."

"You're like a rock," she says, and this time *she* walks away, as the camera pans back with her. And this time it is he that can't yet let it end; he goes to her, and touches her arm and holds it. She must understand, he tells her, that his people have power now and he must show them how to use it.

She turns toward him, but this time to fight him once more, standing even with him, her face in semi-profile, set in anger. Her speech is a rather sudden insight that goes beyond anything suggested in her thoughts to this point. It touches on the possible ambiguity in his belief in power, which is also his need for power. It is the one sign of a complexity that might have been developed. "You don't want that power for your people, you want it for yourself. You're afraid to go there because you won't have it anymore.... People don't count with you. Nothing counts with you but power. You use people, you climb on their backs."

But she immediately recants. She admits she didn't mean it. But he cannot admit that some part of it or what it suggests might be true or important for him or for them.

Standing very close to the edge of the cliff, they can go no further. "That's the end, is it?" "Yes, that's the end."

She reclaims her dignity and walks up an incline — away from him and out of the shot to the right. Alone in the shot, he takes a few steps after her but stops. In a closer shot toward him, he looks after her, the sea crashing below. Then he turns away and walks off in the opposite direction. A final shot shows him walking alone along an inland road. He has chosen his people, his cause, but it is interesting to note that he is not shown among them but alone. Striding with purpose and strength, he is isolated in the striking beauty of his land.

The other interracial *love* affair is just the opposite — nice and affectionate, but so very nice and neat. Margot Seaton (Dorothy Dandridge), both beautiful and bright, comes to the Country Club in an orange dress; she is a warm sun in a staid and drab setting. She comes to the Governor's Ball in a warm yellow dress and brightly asks the governor for a job. When she and the white adjutant to the governor, John Justin, dance, it is clearly love. He has taken her to his small cottage on the government property. They begin to dance there, twirling slowly, her face seen over his shoulder. "You know," he says, "I'm in love with you." "Yes." He pulls back. "You knew from the first, didn't you?" "Yes." Smiling softly, she is pleased. He pulls her in close in an embrace as they dance, her face nestled tight against his shoulder and neck; in love too, her hand comes up on his shoulder, pulling him even more tightly to her as they twirl slowly. It is the most positively emotional, even passionate, scene in the movie. After several minor conflicts, more in love than ever, they leave for England, where his first novel is to be published.

The story of Maxwell Fleury (James Mason) is the most dramatic and fully developed thread; it is, more accurately, a story of love and feelings denied — and almost lost. He is a middle-aged second son who still harbors youthful resentments over being mistreated and undervalued by his family. He rails against his parents still for favoring his brother (who, to make matters worse, is now idolized as a dead hero), while expecting that he, Maxwell, would maintain the family's position in the restrictive hierarchical island society. In Rossen's terms, he is without a skill, a craft, an *élan*; he can define himself only by his sense of deprivation, resulting in a free-floating, unfocused anger and resentment, a sense of familial betrayal. He has set a zone of coldness between him and his wife and of course attributes the conflict to her. He finds one obsessive course of action in pursuing his suspicion that she is having an affair with Hillary Carson (Michael Rennie). He, rather inexplicably, decides to act politically and run for office as a way somehow to define his self and fulfill himself. He runs in part to prove to people that he is somebody of substance, and in part to, paradoxically, stand up for the traditions of the white island culture (basically the inequalities) that he himself finds oppressive.

A sudden plot twist produces earthquake fissures in his already shaky sense of self. A journalist has uncovered and publicly reveals mixed ancestry in the family of Maxwell's father: Maxwell is one-sixteenth black! He responds hysterically. In an interesting scene at the club, he defiantly, uncontrollably asserts his new "identity." Sweating, wild-eyed, he proclaims he is proud! Afterwards, wandering drunk in the street, he encounters Hillary.

In a visually and emotionally strong sequence back at Hillary's house, he is driven by self-pity and gives way to his obsession. Maxwell cannot rationally respond to Hillary's obvious innocence, and in a drunken scuffle he loses all control and chokes Hillary to death.

In a series of repetitious and unlikely encounters, the chief police inspector, certain of Maxwell's guilt, psychologically stalks him with hints and innuendos, even giving him a copy of *Crime and Punishment*!

A beautifully wrought scene (just before the revelation of his family's racial background) captures and exposes the blocked core of Maxwell's troubled self. It takes place, appropriately, in his *parents'* house. With ironic use of décor and the shifting, equilibrium-breaking spatial patterns of character relationships, the sequence conveys the family tensions, the deep knots of unfaced conflict, that lead to the eruption of his brooding resentment — an uncontrollable act of murder.

The spacious living room is full of large pieces of furniture and ostentatious art. A tall sculpture of a crane stands awkwardly at the center of the room, at the apex of an L-shaped seating arrangement in the middle of the room. The walls are full, the floor-to-ceiling shutters are tightly closed — just as he feels he is hemmed in, enclosed, unfairly limited his whole life by his parents and their way of life. Like the petulant child still crying out within him, he is complaining about his plight. He sits on a long sofa, his mother on one side of him, to his left. His father is on the other side of him, in an upholstered chair. Tall floral displays behind the sofa seem to press in on them.

When his father appears wary about Maxwell's running for office, Maxwell says, "You don't think I have a chance of winning, do you?" Unable to just sit there, he stands abruptly (standing against their habitual lack of understanding), turns his back on them and shouts, "Well, I do!" They wait him out, and he asks for a drink. His father crosses past them and out to the right to get the drinks. Maxwell remains standing, staring after his father, not looking at his mother as she talks to him.

Paying no attention to what she's saying, he starts to complain about his father's treatment of him. The basic shot is maintained when he walks to the right past her, as she answers, trying to calm him down. The camera pans with him as he walks to the end of the room, passing all the finery in the room and complaining about never being appreciated. He stops, still facing away from her. He turns slightly and shouts that all he ever rated was this dreary island. The camera shifts to her as she protests he's not being fair and starts to rise.

The scene returns back to the basic long-held shot, *his* controlling shot, as she comes after him and stands near him, but not looking at him directly. He is half-turned away, as though while still denying her closeness, he's waiting for her to soothe him, and she can only go so far. He continues complaining. All he ever got was "a decaying house on a godforsaken tip of the island." But as his railing reaches its crescendo, he turns and cries, "I'd be better off if I'd been born black!" She moves closer and starts to slap him. He grabs her arm.

Just then, as the camera pans slightly to the left, his father walks into the shot, shifting the power relationship. The other two now stand chagrined in front of the father and his control. Maxwell drops her arm and rushes out of the shot away from them, from *him*. The shot is held as, not speaking or glancing at each other, they watch him run away. He will continue to run until he can run from himself no longer — on the verge of suicide and seeing himself truly in his bathroom mirror, turning back to life, his wife, and responsibility for what he has done.

In the fourth story Maxwell's younger sister Jocelyn (Joan Collins) also feels trapped in her pointless role in the island's stratified life; she also carries with her a goading, selfish resentment at what limits her. Unlike Maxwell, she acts out an unfulfilling role as the pampered carefree rebel, but she too has no real sense of what the way to fulfillment might be. Her love affair with Euan Templeton (Stephen Boyd), a rather undefined young man from an important island family, is in part an act of sexual rebellion (the sex mainly hinted at, though it has its consequences), in part an opening to some true emotions and love (at present, in a state of confusion).

In the climactic episode of her story, Jocelyn has an extended, and revelatory, conversation with her mother in the same formally furnished living room of her family. These are the furnishings of the life that has controlled her and blocked her emotionally, but it all now seems a false veneer to her after the revelation of mixed blood in her ancestry. The scene's changing equilibriums project not only attempts at control between them, but also shifting feelings of coldness and warmth, resentment, separating and connecting, withdrawing and sharing — until the deepest truths are let out, and the mother and daughter reach a sympathetic sharing that they have not experienced before.

Significantly, the nature of their usual cold relationship is established when Jocelyn enters the large living room through a glass door that opens out to the lush garden. Her mother, Betty Fleury, stands at another entrance, waiting for her with a stern maternal stance that says Jocelyn is to come to her mother. Jocelyn crosses the whole room to the right and says, "I have something I want to tell you" Betty responds by moving away from her, going back to the left across the room to get a match for her cigarette. She then sits, as we see Jocelyn past her, still across the room, left behind. Jocelyn walks forward, needing to come to her, then walks past her and sits in a chair to her left.

During the course of the scene, changes in the "equilibrium" of the shots — movements, distances, cameras angles — parallel the shifting, uncertain course of their emotional interchanges. At one point Jocelyn tells her mother she is pregnant but is afraid to marry because of the discovery of her partial "negro" ancestry. At the scene's climax, Betty tells her the truth: her husband is not Jocelyn's father; she has no African blood in her body. Jocelyn wants to know the identity of her real father, but Betty answers, "Better you shouldn't know." The visual separation between them is closed during a shot past Jocelyn, held to the end of the scene, as Jocelyn moves further into the shot, the camera moving in closer behind her. She goes to her mother and kneels at her side. Her mother turns her head away, pressing against the back of the chair, and starts to cry. Jocelyn rises and puts her arm around her mother and comforts her. They share a moment of tender sympathy — probably for the first time in their lives.

Seeking success, as did Rossen, the film is too neat and melodramatic, too unfocused in its four stories, too un-probing of the issues raised. Yet it provides polished gems of scenes like these, a foreshadowing of complex character relationships.

When Rossen took on his next job of work, *They Came to Cordura*, for a Columbia Pictures without Harry Cohn, he once again created brilliant scenes of visual and emotional unity, but this time they could not overcome the broad irony of the overall concept and the neat individual ironies of its narrative structure. Though he believed in the meaningfulness of those ironies, he could not build it all into a unified whole that satisfied him.

In the making of *They Came to Cordura* he was caught in a complicated story beyond the complicated story of the film. The film was, of course, another opportunity to work, to prove himself in new terrain, in another genre — the broad sweeping plains of a Western. It offered an opportunity to experiment with another kind of "décor" — how the vast natural setting could be used to interact with the characters, and provide visual correlatives for the human conflicts and dilemmas. But it was also the raw material that he was interested in, a project that he could believe in. And so it was even more painful when that belief turned sour in the battle for power, for control over one's work.

In the film's story and characters he found new constellations of his recurring concerns. Its direct dramatization of the complexity of courage was, in fact, a probing not only of what was courage, who had courage, but also of *why* — the complexity, the ambiguity of motives and human frailty. So at its deepest level he could see it as a study of morality — and the perplexing paradoxes of betrayal.

All of this, as one can readily surmise, had its strong personal impact. From the time of his inner struggles over testifying, and the act and consequences of his testimony, these themes were to take an ever stronger hold on his imagination. Here he could clearly see and interpret the parallels. Major Thorne has been labeled a coward for his conduct during a complex battle situation. He has been ostracized, sent out into the wilderness because he had supposedly betrayed, been immoral. Rossen had been labeled a betrayer and scoundrel for his testifying in the complex situation of the investigations and blacklist. The five soldiers who are to be honored as heroes are tarnished morally not only by their motives during the original situation, but even more by their behavior during the struggles afterward. They carry out a threatening vendetta against Thorne. The Communist Party members who had not testified and are honored as heroes and martyrs are tarnished morally by their continuing silence about, denial of, and thus complicity in the monumental ravages and betrayals of Communism and the Soviet Union. They carried out a vilifying vendetta against Rossen and others who testified.

As things take their course, Thorne acts with honor and courage, but with his own willful obsessiveness. And so, after all, who are the betrayers, and what is it to be moral, to behave decently? One couldn't find a stronger symbolic dramatizing of the moral paradoxes of the blacklist period.

The film was made under the auspices of Columbia Pictures, but not under the control of Harry Cohn. Rossen's old friend and verbal and business sparring partner had died just before the production was arranged. The film was a project of the independent producer William Goetz, with financing and distribution by Columbia. Goetz had been a producer at Columbia, Fox, and Universal, and had experienced commercial success with his first independent ventures, *The Man from Laramie* and especially *Sayonara*, which had come out in December 1957, followed by *Me and the Colonel*, released while negotiating for *Cordura*. His subsequent films were undistinguished.

Goetz believed an adaptation of Glendon Swarthout's novel, a variation on Western themes, would continue his positive run, and paid a reported $250,000 for the popular novel. He negotiated financing of more than four million with Columbia's new hierarchy, the most expensive project they had financed up to that time. The duel was thus set — Goetz and the studio's demands for the "commercial values" of a Western epic with big-name stars (right down to a supposedly audience-pleasing happy ending), and Rossen's concerns for character development and motivations, for the emotional fullness of the story and its people (and a valid ending).

Goetz's choice of big-name stars had its own ironies. Gary Cooper had had good success with roles that had been pretty much suitable for his age in *Love in the Afternoon* (1957) and *Ten North Frederick* (1958). Also in 1958, he had just appeared in Anthony Mann's excellent *Man of the West* (which sustained a powerful sense of tragic inevitability), but his career and his health were waning. After *Cordura* he worked on only two more films before his death in 1961. His weariness, his restrained aura of sadness, did suit the situation of his character, Major Thomas Thorne; he did, however, also seem too old and too phlegmatic to convey the wound-up, spinning energy of Thorne's tensions and conflicts. Rossen admired Cooper as a person and a professional. Rossen's comments about him are revealing, both about Cooper and Rossen's understanding of the nature of screen acting:

> He was a unique person, one of the most likable fellows I've ever known.... He lived in perfect communion with nature; he was a poet, a mystic. But too a true professional to his fingertips. In everything that pertains to the actor's profession, I have never met his like. He had the quality that Burton has in equal measure, of controlling his acting completely, of interiorizing it, in a way....
>
> One must know to what point one should surrender oneself to produce the desired effect. Bogart, too, of course, knew it perfectly, but really Cooper was tremendous. It made you act with him; seeing him, you entered into the acting, and it's succeeding in that that makes the great cinema actor.

Nevertheless, Rossen still felt "he was not really suited to the role of *They Came to Cordura*." For one thing, "there was too much dialogue for him." And "I did not know at the time that he was already a little ill."[2]

The box-office power of Rita Hayworth (Adelaide Geary) had also waned. Before his death, Cohn, always her ardent admirer and champion, had wearied of her wayward emotions and loves, and her internal contradictions about acting. At the height of her popularity she had withdrawn from films for several years; then, after returning for a few years, she had withdrawn again for almost four years. After this, Cohn had placed her in *Pal Joey* (1957) as the older but still glamorous counterpoint to his new young star, Kim Novak; and then, in an attempt to reprise her earlier sultry roles, in *Fire Down Below* (also 1957) and *Miss Sadie Thompson* (1958). About this time she met (and would eventually marry) Jim Hill, who for a time was a partner in the Hecht-Hill-Lancaster independent production company. At first Hill indulged her desperate need to get away from the demands of Hollywood, but then he, like others before him, became determined to rekindle and reshape her career as a serious dramatic actress. It was he who insisted she take the role in *Cordura*.

Hayworth's world-weariness, a brooding melancholy underlying her world-worn beauty, was suitable for the role. Hill called it that "sad, faraway look in her eyes." Yet, with her personal longing to withdraw to some safer place than the making of this movie, she did not project enough of the harder edges of the steely resolve that her character also possessed—a character toughened and hardened by the fortunes and misfortunes of life, yet still possessing a tender, compassionate core somewhere within.

Rossen did some re-working of the final draft of a script originally put together mainly by Ivan Moffat; he managed to effect some compromises through a lengthy and conflicted erratic period of preparation and production through the latter part of 1958 and into 1959. He did not take any screen credit. Goetz controlled the film's conventional Western epic form, including the control of the final cut, and his editing upsets the kind of balance Rossen wanted to achieve among the scenes that were left and those that were lost or reduced.

Still, the film's problems were due to more than the battles for control and the decisions on the final cut. For one thing, the movie falls between two stools: epic Western action in the first section, and character studies and confrontations in the rest of the film. While the central irony of the film lies in the real meanings of the typical heroic derring-do of the men during the cavalry battle, it is not effectively implied in the tone and development of that material. Nor was that section adroitly handled by the second unit filming the battle scene. The result, as Patrick Brion in *Cahiers du Cinema* has pointed out, is not consistent with the tone or even shooting style of the rest of the film.[3] This disjunctive difference of tone between the opening section of typical Western action creates expectations in the audience that are frustrated by the uniquely slow progress of the trek to Cordura. The intense personal struggles of people reduced to their essences in the raw, uncaring wilderness, where there is no place to hide from others or yourself, is in typical Western terrain, but it is not typical Western action. And Goetz did his damnedest to remedy that. He maintained tight control throughout the filming, including demanding some conventional over-explanatory dialogue. Rossen was not consistently able to the make the spontaneous kind of adaptations to the day-to-day circumstances of shooting that he wanted to make (and was able to make when he had more control). To Jean-Louis Noames at *Cahiers du Cinema* Rossen remarked:

> I was an employee on that film. I did not have enough control over it. There were two enormous flaws: The first, it was too explanatory; the second, I wanted to give it the same ending as the book and they kept me from it.... I liked that story very much, but I did not expect to meet such difficulties.[4]

More importantly, however, it is the formulaic neatness of the basic premise that Rossen can't completely go beyond, that he never fully faced or admitted. This premise does provide the basis for the more complex implications of the film's psychological and moral themes. But the core of the plot is too neat and clever; it distracts from and undercuts the development of the more complex themes involving the ambiguities of motivation, moral behavior, and betrayal. Four of the five men (we do not see the fifth) who are to be cited as heroes are not heroic at all; the alleged coward is a hero, and the fallen woman has not fallen at all. The whole, the sum of its parts, is too schematic, too complete an abstract reversal of the moral issues and judgments. The strength of the film is in the parts—fine raw scenes that capture the uneven, often explosive jagged mess of human needs and motives, the elusive capacities for good or evil in human nature.

Released in October of 1959, the film garnered moderate reviews and acceptable success. The French critic Andre Fieschi called it a "*film manqué*, certainly, out of balance and confused, but *attachant* [engaging, involving, or, more colloquially, grabbing]." On re-seeing it, he saw its "mapping points" that connected it to Rossen's often ignored "formal or thematic indications."[5]

Rossen's protagonist this time is not an unformed, uncompleted young man on the way up, on the make. Rather, Thorne is on the other side of the hill, unable to come to terms with something that has already happened, but also, really, with the course of his whole life. It is not that he aggressively crusades or controls; he is impaled on the moral conflict within himself. He doubts himself, questions himself. He begins to define himself as others have defined him—as a coward, a betrayer. His assignment—to choose five heroes and lead them to Cordura ("sanity," in Spanish) to be honored — is given him as a scornful retribution. Yet it becomes the means of his retrieving a sense of his own worth, of recognizing that he does have the *élan*, the spirit, the sanity and courage to act rightly and decently. So in this narrative structure there is a pattern of movement upward, unsteady and halting, toward redemption, not merely a sudden redemption at the end.

But there is another strand — another echo of the dilemmas faced by Rossen's more fully developed characters — in the way that Thorne carries out his assignment. After being immobilized, drifting in both resentment and guilt before the trek, he too becomes a crusader, a zealot in carrying out what he sees now as his duty, a matter of honor. He *will* get them to Cordura — no matter what! He *will* get them to recognize their better selves! He is determined to do his duty even when he learns how flawed and even evil his "heroes" are. This unwavering determination seems to become excessive and obsessive, but it is not clear how we are supposed to see and judge it. Is this really a sign of his new sanity, a dedication to his recovered sense of honor? Or can we see it as an irrational extreme, the unfortunately inevitable tragic flaw in even the best of righteous campaigns and most idealistic crusades? It is satisfying to see this complexity in motivations and needs. Is his nobility driven also by his own selfish need to prove himself — mainly *to* himself — and expiate what he accepts as his sins? Or is this only a complexity we would like to see in the film, that might have been in the film?

Thorne's antagonists, the four heroes he is shepherding to Cordura, follow the opposite course — a steady exposure of their venality, immorality, and betrayal. The bitter irony of their certified heroism is two-fold. Whatever they did in battle had not been driven by a consciously heroic spirit or impulse. But the second level of the irony is more important: their intentional, conscious betrayal of the moral code signified by such concepts as honor and courage. Each, for his own self-protective reasons, does not want to be taken to Cordura to be honored, and it is this motive that will lead *them*, in varying ways, to do whatever is necessary — even murder — to betray Thorne and keep him from fulfilling his assignment.

The opening section of the film — the battle and what precedes and follows it — sets the premise for the action of the main section and the narrative's scheme of ironies and reversals. The American army has entered Mexico to track down and capture Pancho Villa, who had earlier entered the U.S. with his forces and killed soldiers and civilians. The result has not yet been effective — or productive of good newspaper copy. Reporters have been brought in to witness and then publicize an expected victorious battle. And to dramatize the victorious heroism of the American army and shift the focus from the casualties incurred, the public will be given "live heroes to think about." Major Thorne will find the heroes who will be taken to Cordura to receive the Congressional Medal of Honor. (One designate has already been determined.)

This publicity campaign has another purpose: the self-serving aggrandizement of Rogers, the cavalry colonel in command. He's going to prove that the Mounted Cavalry is not obsolete. The classic cavalry charge — "The Regiment in line, a single line abreast!" — is a recipe for disaster, as the formal pattern of the single line is decimated by the Mexicans firing from within the compound. But the visualization of the human cost of the righteous dogma and destructive glory is too brief and abruptly shifts to the isolated single actions, going beyond the prescribed strategy, of the men that Thorne observes and will choose.

In addition to the four heroes, Colonel Rogers orders Thorne to arrest "that woman"

Adelaide Geary and take her to Cordura to be tried for "giving aid and comfort to the enemy. The Mexicans had used her house during the battle. "Treason!" the Colonel insists. One of the most elusive and bothersome of Thorne's ambiguities in doing his duty is his resolute insistence that he must follow the law and take her to have a court determine her culpability or not, even though he has not agreed with the Colonel from the start. For the French critic Patric Brion, Adelaide is "a remarkable female character who, as incarnated by Rita Hayworth ... was the sign of a real achievement in Rossen's career." She is wonderfully contradictory, a tired free spirit just as disillusioned with her rebellions as she is with all she has rebelled against. She has run from the pain of her life in the States — and from herself. She has found a life of easy pleasures and yet more of the same emptiness, which a lot of hard drinking cannot fill, in her life in Mexico. She is cynical and aloof, but all of her mocking cannot fully cover a lingering sense of sadness. After all that she's gone through, she has nowhere that she wants to go. Even here she has moved into the wilderness to be alone and yet has enjoyed having the Mexican troops stay with her. Neither side — no one really — is of that much interest to her. She doesn't want to take part, no matter what it is. Yet the tensions and difficulties of the journey, the choices it raises, bring her back to a self she has ignored, a self that does care.

Adelaide is an interesting variation, an older, more jaded, inwardly troubled version of the "good-bad" girl Hayworth had played to much success in earlier films — whether moving from seemingly bad to good in *Gilda* (1946), or from seemingly good and oppressed to bad and deadly in *The Lady from Shanghai* (1948).

From the start of the journey she keeps her physical distance, and is defiant and taunting of them. She smokes while the men have no cigarettes, and toasts them and drinks from the bottle she's brought along. She almost demands their rising hostility.

As the journey progresses, Thorne interviews each of the men about their motives for their actions and their feelings while performing them. In each overly didactic instance he is disappointed by their responses but continues to insist on the value of their displays of courage. The tougher ironies and impelling conflicts, though, rise from the men's attempts to keep Thorne from taking them to Cordura, as the rigors and pressures of the journey mount. The reason for the refusal of the aggressive Sergeant John Chawk (Van Heflin), for example, is that he had killed a man in a brawl, and so the publicity and his picture in the paper will get him arrested for murder. From the start he is the most hostile, even threatening, toward both Thorne and Adelaide. During the second day they are caught in a canyon, pinned down by a remnant of the Mexicans who had fled. To escape, Thorne agrees to give the Mexicans their horses (which seems a forced plot gambit), and Chawk threatens that it better work or else!

They are now forced to walk, their own water supply diminishing, through the brutal burning brightness of a desert day. The young religious soldier develops a fever, and they construct a litter and carry him. (After the extensive editing, his place in the narrative structure remains incomplete.) Exhausted, they collapse, seen up close with wild empty prairie stretching out, more threatening than the Mexicans, all around them. That night they camp in the dark shadows under the stark, oppressive wall of a stone cliff. Chawk and Trubee explode. Adelaide can't sleep and goes for a walk. They grab her and start to tear at her clothes. Thorne sees them and, pistol out, stops them.

Up to this point Trubee has been seen as a whiner and complainer, a weasel who is used to getting along by making deals. His weakness exacerbates Thorne's need to prove him courageous. But on the night in front of the implacable stone wall, after Trubee and Chawk have attacked Adelaide and Thorne had stopped them, Trubee goes on the attack. He tells them all what he has heard: "He [Thorne] was hiding in a ditch when they were fighting at Columbus. The dirty yellow guts hid out in a ditch. I say blow him full of holes and let's find our own way home. He won't shoot, he's a yellow guts."

After a sequence of cuts have built the rising conflict, the final action of the scene is held in a wide-angle shot that epitomizes the tension among them and the unresolved threat still hovering among them in that darkness. Thorne is to the left, Lt. Fowler (Tab Hunter) is in the middle (beginning to feel caught between them), while Chawk and Trubee are over to the right. Thorne orders Lt. Fowler to take their guns. Fowler is an idealistic believer in the cavalry and its glory. He hesitates but then follows orders and goes to them, the camera panning with him, and takes their guns. He walks back past Thorne, not looking at him, the camera following as he throws the guns into the shadows off to the left. He walks back past Thorne again and is in the middle once more. Chawk mocks Thorne, telling him he won't get them to Cordura, and that he'd better not go to sleep. Chawk turns away and, along with Trubee, walks out of the shot along an even darker section of the cliff wall. Thorne watches, then follows them out. The camera pans back past Fowler, frozen for the moment, until off to the left we see Adelaide still sitting, shamed, on the ground. She rises, pulls herself together, and walks off alone.

Later that night Fowler has made up his mind. He tells Thorne, "As far as I'm concerned, Major, you're on your own." In his case, his belief in the traditions of the cavalry, his belief in the cause of the military, leads him to betray Thorne. For him, "covering up for cowardice is beyond" any requirement of duty. In his version of honor as he sees it, he tells him he won't participate in their rebellion, but he also won't lift a finger to prevent it. But later he does go beyond neutrality to active betrayal, and is even the last, in his righteous military rigidity, to relent.

Chawk and Trubee go on the offensive — Chawk threatening to kill Thorne, Trubee demanding he give him the woman or he'll tell all he knows in Cordura.

The events of the journey have started Adelaide thinking about herself, the problems and mistakes in her life, and about others. The arc of her character has risen in an opposite curve to the descent into selfish betrayal of the heroes. There are three scenes between Adelaide and Thorne which have a touching emotionality that is a calm, open counterpoint to the hostile confrontations of the rest of the narrative. In vulnerable performances (especially by Hayworth), they reveal, if tentatively and still guarded, a tenderness that is not easy for them. Together they take care of the feverish young soldier. They show each other more of themselves than they have to anyone before. It is she who helps him let out things he has kept inside tearing at him beneath his stoic control. She has changed. But he still cannot let go of his almost mad dream, his belief in his now ludicrous cause.

In the first of these scenes between them, Thorne tells her that his father had been a hero who was killed in battle; but at Columbus, when Pancho Villa had attacked suddenly in the night, Thorne had been running through the confusion to regimental headquarters when bullets tore into a tree next to him. He took cover in a culvert. And he stayed there. "There's a moment in life when you stop being several things and become one thing, a coward. After — I became two men. One can't stand living with the other."

She tells him that one act of cowardice doesn't make a man a coward forever, that he's crazy to go on with this mission. They're not heroes, they're no good. They tried to rape her, they'll kill him.

His answer sums up his idealism — or is it his blinding obsession? "They have one thing in them that's a miracle and a mystery — it redeems them. I have to save it."

The next day they reach a railway track and find an abandoned hand-pump car. They put the sick boy on it. Chawk agrees to help pump it — for awhile, until he finds the opportunity to kill Thorne. They start off in what they hope is the direction to Cordura.

That night (in the second of the three scenes) Adelaide and Thorne sit leaning back against the handcar. Thorne gives her shawl to her and puts it around her shoulders. The feverish boy is lying on the hand car above them, spouting bible passages. Chawk is off to the right, lying on the ground, shouting at them on and off as they talk. She tells him she can't go on, she doesn't care if they all die. "You're all crazy, military crazy." She starts to cry. "I hope they do kill you and put you out of your misery." He wants to touch her but can't. "No," he says, as the camera moves in, holding the two of them within a closer, more intimate frame. "I'm proud of myself, really," he says. "First time in a long time. I've got to stay awake." But he can't.

Chawk shouts. She looks over at him. She stands and looks down at Thorne. "I can give you your sleep," she says. The shot, their shot, is held, and the camera pans to follow her as she walks past him, accepting what she has to do for him, goes to Chawk and drops her shawl on the ground as the scene fades out.

In the scene between them the morning after, their feelings at first are more disturbed, burdened. But then the tempo and the combination of the shots take on the feel of the shared sympathy displayed in their looks and the softened tones of their voices, easing into acceptance and affection. The sexual sacrifice she made for him may have been degrading, but it paradoxically has a nobility; it gave her back herself. The opening shot of this scene is from the same angle as the basic shot utilized in the previous one, but this time he is sitting at one edge of the frame as she enters and stands at the other edge. He jumps up, and the camera cuts to her face in profile, looking at him, not sure of what to expect but wanting to tell him what she feels. The camera moves to him when she says, "I'm ashamed of what I've been all my life," and he answers, "My fault, not yours, my guilt, not yours." The camera pans to her as she can admit to him what she has told nobody, not even herself. The ranch was her culvert, like him in the culvert. "I tried to shut out the world I hated." Cut to a close-up of her as her face reveals she knows that she can trust him. There's even a hint of strength, of pride, in her knowing that *he* can trust *her*. "Most of all," she can now tell him, "I hated myself." The camera looks past her profile to him, revealing the connection between them as he reacts, nodding, understanding, and pleasing her in what he shows. The scene returns to the wider basic shot as he moves closer to her. He gives her the set of citations to give to the officials, wants her to swear she'll do it. The camera first looks past him, close to her now, as she accepts; and then shifts to him, pleased, as she reaches out and touches him, saying, "You're the bravest man I've ever known." Then, in the wider two-shot again, they stand in profile, close, looking at each other, words not necessary, embracing with a look if not their bodies.

A counter-turn of the camera disrupts this moment tenderness, thrusting the sequence forward to a violent, bitter climax. The men begin to argue and fight among themselves. The boy's fever has passed and he can move about. Chawk mocks him, and

They Came to Cordura (1959), Columbia Pictures. Adelaide Geary (Rita Hayworth) gives solace to Major Thomas Thorne (Gary Cooper) after he has collapsed while trying to push the railway flatcar up a hill alone in his idealistic and obsessive attempt to see the undeserving "heroes" in his charge be honored in Cordura.

they fight. Chawk knocks him down. Chawk turns his back, and the boy jumps him. They fall and the boy grabs a rock. Thorne hits the boy in the head with his pistol to save Chawk.

The men now refuse to help man the handcar. Trubee insists that he is too tired to walk and simply sits on the car. Thorne now, crazily and nobly, goes on pumping it by himself. It has become the personal symbol of his quest. In the images of a brilliantly, painfully shot and edited sequence, their final defiance and betrayal of him and his mad, paradoxical determination is acted out, like so many stations of the cross. It is his Calvary—for the questionable ideals of the cavalry, or himself.

He is pumping alone, the others walking along, until his hands are torn and bloody.

Adelaide tears off pieces of her clothes with which she can wrap his hands. Filmed from the front of the car toward him, he pushes the bar up but can't push it down, and almost hangs there. Seen now from the back, he and Adelaide stop the car from slipping back along an incline. He ties a rope to it and pulls from the front. She makes Trubee get off and pushes from the rear. The brutal grotesqueness of the scene is heightened as the others go up on a slope along the track and sit and watch, refusing to help, mocking. As seen by them from above, Adelaide falls and crawls after the car as Thorne pulls on. She gives up and collapses, too weak to get up, and shouts at him, "Let go, you'll kill yourself!" Fowler throws a rock down at him. He falls and is dragged along the track as the car rolls back, past Adelaide, but he refuses to let go of the rope. It finally stops; he lies there.

He is lying face down, between the tracks, too weak to move. He looks up as they gather around him, planning to shoot him and discussing their story. But they need to get the packet of citations and the notes he has written.

Each now reads his own citation, and then Fowler reads Thorne's notes: "Each of them alike to each other, as I am alike to them. In each of us there lives a crippled child. I know they are vicious, treacherous, dishonest. They are also brave, noble. That's why I must make Cordura. To prove something else also lives in men."

Here, at their lowest point of immorality, on the brink of murder, the words of Thorne, now too weak to talk, break the momentum of their selfish betrayal. They are granted a different sense of themselves, of a common humanity that they had denied. It is a scene, a turn and a redemption, that takes a good deal of Coleridge's dictum for art: "suspension of disbelief."

They relent and so are allowed to come to their Cordura, seen finally in the distance from a hill that they then climb, with Adelaide helping Thorne up the slope. Although it is the kind of redemption that Rossen believed in, he didn't believe in it for this ending. As he told Jean-Louis Noames in 1965, the ending was forced upon him. It was too explanatory. But more than that, "It was absolutely necessary that the hero die at the end, but you don't kill Gary Cooper. It was necessary because in the book the hero was partly the symbol of Christ. Thus the story can end in only one way. But not only for that reason."[6]

Rossen lost that battle, and he vowed never to let it happen again. In the interview he summed up what he had learned about creating in the movie *business*:

> When I myself controlled my productions, I made my best films; when I no longer controlled them, I was far from making my best films.... If you have a success, you have more and more control over your films.... If you have a strong position, you can fight, but if you have no power, people walk over you....
>
> It's the combat there has always been between the creators and producers or all those people who work in the studios. They are frustrated people, who dare address themselves to a writer telling him what he is to write. They act the same way towards the director, who has the right of first editing: the "director's cut"—which means nothing because they can re-edit the film after that to show how it should have been done. But they know nothing these people. If the film has success, they profit by it; if not they attribute the failure to the director. There's no rhyme or reason to it. They are idiots.[7]

But we can conjecture about the possible implications had he been allowed to kill Gary Cooper. How would it have affected the resolutions for the other characters? And as for Thorne, would this brutal betrayal have put into sharper focus the foolishness of his idealism that had become a destructive obsession, pursued even for selfish needs and motives he couldn't face? Or would it have illuminated the ambiguities of the human world that can betray the pursuit of a good deed, an ideal? Or would it have merely made more unambiguous, more noble and heroic, his Christ-like belief that "something else lives also in men"?

In any case, that kind of glimpse of truly earned, utterly human redemption amid the wreckage of life would have to wait for Rossen's last two films, *The Hustler* and *Lilith*— and for the artistic control of his work that he had been fighting for. As Rossen said:

> Of course one knows moments of discouragement in the course of which one asks oneself whether it wouldn't be better to drop everything and satisfy oneself with work at fixed hours.
> But if you believe in what you are doing, you must struggle, struggle, and be alone. Who isn't?[8]

17

At the Top of His Game — *The Hustler*

Robert Rossen to Jean-Louis Noames:

And I don't agree with the *Cahiers* lad, a fine fellow — Marcorelles, I think — who said to me ... as we were having lunch, that there were no more "hustlers" in Europe. Then I looked at him: at a nearby table were a group of people who were there for the launching of *Jules and Jim*, starlets, businessmen, photographers, and so on. I pointed them out, saying to him, "And they? They are not 'hustlers'? You don't believe that they try to rob one another, to exploit one another, all day long?"[1]

With *The Hustler*, Robert Rossen came home. He not only returned to his supposed normal "milieu" (as some had carped at him to do), not just literally to the contemporary American Big City (the old neighborhood), but to his deepest feelings and intuitions about the kind of films he wanted to make, what he wanted to say about living as an inevitably tarnished human being and how he wanted to say it. And now he had the power of total creative control of his work that he had struggled for (although not without some "hustling" strategies of an old pro). Here he found greater complexities in narratives and characters, and risked more in revealing more of himself through and in them. He kept the widescreen shape that he had welcomed, but returned to black and white for the complex tones and shadings he could draw from it. Limiting the scale, in *The Hustler*, Rossen focused on a dramatic core of characters — a shifting triangle of emotional vectors of force that takes us beyond easy definitions, that, as Andre Fieschi recognized, "develops as if underground a fragile network of hauntings and obsessions ... [in] the deep inquietude and trouble revealed by the ambiguous relations of the characters."

It was nice and just the way things sometimes come together. Rossen was now able to distill all that he had learned and all that he had lived through into his two final masterworks, and two of the last great monuments to black and white cinematography. The first, *The Hustler*, is generally acclaimed but seldom really fully understood. The second, *Lilith*, is strange and tormented and truly daring, but neither acclaimed nor understood.

Living again on the East Coast, Rossen physically and emotionally was returning to his roots, conscious of making a fresh start, refreshed after passing through this period of fighting his way back. He experimented with writing a stage play, collaborating with

Warren Miller on the dramatization of his novel *The Cool World*, and directing it on Broadway. It depicted the destructive world of young toughs in Harlem — which echoed for Rossen the tough world of the Lower East Side during his youth. Praised by Kenneth Tynan in *The New Yorker* for a number of good touches and scenes, it nonetheless expired quickly. *The Cool World* did presage, however, Rossen's return to a more familiar milieu — the people, settings, and voices of his own past, and the created world of some of his Warner screenplays and *Body and Soul*. But now he recognized in this milieu something beyond what he had seen in it before. He found his fruitful core in a novel by Walter Tevis and an old interest:

> I tried as I do always when I adapt a book that I like, to render the spirit of it rather than the letter. Nor was *The Hustler*, either, a literal translation of the book. Only, there my task was easier to the extent that I had spent many years of my life in billiard rooms. I even wrote a play on that theme when I was twenty-five or twenty-six. I never staged it because I was not satisfied with it; it seemed to me that it didn't succeed in saying what I wanted to express. Then thirty years later I read *The Hustler*...[2]

For financing and distribution, Rossen turned to Twentieth Century–Fox. He had made money for the studio with *Island in the Sun*, and he knew some executives there. Even though Darryl Zanuck had moved into independent production, he usually still worked in conjunction with Fox. Zanuck was useful in getting the studio to back the production, but it all took time. A good part of the basis of the deal that emerged was the box-office value of Paul Newman as the star. When the film was released in September 1961, in the opening credits, after the obligatory panel of "Twentieth Century–Fox Presents," the next panel states in large, bold, capital letters:

PAUL NEWMAN
IN

while it is only on the third panel that we see:

Robert
Rossen's
THE HUSTLER

It is not quite the bold assertion of *Alexander the Great* but a necessary deployment of one's forces for the major battles ahead. Rossen produced, directed, and wrote the screenplay with Sidney Carroll, an old friend whose other screen credits were not particularly noteworthy, including *A Big Hand for the Little Lady*, the little known *You Killed Elizabeth*, and a British crime series, *Three Cases of Murder*. Carroll worked on structuring the material from the novel into an initial treatment and script, which Rossen then rewrote and, as he always did, continued to adapt extensively as he shot the film.

While the production was underway, the studio was not at all positive about its commercial prospects. An executive quoted in the *New York Times* said the film's appeal "might be limited because it deals with an almost unknown and rather shabby aspect of American life — the poolroom hustle." They were planning, and even had prepared an ad with Paul Newman in a sexy torn tee-shirt (*à la* Marlon Brando in *A Streetcar Named Desire*). Newman vetoed the ad. When the film previewed extremely well and then opened to good critical and audience response, the studio began to promote it more energetically. As one executive said, "We came to the conclusion that this picture had much wider appeal than we originally thought." They were pleasantly surprised when *The Hustler* became one of Fox's most successful products of the period. As studio head Spyros Skouras said, "For the first time in two years, I am smiling."[3]

Fox's publicity synopsis of the film is a striking and unusual indication of Rossen's strategies in making the picture — and the studio's apparent lack of understanding of the project. The press release was apparently based on the early summary treatment of the novel put together by Carroll. Rossen then used their acceptance, and distribution to the press, of this version as part of a ploy to get the film made the way he wanted to make it. According to that studio synopsis, the theme of the picture is that a young pool "shark" loses his head while playing the champ and so loses the game, but he is then "taken in hand by a manager who teaches him the psychology of being a winner. He then plays a return match with the Chicago man and wins." The plot summary involves nothing more: Eddie arrives and loses, is taken under the wing of the amateur psychologist Bert, but refuses to go to Louisville for a match when Bert demands 75 percent of the take. In a cheap pool hall his thumbs are broken, and while he recovers he meets the girl Sarah. He then goes to Louisville with Bert, is taken aback when the game is billiards instead of pool, wins anyway, and returns to Chicago to reject Sarah, whom he recognizes is a born loser, and beats Fats for the championship.

That is not, of course, a synopsis of the film Rossen actually made. By the time of the picture's completion, Rossen summed up one capsule version of his intentions in this way: "The game represents a form of creative expression. My protagonist, Fast Eddie, wants to become a great pool player, but the film is really about the obstacles he encounters in attempting to fulfill himself as a human being. He attains self-awareness only after a terrible personal tragedy which he has caused — and then he wins his pool game." And further: "He [Eddie] needs to win before everything else; that is his tragedy."[4]

In later discussions, Rossen touched on more intertwined aspects of the themes. Reading the book and "re-reading" his life and work, he now knew what he wanted to express in this familiar story of Fast Eddie the pool hustler. "Filming *The Hustler*, I was extremely conscious of what I was doing from beginning to end. In every region, on every level, from that of billiards ... to the fact that Newman associates with a cripple. In fact, why is she lame? It is hard to say, and yet it could not be otherwise. He too is a cripple, but on the level of feeling, while she is one even physically."

He spoke of this again when he was asked about his tendency to speak of disability in his last films. He replied, "It is because if I look at the world in which we live, if I think about this world of today, I cannot keep from seeing in it a great number of cripples, and I cannot speak of them as if it were a matter of contemptibly depraved beings. I want to speak of them with sympathy, to try to understand them."[5]

In April 1966 the influential French journal *Cahiers du Cinema* devoted a special issue to Rossen's work, two months after his death. It was an important, if still limited, re-claiming of the value of his work — at least in Europe. In his homage to *The Hustler*, Jacques Bontemps poetically evoked this motif of being "crippled" and its relationship to a central theme of knowing yourself, of attempting to know and connect to others:

> This was a story of wounded ones, of isolated ones, of unknowns. Constrained to limp alone.
> At the threshold of the insurmountable strangeness of the other was revealed an irremediable strangeness to one-self.

And, of course, there are all the echoes emanating from the central word itself—and the actions of—the *hustler*. Bontemps wrote of one provocative sense of these resonances: "The film, its story full of digressions and lacunae, said that, essentially 'hustled,' each person was perhaps most deeply his own 'hustler' forever."

For Rossen, the materials of the story, as he adapted them, resonated on a personal level. With the ideological turmoil of the blacklist and testifying somewhat loosening its hold on his imagination, he sensed in this narrative a parable on the hustlers of Hollywood—at any time. Bontemps, again, was insightful on this implication, writing that in "a universe dulled with leveling ... the one who wins is not the one who concerns himself with the beauty of the gesture, but he for whom everything poses itself in terms of efficacy of return. Creator: forbidden a stay. Compromise or resignation are required. There is a place only for Bert or for Minnesota Fats."[6]

The gesture of *The Hustler*, with its own kind of beauty, is jagged and unsettling, a paradox. As Claude Ollier had perceptively written when the film first came out, what gives *The Hustler* its special quality, its staying power, goes beyond its "ultra-classical skill." It is that "one has the constant impression that something else is happening that is escaping, being only briefly suggested by acting and dialogues with two meanings.... A sense of indecision hovers permanently over this strange film, and the final explanations are not enough to dispel it."[7] As, rightly, deeply, they should not.

Nevertheless, the familiarity of the materials and the preconceptions of the critics kept most from seeing *The Hustler* for what it was. Most critics, while praising it, did not allow it to resonate on these terms. Some even complained that the whole affair with Sarah—the crux of the film's deepest feelings and insights—is irrelevant and destructive. Brendan Gill in *The New Yorker* felt Rossen had become "over-ambitious." He bemoaned "the marvelous picture it might have been if it hadn't got so big and diffuse," and had stayed within the realistic depiction of the tricks of the trade of the pool hall. For him, Bert Gordon was another "tough gangster-gambler."

In 1962 Henry Hart, for one, did see it as more than a sports story, but emphasized its treatment of "low life subject matter." He still could not escape the limitations of his own premise of Rossen as a maker of exposé films, would not go beyond the limiting boundaries that he saw in the earlier films and interests. "His last picture [at the time of the article], *The Hustler*, is an *exposé* of the underworld modern society allows to exist."[8]

Pauline Kael dug a bit deeper into it: "George C. Scott in *The Hustler* suggests a personification of the power of money." Kael, in another article, wrote, "*The Last American Hero* isn't just about stock-car racing, any more than *The Hustler* was only about shooting pool."[9] She does not, however, go on to differentiate the vast differences in insight and artistry in dealing with what else the two films were about.

As usual, Bosley Crowther in the *New York Times* was perceptive in defining the skill and power and energy of Rossen's work, but not in pursuing what the film was really about. "Under Robert Rossen's strong direction, its ruthless and odorous account of one young hustler's eventual emancipation is primitive and alive. It crackles with credible passions. It comes briskly to sharp points."[10]

The film received eight Academy Award nominations, winning for Eugen Shuftan's cinematography and the art direction of Harry Horner and Gene Callahan, but losing the Best Picture award to *West Side Story*. Rossen lost to Robert Wise and Jerome Robbins (for *West Side Story*) for Best Director, but won the New York Film Critics award in that category. He and Sidney Carroll lost to Abby Mann (for *Judgment at Nuremberg*) for Best Screenplay. Newman, Scott, Laurie, and Jackie Gleason were nominated in the acting categories.

The Hustler is the most achieved and fulfilled of Rossen's films. It is the quintessential version of Rossen's deepest, abiding interests and insights, his core sense of the shape of things, and his unflagging hopes. Rossen felt that we could all be driven through the turbulent, often inexplicable flux of our motives, our inner weaknesses and external pressures, to violate and betray others—and ourselves. But even after the most careless and hurtful of betrayals, one was human still, and could find some enduring form of his better self and some form, however complex and paradoxical, of redemption.

Certainly part of the work's artistic fulfillment was his writing the best dialogue of his career—credible and moving, yet thoughtful, meaningful, and even iconic. And furthering this was his working with the three very disparate actors to project its nuances and its accompaniment in movement, gesture, and expression. Part of it was his continuing refinement of the elements of *mise en scène*—the expressive fusion of characters and their surroundings, their shifting patterns in space—to convey his increasing emphasis on, and discovery of, the ambiguities of "the inner life," which he later commented was what he more and more wanted to reveal. As he had seen developing in the later stages of the work of Roberto Rossellini as the Neo-realist director turned to the "introspective neo-realism of the person," the images and the décor are an integral part of the dramatic action; but they also have the paradoxical "opaqueness" that Andre Bazin talked about, revealing their own truths yet being able to "bounce back," holding back meaning and reflections also of the intangible, even undefined level of the characters' inner lives. The sets are designed to both immediate and echoing perfection by Harry Horner. All is real and alive in the dramatic scene, and yet all is quietly and deeply metaphoric—of character, conflict, and theme.

Michael Wood made a nice comment on one instance of this visual resonance:

> Rossen's wonderful use of Cinemascope (in black and white) to create an oppressive, elongated world in which ceilings always seem terribly low; and people terribly separate from each other; in one shot Newman is even separated from his own image in a mirror by almost the whole width of a very wide screen. It is a world in which the pool table seems the one natural shape, while human beings seem untidy intruders, and that, of course, is the film's chief concern: the human cost of being the greatest pool player in America.[11]

This sense of oppressive, enclosing settings—décor in the broadest sense—is one of the central constellations of visual motifs that span the structure of the film. These settings help to shape the restricting pressures of the world in which the characters live—their enclosed trap and arena. Only one major scene—and appropriately so—takes place within an outdoor (and lovely) setting. The sensitive, quietly magnificent cinematography of Eugen Shuftan captures and projects every nuance.

The film's characters—like so many in the whole family of Rossen characters—are locked together in the dynamic, ambiguous welter of their needs and desires. Entangled and trapped, embarking together, they are bound for hell (or a decadent downstairs billiards room) or given a glimpse of heaven (a summer moment in the park and its fleeting glimpse of possible love, and the thrilling fulfillment of one's own métier, even if it's playing pool).

Fast Eddie Felson (Newman) is the fullest, most enigmatic of Rossen's vital young seekers, wandering from town to town, pool game to pool game, hustle to hustle. He has the *élan*, he has the craft, but he is driven by an obsessive need for the power felt in winning that warps his potential. It not only mars him as a human being, warping his ability to love and connect, it even distorts the very act of attempting to win. It is more than a practical competitive edge. And it is not a desire for money or the typical accoutrements of success—whether women, fancy apartments, or overcoats. He just *needs* to win, whether in minor games or major. He needs to show them all—whoever they are. For he is a hustler, and hustlers are out there on a risky ride of illusory bravado—you must control or be controlled, that's the equation. And so he loses control of himself and goes too far, one way or another, hustling others or himself. And so he loses and gets his thumbs broken; but worse, he betrays and destroys—his gift, his *élan*, his friend Charley, and Sarah. There is an ambiguity in the ways that winning just means too much to Eddie that is never fully contained and defined (as there is in the other characters as well). It is an ambiguity that has been criticized as muddled, the result of over-reaching. Rightly viewed, it creates a powerful emotional aura, disquieting, probing, and true of human character beyond neat movie definitions.

The unsettling emotional aura of this ambiguity, this disquieting probing of human motives, illustrates the distance that Rossen has traveled—conceptually, emotionally, and artistically—from the similar pattern in *Body and Soul*: the struggle between the gambler and the woman for the unshaped energies and troubled soul of the young American seeker of success, and of the illusory symbols of his identity. The struggle here is much more paradoxical and disturbing. A resonant re-seeing through the burning lens of one's own painful, even unrelenting personal experience.

The film is certainly not directly about the period of Communism, the investigations, the testimony and the silence of the blacklist period in Hollywood. And yet in its deepest emotions and implications it resonates with the wounds and woundings of that time of turmoil and jagged damage. This time Rossen's young seeker echoes some of the same ragged, paradoxical conflicts that Rossen had been living through himself—commercial, political, and personal. In Rossen's parable of the artist in Hollywood, all are merely human, all are hustlers. They *need*—to win, to be right, to believe. The artist strives too much to hustle and win, to be a success; the Party member goes beyond reason to hold on to his beliefs. The more either (or both in one) hustles and strives, the more he betrays his gift, his *élan*, betraying his ideals and dreams of a better world. And the more he strives, the more he ends up placing himself in the hands of the moguls who not only want to control the product, but, like the gambler Bert Gordon, want to own and control the people who *create* it for them—or in the bloody hands of political tyrants, who, too, must control all in ways that have even more dire and dreadful results.

Certainly the corrupting influence of money still infects Eddie's world, but even on that level the film has greater complexity. We no longer have the standard symbol of the corruption of capitalism in the gambler-promoter. In Bert Gordon we have a man of both satanic power and human weakness. His lust for money is only a segment of a syndrome of his illusory symbols of identity. There is in him the need for possession and violation of other human beings as objects of one's ego. His lust for power is not just for winning or making money. Ownership—still capitalist ownership—is more than success and profit. To win is to beat somebody. To own is to possess fully—dominating, controlling, breaking the spirit of another human being. He recognizes in Eddie the kind of winner he needs as a gambler, but also the kind of loser he needs as a man. He becomes a manipulating, contradictory father-figure for Eddie, who throws away a truly loving father-figure, his long-time manager Charlie (just as Charley in *Body and Soul* threw away Shorty, but here with much more emotional development and pain).

Bert has the kind of cynical understanding, even of himself, that can allow him to see and live with the fact that what he sees in others he can recognize within himself. At one point, after Eddie has had his thumbs broken down at the docks, Bert tells him that they're all out there like Turk, the bartender who led the pack. They all (*we* all?) will break you one way or the other. Especially if you are an artist at something or another.

But Bert is a more subtle and ultimately destructive Turk. He is a Hollywood power broker, a Congressional Committee member, a Communist Party manipulator. He too is one of those who will use you and break your spirit (or your thumbs) if he has to.

Bert's drive for power rises from an ego that is paradoxically both strong and uncertain. It reflects as well a sexual lust (portrayed for the first time in a Rossen film) that is distorted into the same terms of domination and violation, a sexual lust that is sadistic and perverse, twisted by insecurity and ending in failure.

The woman in this strange triangle of struggle and power also is more fully, and ambiguously, developed than any of Rossen's previous female characters. Patric Brion even saw "the center of interest displaced from Paul Newman to Piper Laurie and, indeed thereby, acquiring a very attaching [*attachant*, engaging] truth and tenderness." He saw Sarah as a mid-point in an important new strain of interest, from Adelaide in *Cordura* to Lilith. Sarah is a potential artist, a writer, but far from the perfection of her counterpart, Peg, in *Body and Soul*. She understands and spreads the value and joy of love (a scene lovely in her awkwardly winning openness when she goes shopping for herself and Eddie and girlishly proclaims, "I've got a fella"). But, lame and alcoholic, she too is psychologically crippled. With rejection her only long-time friend, she is too lonely, too precariously needy to use her gift, her loving, well. She is, as Bert Gordon recognizes and cruelly plays upon, a born loser. Too familiar with defeat, Sarah is drawn to it, almost seems to need it, and its way of helping her evade what she calls her "troubles." Life-giving as love is, she knows it is doomed. When she scrawls, "Twisted, Crippled, Perverted" on the mirror of that final hotel bathroom, she knows she is one of them and hates herself for it, for her weakness and her pain. And so she cannot help herself; she lets Bert Gordon win, and lets herself betray Eddie and herself, as though she just couldn't fight anymore, as though that were the only cruel and tragic way left for her to win.

Pool is Eddie's craft, his way of expressing himself. Significant as a deep structural motif are the six games (one, significantly, is billiards) that Eddie plays. Each is seen within an evocative, paralleling setting and décor. Each dramatizes his emotional state at the time, a stage of the fragmented, even warring aspects of his nature and self, the nature of his quest and of his discontents. It is what he does best; yet, until the very last game, it reveals the worst and most destructive drives and needs within him.

The first (added after Rossen's final version of the shooting script was written) is shown in the midst of the opening titles. It is a casual foreshadowing, a glimpse of the habitual resentment within Eddie, his need to show *them*, even if they are nobody important. He needs to win not just for the few bucks involved, but for the act of shoving his win down the throat of somebody who's triggered his anger. He and Charlie (Myron McCormick) stop for gas and go into a typical small-town pool hall, bar and short-order café. Eddie hustles by blowing a couple of games, pretending to be drunk. The owner scoffs, and Eddie bridles. At the showdown, he wants only the owner's money. "No, I want *him*!" he says, a wise-ass smirk on his face. He shoots, and Rossen doesn't bother to reveal the end of the shot but cuts to the car as Eddie hands Charlie the money. The jazz score (by Kenyon Hopkins) comes up, and they're off to New York.

In contrast, the next game is in the cathedral of pool, Ames, the grandest arena for the biggest game of Eddie's life — and for the exposure of the conflicts in the pattern of that life. It is mid-day. The blinds over the high front windows are drawn up, and the light streams in. "This is Ames, Mister." Eddie is in awe, thrilled: "Yeah, like a church — Church of the Good Hustler." But Eddie is also cocky. "How much am I going to win?" he asks Charlie as he "works out" on an immaculate table that he touches admiringly. "Ten grand," he answers himself. "I'm gonna win ten grand in one night." Yet he can't help it, still thinks he can hustle someone to play him, who responds, "You're Eddie Felson, aren't you? Look friend, I'm not trying to hustle.... Don't try to hustle me."

At the stroke of eight a regally serene Minnesota Fats (Jackie Gleason) arrives, immaculate as the tables. He is gracious, polite, calm and controlled. He is a proficient, elegant machine, balanced and graceful in his every move. He is content under Bert Gordon's ownership and all it can bring him, but there is in his methodical reserve an inkling of sad loss — over the willing surrender of his independent spirit, his soul to the Bert Gordons of the world (to work, efficiently but soul-less, in the studio system).

Eddie plays beyond himself and is beating the champ! The games go on and on, night into day and again into night. The more games, and money, he wins, the more Eddie drinks. He insists on playing on until Fats surrenders. Gordon has been summoned from a card game, and sits mysterious and intimidating on a high stool near the center of the table. After watching a while, he says to Fats, "Stay with this kid. He's a loser."

Early the next morning, after losing it all, Eddie leaves a few leftover bills for Charlie and deserts him in a tiny hotel room, just right for people at the low ebb of their lives, right across the street from the flashing promise of the AMES BILLIARDS neon sign. In the large, lonely lunchroom of the Greyhound bus station, after putting what's left of his life in one of the lockers that lines the room, Eddie sits at the counter. He sees Sarah, at the rear of the frame, separated from him by empty tables, sitting with a cup of coffee and reading. He crosses the void to her, flirts, but falls asleep across the table from her. He sees her again in a bar the next day.

The aimless hole he's lost in is shown in brief sequences in which he's first denied a game because he's too clearly a hustler, and then (for the film's third game) in a small bar he wins some petty cash and, without any arrogance or scorn (and certainly without any pride), picks up the sparse pile of bills from the beat-up, ragged table. This time, the game, the playing, is not even shown. It's managing to live; it's not playing the game that is his life.

He finds Sarah again on another lonely, early morning at the bus station, and this time she crosses the room, limping, passing all the empty tables, to him. With a bottle in a paper bag in one hand and his arm around her, they walk to her apartment.

From the outside we next see the shutters of a window in her small apartment open. Eddie is lying on a bed next to the window, and she walks forward and lies next to him. They turn and look out. It is a bright sunny beginning, an opening for them, but when he says he'll bring his clothes over, she is worried. "Eddie, listen. I've got troubles, and I think maybe you've got troubles. Maybe it would be better if we just leave each other alone." He kisses her, and, staying close, she murmurs, "I'm not sure.... I don't know." He closes the shutters and says, "Well, what do you want to know? And why?"

She is willing to accept that — needs to and is happy with it. As she crosses the street with a bag of groceries, a gracefully sweeping panning shot follows her walk of joy. When she comes back with the groceries for *them*, she tells him she wanted to tell everybody, "Hey, I've got a fella."

The idyll cannot last. Eddie is not sure he wants it, and Sarah wants it too much.

The crucial scene of conflicted emotions that develops and reaches a climactic foreboding of what is to come is shot in a beautifully articulated *plan sequence* from the back end of the narrow kitchen looking out toward the living room–bedroom and the windows beyond. Rossen uses the tight, limited space of the kitchen as the core of Sarah's feeling of domestic happiness (canned goods style), but also as the physical correlative of Eddie's nagging sense of being hemmed in by the demands of this domestic sharing—and then by the demands of Charlie's practicality and loyalty.

In the first segment of this scene there are secrets being evaded, as they move back and forth in the narrow space. She is putting away the groceries, and he comes forward into the kitchen and holds her from behind, telling her he wants to "keep score" on the expenses. She passes him to go to the other side of the kitchen to put away some cans. Opening one, she cuts her finger. He crosses back toward the rear to get a bandage from his suitcase, and she moves back to the original side, asking him about what's in his other bag. Staying back, he kids her that it's a machine gun. Then, walking forward to her, he shifts the focus to where she gets her money. As he bandages her finger, she says, "From a rich old man who used to be my lover." The suspicions are dropped and they kiss. At a knock on the door, she crosses to the door, which opens into the main room just beyond the kitchen. The camera stays on Eddie; he keeps his back to the door, shakes his head and smiles wearily as he knows it's Charlie before Charlie says, "Hello, Eddie." He waits and then turns. The camera pans to meet Charlie walking to him, stopping now between the two of them, with Sarah further back, watching and wondering.

The new wider-angle shot is held as Charlie sits at the side of a small table in a nook just at the end of the kitchen and just past Eddie, who stays standing. Sarah gets drinks and brings him one, standing across from him, with Charlie seen between them. Charlie complains that Eddie deserted him, telling him that he "walked out on me like that. No goodbye, no nothing. Like a thief in the dark. We were partners. We were more than partners." And then Charlie shifts and speaks directly to Sarah, "I've known this boy since he was sixteen. The first time I saw him, back in Oakland, I said, 'This is a talented boy. This is a smart boy.'"

"Talk to *me*, Charlie," Eddie says.

"I want you to go back on the road with me." As Sarah walks forward and out of the shot, the scene shifts to a subset of alternating close-ups of Eddie and Charlie as they argue about his wanting to play Minnesota Fats again. As they talk about hustling and pool, we cut to a close-up of Sarah, troubled and confused, then back to the original wide shot from the end of the kitchen that includes her, as Charlie talks to her: "This boy is the greatest pool hustler you ever saw. A real high class con man. He could charm anybody into anything."

Carried away talking about going to Florida and getting some sun, Charlie lets slip

The Hustler **(1961), Twentieth Century–Fox. In the oppressive and tight confines of the kitchen of Sarah's apartment, Fast Eddie Felson (Paul Newman) denies and betrays, and verbally destroys, his long-time manager and friend Charlie Burns (Myron McCormick), while Sarah Packard (Piper Laurie) watches, shaken and frightened.**

he kept some of the money. Eddie is furious and rushes at him. Charlie rises, and Eddie, now in front of him, pushes him back down. It's the final showdown after all their years together. The intensity and finality is captured in a set of alternating reversing shots that insist on Eddie's fury and his dominance, his defeat and betrayal of Charlie: past the seated Charlie up to Eddie; past Eddie's hip to the seated Charlie. Finally, Charlie says he just wants to slow down. "Getting old."

Shown from the angle that faces Charlie, Eddie moves out of the shot, separating himself from Charlie, who is left defeated in the chair as Eddie delivers the final blow. "Then lay down and die by yourself. Don't take me with you."

Still on Charlie: "Just like that?"

Cut to Eddie: "Yeah, just like that."

The camera then shifts to Charlie, back to Eddie, and then to Sarah, turned from them, tears on her cheeks, before returning to Charlie and then Eddie. All are silent.

It is done. We come back to the original basic wide-angle shot, but everything has changed. Charlie leaves, saying, "Thanks for the drink, Eddie's girl." Eddie and Sarah are left on opposite sides of the narrow room. Eddie is still complaining. She pours him a drink. He takes it and walks back to the other room and then comes forward again. She pours herself another drink but doesn't move and says nothing. "C'mere," he says, finally, and she crosses to him. They kiss, but there is anger and desperation in it, not tenderness. They still hold their glasses.

With a whiplash of a cut, all is changed, changed utterly. Sarah is on the floor in the living room, in a robe, pecking at her typewriter, drunk. Eddie is in the kitchen, throwing even more cans on the pile of empty cans and bottles; dirty dishes, papers, and trash are everywhere. Sarah knocks over the whiskey bottle next to her on the floor. He is going out to find a game. The shutters are closed.

With another cut, he's reading something she wrote: "We have a contract of depravity. All we have to do is pull the blinds down." He crumples the paper.

""Well, what else have we got? ... We're strangers. What happens when the liquor and the money run out, Eddie? You told Charlie to lay down and die. Will you say that to me too?" When he slaps her, she says, "You waiting for me to cry?"

Eddie's obsession pulls him back to Bert Gordon. They spar over Bert's demanding terms. Bert tells him he's never seen him do anything but lose, but he likes action and Eddie's good for action. He'll take 25 percent. Eddie walks out.

Eddie may have stood up to Bert, but he's impatient, frustrated, and feeling trapped by Sarah. He acts impulsively, excessively, swept away again toward self-destruction. In a grungy pool hall down on the waterfront (in the film's fourth game) he vents it all on a minor-league hustler who's taunted him. Forgetting the con man's strategy, he wins game after game, quickly, and brilliantly — too brilliantly. Beefy guys drag him into the men's room. Seen dimly through the clouded glass partition, shadowy figures around him, Eddie's face is forced up against the glass. He screams once and then again. He drops to the floor, the shadows remain above him.

Eddie returns to Sarah. In the opened doorway of the apartment, she is to the right, Eddie to the left, slumped against the side of the doorway, head down, hands up to his chest, one cradling the other. "What happened?" "I got beat up. They broke my thumbs." The camera cuts to her as she cringes, cuts back to him. In pain, he throws his head back. She comes into the shot, to him, and takes him in her arms as he drops his head to her breast and starts to cry. "They broke my thumbs."

Eddie's hands are encased in white casts — his game, his craft, has been taken away from him. He holds them awkwardly, not quite knowing what to do with them, not knowing what to do with himself. It's left him frustrated but also more open to the possible works of love. He accepts Sarah's constant helpfulness, her love; but, impatient and even petulant, he resents it. He chafes at his inaction and hates his own helplessness. Sarah is in her glory because he *needs* her. The apartment reflects her joy. The shutters are open and sunlight spreads through the room. All is neat and clean. She is dressed, sitting at a table typing, writing. He paces, a caged tiger. He walks to the kitchen, ready for a drink, and asks her if she wants one. When she says "No," he shrugs and puts the bottle down.

They have a picnic on a grassy slope, the only open natural setting in the film. As they talk, they are first seen from the side, he stretched out across the screen, leaning on an elbow, she sitting up. He tells her about Bert Gordon calling him a loser. "Is he a winner?" "He owns things." "Is that what makes a winner?" "Well, what else does?"

But Eddie does know what else does, and he can tell her now about his feeling for his craft, his thrill when it's going right:

I mean when I'm goin'—I mean when I'm really goin'—I feel like, like what a jockey must feel ... and he knows. Just feels, when to let go, and how much. So he's got everything working for him—timing, touch. It's a great feeling, boy, it's a really great feeling when you're right, and you know you're right. Like all of a sudden I got oil in my arm.

The camera cuts from him to a close-up of Sarah: "You're not a loser, Eddie. You're a winner. Some men never get to feel that way about anything.... I love you, Eddie."

In close-up, Eddie is silent, uneasy. Then he asks, "You need the words?"

"Yes, I need them very much," she answers. "If you ever say them, I'll never let you take them back."

The scene's final cut shot is of Eddie, silent. Love is there for him, out on the sunny slope of green grass, but he doesn't know what to do with it, and cannot let it change his life.

The scene dissolves to Eddie standing in front of the apartment door, looking at his hands, now without the casts. When Sarah opens the door and he holds up his hands, she shows fleeting disappointment, even fear, then gives a small sweet smile.

But what Eddie does best—the way he believes he has to do it—leaves no path but to betrayal. He gives himself to Bert Gordon and accepts his deal of twenty-five percent. His first match is in Louisville. It is Derby Week in Louisville.

The Hustler (1961), Twentieth Century–Fox. In the one scene out in nature in the film, his broken thumbs in casts, Fast Eddie (Paul Newman) is able to tell Sarah (Piper Laurie) about the deepest positive spirit and feelings of his craft, his art; but when she asks, he cannot tell her that he loves her.

17. At the Top of His Game—The Hustler

Eddie tries to tell Sarah he needs to go but will come back to her. It's been a bad hustle. Wearing a jacket and tie, he had taken her to a fancy French restaurant. She won't believe him, can't. "Is that your idea of love?"

"I got no idea of love," he answers. "And neither have you. I mean, neither one of us would know what it is if it was coming down the street."

"I'm so scared, Eddie ... I'm scared." He holds her hands, and she puts her face down against their hands. He touches her hair and presses his cheek against her hair.

The next morning he has given in. They meet Bert Gordon together. From the start of the trip — in all the places and palaces of pleasure, of getting and spending — we watch the terrible disjunction developing between the feel of the crowded, fast-moving energy and excitement of Derby Week in Louisville and the building feeling of isolation, dislocation, and loss within Sarah.

Bert knows the battle — for Eddie and his soul — is on; from the start he knows there's weakness there in his opponent and works to keep Sarah off balance and vulnerable. He's enjoying it, excited himself by Derby Week. Bert sinks his barbs, relishing with a hard smile each time he hurts her, draws just a little more blood. When he asks Eddie how his hands feel and then says, "Good, I'd hate to think I was betting all my money on a cripple," he's staring right at her.

But it is in the privacy of their hotel suite that he makes his first direct attack (and, later, his last). Eddie has left her alone and gone off to join the boys in the hotel's "Billiard Room." As Sarah comes into her and Eddie's room, we see Bert in the adjoining room (as we will see him more ominously at the start of their final encounter). She starts to close the connecting door, but he comes to the doorway and leans back against the door frame. She backs off to the right and sits on the edge of the bed. He lays down the terms of his more deadly game. The scene is brilliantly acted. He is smooth, oily and wily, his voice getting more insistent as their exchanges build. She stands up to him, trying to maintain a controlled calm, but then weakens, her voice tighter and weaker even when she finally calls him a bastard.

He proposes a truce, which is a really a surrender. She should back off, or it would be bad for Eddie. He needs to win.

"For whom and for what?"

"For what makes the world go round. For money, and for glory."

"You didn't answer my first question. For whom?"

"Today for me, tomorrow for himself."

"No, there's no tomorrow. Not with you. You own all the tomorrows because you buy them today. And you buy them cheap."

"Nobody has to sell."

"You bastard" (but half-choked).

The camera stays on Bert for his climactic speech, as he leans in close to her and over her. With his head tilted down, he establishes his domination and revels in owning the moment: "Listen, Miss Ladybird, you're here on a raincheck and I know it. You're hanging on by your nails.... You're a horse that finished last. So don't make trouble, Miss Ladybird. Live and let live. While you can."

The culmination of the power struggle and the defeat of Sarah — and of Eddie, even as he wins his match — is the party at the palatial mansion of the mark, Findley (Murray Hamilton). It may be the finest set of sequences in Rossen's work. Findley is throwing a gigantic party and everybody has come, even those who weren't invited. They buzz and circulate, drinking and eating all they can, meeting and greeting, celebrating. Dixieland jazz fills the rooms with a bouncy, happy beat; the dancers dance the night away, dance the blues away. The sequence is a powerful synthesis of image and movement, dialogue and conflict. In the midst of the party, while nobody notices or cares, the terrifying mixture of carelessness and obsessive power, of emotional brutality and weakness, builds the inevitable momentum of betrayal.

The first segment at the party is one of the greatest of Rossen's *plan sequences*—a basic long-held shot intercut with several medium shots at points of emphasis. Powerful in its immediate impact, it is enigmatic and yet reveals all, prophesying the looming defeats ahead and illuminating their causes. The camera pans up from the musicians and dancers to Sarah, starting to come down a long staircase, the ornate grillwork of the railing throwing magnified shadows on the wall behind her. She has a glass in her hand, is unsteady and limping, already drunk (already drinking herself to the defeat that she awaits?). She passes a maid with a tray of drinks and takes a fresh glass. The camera cuts to her point of view, and she sees Eddie chatting with obvious pleasure with a woman. The camera switches back to her, panning down and then across the room with her as she passes between the band and a group of men, who eye her, and as she approaches a wide doorway where she sees Eddie being kidded and touched by a blonde in a black dress. The two of them are laughing. She crosses to the other edge of the doorway. Champagne glass to her lips, she turns from them and walks forward as the camera pulls back before her. She passes through dancers and groups of chattering people, almost unseen, as all are so busy being happy, even though she stands out in a light floral dress (the dress Eddie gave her) in this roiling sea of dark suits and dresses. Still coming forward, she approaches another wide doorway, passes Findley, who is lounging against one edge and turns to look at her as she goes to a bar just past the door to the right. She finds Bert standing there. Findley and Bert, on either side of her, both look at her then share a glance. She abruptly turns from Bert and, with stiff, drunken steps, walks back past Findley and out of the shot. As the camera pans, Bert follows her, looks back, gives a hint of a nod to Findley, and goes past her to her left, as she has stopped against a wall. The scene cuts to a closer shot of them as he leans close and whispers in her ear. The camera cuts back to the basic shot on them as Findley watches from the far edge of the doorway and she throws a drink in Bert's face, starts to cry, and sags. Bert catches her, and Eddie enters the shot. He takes her, and she beats on his chest and then collapses as he half drags her back through the wide doorway, past Findley, and out of sight. Bert pats the liquid from his face. The scene cuts to the band and the dancers dancing like hell to the Dixieland beat.

The match with Findley (the fifth in the film) is played in a decadent lower circle of hell, a downstairs billiard room for the corrupted—wood-paneled, stuffed with stuffed chairs and sofas, frilly bric-a-brac, antique wall sconces and lamps, terra cotta copies of Roman busts, nude male sculptures, and a bar on a mid-level landing. Over the billiard table the three hanging lamps have pleated, pebbly cloth shades. Bert sits next to a figure of Pan, standing on goat's legs, horns rising from his curly head. Findley: "Have you noticed, Bert? This fellow here bears a striking resemblance to you."

Findley surprises them by announcing the game will be billiards, not the expected pool. It also becomes as much a devious battle of wills as of skill. They are hustling each other in their own enigmatic triangle of power. Eddie claims he's played billiards before and knows he can beat him. Bert doesn't believe him and says he's never seen him do anything but lose. Findley smiles mischievously and drinks. Eddie doesn't. Findley loses at first, probably out-hustling the hustler, and then comes on strong, as he raises the bet and keeps on drinking, and keeps on winning.

Eddie is leaning against the wall along the side of the table, rubbing his hands, when Bert gets up and says he's had enough. He goes up to the landing to join Findley at the bar, leaving Eddie behind and below. Bert is looking down at him, with Eddie looking up, beseeching, "I can beat him, Bert." Bert denies him, and Eddie says he'll play with his own money. He goes up to the bedroom where Sarah is passed out on a bed. He takes his money from her purse, pauses, but doesn't look at her. As he leaves, she stirs.

Eddie continues to lose. Bert is lounging on a sofa on the landing, with his feet up. Below him, below the railing at the edge of the landing, Eddie is kneeling—his soul at its lowest level, broken and deserted. "What do you want me to do? What do you want me to do, huh? *Please*— don't get off me now." Behind them, Sarah has come down the stairs, steady but careful, determined to make one last effort to save Eddie and herself. "Don't beg him," she says. In a wide shot she is for this moment above them, with Bert on the sofa at the middle level, Eddie below him, and Findley off to the left leaning back against a wall, drinking. She walks forward. "Doesn't any of this mean anything to you, Eddie? That man, this place, the people."

The camera cuts to a tight close-up of Eddie's face. His hands are clasped tight, pressed tight against his mouth. He's looking down, his eyes squeezed screaming tight, in pain from more than his hands, making a decision and he knows it. She says, "They wear masks, Eddie. And underneath they're perverted, twisted, crippled."

She comes down the last step and kneels now below him, with Bert now sitting up on the sofa above them. "That's Turk, Eddie, the man who broke your thumbs. Only he's not going to break your thumbs. He'll break your heart, your guts."

Eddie raises his head, his features straining in anguish, and then with a sudden movement he fully stands and turns on her, shouting, "Once and for all, will you get out, will you GET OFF MY BACK!" The camera cuts to a shot past his hips as she cringes and turns her face against the railing, and we hear Bert say, "Go ahead and play him, Eddie. For a thousand dollars a game." Cut to Bert. He knows he's won, has beaten her—and Eddie, has him mad enough to beat Findley. A wide-angle shot crystallizes the meaning of the moment. On the landing, Bert stands up. Below him, Eddie is standing over Sarah. Findley is lowest, in the lower left, drinking. Eddie walks past Sarah to the billiard table and picks up his cue. Sarah gets up and goes up the stairs. Bert comes down from the landing into the center of the frame as she leaves it at the top.

Findley does succumb, as he seems to have known he would. He seems content as he pays off— twelve thousand —as if he's enjoyed their battle for power and their final conquest of him. But Eddie and Bert are tense and distant. Eddie is withdrawn, guilty, angry at himself as much as at Bert, knowing what he's done. He had done anything, everything, to win, and now it tastes dirty and he can't swallow it. Bert is drained, even his collar is opened, his tie pulled down, his face drawn. He's won, but it has somehow cost him more than he thought it ever would. Eddie wants to walk back to the hotel—a long way. Bert gives him his share of the winnings.

Back in their hotel suite, Bert needs more. He comes into Sarah's room through that same door. She is sitting on the bed, a drink in her hand, a suitcase beside her. He lies and tells her Eddie wants her to leave, wants her to have some money. The shot is demeaning, the camera pointed toward her from his waist down, a wad of money in his hand. Punishing herself, she tells him to put it on the bed, and he does.

"And the way you're looking at me," she says, "is that the way you look at a man you've just beaten? As if you had just taken his money and now you want his pride?"

"All I want's the money."

"Sure, sure, just the money, and the aristocratic pleasure of seeing him fall apart. You're a Roman, Bert. You have to win them all."

She understands, sees it all, sees herself; but the understanding brings no peace, no release from the pain within. He grabs her and kisses her. She is limp, and he throws her to the bed and walks out. She takes a cigarette and goes into his room.

She's hurt herself as much as she could — and hurt Eddie too? Afterwards, she goes into the bathroom, stares at herself in the mirror, and writes "Perverted, twisted, crippled" on it with her lipstick.

When Eddie gets back to the suite the police let him in. He finds Sarah's body still lying on the bathroom floor. From the side, and looking down from a slightly raised angle, we see him sink to his knees, next to her body, her head blocked from view by the edge of the bathroom sink cabinet. He wants to touch her, but can't. Bert comes to the door from his room beyond, past Eddie, seen only from the waist down, his shirt hanging down loose. He's shaken. Voice plaintive, he tries to explain, to absolve himself. Eddie is rocking, bent over and face down, head sagging from side to side, silent tears tearing at him inside. He sits up, then doubles over again, and then explodes at Bert, driving him back through the door into the bedroom and across the room, pummeling him as the police try to pull him off. All this is seen from the bathroom door, where Sarah's body is lying.

When, months later, Eddie comes back to Ames and plays Minnesota Fats, his victory is shot briskly and cleanly, emphasizing "the beauty of gesture" of his shots with the cue stick — "when you know you're right." And in interspersed two-shots, Eddie is consistently seen above Bert, freed from his domination. He has seen that beating Minnesota Fats, all the Minnesota Fats, is not the main thing anymore. It is winning in the right way for the playing itself and for the right reason. He has won for Sarah — not in a rage for revenge, but for a sense of rightness and justice. And for repentance. He has won because he recognized what he's done to win, what he let happen, what he lost. And so he regains himself, or, rather, for the first time he finds himself.

Despite its being part of a meaningful series of revealing games, the sports metaphor of the triumph in the final game is a familiar motif, and is often too easy a way to generate uplifting feelings. However, critics who have stressed this limitation have themselves not recognized that his *spiritual* victory is more complex.

He has won the pool game, but he will not be Bert's new boy, will not pay him his share. All the elements of the scene — their voices, gestures, expressions; their movement; the confrontational editing — all this gets at the moral intensity and meaning of their final test, going beyond the neatness of the sports metaphor. It is a long way in depth of emotion, insight and implication, and style from the ending of *Body and Soul*, where Charley wins, quickly defies the gambler, and walks off with his love.

Eddie gets ready to walk out. Bert yells, "You owe me money!" He threatens to break his thumbs and much more if he doesn't pay. But Bert is rattled, unsettled. He gets up and paces, carrying his glass of milk. He sits again and negotiates. "I'm a business man, kid." He'll change their percentages, take thirty, even twenty-five.

"We really stuck the knife into her, didn't we, Bert?" Eddie accuses. Bert defends himself: "If it didn't happen now, it'd happen six months from now. That's the kinda dame she was."

As Eddie speaks his heart, the camera cuts between the three of them, interspersed with wider shots of all three and particularly two-shots of Bert and Eddie. The beautifully modulated sequence enhances the intensity of his words and impact on the others:

> And we twisted it, didn't we, Bert? ... I loved her, Bert. I traded her in on a pool game. But that wouldn't mean anything to you. Because who did you ever care about? Just win, win, you said, win.... You don't know what winnin' is, Bert. You're a loser. 'Cause you're dead inside, and you can't live unless you make everything else dead around you.
>
> Too high, Bert. The price is too high. Because if I take it, she never lived, she never died. [Eddie pauses, almost cries.] And we both know that's not true, don't we, Bert? She lived, she died.

He tells Bert his boys better not just bust him up, because if they do, he'll come back and kill him. Bert accepts, but, "Only don't ever walk into a big-time pool hall again."

After this most careless and brutal of betrayals, Rossen hopes to see an enduring possibility of redemption. Eddie's redemption is not in his winning, but in *why* he wins, in what he recognizes and accepts about himself. And so he will not play their game anymore—the Bert Gordons, the dominators, the moguls, the tyrants of the world.

It is not the easy redemption of proletarian drama and film. It is not without its seemingly inevitable bitter irony. It comes not only from what he has won for her, but what he is willing to lose for her. It has left him exiled from the world of pool playing that he now for the first time really understands.

He will never be able to play pool in the places and competitions that he deserves. He gives up all that he has left to love. He has no lover to walk home with, no lover to share a lifeboat with, no deep friends and comrades to walk home with, no love to drive off with or brother to walk off with into the sunlight, no one even to come to Cordura with. He is alone and has given up what he does best, and he accepts that. He has paid his debt—by winning and losing.

One can sense the personal echoes for Rossen in this final resignation: Eddie's acceptance of this risk and his banishment, his exile, for the sake of what he believes in.

18

The Forgotten Masterwork and Enigma — *Lilith*

Lilith: Robert Rossen's biggest artistic gamble, his furthest exploration into the deepest, most disturbing ambiguities of human nature — and the potentials of filmmaking. It was his biggest, most disappointing commercial failure and his biggest mistake (as the close-minded attacks, hurtful and hateful, by most American critics had it). It was deemed unacceptable for Venice Film Festival participation, as the ideology of its director, Luigi Chiarini, insisted. The critics' responses may have been the most painful, as the film may be — for all its flaws so intrinsically wrapped within its wonders — Rossen's best, though strangest, work. It is "his incontestable masterpiece," as Andre Fieschi saw it.[1]

Lilith: butterfly and spider. She *is* a human paradox. Artist and seductress; passionate, impulsive, free and liberating; driven, trapped and entrapping. She is sweet and lovely as her lilting song, irresistibly spontaneous, yet also manipulating and demanding. Open to love, she is an opening for others, yet selfish and cruel. Full of joy, and of pain, she is destructive and destroyed. In Lilith is glimpsed, broken and glinting like the cut facets of a deadly diamond, the demanding allure of love and passion, of rapture — its wonder, its battles of possession and dominance, its seemingly inevitable betrayals.

But Lilith, of course, is mad. Sick, crazy, twisted, damaged, crippled; still, for all that, she is so utterly human. If she causes others to suffer and creates victims, she is a victim herself of her own unfathomable traumas and emotions. She promises the wondrous passions we all dream of, yet she breaks — must break — those promises. She can't help it. We wish that she could (that we all could).

Lilith and her beautiful *asylum* and its sharers of pain seem far from the world of Hollywood, its blacklist years and its dark, painful turmoil and hatreds. Gone are the conflicts over ideology, the judgments of actions that are, or seem to be, necessary. Absent are the allusions to the venality of Hollywood, the corrupted violations of political action. Yet *Lilith*, through artistic indirection and personal, saddened insight, bears the scars of those years; in its lyrical compassion the film reaches for some path, wandering and unsettling, that can lead to a way of living with those still-open wounds.

There is this time a compassionate sadness in Rossen's treatment of the forces that lead to betrayal and destruction. Easily fatigued, in constant physical pain, and still affected by the years of tension and conflict over his testifying, and the loss and destruction of friendships, Rossen risks the attempt to express openly, yet with all the mystery of their complexity, pure non-political *human* emotions. With rueful regret, the film is suffused with a sympathy for the inevitability of human frailty. It has the embracing compassion, the sad, tender ache of loss and waste that James Joyce captures in the lovely last phrases at the end of "The Dead." After Gretta and Gabriel, married for so many years, had for the first time opened their deepest feelings to each other, Joyce writes, "His soul swooned slowly as he heard the snow falling faintly through the universe and faintly falling, like the descent of their last end, upon all the living and the dead."

Despite the film's title, it is Vincent who is the protagonist, the troubled and troubling moral center of the film, and the intense focus for Rossen's compelling need to examine what it is to try to behave decently. Lilith, for all her painful complexity, is the wonderful, terrible and overpowering object of desire. Vincent is Rossen's loneliest, most isolated seeker of himself— most separated even from himself. And he is a significantly different seeker. He has no particular gift beyond being shyly likable. He is not driven by a desire for money or success — the usual illusory symbols of identity that are fostered within society. He is an empty vessel. But his emptiness, his lack of knowledge of himself, his elusive sense that he needs and *wants* but doesn't really know what or why — all this derives from the dulling emptiness of the small-town life he has grown up in and comes back to after serving in the Korean War. His one unexamined impulse is to "help people directly." Not the masses, the people, the "hicks," like Willie Stark; not for glory or culture, like Alexander; not for honor and principle, like Major Thorne. Driven by unfaced memories of the troubles of his dead mother, he is drawn to those who are also troubled — the insane, the mad. He does not betray people because of his lust for power, control, or glory. The tragic irony of his betrayals is that, as he seeks to live more fully, his helping helplessly ends up hurting, killing and destroying.

Vincent's inevitable betrayals of the principles he had started with, and, of course, even worse, his betrayals of Lilith and the young man Stephen, rise not from a denial of love for the sake of one's quest for success or skill, as in Rossen's previous films. Dreadfully, instead they rise from a total obsessive immersion in love. Love itself, the deepest of loyalties, can bring into question the deepest dilemmas of loyalty. In Rossen's earlier films there was a clear demarcation between false love and true love, and in the relation of the two types to the moral being of the protagonist, his loyalty to himself and his principles, and to others. In *The Hustler*, Sarah was Rossen's most complex, fully human source of love to that point. As troubled as her offering of love was, she and her loving were a force for good in Eddie's life. In *Lilith*, love itself is an unsolvable paradox, its liberation leading to enslavement, its rapture becoming obsession, its seductive source a mad lure to destruction. To use one of the film's central metaphors, Vincent is caught in the spider's web of wondrous passion, yet the overwhelming demands of his desire make him, after all, a deadly spider himself.

Similarly, Vincent's motives are not neatly definable, whether in seeking to help the mad or in acting from the demands of his own form of madness. He begins with both conscious reasons and confused emotional needs; he ends swept away beyond reasons into uncontrollable fears and desires. Lilith's motives elude our categories. We seem to know, or think we know, why she is doing what she is doing and judge her for it. But then we realize that she is driven by inner demons that are beyond those neat definitions and judgments. She has no gatekeeper for her raw needs and desires. Her madness is the extreme metaphor, as seen through a glass magnified and distorted, for the opaqueness of human motivation. And when do the Vincents cross over into the world of the Liliths — only when they are so clearly swept into madness themselves? In Rossen's final film any attempt at definitive understanding is inextricably bound up with the unknowability, the ultimate ambiguity of human motivation and desire, and of betrayal. It is that inner world where, as Andre Fieschi saw, "desire and anguish are confounded."

As for redemption, all that is allowed in this bleaker view of the potential for change is a glimmer of hope, an admission of needing help, and an expectation of receiving it. It is not based on an assertion of principled action but on an acknowledged weakness.

As he had been refining in previous films, Rossen wanted to evoke with the reality of moving images more than a perfect representation of the way something looks, the way someone moves and acts:

> I think what it [*Lilith*] had to say was an important comment to make for today's society, because I don't think it has even been touched yet — this whole question of inner life. I think there is only one man that I know of in films who really understands how to do it, and that's Bergman....
>
> Brains — what the hell, I know a lot of brainy guys that can't make a picture around the corner. I'm making intent a prerequisite. I think Bergman does things that are really trying to get into the twentieth century. The whole approach to the part of life which is subjective and yet has to be objective because we have no other defense.[2]

In defining the approach he was now risking, Rossen said:

> It is not a matter of a servile reproduction of reality. Rather it will be necessary to capture things as they are and modify them so as to give them a poetic significance. Furthermore, it matters little whether you call it poetic or not; what matters is that in this way something situated beyond and above life be delivered, and that thus one should feel what one deeply thinks. To reach through the objective become universal.[3]

Using the cinematography of Eugen Shuftan at his lyrical, evocative, and provocative best, Rossen creates a visual "universe" that in the unsettling ironies of beauty and suffering merges what he described as the two universes of the madness of Lilith and the normality of Vincent. The lighting captures this evanescent, ethereal, and ineffable dimension beyond by clothing the surface reality in half-light, mists, and strong contrasts of pervasive gray and releasing brightness, the gloomy darkness and blacks of Vincent's "normal" world contrasting with the lighter (and entrancing and misleading) whites of Lilith's.

Rossen's use of setting and décor is the most emotional and metaphoric in his films. Architectural settings and landscapes, objects, bars and screens, webs, water and weaving, cotton candy and small wooden boxes, dolls, a dinner table and a bowl of soup, patterns of people and the colors of their clothing — these images are, again, not merely abstract symbols. The settings and decor interact dramatically with the characters — they are lived-in and lived-with. In a hallucinatory way, the settings seem to seep into and pervade the feelings of the characters, even while they serve as physical correlatives of the elusive inner life. The spatial, again, becomes psychological. But this time, as befits the film's disturbing dislocations of neat and easy patterns of definitions and judgments, the structuring of the images builds patterns of unstable motifs; the images shift in meanings and implications, in emotional tenor, as they appear and reappear.

The magical score by Kenyon Hopkins creates an immersing lyrical surround for the shifting, unsettling moods of the film. For *The Hustler,* Hopkins had emphasized the strong rhythms, phrasings, and tones of the saxophone in a syncopated jazz score that conveyed the world of Fast Eddie Felson. Here, among other musical motifs, Hopkins focuses on the reed-like, lovely melody of the tune that Lilith plays on her recorder. He expands it orchestrally with shifting moods—from innocent and lilting, to full and romantically seductive, to dark and dangerous, even tragic.

The insistence on seeing the reality beyond easy responses leads to elliptical, disrupting narrative structure within scenes, between scenes, and in the overall narrative sequence. Yet equally insistent in developing the central theme of dominance, control and possession are some tightly edited sequences. In an intense pattern of reverse shots, each shot is often held with more duration than is usual in this type of pattern. One person is seen past the head or form of the other in ways that emphasize dominance and, conversely, evasion, of holding back. The space between shifts as well, as the confrontations become more combative.

One last element of editing helps create the evanescent mood of floating and shifting, blending and blurring emotions: dissolves. Rossen uses many more of them here than in his previous films, often with significant musical motifs. They too help to develop the blurring of time and actions, the motives of actions, the over-lapping and merging of identities, and seemingly separate and independent worlds. All is dissolved together, the normal and the insane.

Rossen's sense of irony—in life and in art—also takes on an important and new dimension: a doubleness, a duplicity. The basic structural irony is embodied in the visual contrasts between the asylum, Poplar Lodge, and the neighboring town, Stonemount. The mysterious, romantic beauty of the madhouse, and the exciting beauty of a nearby park and its cascading waterfall, are posed against the harsh, dull realism of the neighboring town, the normal. The world of the insane has lovely, light-softened, haunting landscapes; the world of the normal has the ugly, damp, gray, second-hand sadness of dreary store fronts, diners, cheap dime stores, and Laundromats, not to mention the dark joyless dining room of Vincent's grandmother's house and the cluttered emptiness of the house of Vincent's old girlfriend. But in the counterpoint of the double irony, within the asylum side of the equation, despite the loveliness, nobody seems to get well, no-one is immunized against the destructive weaknesses of human nature.

With the images of beauty (both Lilith and her landscape), Rossen is not setting up the neat irony that the insane live creative, passionate lives, while the normal live dull, tawdry, empty lives—or that the insane can love and the normal can't. (This is not the old social drama structure of the noble poor versus the terrible rich, the workers versus the bosses.) That reversal of the conventional definition of the insane and the normal is part of the provocations of the human complexity, but it is certainly not the whole of the ambiguities he is after. Vincent wants to escape from the petty defeats of the life of the ugly drab sanity of the town to the ecstatic fullness of the passions and loveliness of Lilith and her lyrical world; but that beauty is a siren song that carries him away past the boundaries of moral behavior, beyond his own necessary hold on sanity. At one point the psychiatrist shows the staff a slide of the web of a maddened spider. The web of the insane spider is the most beautiful web of all. And as an indication of the carefulness of Rossen's choice of composition and editing patterns, that shot is immediately followed by one of Vincent, seen standing within the eaves in a constricting alcove of Lilith's room—in her web. He is in the same position within the frame as was the apex, the innermost point, of the spider web displayed in the previous shot.

Lilith's irony is in another dimension beyond the formulaic reversals of *They Came to Cordura*. Lilith's rapture may have more wonder in it than sanity can usually provide, but it also has devastating madness. The nature of love is left a welter of irreconcilable opposites. It is not finally classified for our neat response, as was the nature of courage in *Cordura*, or, in Rossen's earlier films, the nature of economic corruption or the drive for power.

This intentionally ambiguous approach to capturing the ineffable — feelings and needs beyond control and definition, phantom impulses — was admired in France. But it was frequently derided in America, where reviewers seemed delighted to tell Rossen: Go back to your gamblers and gangsters, boxers and pool players. Who do you think you are, Ingmar Bergman? *Lilith* was first shown at the New York Film Festival on September 20, 1964 — three hard-fought years after the opening of *The Hustler* — and then put into general (and commercially doomed) release. In the *New York Times*, Bosley Crowther issued a complaint typical of his usual approach to films. While he was again perceptive in praising the "vivid structuring of striking images by Mr. Rossen, who is a master at catching the American look of things," he nonetheless protested that there was no "lucid demonstration of what the whole thing means. Is he saying that madness is monstrous or that insanity is good for you?"[4] That Rossen may have been saying both or neither did not occur to him. Others protested that Rossen was cheating by "hurling symbols" at the audience, attempting "to deliver the same old Hollywood sexology in a fancy wrapper"; and that the recent *David and Lisa*, a film of conventional, simplified realism, in which the love between two mentally ill young people nicely leads to the improvement of their psyches, had "already explored the same gray area between sanity and madness with greater simplicity and directness."

Rossen's angry disappointment, and the nature of his own intentions, were indicated in his remarks during his final interview. When asked about the comparison to *David and Lisa*, he replied, "The theme of *David and Lisa* is completely antithetical to the theme of *Lilith*. I understand *David and Lisa* is very well made but it is a very small story and has no implications of any size outside of its immediate story. *Lilith*, I thought, had enormous implications. I think the critics were shocked by it, shocked because I made it. They never expected me to make that kind of picture, because they associated me with something else." When the interviewer asked, "With the tough type of *The Hustler*?" Rossen replied, "That's right — and I knocked them right on their ass, because critics, once they set you up in their minds, and they have created the image, don't want you to destroy that image.... That makes them work, and critics don't like work.... Of course, I don't think a lot of American critics got *The Hustler*, but the European critics did. I don't think Archer Winsten still knows what the picture was about."[5]

The British critical response to *Lilith* was somewhat better, and in France it won high placement on the *Cahiers du Cinema* yearly listings. The film's acceptance in France was not surprising, since in it Rossen reveals a development of thought and technique toward the approach to character, plot, imagery, and editing used by Continental directors. In his fulsome praise of the film, Fieschi recognized and defined (with the flourishes typical of French critics) the essence of Rossen's approach, "to render them [people] in their complexity" and his central pattern of shifting implications:

And so *Lilith* is, with [Alfred Hitchcock's] *Vertigo*, the most complete realization in cinematographic form of the indefinable, the inaccessible, which the coupled plays of beauty and illusion shape into a sumptuous fatal mirage....

It is the fairy tale in reverse.... And like *Vertigo*, *Lilith* develops in its first part the elements of the crystallization of the passions close to hallucination, or out and out hallucinatory, and in its second part destroys or reverses these elements, which it desublimizes up to the final, unbearable rupture.[6]

For major financing and eventual disinterested distribution, Rossen had gone back to Columbia Pictures. Once again he shot the film almost entirely on location. One week of the shooting was done in a studio. The six weeks of location shooting were on Long Island, where Rossen rented an old boarding house and the Killingsworth Taylor mansion, and in Rockland, Maryland, where the clinic was located. Once again he used a skillful craftsman, Robert Alan Aurthur, to block out material from the novel, by J.R. Salamanca, and provide an initial structure for the screenplay. Rossen said he had been drawn to the book's paradoxical comparison of those "whom people call 'adjusted' to someone called 'maladjusted' in our society." But he found the prose "precious, *recherché*, it was hard to uncover what was image, what was not.... That is, indeed, why, moreover, I made efforts to transpose many descriptions and dialogues in visual terms. I reshaped the book along those lines."[7] He worked on the screenplay extensively (one could say obsessively) himself, both before and during production. Oddly, in a minor industry paradox of technicalities, Aurthur is not listed in the credits on the film itself but was granted credit later.

It was the actress Yvette Mimieux who first introduced the novel to Rossen, but it was Jean Seberg who Rossen, after considering a number of women, felt was the actress for the role. She exuded an innocence of look and manner; yet within her natural beauty he saw — and elicited in her performance — a paradoxical mystery, a glimpse of inner separateness, an ornery strength, and a surprising sadness and instability. As he told her during filming, he did not want her to be a mad Ophelia, too purely feminine; he wanted to see in her a certain virility. The role was deeper, fuller, more exposing than any she had performed before (or after). It was certainly the performance of her career, but the deep disturbances of the inner life in Lilith were too prophetic a foreshadowing of the emotional troubles in the later life of Jean Seberg.

Seberg had begun her career, young and overwhelmed, in Otto Preminger's *Saint Joan*, and had gone on to more fitting roles in *Bonjour Tristesse* and Jean Luc Godard's *Breathless*. Her career after *Lilith* wandered through a disparate set of films, in which she was invariably real and palpable. Her life followed a troubled arc, as she was beset by her own demons, from marriage to the French novelist Romain Gary to rebellious affairs and episodes in the sixties and seventies, and to her death in a parked car (which was never explained without lingering discrepancy and mystery).

Rossen was already seriously ill when he began work on the film, weakened by an unusual skin disease that was to plague him for his remaining years, and by the side effects of the cortisone used to treat it. As Seberg recalled, "At the end of the filming, he was in a complete state of exhaustion, the state of someone who has given all he could."[8]

In a tender and insightful essay that she wrote about Rossen and the making of the film, Seberg remembered how his troubled relationship with her co-star Warren Beatty during the production contributed to his exhaustion:

At the start, Rossen and he had a relationship which was strangely fraternal, very intimate, very like accomplices even. Oddly, this relationship of intimacy stopped at the first day of filming, and from then on, it did nothing but deteriorate more and more and more....

Now, Rossen singularly escaped labels. He was a very complicated man, agonized even, who continually asked himself questions about himself.... Rossen truly approached this film with a pure viewpoint, which under American conditions is an immense thing. At the end of the filming, he was in a complete state of exhaustion, in the state of someone who has given all he could. And the permanent confrontation that opposed him to Warren did not help matters; he even wanted to bring a lawsuit against him, and other childish things.[9]

After just three films, Beatty had already established himself as a major and iconic figure with a particular image and presence. In *Splendor in the Grass*, *The Roman Spring of Mrs. Stone*, and *All Fall Down*, he had already developed a manner — and some mannerisms — that combined a partly revealed sense of inner emotional disturbance with the covering flair of a natural, youthful and winning arrogance. During the filming of *Lilith* it was clear that the arrogance came naturally to the actor, and not just his characters. He and Rossen fought over a basic conception of the role and over specific performance elements, such as Beatty's trademark looking down and away as a means of showing some inner disturbance, uncertainty, or withdrawal. It was an effective gesture, used too much, Rossen felt, but still used to strong effect in *Lilith*.

From the beginning there is an aura of hesitation, discordance, and confusion (both his and ours) over his feelings, even the manner of displaying — or hiding — them.

In the opening scene we follow Vincent as he enters the beautiful grounds, and the world, of Poplar Lodge, and as he is seen by Lilith through the diamond shapes of the heavy wire grate on her window. She is seen behind her bars; he is seen through and thus behind *her* bars. It is a walk that will be retraced, in the film's final and tragic irony, and with far different feeling and meaning. He comes to the Occupational Therapy Barn as Bea Bruce (Kim Hunter), the head social worker, is opening its wide double doors. He picks up a book she drops and hands it to her. "Thank you," she says, and with a mere formality that will also have poignant echoes at the ending, "Can I help you?"

In his job interview he is hunched forward, face somewhat down, raising his eyes as he answers her questions. He tells her, "I want to do some kind of work where I can be of direct help to people. And..." His eyes drop again and his head dips, still defending against something, still hiding something, some wound? He ends abruptly, "...that's why I decided to come." Bea then takes him on a tour of the main building hallways and its disturbed, and disturbing, inhabitants — a walk that will also be retraced as a nightmarish hell at the end (when all will be revealed but nothing really yet understood).

The first contrast of the idyllic looking Poplar Lodge to the town of Stonemount and the emptiness of Vincent's life is developed in the next three scenes. In a dreary gray rain, Vincent is on the main street of dull, unimposing shops when he sees his former girlfriend, Laura (Jessica Walter), who had married while he was in the Army. In the heavy darkness of the dark-walled dining room of Vincent's grandmother's house, she and Vincent are having a silent dinner. Without looking up from toying with his bowl of soup, he tells his grandmother that he can have the job. In her sweet small voice she tells him, "If your poor mother knew about this job, I think she'd be very glad." Upstairs, in his small room, Vincent is lying in bed watching a war documentary. A picture of his mother as a young blonde woman is on the bedside table. Dead and wounded bodies are strewn all over the screen. He shuts off the set. "You die. She dies. Everybody dies," he mutters.

At Poplar Lodge, Vincent sees Lilith through the grate in her window as she plays her beautiful song. On the terrace below, a shy, sensitive patient, Steven (Peter Fonda), is listening, rapt, and suddenly shouts for the ping pong players to stop playing and making noise. Vincent's first task is to get Lilith to join an outing to a public park.

At the picnic Vincent watches her constantly. Lilith is entranced by the glimmering, rippling rhythm of the quiet water of a river. She looks down and sees stars of light glistening over an image of herself blending into the quiet flow of the water. After a burst of rain, the water, swollen in the storm, is now wild and roiling, crashing over rocks. Lilith has lured Steven to a dangerous spot on the rocks. He slips and grabs rocks to keep from falling, and Vincent must climb down the rocks and rescue him. The water is a dynamic physical correlative for the mercurial moods of Lilith—first lovely and calm, even seductive; then rising to a climax of frothing, surging passion, dangerous but thrilling; then, as if uncontrollable, going beyond to stormy, threatening uproar and to destructive danger. But it is typical of Rossen's method in the film that it is not merely symbolic. It is used dramatically. It draws her to it, excites her. She sees herself in its changing powers and is led to emulate it. After being tender with Steven, she maliciously uses the water to toy with him, to intentionally lead him to danger.

That night Vincent goes to Lilith's room. Several times it will be the setting for their growing intimacy, but also their battle over control and possession. The room is basically a small, askew rectangle, the ceiling sloping to meet with the odd shapes of the eaves that extend into the inner corner of the room. He is often seen hemmed in by the angles of those eaves, which parallel the web of an insane spider shown on a slide by the psychiatrist at a staff seminar. This scene has one long-held shot; throughout, both of them are seen through the grate (like bars, like a web) in Lilith's window. He tries to reason with her, bawling her out for "almost killing a boy. How could you let a paintbrush fall fifteen yards in front of you? ... Why did you make him go after it?"

"Because he's a fool."

"Well, if he's a fool, why lead him on like that?"

"Because I'm mad."

He rushes out.

By the next scene in her room he is already in her thrall. He is standing, hunched forward, hemmed in by the slope of the ceiling and the eaves, seen in the dominant angle of the scene from her point of view as she sits on her bed. We see him past her shoulders and long, lovely hair.

After this scene there are several brief vignettes that show the increasing closeness and tenderness between them, as if they were young lovers and not patient and caretaker. In a key scene there is a lovely early morning mist, and they are at a tranquil pond. She is standing in the water, her dress pulled above her knees, bending to be close to her shadowy reflection rippling in the water. She kisses the water, breaking up the image. "Look at her. She wants to be like me. She's lovely. My kisses kill her. She is like all of them." She straightens and looks up at him. "It destroys them to be loved."

She walks through the water into deeper mist. He follows along on the path, pushing through low branches, another web. He can't see her and calls, "Lilith, Lilith?" Her face appears, barely discernible in the thick mist. She is smiling. "You called me Lilith."

He has entered her world and accepted it. Yet, in her room, when she has caught her hair in the webbing of her loom and he is carefully unloosening it, he says, "I'm going to set you free."

He does try to pull back and talks to the psychiatrist Dr. Lavner about feeling that she wants to pull him in, how she seems so happy. It's like a "rapture," Lavner says, which, he explains, in Shakespeare's time meant both madness and a kind of ecstasy and innocence. He alludes briefly to one of Lilith's traumas — a brother who was killed accidentally in a fall. Lavner feels her chances for recovery are small. Nevertheless, he is pleased at Vincent's positive effect on her.

But Vincent's doubts are swept aside by the momentum of the feelings she has released in him. We follow them gracefully gliding along on bicycles through tree-lined streets and then along the quiet pond. Lilith speeds around a turn, loses control and crashes down. She has cut her hand. As he reaches to look at it, she takes his hand and puts it against her breast. "Don't you think I know how you suffer? I know how terrible it is to love and not be able to confess your love. [Cut to his face, looking down.] But you can tell me. Please, I can't stand it. [The camera looks down at her as she raises herself toward him.] I can't stand it anymore." [She kisses his hand.]

But then, troubled, he pulls his hand away. She rubs her bloody hand across his face, hard, like a slap, and then again, smearing her blood on his face. He grabs her hand, drops it, walks away and leans his head against a tree trunk. Past her and her entrancing hair, we watch him turn and, trying to fight the power of her gaze upon him, say, "Lilith, I've never been able to do anything worthwhile in my life. I wish you would help me do this one thing. Honorably."

The camera cuts to her as she says, "I can't be saved by honor."

He lets go. He lies to Dr. Lavner that everything is fine, it was all just beginner's nerve, and asks permission to take her to the jousting fair in a nearby town.

Their moment of pure joy, of a positive kind of rapture, is reached at the Renaissance pageant, full of gaiety and people in costumes. It is the thematic and emotional fulcrum of the film, a wondrous masquerade in which the two worlds meet. For the magical moment of an afternoon holiday, the disparities are transcended. The mundane truths and normality, the quotidian of the world of the townspeople, are transformed into romance and release, sharing the kind of innocent joy that is there in the world of Lilith's ineffable rapture, her moments of special innocence.

Still, there is an ominous moment, an unsettling sign of her uncontrollable needs. She buys a piece of watermelon from two boys, leans in to help one cut the piece, and takes a piece of ice and sucks on it as he and his friend watch. She takes his hand and touches it to her cold wet lips as he looks at her, frightened and intrigued. She touches him on the temple; he swallows hard, embarrassed, but he likes it. She offers to pay him with a kiss as he says, "Yes, Ma'am." She is kneeling and draws him down to her and kisses him on the lips, and then on the neck and ear as she whispers in his ear. Vincent moves in and hurries her away.

The medieval jousting tournament itself returns us, at a suggestive sexually exciting level, to the joyful burgeoning of their romance, beyond any allowance of ambivalence or doubt. All is a perfectly normal fantasy of love. With her scarf attached to his saddle as his Knight's banner, he (entered as the Knight of Poplar Lodge) rides for his lady. In a sequence of increasingly rapid shots, the riders pound down the course toward the camera and, in ringing close-ups, pierce the hanging rings with their lances, riding and

Lilith (1964), Columbia Pictures. Lilith (Jean Seberg) and Vincent Bruce (Warren Beatty) at the Renaissance pageant in town, where Lilith is excited and joyous as a child, although not without a revelation of her destructive obsessions.

thrusting again and again, as the band bursts into its resounding praise and the crowd cheers. Lilith claps her hands in glee. Vincent wins. She runs joyously to the judge's stand; Vincent puts the victor's wreath on her head. She is proclaimed his victorious lady: "Thou art Queen of Love and Beauty." She turns to accept the crowd's applause. In a wider shot she takes hold of the saddle and sweeps herself up behind him, her long, loose skirt flowing out, graceful as butterfly wings, around her, her legs shining in the sunlight. In a wide angle shot they ride proudly from the crowd toward the camera, which then pans, calm and contented, and watches them as they go by and into the field beyond. We dissolve into them riding gracefully through lovely woods, mottled by the late afternoon sun through the trees. After a dissolve, the camera is closer as they leave the woods and come into a sunlit meadow. Lilith's theme is heard in its sweetest form.

It is their moment of pure love and passion — the only one their fate will allow them to have. Lilith is kneeling, scooping water up from a creek at the side of the meadow. She watches Vincent walk toward her, her scarf in his hand. In a reverse shot we see her past the scarf, the stream shining behind her, the only sound the quietly rippling water. The shot reverses toward him, but stays back, keeping a respectful distance from their freshly tender mystery. He drops the scarf next to her and says softly, "I love you." And he walks out of the shot. She rises and, as the camera follows, goes to him, and they walk from us into the sunlit meadow.

As the afternoon passes, in a series of quiet, caressing dissolves, they make love, walk, talk, are in tender touch. In one set of dissolves they are lying quietly in the meadow, then seeing themselves reflected in the water of a quiet cascade into a silent pool, then embracing on a rocky ledge, light and water darting over them.

The sudden rupture, the irreversible momentum down into pain and betrayal, is signaled by a sudden cut from the serene openness of nature (as in *The Hustler*) to a formal cold scene on an enclosed porch of the Poplar Lodge. It is a simple scene, yet is one of Rossen's finest use of the implications and impact of a series of deep, reversing two-shots that maintain an unexpected, oppressive distance between characters. In this instance there is an unexplained threat and intimidation, a sudden surprising sense of the sparring of two adversaries. Though dropping hints, the scene holds back what is still to be revealed. At either end of the rectangular porch, Vincent and Mrs. Meaghan are sitting. She is, as usual, alone and keeping to herself. Dressed formally, she speaks in a patrician, haughty tone. Both are in black, and we see each at some distance past the dark shape of the other, as Vincent warily observes her and evasively answers her questions about Lilith and him. Concluding the audience, she rises abruptly. "You seem to be a man of principle. That's less flattering than you think.... Principles, Mr. Bruce, should always be examined." As Vincent watches, she strides out, high heels clacking against the floor.

Lilith's passions, her whole warring syndrome of desires, cannot be contained, even by her love for Vincent; they are even impelled further by that love. Vincent's love is driven, by her and something uncontrollable within him, to possess her, jealously and zealously. But to keep her love, to possess her, however incomplete that must be, he must be complicit in her betrayal of him and his feelings.

In a sequence of elliptical, disjunctive scenes, Vincent helps Lilith keep her assignations with Mrs. Meaghan. He follows the pair of them, holding hands, as they pass through the now-mocking settings of woods, meadows, and stream. They go into a barn and close the doors behind them. There is a time-blurring dissolve, and Vincent can't take it any more. He bursts into the barn as Mrs. Meaghan is buttoning her blouse, Lilith lying back on a pile of hay. He pulls her up, throws her back down, rushes Mrs. Meaghan out and slams the door. From close in behind him we see him move wildly forward—furious yet sexually aroused—and pull her up into the shot and kiss her. He pushes her back onto the straw, roughly but passionately, this time to make love.

At night Vincent is waiting on a stone bench in the park in the town square, across from a movie theater. When the movie is over, and Lilith and Mrs. Meaghan emerge, he follows and takes them home.

Interspersed are brief, intense scenes, increasingly disturbing, with Vincent and Lilith. Loving is intensifying her madness; loving is pulling Vincent into madness. In one scene her room seems smaller than ever; trapped, caged, they move back and forth in a fretful discord. He walks toward the window, passes her, and then goes back to the door and shuts it. He passes her again, a torso, and sits down into the shot and onto the bed, half resigned, half angry. She crosses forward, goes to the window, and says, "Do you think loving me is sinful? Do you think I have a talent for love?" We cut to see Mrs. Meaghan walking below, seen through the grate on Lilith's window. The camera focuses back on Lilith through the grate, and reveals Vincent past her and below her on the bed, depleted, futilely angry. "If my talent were greater than you think, would you stop loving me?" And yet in a scene on the porch, while they play Scrabble, she says quietly, tenderly, "I love you, Vincent."

Lilith (1964), Columbia Pictures. Obsessed with the wondrous, destructive, insane Lilith (Jean Seberg) and his love for her, Vincent Bruce (Warren Beatty) must help her with her rendezvous with Mrs. Yvonne Meagham (Anne Meacham) but then explodes in anger and jealousy.

Vincent makes one last half-hearted, futile attempt to escape, to find a way back to the normal, to the dark gray world of the town he had run from. Seemingly wandering, he ends up at the house of his old girlfriend, Laura. At her house the scene is a brilliant ironic mocking of the defeating trap of normality. It is bitterly, obliquely comic, yet so gently sad and rueful over those caught with no way out.

Three main shot patterns capture the oppressive architecture of the facets of Laura's life: from Laura's kitchen, the core of her cage, down the main hallway toward the front door; from the middle of that hallway across into the corner of the living room, so dully, so tastelessly, so normally furnished; and from that same point in the hallway into, and then in, the dining room on the other side of the hall. Seen oddly and intentionally from the kitchen, Laura is helping Vincent off with his raincoat in the hall when Norman (Gene Hackman) comes into the hallway from the living room. He takes Vincent out of the shot and into the living room. Laura — her expression dulled — walks back to the kitchen and starts to make coffee. The scene cuts to the shot of the men in the corner of the living room as Norman starts to talk — and doesn't stop. He is crass, pompous, and insensitive. It is impossible to convey the wonderful texture of Hackman's delivery.

He is lip-smackingly, insistently pushing, salacious, and sporting a baldly arrogant grin, yet through it runs a tension, a grating resentment. It is just enough, not over the top. Hackman is perfect as a loud, thoughtless counterpoint to the silent anguish that is knotted there, unreleased, in Vincent as Vincent manages: "Yes, I guess they do." — "Yeah" — "Yes, it was" — "No. No, I don't" — "Great" — "Yes" — "No." Norman talks about the war, and Vincent squirms. Norman tells a bad joke and can hardly finish it as he starts laughing. Vincent stares. Norman talks about a salesman he knows who has lots of money and is on the road all the time. He winks, chewing candy the whole time.

"HONEY!" he yells.

In the kitchen, from the original angle, "Honey" starts to pour the coffee, stops, leans back against the counter, and sags into the sad disappointment of her life.

In the living room Norman starts to talk about Vincent's job at the asylum. With a leering grin he says, "Hey, must be some pretty funny stuff goin' on in a place like that, huh?" His voice, his smirk, is almost a nudging elbow in the ribs. Vincent stares at him. "Huh? Right?" Still chewing: "Come to think of it, Laura was telling me your mother used to be a little ... ah..." And he points his fingers at the side of his head and makes the circling gesture of being crazy in the head.

Laura interrupts with the coffee, glaring at Norman. After an awkward moment or two, Norman decides to leave — he has a meeting to go to.

At the wide doorway from the living room to the hall, Laura and Norman are at the front of the shot, at either side of the doorway. Vincent is still seated, back in the corner of the living room, looking down, then up at them, then down again. Laura asks Norman if he put out the garbage. He grouses at her, voice biting in petty resentment, "I can't think of everything. Now I just can't think of everything. I got more important things on my mind than garbage."

He says goodbye to Vincent and leaves. The shot holds as Laura looks at Vincent, a wide gap between them. In the reverse shot past Vincent the distance increases as she goes into the dining room across the hall and he watches her take a drink. They look at each other across the divide of a lost hope. She finishes her drink.

In the dining room now, she is sitting at a table, topped with several bottles of whiskey. He comes in, fiddles with the piano, his back to her. He sits, seen past the bottles, and has a drink with her. She tries to bridge the gap between them. He tries to smile, is in pain. She notices and asks him what's wrong. When he says he should leave, she stands and says, "Vincent, do you remember when I said I'd never really let you make love to me until I was married. Well, I'm married now."

He can't respond. Hurt, exposed, she walks past him and out to the hall.

The final, long-held shot of the sequence is from the original angle in the kitchen.

She comes down the hall and goes off to the side to the stairs to the second floor. The hall is empty. Vincent enters the shot, takes his coat, pauses at the door, and leaves. The shot holds on the hall's deadly domestic emptiness. They are all isolated — in their passionate, destroying madness, anguished by too much within them; or in their lonely, crushing mediocrity, deadened by the emptiness within, the loss of feelings they still yearn to regain or never even noticed were missing.

There is nowhere else for Vincent to go. He succumbs to Lilith and himself. Giving way, he careens on past any boundaries. He buys an aquarium in the general store. While Lilith is asleep he steals a doll he bought her at the fair. He holds the doll face down in the water of the aquarium — as he hears the fairground music — and its long blonde hair and white dress are billowing in the water.

He knows she is slipping away from him, into love for others, into deeper madness. He dreads it, is holding it all in but bursting inside. She is volatile, erratic, lurching between her two worlds. In the next two scenes in her room we are thrust into tense, desperate individual close-ups and close two-shots, even as they move jaggedly to each other or away from each other in the tight confines of the room.

In the second of these she is in a corner by the window; he is across the room back under the eaves, tightly hemmed in, leaning down on the top of a dresser. Close-ups alternate. She knows he stole her doll. He denies it. The camera uneasily follows her as she moves around the room in strident anger, screaming at him. Finally, he admits it. "I took it. Because I love you."

Her anger passes; she's won and sits. In a close-up only of her chest and face, she gets up and admires a box Steven had made for her; but she calls him Ronnie, who is her dead brother. She mixes the two as she taunts Vincent. "His hands are warm, not cold and dead like yours. He's very sweet. I've been cruel to him." She wants him to take her walking with Steven. In a sequence of tight, alternating close-ups, she says, demon intense, "You will take us walking tomorrow, won't you?" He can't answer; his lips work and press together. He squeezes back tears. She leans forward, softer now, but triumphant, "You will take us walking, won't you?"

It is night. Vincent comes out of the darkness into an outside seating area. Steven invites him to sit. He sits, slouched, and looks at Steven coldly, silent and cryptic when he answers a question. Steven asks him if Lilith showed him the box he made for her, and wants to know if she seemed pleased. "She showed it to me." And Steven takes that as her being pleased. Shots have alternated past each to the other, but as Steven expresses how happy he is, how wonderful life now feels, the shot stays past Steven to the tightened anger hidden in Vincent's unmoving glance, half of his face in a slight shadow. Steven is joyous; he doesn't see Vincent's coldness and tells him he trusts him. He has to hear more about her response to his gift. "Did she like it? Did she talk about it?"

Vincent reaches into his pocket, takes out the box, and lays it on the table. As he gets up and leaves, his shadow falls across the sudden pain on Steven's face. He walks out into the darkness.

In the morning Steven is being taken away in an ambulance. He has killed himself. Looking as if he's been walking all night, Vincent, in his dark blazer, watches the ambulance leave. Lilith watches from her window, clinging tightly to the grate, staring out. She turns her head away, fingers clutching the mesh.

Vincent is unable to bear what he has done and rushes to Lilith for — something, anything. He needs it so badly he is unable to recognize, or at least admit, that she too has been shattered. In a powerful series that alternates shots from several disturbing angles, we are again thrust in close to the tearing anguish in the web of her room.

She is at her window, her hair seen from the back in close-up as his dark arm and then his back in his dark jacket cover her. The camera cuts to showing them through the grate, behind their bars. He kisses her shoulder, slides down, kisses her bare arm, and rubs his face on her arm, as if he could rub it all away. She is talking wildly — to her mother, about her brother being taken away. "It was Steven," he mutters, face pressed against her arm.

The scene shifts to an angle from the inside looking out. The shot is in tight and tense on her face as she half turns from the window, and we can see only her eyes above the dark mass of the back of his head. "Steven? You're lying. Why are you always lying?"

The camera cuts to a second poignantly, painfully beautiful, very tight pattern — of her back and his face from the side pressing against her arm and then her side, burrowing in even when he speaks. These last two shots are alternated four times in building intensity as he tries to keep her in reality and accept that Steven is dead.

She can't take it any longer. In the one long, wider angle view of the scene, from the back of the room toward them at the window, she breaks away from him. She walks to the bed in the foreground, covering herself totally with the sheet. Vincent is seen at the window past her. As she slips deeper into her own mind, and Vincent's desperation drives him too far, the scene shifts to a second set of powerful alternating close-ups: Vincent's face, almost immobile, emotions jammed in tight, at the window; Lilith's face, almost out of the covers, pressing against a pillow, thrashing from side to side.

He must demand that she share his guilt, take it from him.

"I did the right thing. Tell me that. Say that."

"That isn't why they die."

"Just say I did the right thing. Tell me that. Say you wanted me to do it."

"I don't kill the things I love. Didn't kill my brother. He jumped. He jumped because he couldn't bear to love me. I wanted him to. I wanted him to."

She starts talking to her doctor. She calls Vincent "Doctor" and buries her head totally under the sheet. "Leave me alone, please."

Vincent runs away, gets drunk in a bar, and slams a glass on the bar in front of a blonde woman: "This one's for you ... bitch!" At this we hear mysterious, confusing sounds of glass shattering, wood cracking, things crashing to the floor.

The scene dissolves to Lilith's room as the sounds subside. In one very slow panning shot, circling the room, we see, and feel, the final brutal wreckage of Vincent's headlong series of betrayals — the final betrayals depicted in Rossen's films, vicious and yet seen (and felt) with a painful, compassionate regret, like a damp leaf around the heart. All of Lilith's things are broken, smashed, torn off the walls, strewn in clumps and piles all over the floor. We suddenly hear muffled sobbing, a gasping for breath, and the melody of her song creeps in quietly, sadly. The camera passes the tipped and torn wreck of her loom and finds Vincent in that same corner of the eaves, hemmed in by the slanted ceiling and jutting angles of the wall, caught in the horror of what he has done. He leaves.

He looks in through the wire mesh of a window in the door of a different room, an observation cell, where Lilith now resides. She is on the floor, sprawled back against a cot, mouth open, head tilted to one side, her eyes staring up blankly. He has driven her into the living death of a complete catatonic state.

The last sequence is almost totally silent, a mourning, an aching requiem — and a final reaching toward the beginning of a possible atonement. It offers a tender glimmer of redemption through pain and a recognition of the pain one has inflicted on others. At first, however, Vincent flees, retracing in bitter contrasts his path on his first visit to Poplar Lodge. All has been so utterly changed. He passes through the halls of the most disturbed patients, seeming more grotesque now. Clamorous, they grab at him. He strides away across the wide expanse of lawn, seen suddenly through the grate of Lilith's room (as she saw him on his first visit). He walks on as Bea and Dr. Lavner come to the door of the main building and watch him. The camera cuts closer to him as he stops, looks back, and sees them standing on the steps of the entrance. He starts to walk back; the doctor and Bea are waiting on the steps. The final, long-held, graceful and grace-granting shot is seen past the two of them, holding on Vincent as he walks back across the unchanged, uncaring, lovely lawn to them. He slows and stops at the base of the steps. Seen between them, he looks up at them, and the camera gently moves in to a close-up of his lonely sorrow as he says to them, to us all — and for us all, "Help me."

These are the last words in the film. The last words of Robert Rossen in a film. In them we can sense and feel the recognition of human frailty and the possibility for human compassion that W.H. Auden caught so beautifully in these lines:

> Lay your sleeping head, my love,
> Human, on my faithless arm.

In Rossen's final film, in his most lyrical and tragic film, we are beyond all simplistic cant and pompous pride about behaving decently. Why we do what we do as we seek to define ourselves and find our truest selves, even as we seek love and rapture, is left an awful, if strangely beautiful, mystery.

In her lovely tribute to the film and the man, Jean Seberg wrote:

> *Lilith* is a magnificent crystal, so clear and so pure that it can only break itself. Madness is often sordid; he knew, in this, his last film, how to go beyond appearances, towards something very beautiful, in which all his personal unhappinesses were buried. *Lilith* was a defiance....
> I remember the unbelievable camaraderie that bound us all towards the same end.... I remember the Jewish Passover spent among Rossen's family, the Jewish dinner, the thousand candles that burned in the room, while Rossen chanted the ritual songs with his children, and I had the impression that there was in Rossen, and in his film, something very precious and very secret that I would never find again.[10]

In the months following the release of *Lilith*, Rossen faced, along with the burden of disappointment, the deepening of his illness. He grew weaker and was easily tired, but persevered slowly in working on a script (tentatively entitled *Cocoa Beach*) that was to depict the contrast between the lives of those living near the rocket site at Cape Kennedy and the kind of scientific progress symbolized by the site. He was hospitalized a number of times in his last year, and stayed a good deal within the circle of his own family and close friends. He underwent surgery in November 1965, and then, while in the hospital as a result of complications arising from the surgery, he died of a coronary occlusion on February 18, 1966, a month before his fifty-eighth birthday.

19

An Unfortunate Epilogue — The Legacy Denied

In the creation of *Lilith*, Robert Rossen had left the world of politics behind; that world, the world of political and ideological fervor and bias, was not to follow the same path. The prospect of the legacy envisioned by the publisher Nan Talese ("a greater legacy than anyone can normally hope to leave") was denied and betrayed while Rossen was still alive. In a last whirl of the relentless wheel of life's irony, it was an act that was a dire foretelling of the denial of his legacy and stature as a filmmaker, and as a man, in the passing of all the decades since.

In July of 1964 the Motion Picture Association of America had chosen *Lilith* as the official American entry in the International Venice Film Festival, scheduled to open in mid–August. However, by the second week of August the Italian press had referred to "private comments" that, among other derogatory statements, the film "was at a low level of artistic merit." As the *New York Times* reported, there were "festival rumblings over the activities of an Italian official named Luigi Chiarini, head of the Organizing Committee, who reportedly made the publicized criticisms." It was a singular polemic and attack without precedent in the history of the Venice Film Festival. In response to American protests, Chiarini denied that there had been "any official comments derogatory of the American entry."[1] His emphasis on *official* comments is revealing; all knew it had been Chiarini.

Furious, Rossen, from his home in Westport, Connecticut, called Chiarini's action "tyrannical" and "typical of the new cult of snobs." He demanded Chiarini's resignation.[2] Instead, the MPAA withdrew the film, ostensibly as their protest. As an alternate, they chose Michael Roemer's *Nothing but a Man*, a small-scale, straightforward dramatization of African American family life, nicely articulated but minor. It is not without significance that they picked a representative of an independent American cinema strongly influenced by the films and theories of Italian Neo-realism.

It is valuable and necessary to look at the background of Chiarini — the arc of his career to this point, and the consistent and insistent aesthetic and ideological stance throughout this career — to see the full motives and meanings of this intentional act of provocation. It is an action, a personal affront made blatantly public, that can provide a useful epitome of the ways that the combination of personal bias and ideology can shape and distort aesthetic judgments, and the patterns of conventional film criticism and history.

While Chiarini was director of the Festival from 1962 to 1968, his reign was "marked by controversy and criticism of his flamboyance and dictatorial one-man polices" (a consensus opinion summed up by Ephraim Katz in *The Film Encyclopedia*).[3] He was a longtime advocate and historian of Italian Neo-realism and its political implications. An ardent defender of the faith, he had previously turned against those like Federico Fellini and Luchino Visconti whom he felt had betrayed their principles of objective realism by moving into the realms of evanescent subjectivity and the ambiguities of the inner life. Although never revealed as a member of the Communist Party, he was equally firm in his defense of the true causes of the Italian Left. For Chiarini, Rossen's venture into that other reality of the slippery, paradoxical inner life was a shock, an unacceptable betrayal, especially by a man who had earlier displayed a praiseworthy affinity for the true Neo-realist way with *All the King's Men*. And for Chiarini, so too was Rossen's known betrayal of the Cause by *testifying*.

The context for Chiarini's action can be found in his role in the history, and the controversies, of Neo-realism. In the 1940s, the early stages of Neo-realism grew from the ground up, from responses to the war and fascist dictatorship of Benito Mussolini, and its forms of film art, and then to the difficulties of the postwar period. Soon the theories that were behind the early films or extrapolated from them began to be codified to maintain the integrity and purity of the movement. Through these stages, the set of principles that were developed — and the theorists, writers, directors — were influenced by Marxist theories that combined aesthetics and ideology, such as the ideas of the major European theoretician George Lukacs. And they were influenced more directly by the political bases and strategies for art defined in the late forties by the Soviets in what was known as "Zhdanovism" (see Chapter 10).

In response to the perceived needs of the Soviet Union in the developing Cold War between the Soviets and the Western nations, Andre Zhdanov (and his staff) defined the active role that art must take in defending the rights of the people and, of course, the interest of the Soviet Union. The principles of this Cold War adaptation of basic Marxist attitudes toward artists were the commanding core of a cinema conference held in Perugia, Italy, in 1949 and a second conference in Parma. Before the Zhdanov campaign, similar issues had already been raised in arguments over the purity and integrity of Neo-realism and its relationship to the ideology of Communism; but the issues were given new and long-lasting importance by the new campaign and its prominent proponents. As the debate continued, the arguments produced attacks not only on the works themselves, but also the moral stature of the men behind them and the morality of their work. The unflagging vitality and volatility of these collisions between politics and art continued for decades and set the context for the eventual controversy over *Lilith* in 1964.

At the International Film Conference in Perugia in 1949, V.I. Pudovkin, the legendary Soviet film director, gave the keynote address and personally delivered the Zhdanov demands to the Italian filmmakers and scholars. For the film medium (as well as all art), content was supreme; film must be used in the struggle against capitalism, and it must create "positive heroes," embodying "the people's" fight for freedom. "One of the main tasks of the cinema, " Pudovkin stressed at the conference," is to bring to the screen the characters of positive people and to show them as an example to follow." The cinema must present the determining pressures and structures of society (capitalist society) on people, and the people's ability to overcome them. To be avoided were the "bourgeois and cosmopolitan" artistic evils of "formalism, pessimism, subjectivism, and insufficient social commitment."[4]

Chiarini and his friend and long-time colleague Umberto Barbaro delivered major speeches at the conference in Perugia, for which they had been among the chief organizers. Barbaro, a member of the Party who had earlier fled an anti-communist crusade in Italy, was teaching at the Polish Film Academy at Lodz. In his speech at the conference he delivered a scathing attack on "bourgeois and cosmopolitan" tendencies in some filmmakers, including Luchino Visconti, whose early film *La Terra Trema*, he declared, "is a film which lacks any lucid idea [translate as any clear political analysis and commitment]."[5]

Chiarini, in his address, defined in similar terms what he believed Neo-realism should be, principles which he continued to stress and act upon for years to come. Among his books, Chiarini's *Il Film nel Problemi dell'Arte* of 1954 defined more fully his belief in the interaction of film art and social progress, and the artistic and social characteristics and importance of the Neo-realist movement. Along with Guido Aristarco and Carlo Lizzani, both dedicated Communists, Chiarini and Barbaro were among the most important and respected commentators on the Neo-realist movement and its social and psychological imperatives.

For these critics and filmmakers, Neo-realism was more than art; it was a crusade. Its roots were in the wartime resistance against the fascists and Nazis, and in the postwar struggle for a new and better society. Its art was to reflect the purity and integrity of the common people that it, for the first time, brought into central focus in Italian cinema. Its technique was the naturalism of watching with respectful and unforced images (in a Chiarini definition, "without rhetoric") the lives of people in the everyday setting of their lives. But from the start there was a more pointed, defined ideology. Placing *the people* in the real contexts of their society meant having and showing the *proper* "analysis" of that interaction — a clear and, of course, correct evoking of economic and class structures. For technique was not enough. Chiarini made the important distinction in his book *Il Film nella Bataglia delle Idee* in 1954: "The greatest misunderstanding consists in confusing neo-realism with cinematic *verismo* and in the belief that a neo-realist film can be created just by shooting on location without actors and with people picked from real life. That was a mistake that led to the confusion between the demands postulated by a spiritual attitude and a technical fact." He stated his agreement with his colleague Barbaro's formulation of this belief in his typically more programmatic way: "Art was on one hand conditioned and determined (i.e., tied to an epoch), expressing determined reality, and on the other hand turned toward the future, anticipating and contributing to the creation of a new epoch." As Barbaro defined the Marxist idealism in a central dictum in 1961, film must present "a section of humanity whose living conditions are determined in the first instance by their work.... Italian film will attain the peak of perfection" once it deals with these people.[6]

Major filmmakers were attacked for wandering from the demands of the new era of greater artistic purity, including on occasion, Neo-realist stalwarts Vittorio De Sica and Roberto Rossellini when they strayed. Artistarco, long-time editor of the influential journal

Cinema Nuova, reflects this whole milieu of ideologically determined aesthetics in his criticism in 1961 of Michelangelo Antonioni and his negative influence on younger filmmakers. For Antonioni, along with Federico Fellini, embodies "contemporary Italian cinema [that] refuses critical realism: the depiction of phenomena as well as the search for and the analysis of *their determining circumstances*" [emphasis added]. Aristarco faults them both for showing a "fundamental conflict between the paradoxes within a human being" and thus producing "the destruction of characters"[7] in any valuable sense. In other words, they became too concerned with depicting the complex inner realities of people and not their place in the structures of society.

Chiarini joined Aristarco, after a showing of *Stromboli* at the Venice festival, in attacking Rossellini's turn toward "involutions"—that is, turning inward, toward the subjective, the inner life. In an essay stressing the continuing need to maintain the ideals of Neo-realism, Chiarini complains that Rossellini has shifted "the theme of his inspiration" away from the real people, the islanders, onto the "subjectivity" of the bourgeois "unjustifiable and gratuitous Karin."[8] It is these very positions that are the basis for his later dismissal of *Lilith*; as are the terms of Barbaro's attack on Visconti's *White Nights* as "a formalistic nightmare," for Visconti had betrayed normal "verisimilitude" for a reworked artificial kind of reality, had reduced meaningful film images to empty displays of "the evanescence of life."[9]

In 1959 Chiarini achieved a victory in fighting for the resurgence of the Neo-realist tradition in the face of the competition of newer styles. As that year's president of the award jury, he forcefully dominated the award process that gained a dual Grand Prize for two films that still embodied the style and principles of the earlier era of Neo-realism and especially the belief in the power of positive heroes to act and energize the common people — Rossellini's *Generale delle Rovere* and Mario Monicelli's *La Grande Guerra (The Great War)*.[10]

Within this background of Italian film culture and the consistent pattern of Chiarini's beliefs and determination in acting upon them, the contretemps over *Lilith* can be seen more clearly—and almost as inevitable. What he was reported to have said about it echoes the kind of criticisms alluded to above that he and his colleagues had been regularly bringing to bear during the earlier battles over keeping the Neo-realist faith. For (on an impatient and unsympathetic viewing, a shallow Zhdanovist reading) the film clearly violated every one of the aesthetic and moral values Chiarini's ideology demanded in a film; and it possessed almost all of the vices. It could be said to have no faith in people, no analysis of "determining circumstances," of economic and class structures, no positive heroes. It was, indeed, a film of "involutions," subjectivity, the inner life, reflecting the ambiguities and paradoxes within a human being. It was all too formalistic and lyrical — and in the phrase used for Visconti's flaw in *White Nights*, too full of "the evanescence of life." Even its ironies contained unresolved paradoxes, and did not have the clear certainties and meanings of the ironies in such films as *The Bicycle Thief* (i.e., the man whose bicycle is stolen is forced by society's pressures to steal a bicycle himself).

However, for an ideologue like Chiarini, these cinematic sins within the film would be more egregious when committed by a man who in his earlier films had seemed committed to the Neo-realist traditions that he had now "betrayed." But even if Chiarini may well have not liked the film and been disappointed by it — even if he had felt betrayed that the creator of *All the King's Men* had perpetrated this — why create such a unique, demeaning public attack on it, and thus on its creator? There is, in Chiarini's response, a righteous emotional and personal dynamic — as was to be the case for much of the later reductive approaches to Rossen and his work. It is his response to his "reading" of the *man*, not just the film, to the former Communist who in 1953 had *testified* before the House Un-American Activities Committee — who had thus by this ingrained ideological definition "betrayed" more than film theory.

This attack on Rossen's final work — as it became part of accepted assumptions and unexamined conventional wisdom — both prefigured and influenced how this combination of ideology, aesthetic theory and personalized politics distorted the perception (and even notice) of Rossen and his work, especially when within the broader context of the generally Left-oriented, academically fashionable cinematic aesthetics and post-structuralism.

From these premises, this way of defining Rossen influenced the assumptions of academia, curators of festivals and forums, and writers of criticism and film history (particularly apparent in the reductive or absent treatment of Rossen in standard histories for college film courses). These representations then filter down into the unexamined and often unknowledgeable conventions and premises of popular culture. A reminder of the hyperbolic and destructive level of the invective toward those who testified is indicated by another iconic quotation from Victor Navasky's image-influencing *Naming Names*:

> The blacklist savaged private lives, but the informer's particular contribution was to pollute the public well, to poison social life in general, to destroy the very possibility of a community; for the informer operates on the principle of betrayal and a community survives on the principle of trust.[11]

Or, as seen in a more personal manner in a letter from Ring Lardner, Jr. to Albert Maltz in October of 1977, "The choice we faced was between being 'heroes' and being complete shits." Later, in the interview anthology, *Tender Comrades*, Lardner insisted that Rossen "decided to preserve that career at the expense of his former values." And from Walter Bernstein: "The first time he [Rossen] testified, he only gave the Committee the Fifth Amendment [not accurate] and was excused. The second time he gave them a lot of junk, rationalizations about why he was testifying now. I felt the same as I did while rereading Kazan's testimony: the two of them didn't believe anything that they were saying." And, "I felt there was something essentially corrupt about him on a personal level.... You could tell that there was something slippery about him."

Similarly, Abraham Polonsky: "You wouldn't want to be on a desert island with Rossen, because if the two of you didn't have any food, he might want to have you for lunch tomorrow." A comment by director Jules Dassin takes a direction that others followed through the years: "And his kids had to live with what he did ... simply placed career above honor."[12]

Another dimension of the vendetta came through anecdotes of (claimed) personal experience. An example from John Bright, a writer on *The Brave Bulls*, is indicative also of the spread of a claim or judgment into the assumptions of the popular culture. As Victor Navasky in *Naming Names* describes an anecdote told by Bright:

> In 1953 Rossen was living in Mexico with a colony of political refugees, and when he was subpoenaed he told his friend the screenwriter John Bright that he was going to challenge the Committee "just like Dimitroff challenged the Nazis' attempt to frame him for the Reichstag fire." When Rossen named the names, Bright sent him a wire, "How do you spell Dimitroff?"[13]

Rossen was not living Mexico in 1953 and so could not have told Bright that at that time — and as we have seen, that kind of statement did not at all match his troubled, deeply concerned attitude in 1953. In 1951, by the time he was called to testify (and did not name the names), work on *The Brave Bulls* was over. Rossen had gone to and returned from Europe, but not to Mexico. As shown in Chapter 12, in 1951 his way of "challenging" the committee was a strategic attempt to avoid meaningful factual testifying — the "Diminished Fifth." If he had at that time blustered to Bright about this Dimitroff-like challenge (as he was wont to do, but not likely to Bright by 1951 because of their increasing political differences), Bright's alleged response would have been caused by Rossen's strong criticism at those hearings of Bright's still sacred communism, not by his naming names (which he did not do). In turn, Bright's anecdotes about Mexico enjoy a continued existence in Bruce Cook's popularized biography of Dalton Trumbo.

Navasky's Rossen-Bright reference occurs, meaningfully, in a section in which he quotes Rossen's widow Sue. After publication of the book, Sue Rossen was hurt and furious at what she believed was his ideological and immoral way of selecting material from her interview (after feigning impartiality) and so distorting her statements, beliefs, and intentions. What he used of her statements allied her with the negative premises of his chapter on "The Reasons Considered"; It stressed only that Rossen testified because he needed to work (i.e., "in my book if he couldn't write he couldn't live"). What he omitted was her explanation of the important other side of his reasons: his growing disillusionment with, his strong opposition to communism and the Communist Party, and his dilemma of wanting to expose the Communist claims of nobility but still not wanting to testify.[14]

An example of the trickle down, and even acceleration, of unexamined assumptions and inaccurate data in the books and articles of non-ideological writers is Joan Mellen's offhand remark in her biography of Lillian Hellman and Dashiell Hammett: "One day as [a group of people] were chatting about the Korean War on the Rosen porch, filmmaker Robert Rossen, a *government informer*, appeared" [emphasis added].[15]

Parallels in the case of Elia Kazan provide a useful context for this kind of reductive approach to Rossen and a glimpse of the full spread of assumptions and false facts in this region of film history. Overall, the case of Kazan has had a slightly different trajectory. Despite continuing personal vilification, his work has been given more attention. In great part this difference is due to the fact that he had lived on and continued to work in film and theater (where he was a dominant presence for several decades), had been an active presence in the culture wars, had continued to battle aggressively those who attacked him, and had forcefully and cogently asserted his position and beliefs. The momentum of the relentless decrying of Kazan's moral turpitude has continued through the decades, however, even though he was a member of the Party for only a short period in the mid-thirties and actually named only a handful of people he knew at that time in the Group Theatre. When, late in his life (far too late), Kazan was given a Life Achievement Award by the Hollywood Academy, the leftover Left garnered much coverage with speeches, conferences, and interviews. A full-page ad in *Daily Variety*, for example, recruited some new signators, like Sean Penn, and attacked Kazan and the award, claiming he had given HUAC its creditability and that his testimony (naming eight people in 1952) had "validated the blacklisting of *thousands*" [emphasis added].[16]

When Kazan died in September 2003, the emphasis in an editorial in the *Philadelphia*

Inquirer was not on his amazing accomplishments on both stage and screen, but on how his reputation was "tarnished by his betrayals." Moreover, a subsequent news article actually drew a parallel between Kazan and the German director Leni Riefenstahl, associating him — on no logical or factual basis whatsoever — with the artful propagandist who, the reporter neatly defined, glorified "the perverted ideals of Nazism."[17]

The conventional wisdom travels worldwide. Budd Schulberg, who wrote the screenplays for Kazan's *On the Waterfront* and *A Face in the Crowd*, and noted novels, including *What Makes Sammy Run*, *The Harder They Fall*, and *The Disenchanted*, died at age 95 in 2009. In Italy, the *La Repubblica* newspaper picked up the emphasis of the reports in the American news services. In large boxed type under his photo was printed:

> Iscritto al Partito Comunista, era stato uno delatori del maccartismo
> [Enrolled in the Communist Party, he was one of those testifiers of McCarthyism]

Edward Dmytryk had gone to prison with the Hollywood Ten, and had then rebelled against the Party and testified. For decades he too was one of the most vilified. After many years his fine and historically ignored film *Salt to the Devil/Christ in Concrete*, made in England in 1949, was finally released on DVD. In the DVD package, even its producer, David Kalat, added to the years of attack: "To rescue his Hollywood career, Dmytryk defected from the Ten and testified, naming names, betraying all those who had hailed him as a martyred hero.... *Christ in Concrete* suffered from his part in its creation." When Dmytryk died in 1999, the obituary in the *Los Angeles Times* was headlined "DIRECTOR EDWARD DMYTRYK DIES. TESTIFIED IN BLACKLIST ERA."[18]

Rossen's obituary in the *New York Times* stands in sharp contrast to those later positions. It, of course, was written before the development of the conventional wisdom through these decades, and it was clearly based on the writing of Bosley Crowther in the *Times* through the years. It does not have the slant and bias of the later approaches, but it also shows little understanding of Rossen's films past some generalized praise. In this too it was indicative and influential. From its subhead on, it uses phrases Crowther had applied to his kind of praise of Rossen's films: "Writer, Director, Producer Won International Fame for Trenchant Realism." It is full of phrases such as "hard-hitting, crackling realism; stunningly graphic boxing picture; sleazy world of pool sharks, stunningly imprinted with the Rossen brand of movie realism; diamond-hard depiction; high-voltage drama; crackling retrospective; powerful anti-lynching drama; trenchant drama; glamorous hard-bitten Rita Hayworth astride a thirsty horse." While well-meaning, its one attempt at a thematic definition — "concerned with the theme of a man's struggle against his destiny" — is typically Crowtheresque in its rather inaccurate generality and its failure to capture the distinct social and personal strain of Rossen's films.[19]

Still — in another contrast — it is more accurate and less distorting than the later generations of false facts and faulty interpretations, and the trickled-down acceptance of these in discussions of Kazan and Schulberg's important *On the Waterfront*. To see it as a self-serving apologia for testifying before the Committee, ideologues of the Left have distorted its basic facts to have Terry Malloy testifying against his *friends*. In the film, Terry of course testifies against the totalitarian gangster union leaders who are oppressing his friends, who have, in fear, remained silent. Navasky in *Naming Names* sees it as a dishonest defense of informing "in which Terry Malloy comes to maturity when he realizes his obligation to fink on his fellow hoods." In their widely circulated *Inquisition in Hollywood*,

Larry Ceplair and Steven Englund pick up on Navasky's phrasing and distort the point further. They have Kazan exculpating his own immorality with a film that "glorified the hero's decision to testify against his former *friends* and union *comrades*" [emphasis added]. Paul Buhle, in a long and distorting analysis, takes the same tack, stressing, for example, that the union members regard Terry as an informer.[20] In the film, testifying is seen as dangerous to one's life, not immoral.

These distortions have set the pattern and have been passed on thoughtlessly or intentionally in the popular media and in books. In 2011, for example, Manola Darghis, one of the two main film critics at the *New York Times*, did a piece on the difficulty of dealing with directors who have committed immoral acts. Kazan is her next-to-last example, just before her climactic Leni Riefenstahl, Hitler's favorite filmmaker (and who was linked to Kazan in that 2003 *Philadelphia Enquirer* piece). With even more scornful terms, she follows, and thus passes on, the thrust and detail of this sequence of distortions: "In 1952 Elia Kazan gave up old colleagues to the House Un-American Activities Committee. And then went on to direct a handful of movies about betrayal, including one about selling out your nearest and dearest: *On the Waterfront.* It's a classic."[21]

As the conventional wisdom of this extreme moralistic dualism has been passed down through these cultural "gatekeepers," a further important, and damaging, layer of unexamined assumptions has accrued: These political betrayals, these moral failures, are, in turn, linked to artistic failures in the films of those who testified.

Rossen and Kazan, the most important filmmakers among those in the Party and its orbit, are often linked in this next stage of disparagement. Abraham Polonsky, for instance, claimed, "He [Rossen] was talented, but like Kazan he also had a rotten character." And so their films after they testified were "marred by bad conscience." It was a repeated refrain — the moral stain debilitating the whole man and his talent and work — as in the judgment of Martin Ritt: "And I know a lot of guys [emphasizing Rossen and Kazan] who behaved badly, and who have not fully realized themselves as artists or human beings since that time.... They violated themselves." And Bernstein: "It is important, too, what testimony did to his [Rossen's] work."[22]

Buhle, the left-wing political author, activist and film historian (and the promulgator of the legend of Polonsky and the attempt by Rossen to destroy *Body and Soul*), is a prolific producer of articles and books combining ideological, moral and artistic criticism. He is among the most influential (possibly *the* most influential) in spreading this gospel through the years — through his own statements and those of the Left who he has interviewed and quoted. The influence of Buhle and similar advocates is felt not only in the academic bastions of the Left, and in the subsequent assumptions of the students who become writers and teachers themselves, but also in the received assumptions of reviewers and critics, curators of film programs, and strikingly, in the extensive, journal-approved placement of his books in public libraries and those of schools at all levels. They are a source of information and opinion for the public and for the purveyors of information and opinion in the popular media.

The repeated essence of Buhle's influential treatment of Rossen and his films is captured in this exchange with Polonsky:

POLONSKY: In the end they both [Rossen and Kazan] became stool pigeons. I figured all along that Rossen couldn't be trusted, but no one asked me....
BUHLE: His pictures frequently seem a mishmash of blue-collar melodrama and art film,

as though he had always wanted to do both types of films and constantly mixed them up.

POLONSKY: You have him down cold.[23]

This tone, and combination of ideological and moral bias and critical claim, are a constant in Buhle's references to Rossen and his work. In *Radical Hollywood*, with Dave Wagner, he wrote: "[After testifying], Rossen made several unsuccessful films hitching avant-garde themes to blue-collar backgrounds — the best of them was *Mambo*."[24]

The treatment of *All the King's Men* in several of Buhle's books is indicative of the grudging praise, reductive ideological interpretation, and caustic personal barbs in his approach to Rossen's films. In *Radical Hollywood* Buhle wrote:

> The most highly awarded movie by a prospective blacklistee, *King's Men* was Robert Rossen's triumph and very likely his corruption. Succeeding brilliantly on his own terms as writer-director, Rossen delivered the artistic self-congratulations of the parliamentary democratic system that rightward-drifting American liberals longed to hear by this time.

While there is no direct explanation of why it was his *corruption*, in context it is clearly because its success encouraged his aggressiveness, fed his ego, and led to his seeking success only, which in turn led to his selling out by testifying for more success. In *Blacklisted* (2003), the widely-distributed encyclopedic listing of Left-wing movies, Buhle wrote, "It was voted best film of the year by the New York critics eager to make a safely liberal political choice."[25]

In another passage of *Radical Hollywood* the film is even used as an unfavorable example in contrast to a weak and minor movie called *Honky Tonk* because of its failure to consider "issues of class: ...the true character of politics and government.... Unlike the popular critique of demagoguery made repeatedly during the Cold War era (the first time by Robert Rossen's award-winning *All the King's Men*, in 1949), Roberts and Sanford [in *Honky Tonk*] went deeper, beyond easy individualist moralisms."[26]

Again and again, while dropping in a bit of praise, Buhle refers to Rossen's limitations and his failure to develop. The following is a premier example, for several reasons: "Almost overnight Rossen perfected the distinctive Warners style — a success that arguably confined him to its limits all the way to its final triumph in *The Hustler*." In this admittedly odd praise of *The Hustler*, we need to note that the grammar's emphasis on "its" indicates it is the *Warners style* that has triumphed, indicating a rather ironic use of "triumph" in the context of his being stuck in repetitions of the same old thirties fashion. This qualification is defined more explicitly in *The Hustler*'s entry in *Blacklisted*: "The speeches had arguably been better ten or fifteen years earlier, and the black-and-white cinematography was by now self-conscious."[27]

In the wider world of film history and criticism, a respected film like *The Hustler* has been left floating independently in the historical air, unrelated to a creator and his significant body of work. In this paradoxical historical universe, four of Rossen's films have been subject to inferior remakes — *Body and Soul*, *All the Kings Men*, *Alexander the Great*, *The Hustler* — with little or no attention to their original filmmaker, and with a paucity of honoring or interpreting the nature of the originals and their place in the context of their creator's career, or his place in the history of film in Hollywood.

In a revealing contrast, in Europe in 2008 the centennial of Rossen's birth was celebrated in a number of series and festivals. In Northern Italy alone there was a retrospective in Torino at the National Museum of Cinema, featuring all the films he directed; and in Trieste, the Festival of a Thousand Eyes focused on a selection of films written by Rossen as well as directed by him, including (in the words of their announcements) "the two masterpieces *The Hustler* and *Lilith*." In America, however, there was not a single celebration of, or even reference to, the centennial of Rossen's birth — while a play and a film about Dalton Trumbo and a film about Herbert Biberman of the Hollywood Ten were made and received some distribution before going onto the circuit of college campuses, film schools, societies, and festivals.

Was this, then, a man who was so slippery you wouldn't dare being on a desert island with him, who was essentially corrupt, who had no belief beyond his own ego, and whose films were marred by his bad conscience? Or...

Was this a man who could create the most complete realization in cinematographic form of the indefinable, who learned to use the surface realism of the film image to reveal a reality of another kind — the complexity of the inner life? Was this a man who saw that each person was perhaps most deeply, and sadly, his own hustler and betrayer; and who saw also that if you have no power, people pass over you and so you must fight? Was this a man who could clearly define the nature of his ideals and the violation of them, who believed that his art spoke to and for the American people and spirit and experience, who transmitted not only his own experiences but his painful sense of his own troubled and conflicting motives and actions into a valuable deepening of the art and humanity of his films?

Which, then, is Robert Rossen? What human complexity, ambiguity, or paradox does he embody as a man — and as an artist transmute into the shape and fabric of the twelve screenplays he wrote and the ten films that he directed?

In Rossen's own words:

> I tried to be as honest in my portrayal of the American scene as I possibly could and I believe, now, that whatever success I had was due to the fact that I was so deeply embedded in that scene, that my roots received the same nourishment as millions of other Americans, that my hopes were theirs, and so were my fears, and that they recognized this quality in my work.[28]

Chapter Notes

Introduction

1. Nan A. Talese, unpublished letter, property of the Robert and Sue Rossen family.
2. Robert Rossen, "Testimony of Robert Rossen," in U.S. Congress, House Committee on Un-American Activities, *Investigation of Communist Activities in the New York City Area Hearings*, Eighty-Third Congress, 7 May 1953, 1457–58 [hereafter cited as *New York City Area: Hearings*]. "Testimony of Robert Rossen," *New York City Area: Hearings*, 1953, 1458–59.
3. Robert Rossen, unpublished statement, 1–2, property of the Robert and Sue Rossen family.
4. Robert Rossen interview, Jean-Louis Noames, "Lessons Learned in Combat," *Cahiers du Cinema in English*, Jan. 1967, 22.
5. Victor Navasky, *Naming Names* (New York: Viking, 1980), xii.
6. Walter Bernstein interview, Patrick McGilligan and Paul Buhle, *Tender Comrades: A Backstory of the Blacklist* (New York: St. Martin's Griffin, 1999), 46–47.
7. Abraham Polonsky interview, McGilligan and Buhle, *Tender Comrades*, 486.
8. Lester Cole, *Hollywood Red* (Palo Alto: Ramparts Press, 1981), 346.
9. Maltz letter, see the *Hollywood Reporter*, 29 May 1951, reprinted in Eric Bentley, *Thirty Years of Treason* (New York: Viking, 1973), 400–405.
10. Abraham Polonsky interview, McGilligan and Buhle, *Tender Comrades*, 486.
11. Walter Bernstein interview, McGilligan and Buhle, *Tender Comrades*, 49.
12. Martin Ritt interview, McGilligan and Buhle, *Tender Comrades*, 563.
13. "Testimony of Robert Rossen," *New York City Area: Hearings*, 7 May 1953, 1456, 1459.
14. Written statement of Elia Kazan, *New York City Area: Hearings*, 10 April 1952, reprinted in Bentley, *Thirty Years of Treason*, 485 (full statement 485–95). Also see Elia Kazan, *A Life* (New York: Alfred A. Knopf, 1998), 458–60.
15. Kazan, *A Life*, 460.
16. *Ibid.*, 458–60.
17. Edward Dmytryk, "Testimony of Edward Dmytryk," U.S. Congress, House Committee on Un-American Activities, *Communism in the Motion Picture Industry Hearings*, Eighty-Third Congress, 25 April 1951 [hereafter cited as *Motion Picture Industry: Hearings*], reprinted in Eric Bentley, *Thirty Years of Treason* (New York: Viking, 1973), 398.
18. Dmytryk: See footnote, Ceplair and Englund, *The Inquisition in Hollywood*, 374.
19. Walter Bernstein interview, McGilligan and Buhle, *Tender Comrades*, 47.
20. Helen Manfull, ed., *Additional Dialogue: Letters of Dalton Trumbo, 1942–1962* (New York: Bantam Books, 1972), 379. This is in a long letter to Guy Endore, December 30, 1956, 378–93. See also Trumbo's correspondence with Endore in Ronald Radosh and Allis Radosh, *Red Star Over Hollywood: The Movie Colony's Long Romance with the Left* (San Francisco: Encounter Books, 2005), 222–24 and notes 31 and 32, 287.
21. Ring Lardner interview, McGilligan and Buhle, *Tender Comrades*, 405.
22. Lardner: Quoted in Nancy Lynn Schwartz, *The Hollywood Writers' Wars* (New York: McGraw Hill, 1983), 39, from Ring Lardner, Jr., *The Lardners: My Family Remembered* (New York: Harper & Row, 1976). Lawson: See Otto Friedrich, *City of Nets: A Portrait of Hollywood in the 1940's* (New York: Harper & Row, 1986), 254. Polonsky: Quoted in Brian Neve, *Film and Politics in America: A Social Tradition* (New York: Routledge, 1992), 203. Maltz: Quoted in Larry Ceplair and Steven Englund, *The Inquisition in Hollywood: Politics in the Film Community, 1930–1960* (Berkeley: University of California Press, 1983), 235 and 77. See also interview in *Cineaste* 8, No. 3, 1978, by B. Zeitlin and David Talbot, 2–24; Radosh and Radosh, *Red Star Over Hollywood*, 172, 233; Navasky, *Naming Names*, 296.
23. On the Call: Carl Rollyson, *Lillian Hellman: Her Legend and Her Legacy* (New York: St. Martin's

Press, 1986), 146. See also Rollyson, *Lillian Hellman*, 184; Joan Mellen, *Hellman and Hammett: The Legendary Passion of Lillian Hellman and Dashiell Hammet* (New York: HarperCollins, 1996), 169.

24. Mellen, *Hellman and Hammett*, 307.

Chapter 1

1. Daniel Stein, "An Interview with Robert Rossen," *Arts in Society*, Winter 1966-67, 3.
2. Robert Rossen, unpublished statement, 2.
3. Robert Rossen interview, Jean-Louis Noames, "Lessons Learned in Combat," *Cahiers du Cinema in English*, January 1967, 22–23.
4. Ibid., 25.
5. Albert Fried, *The Rise and Fall of the Jewish Gangster in America* (New York: Columbia University Press, 1974), 31.
6. Quoted in unsigned obituary, "Robert Rossen Is Dead at 57; Maker of Films for 30 Years," *New York Times*, February 19, 1966, 27.
7. Fried, *The Jewish Gangster*, 32.
8. Ibid., 117, and *passim*.
9. Ibid., 9.
10. Ibid., 119.
11. Ibid., 11.
12. Rossen's years in New York are discussed in Henry Hart, "Notes on Robert Rossen," *Films in Review*, June-July 1962, 333–34; Patrick Brion, "Biofilmography," *Cahiers du Cinema in English*, January 1967, 38; Robert Rossen, "Testimony of Robert Rossen," *Motion Picture Industry: Hearings*, June 25, 1951, 662ff.
13. Rossen, "Testimony of Robert Rossen," *Motion Picture Industry: Hearings*, June 25, 1951, 666.
14. Mike Gold, *A Literary Anthology* (New York: International, 1972), 163. See also Gerald Rabkin, *Drama and Commitment: Politics in the American Theater of the Thirties* (Bloomington: Indiana University Press, 1964).
15. Nathaniel Buchwald quoted in Eric Bentley, *Thirty Years of Treason* (New York: Viking, 1973), 518.
16. Stein, "An Interview with Robert Rossen," 46.
17. Quoted in Bentley, *Thirty Years of Treason*, 465.
18. Hart, "Notes on Robert Rossen," 334.

Chapter 2

1. Graham Greene, *Graham Greene Film Reader*, edited by David Parkinson (New York: Applause Theatre and Cinema Books, 2000), 235–6.
2. Rudy Behlmer, *Inside Warner Bros.* (New York: Viking, 1985), 61–62.
3. Ibid., 39.
4. Greene, *Graham Greene Film Reader*, 220.
5. For a feminist criticism viewpoint, see Karyn Kay, "Sisters of the Night," *The Velvet Light Trap*, Fall 1972, 20–25.

Chapter 3

1. Robert Rossen, unpublished statement, 1951, 2.
2. Robert Rossen, "Testimony of Robert Rossen," *New York City Area: Hearings*, May 7, 1953, 1457–58.
3. Robert Rossen, "Testimony of Robert Rossen," *Motion Picture Industry: Hearings*, June 25, 1951, 672, 681, 709.
4. Rossen, "Testimony of Robert Rossen," *New York City Area: Hearings*, May 7, 1963, 1460.
5. Larry Ceplair and Stephen Englund, *The Inquisition in Hollywood: Politics in the Film Community, 1930–1960* (Berkeley: University of California Press, 1983), 107, 108–9.
6. Ceplair and Englund, *The Inquisition in Hollywood*, 115. Stander Party: Martin Berkeley, *Motion Picture Industry: Hearings*, Sept. 19, 1951; John Russell Taylor, *Strangers in Paradise: The Hollywood Emigres, 1933–1950* (New York: Holt, Rinehart, and Winston, 1983), 118–19; Salka Viertel, *The Kindness of Strangers* (New York: Holt, Rinehart, and Winston, 1969), 215 and *passim* for a personal view of the times and events; Malraux: Curtis Cate, *Andre Malraux* (New York: Fromm International, 1998), 255–57. See also Budd Schulberg, *Writers in America: The Four Seasons of Success* (New York: McGraw-Hill, 1983), 82–83.
7. Leonardo Bercovici interview, Patrick McGilligan and Paul Buhle, *Tender Comrades: A Backstory of the Blacklist* (New York: St. Martin's Griffin, 1999), 33–34 and 39.
8. Quoted in Henry Burton, "Notes on Rossen Films," *Films in Review*, June-July 1962, 339.
9. On the ending: Rudy Behlmer, *Inside Warner Bros.* (New York: Viking, 1985), 71. On combat: Robert Rossen interview, Jean-Louis Noames, "Lessons Learned in Combat," *Cahiers du Cinema in English*, January 1967, 28.
10. Larry Swindell, *Body and Soul: The Story of John Garfield* (New York: William Morrow, 1975), 251.
11. Swindell, *Body and Soul*, 254.

Chapter 4

1. Rudy Behlmer, *Inside Warner Bros.* (New York: Viking, 1985), 90–94. On Wald: 256ff.
2. Larry Swindell, *Body and Soul: The Story of John Garfield* (New York: William Morrow, 1975), 147.
3. Behlmer, *Inside Warner Bros.*, 92–94.
4. Ibid., 122, 130, 177.
5. Quoted in Henry Burton, "Notes on Rossen Films," *Films in Review*, June-July 1962, 336.
6. Robert Rossen, "The Face of Independence," *Films and Film-making*, August 1962, 7.
7. Graham Greene, *Graham Greene Film Reader*, edited by David Parkinson (New York: Applause Theatre and Cinema Books, 2000), 336.

Chapter 5

1. See Harvey Klehr, John Earl Haynes and Fridrikh Igorevich Firsov, *The Secret World of American Communism* (New Haven: Yale University Press, 1995), 81–83.
2. These and other activities are described in Nancy Lynn Schwartz, *The Hollywood Writers' Wars* (New York: McGraw-Hill, 1983), 150–51 and Larry Ceplair and Stephen Englund, *The Inquisition in Hollywood: Politics in the Film Community, 1930–1960* (Berkeley: University of California Press, 1983), 165–68.
3. Ceplair and Englund, *The Inquisition in Hollywood*, 166.
4. Irving Howe and Lewis Coser, *The American Communist Party: A Critical History (1919–1957)* (New York: Praeger, 1962), 394ff. Ceplair and Englund, *The Inquisition in Hollywood*, 174.
5. Howe and Coser, *The American Communist Party*, 398.
6. Joyce Milton, *Tramp: The Life of Charlie Chaplin* (New York: HarperCollins, 1996), 400.
7. Andre Bazin, *What is Cinema?*, edited by Hugh Grant (Berkeley: University of California Press, 2004). On décor: 11, 133. On space: 34–37, 50ff, 138.
8. Rudy Behlmer, *Inside Warner Bros.* (New York: Viking, 1985), 131.
9. *Ibid.*, 132.
10. Larry Swindell, *Body and Soul: The Story of John Garfield* (New York: William Morrow, 1975), 174.

Chapter 6

1. Robert Rossen, "Testimony of Robert Rossen," *New York City Area: Hearings*, 1472–80. See also Robert Rossen, unpublished statement, 1951, 5–6.
2. Nancy Lynn Schwartz, *The Hollywood Writers' Wars* (New York: McGraw-Hill, 1983), 198–202. Larry Ceplair and Stephen Englund, *The Inquisition in Hollywood: Politics in the Film Community, 1930–1960* (Berkeley: University of California Press, 1983), 187–90.
3. Rossen, "Testimony of Robert Rossen," *New York City Area: Hearings*, 1476 and 1479–80.
4. Rossen, "New Characters for the Screen," *New Masses*, January 18, 1944, 18–19.
5. Rossen, "Testimony of Robert Rossen," *New York City Area: Hearings*, 1473–74.
6. Rossen, "Testimony of Robert Rossen," *Motion Picture Industry: Hearings*, 695.
7. Rossen, "Testimony of Robert Rossen," *Motion Picture Industry: Hearings*, 687–88.
8. Rossen, "Testimony of Robert Rossen," *New York City Area: Hearings*, 1489.
9. Review reprinted in James Agee, *Agee on Film* (Boston: Beacon Press, 1958), 185–86.
10. Schwartz, *The Hollywood Writers' Wars*, 250.
11. *Ibid.*, 223–27; Ceplair and Englund, *The Inquisition in Hollywood*, 218; David F. Prindle, *The Politics of Glamour: Ideology and Democracy in the Screen Actors Guild* (Madison: University of Wisconsin Press, 1988), 42–43; Otto Friedrich, *City of Nets: A Portrait of Hollywood in the 1940's* (New York: Harper & Row, 1986), 248–49.
12. Friedrich, *City of Nets*, 249–50; Bruce Cook, *Dalton Trumbo* (New York: Charles Scribner's Sons, 1977), 227–28.
13. Friedrich, *City of Nets*, 276–83; Schwartz, *The Hollywood Writers' Wars*, 244–50.
14. Prindle, *The Politics of Glamour*, 47–49 and 41.
15. Schwartz, *The Hollywood Writers' Wars*, 263–66; Ceplair and Englund, *The Inquisition in Hollywood*, 292–96; Friedrich, *City of Nets*, 332, 378.
16. For Maltz article, see, for example, Friedrich, *City of Nets*; Mike Gold, *Mike Gold: A Literary Anthology* (New York: International, 1972), 283–4; Victor Navasky, *Naming Names* (New York: Viking, 1980), 288; Robert Vaughn, *Only Victims: A Study in Show Business Blacklisting* (New York: G.P. Putnam and Sons, 1972), 191. Article is reprinted in Kenneth Lloyd Billingsley, *Hollywood Party: How Communism Seduced the American Film Industry in the 1930's and 1940's* (Rocklin, CA: Prima, 1998), 290ff.
17. Zhdanov: Quoted in Dwight Macdonald, *Memoirs of a Revolutionist* (New York: Farrar, Straus and Cudahy, 1957), 238–9. For the article and response, especially Sillen and Dennis; see Joseph R. Starobin, *American Communism in Crisis 1943–1975* (Berkeley: University of California Press, 1975), 136–38. Gold and Sillen: Gold, *A Literary Anthology*, 283–91, Ceplair and Englund, *The Inquisition in Hollywood: Politics in the Film Community, 1930–1960*, 233–235; and see also Robert K. Landers, *An Honest Writer: The Life and Times of James T. Farrell* (San Francisco: Encounter Books, 2004), 279–80.
18. Article: Albert Maltz, "Moving Forward," *New Masses*, 19 April 1946. Quoted and discussed in Landers, *An Honest Writer*, 281. Meeting: In "Albert Maltz: Portrait of a Hollywood Dissident," *Cineaste*, Winter 1977-78, 114.

Chapter 7

1. Bob Thomas, *King Cohn: The Life and Times of Harry Cohn* (New York: G.P. Putnam's Sons), 182.
2. *Ibid.*, 188.
3. *Ibid.*, 196.

Chapter 8

1. Quoted in Paul Buhle and Dave Wagner, *A Very Dangerous Citizen: Abraham Lincoln Polonsky and the Hollywood Left* (Berkeley: University of California Press, 2001), 137.
2. Stanley Roberts, "Testimony of Stanley Roberts," *Motion Picture Industry: Hearings*, May 20, 1952, 3335–36.
3. Raymond Durgnant, "Ways of Melodrama," in *Imitations of Life: A Reader on Film and Television*

Melodrama, ed. Marcia Landy (Detroit: Wayne University Press, 1991), 43.

4. On Buhle's comments on *noir*, see Buhle and Wagner, *A Very Dangerous Citizen*, 1, 3, 101, and 189.

5. Quoted in Buhle and Wagner, *A Very Dangerous Citizen*, 137.

6. John Simon, *Movies Into Film: Film Criticism, 1967–1970* (New York: Dell, 1972), 104.

7. Paul Buhle and Dave Wagner, *Blacklisted: The Film Lover's Guide to the Hollywood Blacklist* (New York: Palgrave Macmillan, 2003), 36 On achievement, see Buhle and Wagner, *A Very Dangerous Citizen*, 102.

8. Abraham Polonsky interview, Patrick McGilligan and Paul Buhle, *Tender Comrades: A Backstory of the Blacklist* (New York: St. Martin's Griffin, 1999), 485.

9. Polonsky, quoted in Buhle and Wagner, *A Very Dangerous Citizen*, 115–16.

10. Abraham Polonsky interview, McGilligan and Buhle, *Tender Comrades*, 486. For Buhle, see Buhle and Wagner, *A Very Dangerous Citizen*, 113.

11. McGilligan and Buhle, *Tender Comrades*, 486.

12. Reservations: Discussed with Tony Williams, *The Cinematic Vision of Robert Aldrich* (Lanham, MD: Scarecrow Press, 2004), 52. Wong Howe: Daniel Stern, "An Interview with Robert Rossen," *Arts in Society*, Winter 1966, 7. See also Williams, *The Cinematic Vision of Robert Aldrich*, 138.

13. Quoted in Eugene L. Miller, Jr., and Edwin T. Arnold, *Robert Aldrich Interviews* (Jackson: University Press of Mississippi Press, 2004), 42.

14. Wong Howe: Daniel Stern, "An Interview with Robert Rossen," *Arts in Society*, Winter 1966, 7. See also Williams, *The Cinematic Vision of Robert Aldrich*, 138.

15. Rossen quoted in Patrick Brion, "Biofilmography," *Cahiers du Cinema in English*, January 1967, 40.

16. Robert Rossen interviews: Daniel Stern, "An Interview with Robert Rossen," 4; Jean-Louis Noames, "Lessons Learned in Combat," *Cahiers du Cinema in English*, 26.

17. Robert Rossen interview, Stern, "An Interview with Robert Rossen," 6.

18. Andre Bazin, *What Is Cinema?*, ed. Hugh Gray (Berkeley: University of California Press, 2004). Godard in Richard Roud, *Godard* (New York: Dutton, 1967), 86–87.

Chapter 9

1. Katz is quoted in Nancy Lynn Schwartz, *The Hollywood Writers' Wars* (New York: McGraw-Hill, 1983), 269. On the Margolis letter to Kenny, see Ted Morgan, *Reds: McCarthyism in Twentieth Century America* (New York: Random House, 2003), 520. For Margolis speech, see Robert Rossen, "Testimony of Robert Rossen," *Motion Picture Industry: Hearings*, 1951, 696–97, and Morgan, *Reds*, 518–19.

2. Edward Dmytryk, "Testimony of Edward Dmytryk," *Motion Picture Industry: Hearings*, 1951, 427–28, and Edward Dmytryk, *Odd Man Out: A Memoir of the Hollywood Ten* (Carbondale: Southern Illinois University Press, 1956), 38, 53–54. Also see Roy Brewer, "Written Statement of Roy Brewer," *Motion Picture Industry: Hearings*, 1947, reprinted in Eric Bentley, *Thirty Years of Treason* (New York: Viking, 1973), 199.

3. Rossen quoted in Victor Navasky, *Naming Names* (New York: Viking, 1980), 303.

4. John Howard Lawson's testimony is reprinted in Bentley, *Thirty Years of Treason*, 153–65, and partially in Gordon Kahn, *Hollywood on Trial: The Story of the Ten Who Were Indicted* (New York: Boni & Gaer, 1948), 68–77.

5. Herbert Biberman testimony and written statement are reprinted in Kahn, *Hollywood on Trial*, 100–104.

6. John Howard Lawson, "Written Statement of John Howard Lawson," in Kahn, *Hollywood on Trial*, 72–73.

7. Samuel Ornitz, "Written Statement of Samuel Ornitz," Kahn, *Hollywood on Trial*, 98–99.

8. Jarrico quoted in Schwartz, *The Hollywood Writers' Wars*, 185–86.

9. Dalton Trumbo testimony, reprinted in Kahn, *Hollywood on Trial*, 78–85; see also Bruce Cook, *Dalton Trumbo* (New York: Charles Scribner's Sons, 1977), 179–81.

10. Stephane Courtois, et al., *The Black Book of Communism: Crimes, Terror, Repression* (Cambridge: Harvard University Press, 1999), 231 and 320.

11. Anne Applebaum, *Gulag: A History* (New York: Doubleday, 2003), 463; Courtois, *The Black Book*, Chapter 11, "The Other Side of Victory."

12. Applebaum, *Gulag*, 45–67. See Courtois, *The Black Book*, 230–38, 379–82, 395–99, 415–20. See also George Hodos, *Show Trials: Stalinist Purges in Eastern Europe, 1948–54* (New York: Praeger, 1987), *passim*, and Simon Sebag Montefiore, *Stalin: The Court of the Red Tsar* (New York: Alfred A. Knopf, 2004), 597–61.

13. Philip Dunne, *Take Two: A Life in Movies and Politics* (New York: McGraw-Hill, 1990), 197–200.

14. Schary is quoted in Schwartz, *The Hollywood Writers' Wars*, note 280 on 300. Rovere is quoted in Michael Ybarra, "Blacklist Whitewash," *New Republic*, January 5 and 12, 1998, 23. Healey is quoted in Cook, *Dalton Trumbo*, 259.

15. Dunne, *Take Two*, 197–200.

16. Huston quoted in Lawrence Grobel, *The Houstons* (New York: Charles Scribner's Sons, 1989), 302–3.

17. Dunne, *Take Two*, 217.

18. Schary quoted in Schwartz, *The Hollywood Writers' Wars*, note 280 on 300.

19. The statement is reprinted Larry Ceplair and Steven Englund, *Inquisition in Hollywood: Politics in the Film Community, 1930–1960* (Berkeley: University of California Press, 1983), 455, discussed 328–31. See also Dore Schary, *Heyday: An Autobiography*

(New York: Little, Brown, 1979), 165–67, and Otto Friedrich, *City of Nets: A Portrait of Hollywood in the 1940's* (New York: Harper & Row, 1965), 332–34.

20. Neal Gabler, *An Empire of Their Own: How the Jews Invented Hollywood* (New York: Anchor Books, 1988), 37–74.

21. See Schwartz, *The Hollywood Writers' Wars*, 279–80.

22. Robert Rossen, "Testimony of Robert Rossen," *Motion Picture Industry: Hearings*, 1951, 695–6.

23. Rossen, "Testimony of Robert Rossen," 696–98.

24. Ceplair and Englund, *The Inquisition in Hollywood*, 345.

25. *Ibid.*, 288–89; Friedrich, *City of Nets*, 306–7, 320–21; Grobel, *The Houstons*, 300–305; Dunne, *Take Two*, 197–200.

26. Ceplair and Englund, *The Inquisition in Hollywood*, 339–40.

Chapter 10

1. Bob Thomas, *King Cohn: The Life and Times of Harry Cohn* (New York: G.P. Putnam's Sons, 1967), 262–65. See also 299.

2. *Ibid.*, 263.

3. Robert Rossen interview, Jean-Louis Noames, "Lessons Learned in Combat," *Cahiers du Cinema in English*, Winter 1966-67, 31.

4. Quoted in Alan Casty, "The Films of Robert Rossen," *Film Quarterly*, Winter 1966-67, 9.

5. Rossen interview, Noames, "Lessons Learned in Combat," 23 and 25.

6. Thomas, *King Cohn*, 262–65.

7. Rossen interview, Noames, "Lessons Learned in Combat," 26.

8. Neal Gabler, *An Empire of Their Own: How the Jews Invented Hollywood* (New York: Anchor Books, 1988), 183.

9. For Zhdanov's speech, see Andrei Zhdanov, *Essays on Literature, Philosophy and Music* (New York: International, 1950). For broad discussion, see Gunter Lewy, *The Cause That Failed: Communism in American Political Life* (New York: Oxford University Press, 1990), 81ff. For Zhdanovschina and the film, see Mira Liehm, *Passion and Defiance: Film in Italy from 1942 to the Present* (Berkeley: University of California Press, 1984), 92–95, 334–35.

10. Healey quoted in Nancy Lynn Schwartz, *The Hollywood Writers' Wars* (New York: McGraw-Hill, 1983), 153.

11. Howard Fast, *Being Red* (Boston: Houghton Mifflin, 1990), 300.

12. Edward Dmytryk, *Odd Man Out: A Memoir of the Hollywood Ten* (Carbondale: Southern Illinois University Press, 1956) 114–15.

13. Bosley Crowther, review of November 9, 1949, reprinted in *New York Times Directory of Film* (New York: New York Times, 1974), 100.

14. Robert Rossen interview, Daniel Stein, "An Interview with Robert Rossen," *Arts in Society*, Winter 1966-67, 47 and 52.

15. *Ibid.*, 47.

16. Rossen interview, Noames, "Lessons Learned in Combat," 28.

17. Robert Parrish, *Growing Up in Hollywood* (Boston: Little, Brown, 1988), 187.

18. *Newsweek*, November 21, 1949, 91; Henry Burton, "Notes on Rossen Films," *Films in Review*, June-July 1962, 337.

Chapter 11

1. Peter Bondanella, *The Films of Roberto Rossellini* (Cambridge: Cambridge University Press, 1993), 87.

2. *Ibid.*, 111.

3. Antonioni quoted in Mira Liehm, *Passion and Defiance: Film in Italy from 1942 to the Present* (Berkeley: University of California Press, 1984), 107.

4. Robert Rossen interview, Daniel Stern, "An Interview with Robert Rossen," *Arts in Society*, Winter 1966-67, 58.

5. Bosley Crowther review of April 19, 1951, reprinted in *The New York Times Film Directory* (New York: New York Times, 1974), 108–9.

6. Bob Thomas, *King Cohn: The Life and Times of Harry Cohn* (New York: G.P. Putnam's Sons, 1967), 189–90.

Chapter 12

1. Robert Rossen, unpublished statement, 1951, 1.

2. *Ibid.*

3. *Ibid.*, 2–7.

4. *Ibid.*, 8.

5. On Scott, see Helen Manfull, ed., *Additional Dialogue: Letters of Dalton Trumbo, 1942–1962* (New York: Bantam Books, 1972), 307; David F. Prindle, *The Politics of Glamour: Ideology and Democracy in the Screen Actors Guild* (Madison: University of Wisconsin Press, 1988), 61. On HUAC and the American Legion, see Otto Friedrich, *City of Nets: A Portrait of Hollywood in the 1940's* (New York: Harper & Row, 1986), 379; and Richard Gid Powers, *Not Without Honor: The History of American Anti-Communism* (New York: The Free Press, 1995), 246. Both use figures from John Cogley, *Report on Blacklisting, 1—Movies* (New York: Fund for the Republic, 1956).

6. Robert Rossen, "Testimony of Robert Rossen," *Motion Picture Industry: Hearings*, 1951, 704, 707.

7. Rossen, "Testimony of Robert Rossen," 676.

8. Rossen, "Testimony of Robert Rossen," 702, 707.

9. Bob Thomas, *King Cohn: The Life and Times of Harry* Cohn (New York: G.P. Putnam's Sons, 1967), 302.

10. Larry Swindell, *Body and Soul: The Story of John Garfield* (New York: William Morrow, 1975), 254–5.

11. Robert Rossen, "Testimony of Robert Rossen," *New York City Area: Hearings,* 1953, 1490.

12. Lardner quoted in Nancy Lynn Schwartz, *The Hollywood Writers' Wars* (New York: McGraw-Hill, 1983), 170.

13. On the Hollywood campaign and Dunne quote, seen Lawrence Grobel, *The Houstons* (New York: Charles Scribner's Sons, 1989), 302–3.

14. Rossen, "Testimony of Robert Rossen," 1953, 1490.

15. See Sydney Hook, *Out of Step: An Unquiet Life in the 20th Century* (New York: Harper & Row, 1987), 385–86; and Robert K. Landers, *An Honest Writer: The Life and Times of James T. Farrell* (San Francisco: Encounter Books, 2004), 306–9.

16. For details of the Soviet campaign, see HUAC, *Report on the Communist Peace Offensive,* April 1951. See also Hook, *Out of Step,* 382–87; and Gunter Lewy, *The Cause That Failed: Communism in American Life* (New York: Oxford University Press, 1990), 181–83.

17. See HUAC, *Report on the Communist Peace Offensive*; Hook, *Out of Step,* 387–96; Lewy, *The Cause That Failed,* 108–14. See also William Barrett, "Culture Conference at the Waldorf," *Commentary,* May, 1949, 37–46.

18. Maltz speeches are reprinted in Albert Maltz, *The Citizen Writer* (New York: International, 1950), see 33, 39, 47.

19. HUAC, *Report on the Communist Peace Offensive,* 34–41; quote, 41; Lewy, *The Cause That Failed,* 183–85. On Seeger: Ronald Radosh, *Commies: A Journey Through the Old Left, The New Left, and the Leftover Left* (San Francisco: Encounter Books, 2001), 35.

20. HUAC, *Report on the Communist Peace Offensive,* 34.

21. *Ibid.,* 70ff.

22. Czeslaw Milosz, "A Letter to Picasso," in *Voices of Dissent: A Collection of Articles from Dissent Magazine* (New York: Grove Press, 1958), 381–84; quote on 384.

Chapter 13

1. Carey McWilliams, *The Education of Carey McWilliams* (New York: Simon & Schuster, 1979), 137.

2. Robert Rossen, "Testimony of Robert Rossen," *New York City Area: Hearings,* 1953, 1456.

3. Rossen, "Testimony of Robert Rossen," 1491.

4. Victor Navasky, *Naming Names* (New York: Viking, 1980), 85.

5. Jean Seberg, "Lilith and I," *Cahiers du Cinema in English,* January 1967, 35.

6. Rossen, "Testimony of Robert Rossen," 1465.

7. Rossen, "Testimony of Robert Rossen," 1467.

8. Rossen, "Testimony of Robert Rossen," 1467 and 1465.

9. Rossen, "Testimony of Robert Rossen," 1468 and 1470.

10. Robert Rossen, unsent letter, dated January 31, 1953, 1, property of the Family of Robert and Sue Rossen.

11. See, for example, Robert Conquest, *The Great Terror: A Reassessment* (New York: Oxford University Press, 1940), 337, 401–2, and 462–63; Robert C. Tucker, *Stalin in Power* (New York: W.W. Norton, 1990), 490–91; Stephane Courtois, *The Black Book of Communism: Crimes, Terror, Repression* (Cambridge: Harvard University Press, 1999), 302–4, 317–18. Simon Sebag Montefiore, *Stalin: The Court of the Red Tsar* (New York: Alfred A. Knopf, 2004), 545–7; and Pavel Sudoplatov and Anatoli Sudoplatov, *Special Tasks* (Boston: Little, Brown, 1994), 294; and see also Chapter 10, "The Jews: California in the Crimea."

12. See Sudoplatov and Sudoplatov, *Special Tasks,* 296–97; Montefiore, *Stalin,* 588.

13. See Stephane Courtois, *The Black Book,* 242–49; on Pravda question: 242. On Lubianka and Komarov's comment: Montefiore, *Stalin,* 588.

14. Courtois, *The Black Book,* 248.

15. On the Doctors' Plot, see Amy Knight, *Beria: Stalin's First Lieutenant* (Princeton: Princeton University Press, 1983), 169–75; Sudoplatov and Sudoplatov, *Special Tasks,* 298–309; Courtois, *The Black Book,* 247–48; Montefiore, *Stalin,* 612–13 and 634–35. On Zhdanov's death, see Montefiore, *Stalin,* 634–35.

16. See Courtois, *The Black Book,* Chapter 20, "Central and Eastern Europe."

17. Adrian Scott, "Testimony of Adrian Scott," *Motion Picture Industry: Hearings,* 1947, reprinted in Gordon Kahn, *Hollywood on Trial: The Story of the Ten* (New York: Boni and Gaser, 1948), 106 and 108.

18. Edward Dmytryk, "Testimony of Edward Dmytryk," *Motion Picture Industry: Hearings,* 1947, reprinted in Kahn, *Hollywood on Trial,* 111.

19. Samuel Ornitz, "Testimony of Samuel Ornitz," *Motion Picture Industry: Hearings,* 1947, reprinted in Kahn, *Hollywood on Trial,* 98–99.

20. Trumbo quote in Dalton Trumbo, *Time of the Toad: A Study of Inquisition in America* (New York: Perennial Library, Harper & Row, 1972), 8–9.

21. Howard Fast, *Being Red* (Boston: Houghton Mifflin, 1990), 239.

22. On Pat survey, see Courtois, *The Black Book,* 319.

23. Rossen, "Testimony of Robert Rossen, 1458–9.

24. Rossen, "Testimony of Robert Rossen," 1489.

25. Rossen, "Testimony of Robert Rossen," 1487–89. See also 1490.

26. Rossen, unsent letter, 1.

27. Rossen, "Testimony of Robert Rossen," 1489.

28. Rossen, "Testimony of Robert Rossen," 1489.

29. On the two orders, see Montefiore, *Stalin,* 228–35; see also Courtois, *The Black Book,* 87–88, 249, 20–51, 252. For a broader picture of oppression, see Martin Amis, *Koba and The Dread: Laughter and the Twenty Million* (New York: Hyperion, 2002), 14,

127–29, 147; Robert Conquest, *Harvest of Sorrow: Soviet Collectivization and the Terror-Famine* (New York: Oxford University Press, 1986), Ch. 16, "The Death Roll." On the camps, see Anne Applebaum, *Gulag: A History* (New York: Doubleday, 2003), especially summary in Appendix; *How Many?*, and Courtois, *The Black Book*, Ch. 11, "The Empire of the Camps," and the summary, 206–7.

30. Lawson is quoted in Otto Friedrich, *City of Nets: A Portrait of Hollywood in the 1940's* (New York: Harper & Row, 1986), 254; Lardner in Nancy Lynn Schwartz, *The Hollywood Writers' Wars* (New York: McGraw-Hill, 1983), 39; Polonsky in Brian Neve, *Film and Politics in America: A Social Tradition* (New York: Routledge, 1992), 203; Hellman in Lillian Hellman, *Scoundrel Time* (Boston: Little, Brown, 1976), 46; Dassin in Patrick McGilligan and Paul Buhle, *Tender Comrades: A Backstory of the Blacklist* (New York: St. Martin's Griffin, 1999), 209; Maltz in Larry Ceplair and Steven Englund, *The Inquisition in Hollywood: Politics in the Film Community, 1930–1960* (Berkeley: University of California Press, 1983), 235 and 77. See also interview by B. Zeitlin and David Talbot, *Cineaste* 8, No. 3, 1978, 2–24; Trumbo in Ted Morgan, *Reds: McCarthyism in Twentieth Century America* (New York: Random House, 2003), 521. See in Murray Kempton, *Part of Our Time: Some Monuments and Ruins of the Thirties* (New York: Simon & Schuster, 1955), 31; Polonsky in Brian Neve, *Film and Politics in America: A Social Tradition* (New York: Routledge, 1992), 203.

31. Bernstein in Walter Bernstein, *Inside Out: A Memoir of the Blacklist* (New York: Da Capo Press, 1966), 181; Ritt in McGilligan and Buhle, *Tender Comrades*, 563.

32. See Eugene Genovese, "The Question," *Dissent*, Summer 1944, 371–6.

33. Quoted in Roger Kimball, "Leszek Kolakowski & the Anatomy of Terrorism," *New Criterion*, June 2005, 10. From the essay in Leszek Kolakowski, *My Correct Views on Everything* (New York: St. Augustine's Press, 2004).

Chapter 14

1. See Mira Liehm, *Passion and Defiance: Film in Italy from 1942 to the Present*, (Berkeley: University of California Press, 1984), 92–93.

2. Rossen quoted in Henry Burton, "Notes on Rossen Films," *Films in Review*, June–July 1962, 336.

Chapter 15

1. On *Exodus*: See Bruce Cook, *Dalton Trumbo* (New York: Charles Scribner's Sons, 1977), 275ff. On Krim: See Dan E. Moldea, *Dark Victory: Ronald Reagan, MCA, and the Mob* (New York: Viking, 1986), 83ff; Joyce Milton, *Tramp: The Life of Charlie Chaplin* (New York: HarperCollins, 1996), 477–78.

2. Robert Rossen interview, Daniel zStein, "An Interview with Robert Rossen," *Arts in Society*, Winter 1966-67, 47–48, and Rossen interview, Jean-Louis Noames, "Lessons Learned in Combat," *Cahiers du Cinema in English*, January 1967, 28.

3. Stein, "An Interview with Robert Rossen," 48.

4. For discussion of the historical context see Paula Fredrickson, "Beautiful People," *The New Republic*, March 21, 2005, 25–29.

5. Stein, "An Interview with Robert Rossen," 47.

Chapter 16

1. Andre Bazin, *What Is Cinema?*, ed. Hugh Gray (Berkeley: University of California Press, 2004), 133 and 138ff.

2. Robert Rossen interview, Jean-Louis Noames, "Lessons Learned in Combat," *Cahiers du Cinema in English*, January 1967, 22.

3. Patrick Brion, "Biofilmography," *Cahiers du Cinema in English*, January 1967, 39.

4. Noames, "Lessons Learned in Combat," 21.

5. Andre Fieschi, "The Unique Film," *Cahiers du Cinema in English*, January 1967, 32.

6. Noames, "Lessons Learned in Combat," 21.

7. *Ibid.*, 28.

8. *Ibid.*

Chapter 17

1. Robert Rossen interview, Jean-Louis Noames, "Lessons Learned in Combat," *Cahiers du Cinema in English*, January 1967, 22.

2. *Ibid.*, 23.

3. See Mason Wiley and Damien Brown, *Inside Oscar* (New York: Ballantine, 1996), 332.

4. Noames, "Lessons Learned in Combat," 22.

5. *Ibid.*

6. Jacque Bontemps, "Reminiscences," *Cahiers du Cinema in English*, January 1967, 30.

7. Ollier quoted in Andre Fieschi, "The Unique Film," *Cahiers du Cinema in English*, January 1967, 32. Originally published in *N.R.F.*, March 1962.

8. Henry Hart, "Notes on Robert Rossen," *Films in Review*, June-July 1962, 334.

9. Pauline Kael, *Reeling* (New York: Warner Books, 1976), 166–67.

10. Bosley Crowther, review in *The New York Times Film Directory* (New York: New York Times, 1974), 168.

11. Michael Wood, *America in the Movies* (New York: Basic Books, 1975), 99.

Chapter 18

1. Andre Fieschi, "The Unique Film," *Cahiers du Cinema in English*, January 1967, 32.

2. Robert Rossen interview, Daniel Stein, "An Interview with Robert Rossen," *Arts in Society*, Winter 1966-67, 55–56.

3. Robert Rossen interview, Jean-Louis Noames, "Lessons Learned in Combat," *Cahiers du Cinema in English*, January 1967, 23–24.

4. Bosley Crowther, *New York Times*, September 21, 1964, 37.
5. Stein, "An Interview with Robert Rossen," 54.
6. Fieschi, "The Unique Film," 32.
7. Rossen interview, Noames, "Lessons Learned in Combat," 23.
8. Jean Seberg, "Lilith and I," *Cahiers du Cinema in English*, January 1967, 36.
9. *Ibid.*, 35.
10. *Ibid.*, 36.

Chapter 19

1. *New York Times*, August 14, 1964, 15.
2. *New York Times*, August 18, 1964, 22.
3. Ephraim Katz, *The Film Encyclopedia*, rev. Fred Klein and Ronald Dean Nolen (London: Collins, 2001), 86.
4. Mira Liehm, *Passion and Defiance: Film in Italy from 1942 to the Present* (Berkeley: University of California Press, 1984), 92. See also Note 16, 304, and Tag Gallagher, *The Adventures of Roberto Rossellini: His Life and Films* (New York: Da Capo Press, 1988).
5. Barbaro quoted in Liehm, *Passion and Defiance*, 93, and Note 12, 304.
6. Chiarini quoted in Liehm, *Passion and Defiance*, 134; Barbaro on 135 and 79.
7. Aristarco quoted in Liehm, *Passion and Defiance*, 160.
8. Chiarini quoted in Gallagher, "The Adventures of Roberto Rossellini," 358.
9. Barbaro quoted in Liehm, *Passion and Defiance*, 151.
10. Liehm, *Passion and Defiance*, 160.
11. Victor Navasky, *Naming Names* (New York: Viking, 1980), 347.
12. Ring Lardner: Navasky, *Naming Names*, 423, and interview, Paul McGilligan and Paul Buhle, *Tender Comrades: A Backstory of the Blacklist* (New York: St. Martin's Griffin, 1999), 405. Walter Bernstein: interview, McGilligan and Buhle, *Tender Comrades*, 47. Abraham Polonsky: interview, McGilligan and Buhle, *Tender Comrades*, 486. Jules Dassin: interview, McGilligan and Buhle, *Tender Comrades*, 74.
13. Bright quoted in Navasky, *Naming Names*, 303.
14. Interview with Sue Rossen. See also Navasky, *Naming Names*, 303.
15. Joan Mellen, *Hellman and Hammett: The Legendary Passion of Lillian Hellman and Dashiell Hammett* (New York: HarperCollins, 1996), 307.
16. For the *Variety* ad, see Ted Morgan, *Reds: McCarthyism in Twentieth Century America* (New York: Random House, 2003), 524; and Ronald Radosh and Allis Radosh, *Red Star over Hollywood: The Movie Colony's Long Romance with the Left* (San Francisco: Encounter Books, 2005), 240. For details of the campaign, see Norma Barzman, *The Red and the Blacklist* (New York: Nation Books, 2003), 442–43.
17. Editorial, *Philadelphia Inquirer*, September 20, 2003; and *Philadelphia Inquirer*, October 4, 2003, quoted in Ronald Radosh and Allis Radosh, *Red Star over Hollywood: The Film Colony's Long Romance with the Left* (San Francisco: Encounter Books, 2001), 240.
18. *La Repubblica*, August 17, 2009, 56. David Kalak, "Commentary," *Christ in Concrete*, DVD (All Day Entertainment, 2003).
19. Robert Rossen obituary, "Robert Rossen Is Dead at 57; Maker of Films for 30 Years," *New York Times*, February 19, 1966, 27.
20. Larry Ceplair and Steven Englund, *The Inquisition in Hollywood: Politics in the Film Community, 1930–1960* (Berkeley: University of California Press, 1983), 377. Victor Navasky, *Naming Names*, 313. Paul Buhle and Dave Wagner, *Radical Hollywood* (New York: The New Press, 2002), 186–87.
21. Manohla Dargis, "Don't judge a movie by its director?" *International Herald Tribune*, September 24–25, 2011, reprinted from the *New York Times*.
22. Abraham Polonsky, interview McGilligan and Buhle, *Tender Comrades*, 486. Martin Ritt, interview, McGilligan and Buhle, *Tender Comrades*, 563. Walter Bernstein, interview, McGilligan and Buhle, 48.
23. Abraham Polonsky and Paul Buhle, interview, McGilligan and Buhle, *Tender Comrades*, 486.
24. Buhle and Wagner, *Radical Hollywood*, 168.
25. Buhle and Wagner, *Radical Hollywood*, 386–87 Paul Buhle and Dave Wagner, *Blacklisted: The Film Lover's Guide to the Hollywood Blacklist* (New York: Palgrave Macmillan, 2003), 9.
26. Buhle and Wagner, *Radical Hollywood*, 387.
27. *Ibid.*, 141. Buhle and Wagner, *Blacklisted*, 89.
28. Robert Rossen, unpublished statement, 1951, 1.

Bibliography

Amis, Martin. *Koba and the Dread: Laughter and the Twenty Million*. New York: Hyperion, 2002.

Antonov-Ovseyenko, Anton. *The Time of Stalin: Portrait of a Tyranny*. New York: Harper & Row, 1981.

Applebaum, Anne. *Gulag: A History*. New York: Doubleday, 2003.

Arnold, Edwin T., and Eugene L. Miller. *The Films & Career of Robert Aldrich*. Knoxville: University of Tennessee Press, 1986.

Barzman, Norma. *The Red and the Blacklist*. New York: Nation Books, 2003.

Bazin, Andre. *What Is Cinema?* Edited by Hugh Gray. Berkeley: University of California Press, 2004.

Behlmer, Rudy. *Inside Warner Bros*. New York: Viking, 1985.

Bentley, Eric. *Thirty Years of Treason*. New York: Viking, 1973.

Bernstein, Walter. *Inside Out: A Memoir of the Blacklist*. New York: Da Capo Press, 1966.

Bessie, Alvah. *Inquisition in Eden*. New York: Macmillan, 1965.

Billingsley, Kenneth Lloyd. *Hollywood Party: How Communism Seduced the American Film Industry in the 1930s and 1940s*. Rocklin, CA: Prima, 1998.

Bonadella, Peter. *The Films of Roberto Rossellini*. Cambridge: Cambridge University Press, 1993.

Bordwell, David, et al. *The Classical Hollywood Cinema: Film Style and Mode of Production to 1960*. New York: Columbia University Press, 1985.

Brownstein, Ronald. *The Power and the Glitter: The Hollywood-Washington Connection*. New York: Pantheon, 1990.

Buhle, Paul, and Dave Wagner. *Blacklisted: The Film Lover's Guide to the Hollywood Blacklist*. New York: Palgrave Macmillan, 2003.

_____, and _____. *Radical Hollywood*. New York: The New Press, 2002.

_____, and _____. *A Very Dangerous Citizen: Abraham Lincoln Polonsky and the Hollywood Left*. Berkeley: University of California Press, 2001.

Casty, Alan. *The Films of Robert Rossen*. New York: Museum of Modern Art, 1969.

Caute, David. *The Great Fear: The Anti-Communist Purge Under Truman and Eisenhower*. New York: Simon & Schuster, 1977.

_____. *Joseph Losey: A Revenge on Live*. New York: Oxford University Press, 1994.

Ceplair, Larry, and Steven Englund. *The Inquisition in Hollywood: Politics in the Film Community, 1930–1960*. Berkeley: University of California Press, 1983.

Chatman, Seymour. *Antonioni or the Surface of the World*. Berkeley: University of California Press, 1985.

Ciment, Michel. *Kazan on Kazan*. New York: Viking, 1974.

Clurman, Harold. *The Fervent Years: The Story of the Group Theatre and the Thirties*. New York: Hill and Wang, 1957.

Cogley, John. *Report on Blacklisting 1—Movies*. N.p.: Fund for the Republic, 1956.

Cole, Lester. *Hollywood Red*. Palo Alto: Ramparts Press, 1981.

Conquest, Robert. *The Great Terror, A Reassessment*. New York: Oxford University Press, 1940.

_____. *Harvest of Sorrow: Soviet Collectivization and the Terror-Famine*. New York: Oxford University Press, 1986.

Cook, Bruce. *Dalton Trumbo*. New York: Charles Scribner's Sons, 1977.

Cook, Pam, et al. *The Cinema Book*. London: The British Film Institute, 1985.

Courtois, Stephane, et al. *The Black Book of Communism: Crimes, Terror, Repression. Cambridge: Harvard University Press, 1999.

Dallin, David, and Boris I. Nicolaevsky. *Forced Labor in Soviet Russia*. New Haven: Yale University Press, 1947.

Dmytryk, Edward. *It's a Helluva Life But Not a Bad Living*. New York: New York Times Books, 1978.

_____. *Odd Man Out: A Memoir of the Hollywood Ten*. Carbondale: Southern Illinois University Press, 1956.

Dunne, Philip. *Take Two: A Life in Movies and Politics*. New York: McGraw Hill, 1990.

Fast, Howard. *Being Red*. Boston: Houghton Mifflin, 1990.

Ferguson, Otis. *The Otis Ferguson Reader*. Cambridge, MA: Da Capo Press, 1997.

Fried, Albert. *The Rise and Fall of the Jewish Gangster in America*. New York: Columbia University Press, 1974.

Friedrich, Otto. *City of Nets: A Portrait of Hollywood in the 1940's*. New York: Harper & Row, 1986.

Gabler, Neal. *An Empire of Their Own: How the Jews Invented Hollywood*. New York: Anchor Books, 1988.

Gallagher, Tag. *The Adventures of Roberto Rossellini: His Life and Films*. New York: Da Capo Press, 1998.

Goodman, Walter. *The Committee*. New York: Farrar, Straus and Giroux, 1968.

Greene, Graham. *The Graham Greene Film Reader*. Edited by David Parkinson. New York: Applause Theatre and Cinema Books, 2000.

Grierson, Lee, et al., eds. *Mob Culture: Hidden History of the Gangster Film*. New Brunswick, NJ: Rutgers University Press, 2005.

Grobel, Lawrence. *The Houstons*. New York: Charles Scribner's Sons, 1989.

Healy, Dorothy. *Dorothy Healy Remembers*. New York: Oxford University Press, 1990.

Hellman, Lillian. *Scoundrel Time*. Boston: Little, Brown, 1976.

Henderson, Ron, ed. *The Image Maker*. Richmond, VA: John Knox Press, 1971.

Hodos, George. *Show Trials: Stalinist Purges in Eastern Europe—1948–1954*. New York: Praeger, 1987.

Hook, Sydney. *Heresy, Yes—Conspiracy, No*. New York: American Committee for Cultural Freedom, n.d.

_____. *Out of Step: An Unquiet Life in the 20th Century*. New York: Harper & Row, 1987.

Horne, Gerald. *Class Struggle in Hollywood*. Austin: The University Press of Texas.

Howe, Irving, and Lewis Coser. *The American Communist Party: A Critical History (1919–1957)*. New York: Praeger, 1962.

Huston, John. *An Open Book*. New York: Knopf, 1980.

Jerome, V.J. *Intellectuals and the War*. New York: Workers Library, 1940.

Kael, Pauline. *I Lost It at the Movies*. New York: Bantam, 1960.

_____. *Reeling*. New York: Warner, 1976.

Kahn, Gordon. *Hollywood on Trial: The Story of the Ten Who Were Indicted*. New York: Boni & Gaer, 1948.

Katz, Ephraim. *The Film Encyclopedia*. Rev. Fred Klein and Ronald Dean Nolen. London: Collins, 2001.

Kazan, Elia. *A Life*. New York: Alfred A. Knopf, 1998.

Kempton, Murray. *Part of Our Time: Some Monuments and Ruins of the Thirties*. New York: Simon & Schuster, 1955.

Klehr, Harvey, John Earl Haynes, and Fridrikh Igorevich Firsov. *The Secret World of American Communism*. New Haven: Yale University Press, 1995.

_____, _____, and Kyrill Anderson. *The Soviet World of American Communism*. New Haven: Yale University Press, 1998.

Knight, Amy. *Beria: Stalin's First Lieutenant*. Princeton: Princeton University Press, 1983.

Koch, Stephen. *Double Lives: Spies and Writers in Secret Soviet War of Ideas Against the West*. New York: The Free Press, 1994.

Kolakowski, Leszek. *Main Currents of Marxism: The Founders, The Golden Age, The Breakdown*. New York: W.W. Norton, 2004.

_____. *My Correct Views on Everything*. New York: St. Augustine's Press, 2004.

Krutnick, Frank, et al., eds. *Un-American Hollywood: Politics and Film in the Blacklist Era*. New Brunswick, NJ: Rutgers University Press, 2007.

Landers, Robert K. *An Honest Writer: The Life and Times of James T. Farrell*. San Francisco: Encounter Books, 2004.

Lardner, Jr., Ring. *I'd Hate Myself in the Morning*. New York: Nation Books, 2000.

_____. *The Lardners: My Family Remembered*. New York: Harper & Row, 1976.

Lawson, John Howard. *With a Reckless Preface*. New York: Farrar & Rinehart, 1934.

Leprohon, Pierre. *The Italian Cinema*. New York: Praeger, 1972.

Lewy, Gunter. *The Cause That Failed: Communism in American Political Life*. New York: Oxford University Press, 1990.

Liehm, Mira. *Passion and Defiance: Film in Italy from 1942 to the Present*. Berkeley: University of California Press, 1984.

Lyons, Eugene. *The Red Decade: The Stalinist Penetration of America*. New York: Bobbs, Merrill, 1941.

Manfull, Helen, ed. *Additional Dialogue: Letters of Dalton Trumbo, 1942–1962.* New York: Bantam, 1972.

Maltz, Albert. *The Citizen Writer.* New York: International, 1950.

McGilligan, Patrick, and Paul Buhle. *Tender Comrades: A Backstory of the Blacklist.* New York: St. Martin's Griffin, 1999.

McWilliams, Carey. *The Education of Carey McWilliams.* New York: Simon & Schuster, 1979.

Mellen, Joan. *Hellman and Hammett: The Legendary Passion of Lillian Hellman and Dashiell Hammett.* New York: HarperCollins, 1996.

Miller, Arthur. *Timebends: A Life.* New York: Grove Press, 1987.

Miller, Eugene Jr., and Edwin T. Arnold. *Robert Aldrich Interviews.* Jackson: University Press of Mississippi, 2004.

Milne, Tom. *Losey on Losey.* Garden City: Doubleday, 1968.

Milosz, Czeslaw. *Voices of Dissent: A Collection of Articles from Dissent Magazine.* New York: Grove Press, 1958.

Milton, Joyce. *Tramp: The Life of Charlie Chaplin.* New York: HarperCollins, 1996.

Moldea, Dan E. *Dark Victory: Ronald Reagan, MCA, and the Mob.* New York: Viking, 1986.

Montefiore, Simon Sebag. *Stalin: The Court of the Red Tsar.* New York: Alfred A. Knopf, 2004.

Morgan, Ted. *Reds: McCarthyism in Twentieth Century America.* New York: Random House, 2003.

Navasky, Victor. *Naming Names.* New York: Viking, 1980.

Neve, Brian. *Film and Politics in America: A Social Tradition.* New York: Routledge, 1992.

The New York Times Directory of Film. New York: New York Times, 1974.

O'Neill, William L. *A Better World: The Great Schism—Stalinism and the American Intellectuals.* New York: Simon & Schuster, 1982.

Parrish, Robert. *Growing Up in Hollywood.* Boston: Little, Brown, 1988.

Payne, Stanley G. *The Spanish Civil War, The Soviet Union, and Communism.* New Haven: Yale University Press, 2004.

Pizzitola, Louis. *Hearst Over Hollywood: Power, Passion, and Propaganda in the Movies.* New York: Columbia University Press, 2002.

Powers, Richard Gid. *Not Without Honor: The History of American Anti-Communism.* New York: The Free Press, 1995.

Prindle, David F. *The Politics of Glamour: Ideology and Democracy in the Screen Actors Guild.* Madison: University of Wisconsin Press, 1988.

Rabkin, Gerald. *Drama and Commitment: Politics in the American Theatre of the Thirties.* Bloomington: Indiana University Press, 1964.

Radosh, Ronald. *Commies: A Journey Through the Old Left, The New Left, and the Leftover Left.* San Francisco: Encounter Books, 2001.

_____, Mary R. Habeck, and Grigory Sevstianov. *Spain Betrayed: The Soviet Union in the Spanish Civil War.* New Haven: Yale University Press, 2001.

_____, and Allis Radosh. *Red Star Over Hollywood: The Film Colony's Long Romance with The Left.* San Francisco: Encounter Books, 2005.

Reagan, Ronald. *Where's the Rest of Me?* New York: Elsevier-Dutton, 1965.

Rollyson, Carl. *Lillian Hellman: Her Legend and Her Legacy.* New York: St. Martin's Press, 1986.

Rossen, Robert. *Three Screenplays: All the King's Men, The Hustler & Lilith.* Ed. Steve Rossen. Garden City: Anchor Books, 1972.

Roud, Richard. *Godard.* New York: Dutton, 1967.

Schary, Dore. *Heyday: An Autobiography.* New York: Little, Brown, 1979.

Schrecker, Ellen. *Many are the Crimes: McCarthyism in America.* Boston: Little, Brown, 1998.

Schulberg, Budd. *Moving Pictures: Memories of a Hollywood Prince.* New York: Stein and Day, 1981.

_____. *Writers in America: The Four Seasons of Success.* New York: Stein and Day, 1983.

Schwartz, Nancy Lynn. *The Hollywood Writers' Wars.* New York: McGraw-Hill, 1983.

Silver, Alain, and James Ursini. *What Ever Happened to Robert Aldrich: His Life and Films.* New York: Limelight Editions, 1995.

Solzhenitzn, Aleksandr. *The Gulag Archipelago: An Experiment in Literary Investigating, 1918–1956.* 3 vols. Boulder, CO: Westview Press, 1997.

Starobin, Joseph R. *American Communism in Crisis.* Berkeley: University of California Press, 1975.

Sudoplatov, Pavel, and Anatoli Sudoplatov. *Special Tasks.* Boston: Little, Brown, 1994.

Swindell, Larry. *Body and Soul: The Story of John Garfield.* New York: William Morrow, 1975.

Taubman, William. *Krushchev: The Man and His Era.* New York: W.W. Norton, 2003.

Thomas, Bob. *King Cohn: The Life and Times of Harry Cohn.* New York: G.P. Putnam's Sons, 1967.

Thurston, Robert. *Life and Terror in Stalin's Russia, 1934–1941.* New Haven: Yale University Press, 1996.

Trumbo, Dalton. *The Time of the Toad: A Study of Inquisition in America.* New York: Perennial Library, Harper & Row, 1972.

Tucker, Robert C. *Stalin in Power.* New York: W.W. Norton, 1990.

Vaughn, Robert. *Only Victims: A Study in Show Business Blacklisting.* New York: G.P. Putnam and Sons, 1972.

Viertel, Salka. *The Kindness of Strangers.* New York: Holt, Rinehart and Winston, 1969.

Volkogonov, Dimitri. *Stalin: Triumph and Tragedy.* Rocklin, CA: Prima, 1992.

Wat, Aleksander. *My Century: The Odyssey of a Polish Intellectual.* New York: W.W. Norton & Company, 1988.

Wexley, John. *The Judgment of Julius and Ethel Rosenberg.* New York: Cameron and Kahn, 1955.

Wiley, Mason, and Damien Brown. *Inside Oscar.* New York: Ballantine, 1996.

Williams, Jay. *Stage Left.* New York: Charles Scribner's Sons, 1974.

Williams, Tony. *The Cinematic Vision of Robert Aldrich.* Lanham, MD: Scarecrow Press, 2004.

Wood, Michael. *America in the Movies.* New York: Basic Books, 1975.

Wright, William. *Lillian Hellman: The Image, The Woman.* New York: Simon & Schuster, 1986.

Zhdanov, Andrei. *Essays on Literature, Philosophy, and Music.* New York: International, 1950.

Index

Numbers in ***bold italics*** indicate pages with photographs.

Abakunov, Victor 169
Abel, Walter 45
Adler, Luther 102
Agee, James 78, 82, 107–8
Albert, Eddie 62, ***65***
Aldrich, Robert 105–6
Alexander the Great 182–93, ***190***; characters and narrative 185–93; critical/audience response 184, 194; film techniques 183, 189; genre/themes 85, 182, 184–87, 192; political influences 186; post-production 184; preproduction 175, 182–83, 184; remake 252; and Rossen's other films 183, 187, 212
All Fall Down 234
All Quiet on the Western Front 77
All the King's Men 126–42, ***136***; awards 129–31; characters 7, 131–32, 135–42; and Cohn 127–29, 144; critical response 130–31, 245; criticized by the Left 28, 130, 154, 172, 252; film techniques 100, 128, 131, 133–41; narrative 132, 135–42; preproduction 127–29, 133; release 130; remake 252; Rossen and 93, 101, 125, 247; and Rossen's other films 108, 139, 142, 183, 187; themes 24, 131–32; and Zhdanovism 129–30
The Amazing Dr. Clitterhouse 60
American Communist Party 16, 133
American League Against War and Fascism 43
American Legion 154

American Peace Crusade 160
American Peace Mobilization 61–62
American People's Mobilization 62
Anastasia 61
Anderson, Maxwell 27
Andrews, Dana ***81***
Anna 176
Anthony Adverse 31
anti-communism: and anti-Semitism 120, 171; Brewer and 83, 144; and the Cold War 82, 143–44, 153; CSU strike 83–84; and fear 143–44; and Hollywood conservatives 77, 122–24; Screen Playwrights 43; *see also* communism
anti-fascism: as theme in Rossen films 68, 72; *see also* fascism
anti-Nazi themes, in Rossen films 24, 60–61, 68
anti-Semitism: accusations of against HUAC 120, 123, 170–71; and anti-communism 120, 171; and blacklist 170; and fascism 167; Rossen on 168; in Soviet Union 22, 123, 167–71; *see also* Jews
Antonioni, Michelangelo 146, 247
Anything Goes 77
Arch of Triumph 78
Aristarco, Guido 246–47
art: film as 19–20, 128, 154, 245; Marxism and Modernism 22, 245; Zhdanov and 129–30, 245; Zola on 7

The Asphalt Jungle 54, 86
Association of Motion Picture Producers 123
Auden, W.H. 243
Aurthur, Robert Alan 233
Awake and Sing 26
Ayres, Lew 77

Bacon, Lloyd 31, 34, 44, 50
The Bad Seed 31
Baker, Stanley 183
Barbaro, Umberto 246
The Barkers 23
Batista, Henry 145
Battleship Potemkin 24, 28, 74
Bazin, Andre 63, 115, 195, 215
Beach Blanket Bingo 145
Beatty, Warren 233–34, ***237, 239***
behaving decently 201, 229, 243
Being Red 130, 171
Belafonte, Harry 195–96, ***196***
Bell, Ulrich 77
Benjamin, Robert 183
Bercovici, Leonardo 44
Bergman, Ingmar 20, 230, 232
Bergman, Ingrid 78
Berkeley, Busby 31
Berkeley, Martin 155
Berlin Airlift 159
Bernstein, Walter 13–15, 174, 248, 251
Berry, Jack 157
Bessie, Alvah 130
betrayal: in *Alexander the Great* 188; in *All the King's Men* 131–33; in *Body and Soul* 95, 98–99, 108–9, 111, 114, 117; in *The*

267

Brave Bulls 143, 146, 148; degrees of 30–31, 155; Dmytryk and 250; in *Edge of Darkness* 73–74; in *The Hustler* 2, 215; in *Lilith* 229–30, 242; in *Mambo* 179, 180; and moral issues 2, 7, 10, 14, 51, 111, 117, 229–30; and naming names 13, 16, 201, 250; in *Out of the Fog* 62–64; and power 3, 5, 72, 85, 108, 112, 131, 137, 185; in *The Roaring Twenties* 54, 56; Rossen and 2–3, 76, 247–48; in *The Strange Loves of Martha Ivers* 84–86; as theatrical motif 26, 106; in *They Came to Cordura* 201, 203–4; in *They Won't Forget* 32
Biberman, Herbert 119–20, 130, 253
The Bicycle Thief 128, 247
The Big Combo 101
A Big Hand for the Little Lady 212
Birthright 23
Bitter Rice 176, 177
Black Pit 26
blacklist: and anti–Semitism 123, 170; and the film industry 10, 77, 104, 123–24, 154–55; and HUAC testimony 16, 123, 153, 156, 248, 249; the Left on 157, 249; and morality 2, 9–10, 12–16, 81–82, 153–61, 201; Navasky on 248; period of 2–3, 12–13, 77, 126, 153–61; Rossen and 2–3, 9–10, 21, 119, 156, 157, 166–67, 186; victims 16, 23, 104, 126, 144, 154–56, 201, 250; and the Waldorf Statement 123
Blacklisted 104, 252
Blonde Crazy 145
Blood and Sand 144
Bloom, Claire 183, 189, **190**
Blues in the Night 50–51
Body and Soul 102–17, **116**; autobiographical elements 21, 212; and betrayal 108–9, 111, 114, 116–17; characters 21, 104–8, 110–11, 217; critical/audience response 100, 104, 107; direction 93, 101, 105–7, 109; film techniques 106, 109–10, 112–16, 134, 145; financing 102; and Garfield 49, 94, 102, 107; genres/themes 7, 21, 27, 103–4, 105–10, 114, 116–17, 229–30; historical context 21–22, 103, 106; narrative 106, 108–17; political influences 102–5, 251; and Polonsky 102–7, 117, 251; release 100, 102; remake 252; and Rossen's other films 21–22, 27, 50, 56, 73, 79, 108, 110, 152, 216, 217, 226; screenplay 27, 103, 107–8, 212
The Body Beautiful 5, 28
Bogart, Humphrey 38, **39**, 46, 49, 52, 53, 55, 202
Bondanella, Peter 146
Bonjour Tristesse 233
Bontemps, Jacques 213–14
Bower, Anthony 66
boxing films 102, 107
Boyd, Stephen 200
Brando, Marlon 78, 212
The Brave Bulls 143–52, **150**; characters 7, 145–47; critical response 152; film techniques 145, 147–52; narrative 147–52; political influences 143–44; preproduction 144–46, 248; production in Mexico 44, 144–45, 147; release 152; and Rossen's other films 145–46, 149, 152, 183; themes 145–47, 149–52
Breathless 233
Brecht, Bertold 12, 93, 118; HUAC testimony 9, 125
Brent, George 24, 45
Brewer, Roy 83, 144
Bridges, Lloyd **81**
Brief Encounter 183–84
Bright, John 144–45, 248–49
Bright Road 195
Brion, Patrick 202, 205
Brother Orchid 34
Browder, Earl 76, 172
Brown, Harry 78
Brown, Joe E. 31
Brute Force 86
Buchman, Sidney 156
Buchwald, Nathaniel 25
Buhle, Paul 103, 105, 251–52
The Bullfighter and the Lady 144, 152
bullfighting genre 144, 145, 152
Burnshaw, Stanley 26
Burton, Henry 55
Burton, Richard 183, 184, **190**, 202
Butler, Hugo 124, 157

Caesar and Cleopatra 183
Cagney, James 46–49, 52, 53, 55, **58**, 59, 131
Cahiers du Cinéma 20, 128, 203, 211, 213–14, 232
Callahan, Gene 214
Cambridge Encyclopedia of Ancient History 185
Cantor, Eddie 21
capitalism/capitalists: Communist Party and 15, 43, 62, 105, 154, 172; as theme in Rossen films 7, 9, 21, 27, 36–37, 55, 61, 72–73, 84–85, 106, 108, 132; Zhdanovism and 130, 245–46
Capone, Al 101
Carmen Jones 195
Carroll, Sidney 212, 213, 215
Casablanca 53
Castle on the Hudson 60
Ceplair, Larry 251
Champion 131
Chandlee, Harry 35
Chandler, Jeff 96
Chandler, Raymond 94
Chaplin, Charles (Charlie) 62, 159, 183
Chiarini, Luigi 118, 244–48; *see also* Italian Neo-realism
A Child Is Born 40, 49, 50
China (Communist) 186
Cianelli, Eduardo 36, 177
El Cid 183, 184
Cinema Nuova 247
Cinemascope 183, 184, 215
cinematographers 31, 95, 100–101, 106
City for Conquest 31, 60
Civil Rights Congress 119, 124
Clark, Al 131, 134
class consciousness 23–26, 36–37, 45, 71, 84–86, 104–5
Cobb, Lee J. 94, 96, 155
Cocoa Beach 243
Cohn, Harry: and *All the King's Men* 127–29, 133; and the blacklist 156; and *The Brave Bulls* 143–44; and Rossen 93–94, 95, 100, 152, 155, 200, 202
Cold War: international tensions and 82; and Zhdanovism 129, 245
Cole, Lester 13, 15, 159
Collins, Joan 200
Collins, Richard 73, 76
Columbia Pictures 83, 93–95, 100, 127–28, 143, 200–201, 233
comedy, in Rossen's work 5, 28
Comintern (Communist International)/Cominform: and aid to Soviet Union 62; and the Cold War 129; and Germany 83; and Hollywood Communist Party 43–44; and Korea 160; "struggle against war" 61; and Wallace campaign 159
Committee for the First Amendment 124
communism: American fears of 143–44; idealism and 5–6, 174;

morality and 153–54; and Neo-realism 245–48; *see also* Soviet Union

Communist Party: and aid to Soviet Union 62; artistic demands on Rossen 23, 60, 72, 75–77, 102–6; conflicts within 82–83; criticism of 14–15, 153–54; Duclos letter 172; and freedom of thought 15, 119, 171–73; Hollywood Left on 15–16; ideal vs. reality of 14–15, 42, 126, 167–68, 171–74, 186; ideals 8–9, 22, 42; Kazan and 9, 14, 249, 251; and labor unions 83, 105; leaving the Communist Party 82–83, 124–25, 133, 171–72, 186; McCarren Act 144; peace as political objective 61, 157, 159–62; rationales after Nazi-Soviet Pact 60–61, 67, 168; Rossen on 42, 154, 167, 172–73; Rossen's decision to leave 42, 124–27, 130, 153–58, 167–68, 171–73, 186; Rossen's work with 72, 76–77, 102; and Screen Actors Guild 84; and secrecy 14; Smith Act 144; and socialism 42; and Spanish Civil War 43–44; Wallace and 157–60, 158, 159; and Zhdanovism 130, 245; *see also* anti-communism; CPUSA (Communist Party, USA); Hollywood Communist Party; *New Masses*; Soviet Union

Communist Party (Italy) 176; and Chiarini 245–48

Communist Party USA *see* CPUSA (Communist Party, USA)

Communists: HUAC testimony 2, 73, 123; ideological fervor of 23; and liberals 83; in Screen Writers Guild 43

concentration camps 121, 170–71, 173

Conference of Studio Unions (CSU), strike of 1945–46 83–84

control: creative 48, 106, 126, 134, 145, 184, 201, 209–10; Rossen on 134–35, 203, 209–10; as Rossen theme 21, 30–31, 37–38, 55–56, 86, 131–32, 186–87; at Warners 44–45; Zhdanov and 129–30

Cook, Bruce 249
The Cool World 212
Cooper, Gary 201–2, **208**, 209–10

Copland, Aaron 73, 78, 159
Corner Pocket 28
Cornered 94
courtroom genre 30–34
CPUSA (Communist Party, USA): anti-Nazi stance 62; and Hollywood writers (post-war) 75–77; leaders 75–76, 129; Soviet control and 159–60, 167; and Soviet-directed peace effort 159–60; and Waldorf Conference for World Peace 159; *see also* Communist Party; Hollywood Communist Party
Crain, Jeanne 195
Crawford, Broderick 128–29, 131, 133, **136**
crime genre 104
Criss-Cross 54
Crosby, Floyd 145
Crossfire 170
The Crowd Roars 145
Crowther, Bosley 94, 107, 131, 152, 214, 232, 250
Crum, Bartley 119
CSU *see* Conference of Studio Unions (CSU)
Cushing, Peter 189

D.A.-justice (courtroom) films 30–34
Daily Forward 171
Daily Variety 77, 131, 249
The Daily Worker 23, 45, 157, 167, 168
Dandridge, Dorothy 195
Darghis, Manola 251
Darrieux, Danielle 183, 187
Dassin, Jules 159, 166, 174, 248
David and Lisa 232
Davis, Bette 37, **39**, 73
Days to Come 25
"The Dead" 229
Derek, John **136**
De Santis, Giuseppe 176
Desert Fury 100
De Sica, Vittorio 176, 245
detective genre 30
Dewey, Thomas E. 35
Diamond, Legs 22
Dies, Martin 76
Dietrich, Marlene 103
di Laurentiis, Dino 175
"Diminished Fifth" 155, 249
Dingle, Charles 73
The Disenchanted 250
Dmytryk, Edward: *All the King's Men* 130; films 94, 130, 250; and Hollywood Ten 13–14, 125,

155, 170, 250; and Maltz 13–14, 130; and the Nineteen 119, 125; obituary 250; and rallies and conferences 159; reputation 13, 122, 250; and Rossen 125, 130, 250; *Salt to the Devil/Christ in Concrete* 250; testimony 13–15, 122, 125, 155
Doctor Zhivago 195
Double Indemnity 85, 86
Douglas, Kirk 85
Dove of Peace (artwork) 160
Drew, Ellen 96
Dubois, W.E.B. 43
Duclos, Jacques 172
Dunham, Katherine 177
Dunne, Philip 121–22, 158
Durgnant, Raymond 104
Dust Be My Destiny 46–50, **47**

Eagle-Lion Studios 183
Edelman, Lou 35, 44
Edge of Darkness 72–77, 86; characters and narrative 73–75; film techniques 73–75; and Milestone 72, 77; musical score 73; political influences 75–76; release 72; screenplay 24, 72, 77; themes/motifs 72–75
editing: *All the King's Men* 128, 131, 133–34, 141; *Body and Soul* 114–16, 134; *The Brave Bulls* 145; *Edge of Darkness* 74–75; *The Hustler* 215, 219–21, 224–25; *Island in the Sun* 195; *Lilith* 231, 238; *Mambo* 176; *The Roaring Twenties* 54–55, 57–58; Rossen on 133–34; *They Came to Cordura* 202–3, 206–7
Edwards, Blake 61
Einfield, S. Charles 36, 94
Eisenstein, Sergei 24, 28, 74
El Cid 183, 184
Eliot, T.S. 27
Elmer the Great 31
Endore, Guy 15, 157
Englund, Steven 251
Enterprise Pictures 94, 102, 105
Epstein, Phil 49
espionage, cases in the U.S. 144
Etinger, Yakov 169
Exodus 183
eyemos 147

A Face in the Crowd 250
The Fall of the Roman Empire 184
The Fallen Idol 131
Farber, Manny 84
Farewell, My Lovely 94
fascism: and hearings of HUAC 120; and Neo-realism 246;

opposition to 16, 61; theme in Rossen's films 68, 72; *see also* anti-fascism
Fast, Howard 130, 159, 171
Faulkner, William 50
fear: in *Alexander the Great* 187; and anti-communism 143–44; and the blacklist 124, 152; in *The Brave Bulls* 145–47, 149–52; in *Johnny O'Clock* 96, 98; in *Marked Woman* 39–40; Rossen on 76, 253; in *The Sea Wolf* 68; in *The Strange Loves of Martha Ivers* 86, 89
Fellini, Federico 20, 245, 247
Ferguson, Otis 31, 58–59
Ferrer, Mel 147
Festival of a Thousand Eyes 253
Field, Betty 51
Fieschi, Andre 203, 211, 228, 230, 232–33
Fifth Amendment 154–55
film criticism 16, 34, 244–45, 248
The Film Encyclopedia 245
film festivals/conferences 228, 232, 244–46, 247, 248, 252–53
film industry: and the blacklist 10, 77, 104, 123–24, 154–55; business aspects 6, 8; CSU strike 83–84; in Mexico 145; Rossen on 48, 106–7, 209; and studio control 31–32, 44–45, 48, 52, 106–7, 134, 145, 175, 201, 209; and Teamsters Union 45
Il Film nel Problemi dell'Arte 246
film noir 54, 85–86, 98, 101, 103–4, 153
film theory: European Theater of the Absurd 12; film as art form 19–20; French New Wave 12; influenced by theater 27; Italian Neo-realism 128, 133, 146, 176, 215, 244–48; postmodern American film 11–12
filmmaking: as cooperative process 54; Rossen's approach to 7, 19–20, 53, 67, 76, 133, 183, 195, 230, 253
Films in Review 55, 67
Finkel, Abem 34–35
Fire Down Below 202
Fitzgerald, Barry 70
Fitzgerald, Geraldine 50
Five Star Final 32
Flaherty, Robert 145
flashback 73, 109–10, 116, 177–78
Flynn, Errol 73
Foch, Nina 96

Fonda, Henry 48
Fonda, Peter 235
Fontaine, Joan 196, **196**
Force of Evil 103–4, 109
Ford, Glenn 101
Ford, John 25, 31, 33
Foreign Language Press Film Critics Circle 131
Foreman, Carl 145, 166
42nd Street 94
Frank, Leo 32
Fredriksen, Paula 185–86
Free World Association 77
freedom of speech 76–77, 84, 120, 124, 167; and the Waldorf Statement 123
Freedom of the Screen Committee 44
freedom of thought 15, 119, 171–72
The Front Page 77
Fuchs, Daniel 129
Fuchs, Klaus 144
Fury 34

Gabler, Neal 123
Gaines, Harry 168
gangster genre 27, 29, 67, 94; *Body and Soul* 21, 108; and courtroom dramas 30, 34–35; gangster and businessman 30–31, 55; *Golden Boy* 27; historical basis for 7, 21–22; *Johnny O'Clock* 94–96; *Marked Woman* 7, 21, 30, 35, 37; neo-gangster films 54; *Out of the Fog* 60–62; *Racket Busters* 24, 44–45, 53; *The Roaring Twenties* 7, 46–47, 52–55; treatment of women in 7, 25, 35; *The Undercover Man* 101
Garfield, John: in *Body and Soul* 94, 102–3, 105–7, **116**; death 157; in *Dust Be My Destiny* 46–49, **47**; and the Left 183; in *Out of the Fog* 60, 62, **65**; and Polonsky 103–6; and Rossen 44, 49, 105–6, 153; in *The Sea Wolf* 60, 67–68, **69**; testimony of 156–57
Garfield, Julie 49
Garson, Greer 31
Gary, Romain 233
Gassman, Vittorio 176, 177, 178
The General Line 24
Generale delle Rovere 247
Genovese, Eugene 174
genres 7, 29–30
Gentleman Jim 54
George, Gladys 57, **58**
Germany (East) 121

Gilda 205
Gill, Brendan 214
Gleason, Jackie **6**, 215, 218
Godard, Jean-Luc 115, 233
Goetz, William 201–3
Gold, Mike 22, 25
Gold Diggers of 1933 31, 94
Gold Diggers of 1937 34
The Gold of Naples 176
Goldberg, Motche 21
Golden Boy 26–27, 102–3
Golden Earrings 103
Gomez, Thomas 95
Gordon, Ruth 73
Graf, William 129
Gramscli, Antonio 192
La Grande Guerra (The Great War) 247
Grant, Cary 145
The Grapes of Wrath 25, 33
Green, Ward 32
Greene, Graham 34
Griffith, Andy 31
Group Theater 26–27, 102, 157, 249
Guernica (artwork) 44
Guffey, Burnett 95, 100, 131, 133
Gun Crazy 101

Hackman, Gene 239–40
Hallelujah, I'm a Bum 77
Halls of Montezuma 78
Hamilton, Murray 223
Hammett, Dashiell 15, 249
Harburg, E.Y. 159
The Harder They Fall 250
Hart, Henry 214
Hayworth, Rita 150, 202, 205, **208**, 250
He Ran All the Way 157
Healey, Dorothy 122, 129–30
Heaney, Seamus 19
hearings of HUAC: effects of 1, 9–10, 12–14, 16, 122, 130, 167; the Left on 12–13; 1947 hearings 118–25; 1951 hearings 153–61; protests against 118–20, 119–20, 122, 157; strategy for 9, 118–19, 124, 152, 153, 155, 186, 249; subpoenas for 118, 144, 152–53; *see also* House Un-American Activities Committee (HUAC); testimony
Heflin, Van 85, **88**, 205
The Heiress 159
Hellinger, Mark 52
Hellman, Lillian 16, 25, 73, 77–78, 159, 174, 249
Hellman and Hammett 16
Hell's Angels 77
Hemingway, Ernest 24, 44

Henry V 183
The Heroes of Telemark 184
High Noon 145
High Sierra 54
Hill, Jim 202
Hiss, Alger 144
historical epic genre, *Alexander the Great* 182
history genre 29, 52
Hitchcock, Alfred 86
Hitler, Adolf 60, 120, 171
Holden, William 102
Hollywood Anti-Nazi League 43, 44
Hollywood Arts, Sciences, and Professions Council 160
Hollywood Communist Party: and *Body and Soul* 102; Cole and 13, 15, 159; control of 103–4, 122; and CSU strike 83–84; disillusionment with Communist Party 60; Dmytryk and 13–14, 125, 155, 170, 250; Fast and 130, 159, 171; Garfield and 102–3, 105, 156–57; and *Golden Boy* 102–3; and Hollywood writers' groups 28, 42–43, 72, 75–77; and HUAC 15, 118, 124, 127; Jerome and 129; Lawson and 15, 26–28, 75–76, 103, 129–30, 159; Maltz and 15, 84, 129–30, 172, 174; Polonsky and 13, 15, 103–5, 174; Roberts and 102–3; Rossen on 42, 154, 167, 172–73; Rossen's work with 72, 76–77, 102; and support of Soviet Union 122, 170–71; on treatment of Jews 170; *see also* Communist Party; CPUSA (Communist Party, USA); Hollywood Ten; the Left; the Nineteen
Hollywood Left 11, 15–16, 61–62, 103, 159
Hollywood Now 43
Hollywood Reds *see* Hollywood Communist Party
Hollywood Review 154
Hollywood Ten 83, 103, 253; on anti-Semitism 170; and the blacklist 123, 144; Dmytryk, Edward 13–14, 125, 155, 170, 250; hearing strategy of 118–19, 124, 152, 153, 155; and HUAC 9, 93; lack of support for 122, 123; names of 155; prison terms 124–25, 152, 155; support for 119, 124; and Wallace campaign 158; *see also* Hollywood Communist Party; the Nineteen
Hollywood Women's Club 76–77

Hollywood Writers Mobilization 28, 43, 72, 75–77; *see also* Screen Writers Guild
Holmes, Milton 94
Honky Tonk 252
Hopkins, Kenyon 218, 230–31
Hopper, Hedda 122
Horner, Harry 214
House Un-American Activities Committee (HUAC): accusations against 120, 170–71; credibility 249; and democratic principles 119–20; and freedom of speech 120; Hollywood Ten on 9, 93; the Nineteen 9; reports 154; Rossen's 1951 written statement to 19–20, 153–54; strategy of opposition 9, 118–19, 124, 152, 153, 155, 186, 249; *see also* testimony
How to Stuff a Wild Bikini 145
Howard, Sidney 67
Howe, James Wong 104, 106, 145
HUAC *see* House Un-American Activities Committee (HUAC)
Huggins, Roy 155
Hughes, Howard 77
Humoresque 103
Hungary 121
Hunter, Kim 234
Hunter, Tab 206
The Hustler **6**, 211–27, **220**, **222**; characters/narrative 211, 215–27; critical/audience response/awards 212–15, 232, 253; depiction of women in 40, 217; film techniques 215, 219–21, 224; musical score 218, 231; political influences 216; preproduction 28, 212, 213; release 232; remake 252; Rossen's control of production 9, 210, 211; and Rossen's other films 108, 145, 149, 194, 216, 217, 226, 229, 238; themes/motifs 2, 213–17, 223–24, 228–29
Huston, John 35, 93, 122, 158
Huston, Walter 73

I Am a Fugitive from the Chain Gang 31, 67
I Can Get It for You Wholesale 104
IATSE *see* International Alliance of Theatrical Stage Employees (IATSE)
iconography: in *Body and Soul* 106; in *Dust Be My Destiny* 46; of the genres 29; in *Marked Woman* 29, 36; and *plan sequence* 64; in *Racket Busters* 46; in *The Roaring Twenties* 7, 46

identity, sense of, as Rossen theme 2, 7, 21, 36, 55–56, 62, 68, 111, 132–33, 166, 184, 216, 229
individuals: depicted in social drama/film 24–26; treatment of in Soviet Union 173
informers: Rossen as 16, 249; in Rossen's films 40, 70, 101
Inquisition in Hollywood 250
International Alliance of Theatrical Stage Employees (IATSE) 83
International Film Conference 245
The Internationale 27
Invisible Stripes 34
Ireland, John 131, 135, **136**
Island in the Sun 194–200, **196**; characters and narrative 195–200; critical/audience response 195, 212; film techniques 195, 199, 200; racial issues 195, 198, 200; and Rossen's other films 194; themes 194, 198
It Happened Tomorrow 94
Italian Neo-realism 128, 133, 146, 176, 215, 244–48; *see also* Chiarini, Luigi
Ivens, Joris 44

Jackson, Donald 157
Jarrico, Paul 73
Jerome, V.J. 129–30
Jews: and betrayal 10; and the blacklist 123, 170; and Nazis in Eastern Europe 167–68; Rossen's Jewish identity 20–21, 167–68, 243; Soviet Union treatment of 167–71; *see also* anti-Semitism
Jezebel 35
Johnny O'Clock 93–100, **97**; characters and narrative 95–100; critical response 94; film techniques 95, 97, 98–99, 100; and other Rossen films 95–96, 100; preproduction 93–94; release 93; screenplay 95; themes 94
Johnson, Lyndon 132
The Journey 61
Joyce, James 229
Judgment at Nuremberg 215
The Judgment of Julius and Ethel Rosenberg 23
Jules and Jim 211

Kael, Pauline 214
Kandel, Aben 31–32
Katz, Charles 118, 122
Katz, Ephraim 245
Kazan, Elia: in *Blues in the Night*

50; criticism of Communist Party 14; HUAC testimony 155; and the Left 183; as member of Communist Party 9, 249; and *On the Waterfront* 46, 251; reputation 105, 248, 249–50, 251
Kennedy, John 78
Kenney, Robert 118
Key Largo 27
Keyes, Evelyn 95, **97**
Khrushchev, Nikita 173
The Killers 54, 86
Knox, Alexander 68
Knute Rockne, All American 34
Koch, Howard 35
Kolakowski, Leszek 174
Komarov, V.I. 169
Korea 160, 186
Korean War 143
Krasker, Robert 183–84
Krim, Arthur 183

labor films 29
labor unions: in drama/film 25, 29; in Hollywood 43, 105; in *Marked Woman* 45; in *Racket Busters* 44; and Reuther 144
The Lady from Shanghai 150, 205
A Lady Without Passport 101
Lane, Priscilla **47**, 51, 52, 56
Lang, Fritz 34, 48
Lansky, Meyer 20, 22
Lardner, Ring, Jr. 15, 76, 158, 159, 174, 248
The Last American Hero 215
The Last Mile 23
Laurie, Piper 215, 217, **220**, **222**
A Lawless Street 101
Lawrence of Arabia 195
Lawson, John Howard: and *All the King's Men* 28, 129–30; and defense of communism 15, 26–28, 127, 174; as film theorist 28; as Hollywood Communist Party leader 26–28, 75–76, 103, 129–30, 159; and *New Masses* 22, 26; as playwright 27–28; and Rossen 28, 129–30; trial of 119, 124; and Zhdanovism 130
the Left: and *All the King's Men* 28, 130, 154, 172; and anti-Semitism 22; and the blacklist 157; and Dmytryk, Edward 13–14; Hollywood Left 11, 15–16, 61–62, 103, 159; ideology in Rossen's films 45, 47–48; and Kazan 249; and moral dualism of testifying 13–16, 251; reaction to HUAC testimony 121–25; response to subpoenas 118;

theater of 1, 23, 25–27, 36, 74, 106; *see also* Hollywood Communist Party
Lennart, Isobel 155
LeRoy, Mervyn 5, 28, 31, 32
Let Us Now Praise Famous Men 78
A Letter to Three Wives 131
Levy, Melvin 76
Lewis, Joseph H. 101
liberals: and Hollywood Communist Party 75, 83; on HUAC testimony 14; response to HUAC hearings 121–22; and Wallace campaign 158
Life 131
Lilith 228–43, **237**, **239**; characters 7, 228–31; critical/audience response 228, 232–33, 244, 247; film festivals 144, 245, 253; film techniques 230, 231, 236–37, 238–40; musical score 230–31; narrative 234–43; preproduction 127, 233, 233–344; psychological issues 230, 232; release 243; and Rossen's other films 217, 229, 231, 232; themes/motifs 229–31, 232–33, 242
Little Caesar 31, 67
The Little Foxes 73
Litvak, Anatole 50, 60–61
Lizzani, Carlo 246
London, Jack 67, 68
The Long Night 61
Look Achievement Award 131
Lord Jim 195
Los Angeles Daily News 131
Losey, Joseph 124, 159, 166
The Lost Weekend 86
Love in the Afternoon 202
Loyalty Program 144
Luciano, Charles "Lucky" 35
Lukacs, George 245
Lumet, Sidney 106–7
Lupino, Ida 62, **65**, 68, **69**
Lux Radio Theater 94
Lynn, Jeffrey 49, 52, 53

Macaulay, Richard 52–53, 60
Macbeth 55
Maibum, Richard 23
Malraux, Andre 43, 44
Maltz, Albert: and *Black Pit* 26; and the Communist Party 15, 84, 172, 174; and Dmytryk 13–14; and Lawson 130; and *New Masses* 26, 84; and peace conferences 159–60; and Rossen 26, 84, 129–30, 172; and testifying 248; and Zhdanovism 129–30

Mambo 176–81; characters and narrative 176–81; critical response 176; film techniques 177–79; music and dance in 176–77, 179; preproduction 175–76; release 176; and Rossen's other films 183; themes 176, 177, 179, 180, 252
The Man from Laramie 201
Man of the West 202
Mangano, Silvana 175–76
Mankiewicz, Joseph 131
Mann, Abby 215
Mann, Anthony 202
Manpower 54
March, Frederick 183, 187
March of Time 54
Marching Song 27
Margolis, Ben 83, 118, 119
Marked Woman 34–41, **39**; characters and narrative 36–40; co-writers 34–35; critics/audience response 36, 44; depiction of women 7, 34, 35, 40–41; direction 34; film techniques 37, 40–41; genres/themes 21, 30–31, 35–38; historical basis 34, 35; release 31, 36; and Rossen's other films 44–46, 88, 139, 152, 177
Marshall Plan 143, 159
Marxism: defense 174; dialectical materialism 154; and freedom of thought 171–72; and growth of consciousness 40; and Italian neo-Realism 245; Marxist themes in drama/film 1, 7, 22–24, 26–27, 33, 36, 66; and Modernism in art 22, 245
Mason, James 198
masses *see* "the People"
Mauldin, Bill 78
Maverick-Woodstock Players 23
McCambridge, Mercedes 131, 134
McCarren Internal Security Act of 1950 144
McCarten, John 78–79, 84, 107, 131
McCarthy, Joseph 144
McCormick, Myron **6**, 217, **220**
McWilliams, Carey 165
Me and the Colonel 201
Meacham, Anne **239**
Meet the People 94
Mellen, Joan 16, 249
Mercer, Johnny 82
Mexico 44, 144, 152, 248–49
MGM 122
Mikhoels, Solomon 169
Milestone, Lewis 72–90, 107;

and *Edge of Darkness* 72–77;
and Garfield 49; and the Nineteen 78, 93; Rossen on 77;
Rossen's work with 6, 8, 72–90, 84, 94; and *The Strange Loves of Martha Ivers* 79–90;
and *A Walk in the Sun* 77–82
Miller, Arthur 159
Miller, Warren 212
Milosz, Czeslaw 160–61, 165
Milton, John 69
Mimieux, Yvette 233
Miroslava 147–49, **150**
mise en scène: in *All the King's Men* 134; in *Body and Soul* 109, 110, 115; defined 63–64, 115; in *The Hustler* 215; in *Island in the Sun* 194; in *Out of the Fog* 64; and *plan sequence* 63; Rossen's trademark use of 11, 64, 80, 109; in *A Walk in the Sun* 80
Les Misérables 78
Miss Sadie Thompson 202
Mister Roberts 31
Mitchell, Thomas 62
Mobilization Steering Committee *see* Hollywood Writers Mobilization
Modernism 22
Moffatt, Ivan 202
Molotov, Vladimir 169
Monicelli, Mario 247
montage: in *Alexander the Great* 189; in *All the King's Men* 134, 135; in *Blues in the Night* 50; in *Body and Soul* 113; in *The Brave Bulls* 149; Eisenstein's use of 24; in *Mambo* 178; in *Racket Busters* 45; in *The Roaring Twenties* 54–55; in *They Won't Forget* 32
Mooney-Billings trial 23
morality: and the blacklist 2, 9–10, 12–16, 81–82, 153–61, 201; and the Communist Party 153–54; and naming names 13, 166, 167, 250; and refusal to testify 155, 251; and Rossen's decision to testify 1–2, 9–10, 13–16, 19, 165–67; as theme in Rossen's films 7, 24, 45–46, 66, 94, 201
Morgan, Ted 119
Mosher, John 66, 67
Mother 24, 74
Mother's Day Peace Council 61
Motion Picture Alliance for the Preservation of American Ideals 77, 83, 122, 144
Motion Picture Artists Committee to Aid Republican Spain 44

Motion Picture Association of America 244
motion picture industry *see* film industry
Motion Picture Industry Council 144
Mrs. Miniver 31
Muni, Paul 67
Murder My Sweet 93, 94
Mussolini, Benito 245
Mutiny on the Bounty 78

My Name Is Julia Ross 101
The Naked City 86, 101
Naming Names 13, 166, 248–49, 250
naming names: HUAC testimony and 9, 16, 155; as moral question 13, 166, 167, 250
The Nation 66, 78, 165
National Lawyers Guild 124
National Museum of Cinema 253
NATO 159
Navasky, Victor 13, 166, 167, 248–49, 250–51
Nazis: anti-Nazi theme 73; in Eastern Europe 61–62, 167; Nazi-Soviet Pact 61, 67, 71, 167, 168, 171
Neo-realism *see* Italian Neo-realism
New Masses 22, 23, 25, 26, 76, 84
The New Republic 31, 94
New York Film Critics 131, 214–15
New York Post 157
New York Times 31, 104, 107, 131, 152, 168, 214, 232, 244, 250, 251
New York University Center for Research 130–31
The New Yorker 66, 78–79, 107, 131, 212, 214
Newman, Paul **6**, 212, 215, **220, 222**
newspaper headline genre 29, 35, 44, 73
Newsweek 107, 131, 134
Nicholson, Kenny 23
Night of the Generals 61
the Nineteen: and the blacklist 144; and Dmytryk 119, 125; and HUAC 9, 93, 118–19, 124, 158; and Milestone 78; and persecution of minorities 170; and Rossen 9, 100, 124–25; strategy for HUAC hearings 118–19, 124, 152, 153, 155; and Wallace campaign 158; *see also* Hollywood Communist Party; Hollywood Ten
No Sad Songs for Me 143, 144
No Time for Sergeants 31
Noames, Jean-Louis 20, 203, 209, 211
Norma Rae 14
North, Joseph 107
The North Star 73, 77–78
Nothing But a Man 244
Novak, Kim 202
Nugent, Frank 31

O'Brien, Pat 34
Oceans 11 78
Odd Man Out 184
Odets, Clifford 10, 25–27, 49, 102–3, 106, 155, 159, 183
Odlum, Jerome 46
Of Mice and Men 77
Office of War Information 76
O'Hara, Shirley 94
Oil for the Lamps of China 31
The Old Man and the Sea 145
Olivier, Laurence 183
Ollier, Claude 214
On the Waterfront 46, 250, 251
O'Neill, Eugene 67
Open City 128
Orgen, Jacob 22
Orion 183
Ornitz, Samuel 120, 170–71
Out of the Fog 60–66, **65**; characters and narrative 62–66; critical response 66–67; film techniques 63–64; political influences 50, 60–62, 65; release 61, 67; and Rossen's other films 61, 62; themes/motifs 60, 62, 65–66

Paglia, Camille 11
Pal Joey 202
Palmer, Lili 108
Paradise Lost 26, 69
Parker, Dorothy 159
Parrish, Robert 131, 134
Pascal, Gabriel 183
La Pasionaria 44
Pat, Jacques 171
peace: as Communist Party objective 61, 157, 159–62; vs. imperialism 159; issues and conferences 77, 129, 159–62
Pegler, Westbrook 122
Penn, Sean 249
"the People" (masses) 2, 24–25, 33–34, 246
People's World 83
Perle, Jed 11
Peters, Paul 23, 24

The Petrified Forest 27
Philadelphia Inquirer 249–50, 251
Picasso, Pablo 44, 160–61
Pickford, Mary 183
Pinky 195
plan sequence: in *All the King's Men* 140; in *The Brave Bulls* 147, 151; defined 40, 63–64; in *Edge of Darkness* 74; in *The Hustler* 219–20, 224; in *Island in the Sun* 195; in *Marked Woman* 40; and *mise en scène* 63; in *Out of the Fog* 63–64; propagandic 74
Polonsky, Abraham: and *Body and Soul* 13, 27, 102–6; on communism 15, 103, 105, 174; and *film noir* 103–4; and *Force of Evil* 103–4, 109; and Garfield 103; as a Hollywood Communist Party leader 103; on Kazan 13; on Rossen 13–14, 105, 248, 251–52
Ponti, Carlo 175
Popular Front 76
Pork Chop Hill 78
Postmodernism, in American film 11–12
postwar period 72
Powell, Dick 93–94, *97*
power: in *Alexander the Great* 185–88, 190–93; and betrayal 3, 5, 72, 85, 108, 112, 131, 137, 185; in *Body and Soul* 21–22, 108, 112; in *The Brave Bulls* 146; and the gangster 21–22, 35–36, 55, 62, 95; and *hubris* 185; in *The Hustler* 8, 216–17, 224–25; in *Johnny O'Clock* 95, 98; in *Marked Woman* 30–32, 36–38; misuse of 2–3, 84–85; in *Out of the Fog* 62; and "the People" 24, 28, 138, 142, 186; political 32, 60, 83, 122, 131–33, 141–42; in *The Roaring Twenties* 54–56, 58; and Rossen 2, 5, 103, 126, 133–34, 166, 194; Rossen on 55–56, 132, 186; in *The Sea Wolf* 67, 72; in *The Strange Loves of Martha Ivers* 84–85, 88; and *A Walk in the Sun* 196–99
Pravda 169
Precedent 23
Preminger, Otto 183, 233
production code, and interracial couples 195
Progressive Citizens of America 124
Progressive Party 159

prostitution, as theme 35
PT-109 78
The Public Enemy 145
Pudovkin, V.I. 24, 74, 245–46
Pyle, Ernie 78

Qualen, John 62
The Quiet American 184
Quinn, Anthony 147, **150**
Quo Vadis 31

racial issues 24–25, 32, 195, 198
Racket Busters 24, 44–46, 61
Radical Hollywood 104, 105, 252
Raft, George 67
Rain 77
Rains, Claude 32
Reagan, Ronald 34, 83–84, 144
The Red Pony 78
redemption 3, 10–11, 26, 54, 204, 227
Reds 119
Reed, Carol 131
Remarque, Erich Maria 77
Rennie, Michael 178, 198
Renoir, Jean 20, 86, 115
Report on the Communist Peace Offensive 159
La Repubblica 250
Reuther, Walter 105, 144
revenge, as theme in Rossen films 179
Revere, Ann 107
Riefenstahl, Leni 250, 251
Ritt, Martin 159, 174, 251; on Kazan and Rossen 14
The Roaring Twenties 52–59, **58**; characters and narrative 54–58; critical response 58–59; film techniques 54–55, 57–58; gangster genre 7, 21–22, 46, 52, 54–55; preproduction 46, 49, 50–54; release 46, 49, 52; and Rossen's other films 22, 56, 61–62, 110, 134, 142; themes 54, 55–57, 58
Robert Rossen Productions 100
Roberts, Bob 102–3, 157
Roberts, Stanley 103
Roberts Productions 102
Robeson, Paul 159
Robinson, Edward G. 32, 34, 60, 67, 68, **69**
Rocket to the Moon 26
Roemer, Michael 244
The Roman Spring of Mrs. Stone 234
Romeo and Juliet 183
Roosevelt, Franklin D. 44
Rosenberg, Ethel 144, 170
Rosenberg, Julius 144, 170

Ross, Barney 102
Ross, Sam 157
Rossellini, Roberto 146, 215, 246, 247
Rossen, Robert (personal life): birth/death 1, 20, 243, 250; early life in New York City 19–20, 22, 212; family 21, 22, 77, 119, 144; illness 228–29, 233–34, 243; Jewish identity 20–21, 167–68, 243; legacy 5, 11–12, 244; living abroad 144, 156, 166, 175, 249; wife and children 77, 119, 144
Rossen, Robert (political life): attack on *All the King's Men* 28, 130, 158, 172; blacklist 2–3, 9–10, 21, 119, 156, 157, 166–67, 186; in the Communist Party 1, 8–9, 19, 42–51, 72, 76–77, 102; on the Communist Party 42, 154, 167, 172–73; criticized by Lawson 28, 129–30; deciding to leave the Communist Party 42, 124–27, 130, 153–58, 167–68, 171–73, 186; deciding to testify 1–2, 9–10, 13–16, 19, 155, 165–67, 171, 249; disillusionment with the Communist Party 2–3, 5, 14, 19, 77, 82, 119, 126–27, 133, 172–73, 186, 249; effect of testifying 1–3, 9–10, 12–14, 130, 167, 252; and Hollywood Writers Mobilization 28, 75–77; HUAC testimony 2, 9, 13–15, 19–20, 155–56, 157–59, 165–67, 172–73, 248; and Maltz 26, 84, 129–30, 172; and the Nineteen 9, 100, 124–25; and Polonsky 13–14, 105, 248, 251–52; reputation 13–16, 105, 248–49; strategy for HUAC hearings 118–19, 124, 152, 153, 155, 186, 249; on the Wallace campaign 158
Rossen, Robert (producer/director): Academy Award 131; *Alexander the Great* 182–93; *All the King's Men* 126–42, 131; *Body and Soul* 27, 102–17; *Brave Bulls* 143–52; on creative control 48, 106, 126, 134, 145, 184, 201, 209–10; criticized by Neorealists 247–48; *Desert Fury* 100; on film as art 19–20; *The Hustler* **6**, 9, 211–27; *Island in the Sun* 194–200; *Johnny O'Clock* 93–100; *Lilith* 228–43; *Mambo* 175–81; montage 113, 134, 135, 149, 178, 189; plan

sequence 140, 147, 151, 195, 219–20, 224; *They Came to Cordura* 200–210; *The Undercover Man* 100–101, 102; on working abroad 166
Rossen, Robert (screenwriter): *Blues in the Night* 50–51; *A Child Is Born* 49–50; co-writers 35, 44, 53; on creative control 44; *Desert Fury* 100; *Dust Be My Destiny* 46–49, 50; *Edge of Darkness* 72–77; *Marked Woman* 34–41; mise en scène 11, 64; montage 32, 45, 50, 54–55; *Out of the Fog* 60–66; plan sequence 40, 63–64, 74; *Racket Busters* 44–46; *The Roaring Twenties* 49–50, 52–59; in the Screen Writers Guild 43; *The Sea Wolf* 60; *The Strange Loves of Martha Ivers* 84–90; *They Won't Forget* 30–31; *A Walk in the Sun* 78–82; for Warner Bros. 6–8, 28, 29–41, 44–45, 46
Rossen, Robert (theater): *Birthright* 23; *The Body Beautiful* 5; commercial theater 28; *The Cool World* 212; on creative control 48; left-wing theater 1, 23, 106; *Steel* 23; *The Tree* 23
Rossen, Steve 166
Rossen, Sue 77, 119, 249
Rovere, Richard 122
Rozsa, Miklos 86
The Rules of the Game 86
Russia *see* Soviet Union

Sabattini, Rafael 67
Saint Joan 233
Salamanca, J.R. 233
Salt to the Devil/Christ in Concrete 250
Salvameni, Gatano 76–77, 76
The Saturday Evening Post 157
Sayonara 201
Schary, Dore 122–23
Schulberg, Budd 46, 52, 155, 159, 250
Schultz, Dutch 22
Scott, Adrian 119, 122, 154, 170
Scott, Allan 76
Scott, George C. 214, 215
Scott, Lizabeth 87
Scottsboro boys 23
Screen Actors Guild 83–84, 144, 154
Screen Directors Guild 125, 131
Screen Playwrights 43
Screen Writers Guild 43, 75, 103, 144, 154; *see also* Hollywood Writers Mobilization

The Sea Wolf 50, 67–71, **69**
Seberg, Jean 166–67, 233–34, **237, 239**, 243
Seeger, Pete 160
Seiler, Lewis 46
Sellars, Peter 61
Sergeant York 35
Shadoian, Jack 54
Shaw, Irwin, 61, 66
She Done Him Wrong 145
Sheridan, Ann 73
Sherwood, Robert E. 27
Shipmates Forever 94
A Shot in the Dark 61
Show 55
Shuftan, Eugen 214, 215, 230
Sidney, Sylvia 34, 48
Siegel, Benny "Bugsy" 22
Siegel, Don 50
Silberberg, Mendel 123
Simon, John 104
Sklar, George 23, 24
Skouras, Spyros 213
Slansky, Rudoph 168, 170
slum boy films 29
Smart Money 145
Smith Act 144
The Snake Pit 61
So Dark the Night 101
social responsibility in filmmaking 76
social themes: anti-Nazi 73; generally 7; and genre films 29–30; life as struggle 20; Marxist ideals 22–23, 73; social problem films 24, 29–30, 45
socialism/socialist movement: and the Communist Party 42; vs. fascism 43; and lack of anti-Semitism 22
solidarity: in iconic Communist drama 24; as theme in *Edge of Darkness* 75; as theme in *Racket Busters* 46; and women in *Marked Woman* 41
Solomon, Louis 76
Sondergaard, Gale 159
Song of Russia 73
Sorrell, Herbert J. (Herb) 83
Sorry Wrong Number 61
Soviet Central Committee 129
Soviet-style epic genre 27–28, 115
Soviet Union: aid for 62; anti-Semitism in 22, 123, 167–71; and the Cold War 129, 143, 153, 172; concentration camps in 121; depicted in film 73; and Eastern Europe 121, 129, 143, 159, 161, 170–71; films 24, 27, 74; Hollywood Reds on 15–16; and Spanish Civil War 44;

treatment of individuals in 173; treatment of Jews in 167–71; *see also* communism
spaghetti Westerns 183
Spanish Civil War, and Communist organizations and activities 43–44
The Spanish Earth 44
Spartacus 130, 171
Spellbound 86
Splendor in the Grass 234
Springer, John 67
Sproul, Robert Gordon 75
Stalin, Josef 60, 161, 169, 174
Stanwyck, Barbara 85, **88**
Steel 23
Stein, Daniel 19
Steinbeck, John 25, 77, 78
Stevedore 23–25
Stewart, Donald Ogden 159
Sticks and Stones 44
Stockholm peace campaigns 160
The Strange Loves of Martha Ivers 84–90, **88**; characters 84–86; critical response 84; depiction of women 85–86; as film noir 85–86; film techniques 88; and Milestone 84; musical score 86; narrative 86–90; and other Rossen films 86, 88, 95; release 93; themes 72, 84, 86, 88
The Strawberry Blonde 54
A Streetcar Named Desire 212
strikes, CSU strike of 1945–46 83–84
Stripling, Robert 121
Stromboli 247
studio system 7–8, 19, 46, 52, 100
Success Story 28
The Sun Also Rises 144
Swarthout, Glendon 201

Tabu 145
Take Two 122
Talese, Nan A. 5
Taylor, Killingsworth 233
Tell Them Willie Boy Is Here 104
Tello, Antonio 145
Tello, Luis 145
the ten *see* Hollywood Ten
Ten North Frederick 202
Tender Comrades 13, 104, 248
La Terra Trema 246
testimony: against the hearings 170; *All the King's Men* and 130, 172; and betrayal 10, 12–14, 16, 117, 201, 245; of Biberman 120; and the blacklist 16, 123, 153, 156, 248, 249; deciding to testify 2, 9–10, 13–16, 19, 155, 165–67, 171–72; of Dmytryk

13–15, 122, 125, 155, 250; effects of testifying 1, 9–10, 12–16, 130, 166, 167, 201, 245, 249, 251–52; of Garfield 156–57; and *Johnny O'Clock* 101; of Lawson 119; *Marked Woman* and 35, 38–40; moral issues 2, 13–16, 19, 201; naming names 9, 13, 16, 155; Navasky on 13, 248; in *Racket Busters* 45–46; reactions to those who testified 12–13, 15–16, 121–25, 174; refusal to testify 3, 10, 16, 118, 119, 154–55; by Rossen at HUAC 2, 9, 13–16, 19–20, 155–56, 157–59, 165–67, 172–73, 245, 248; by Rossen on Writers' Congress 76; Rossen's written statement 153–54; or silence 3, 10, 165–74; strategy for 9, 118–19, 124, 152, 153, 155, 186, 249; subpoenas to testify 93, 118; of Trumbo 120–21; *see also* hearings of HUAC

Tevis, Walter 212

theater: agit-prop 25; anti-Nazi themes 23; and class consciousness 26; influence on film 27; of the Left 1, 23, 25–27, 36, 74, 106; social protest drama 22–23

Theater Union 23

They Came to Cordura 200–210, **208**; characters 201–6; conflict regarding ending 203, 209–10; critical response 203; film techniques 203, 206–7; narrative 204–10; preproduction 201–2; release 203; Rossen as "director for hire" 194, 203, 209–10; and Rossen's other films 85, 217, 232; themes 85, 201, 203–4, 209–10

They Died with Their Boots On 54
They Drive by Night 54
They Shall Not Die 23
They Won't Forget 31–34, **33**, 107
The Third Man 184
Thirty Seconds Over Tokyo 31
Thompson, E.P. 174
Thompson, Sadie 77
Three Cases of Murder 212
Three Cheers for the Irish 34
Time 31, 107
To Have and Have Not 24
Toller, Ernst 43
tough guy films 7, 29, 46, 52–53, 94

Townsend, Leo 155
Tracy, Spencer 34
Transamerica Corporation 183
The Treasure of Sierra Madre 93
The Tree 23
Trotsky, Leon (Lev) 23
Truman Doctrine 143, 159
Trumbo, Dalton: books/films about 249, 253; HUAC testimony 120–21; on informing 15; on the New Liberals 171; and peace organizations 61, 159; as screenwriter 157, 183; on the Soviet Union 174
Turner, Lana 32
Tuttle, Frank 155
Twentieth Century–Fox 194, 201, 212
Tyler, Parker 78–79
Tynan, Kenneth 212

Ulysses 176
The Undercover Man 100–101, 102
United Artists 183
Universal 201
University of California 75

Variety 157
Venice Film Festival 228, 244–45
Vertigo 233
Vidor, Charles 93
Visconti, Luchino 245, 246, 247
Volkogonov, Dimitri 173
Vorhaus, Bernard 76

Wagner, Dave 252
Waiting for Lefty 25
Wald, Jerry 52–53, 60, 66
Waldorf Conference for World Peace 159, 160
Waldorf Statement 123
A Walk in the Sun 78–82, **81**; characters and narrative 79–82, 131; critical response 78–79, 82; film techniques 79–82; preproduction 78–79, 82; release 82, 84; and Rossen's other films 78–79; theme/motifs 72, 75, 78–79, 81
Wallace, Henry 157–60
Wallis, Hal 49–50, 53–54, 67, 100
Walsh, Raoul 53–54
Walter, Jessica 234
war film genre 79
Warner, Jack L. 36, 94

Warner Bros.: and CSU strike 83; on the lot 49; and proletarian drama 23; Rossen as screenwriter for 5–8, 28, 29–41, 94; Rossen on working for 44–45; studio system 7–8, 128; Warner's style 6–8, 32, 64, 115, 145
Warren, Robert Penn 127
Washington Square Players 23
Wasteland 27
Waugh, Alec 194
Welles, Orson 150
West, Mae 145
West Side Story 214
western genre 29, 201, 203
Wexley, John 23, 31, 76
Wharf Nigger 23
What Makes Sammy Run 52, 250
White Heat 54, 64
White Nights 247
Whitmore, James 101
Whorf, Richard 51
Wilson, Frank J. 100
Winsten, Archer 157, 232
Winters, Shelley 177
Winterset 27
women: in *The Hustler* 40, 217; as leaders of "the People" 28; in *Mambo* 176–77; in *Marked Woman* 7, 34, 35, 40–41; prostitution as theme 35, 36; as protagonists 35, 176; in *The Roaring Twenties* 50; in *The Strange Loves of Martha Ivers* 85–86; in union plays 26
Wood, Michael 215
Woods, Sam 143
Workers School 23
Workers Theater 23
The World Moves On 52
Writers Conference (1943) 72, 75
Writers' Congress 76

You Killed Elizabeth 212
You Only Live Once 48
Young, Freddie 195

Zanuck, Darryl F. 25, 194–95, 212
Zhdanov, Andre 129–30, 169, 245
Zhdanovism 129–30, 245–46
Zionists 169, 170
Zola, Emile 7
Zwillman, Longy 22

www.ingramcontent.com/pod-product-compliance
Lightning Source LLC
Chambersburg PA
CBHW081545300426
44116CB00015B/2756